NATIONAL GEOGRAPHIC

TRAVELER
Prague
& the Czech Republic

NATIONAL GEOGRAPHIC

TRAVELER
Prague
&
the Czech Republic

Stephen Brook

Contents

How to use this guide 6–7 About the author 8
The regions 52–294 Travelwise 295–326
Index 327–333 Credits 334–335

Page 1: A budding musician at work
Pages 2–3: A winter view of Prague's
Charles Bridge
Left: Folk dancing at a rural festival

How to use this guide

See back flap for keys to text and map symbols

The *National Geographic Traveler* brings you the best of Prague and the Czech Republic in text, pictures, and maps. Divided into three main sections, the guide begins with an overview of history and culture. Following are four chapters devoted to Prague and six to the Czech Republic, with featured sites selected by the author for their particular interest.

The city and regions, and sites within them, are arranged geographically. Prague is divided into areas. A map introduces each area or region, highlighting the featured sites. Walks and drives, plotted on their own maps, suggest routes for discovering an area. Features and sidebars give intriguing detail on history, culture, or contemporary life.

The final section, Travelwise, lists essential information for the traveler—pretrip planning, getting around, money matters, and what to do in emergencies—along with a selection of hotels, restaurants, shops, entertainment, and activities.

To the best of our knowledge, all information is accurate as of the press date. However, it is always advisable to call ahead when possible.

Color coding

186

Each region is color coded for easy reference. Find the region you want on the map on the front flap, and look for the color flash at the top of the pages of the relevant chapter. Information in **Travelwise** is also color coded to each region.

Visitor information

Convent of St. Agnes

- Map p. 85
- U Milosrdných 17
- 221 879 111
- Closed Mon.
- $$
- Tram: 5, 8, 14 (Dlouhá). Metro: Náměstí Republiky

Practical information for most sites is given in the side column (see key to symbols on back flap). The map reference gives the page number of the map and usually a grid reference. Other details are address, telephone number, days closed, entrance charge in a range from $ (under $2) to $$$$$ (over $8), and nearest public transportation in Prague. Other sites have information in italics and parentheses in the text.

TRAVELWISE

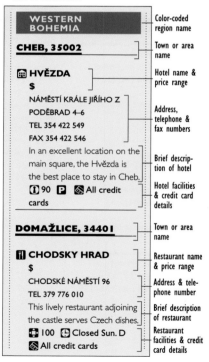

Color-coded region name — WESTERN BOHEMIA

Town or area name — CHEB, 35002

Hotel name & price range — HVĚZDA $

Address, telephone & fax numbers — NÁMĚSTÍ KRÁLE JIŘÍHO Z PODĚBRAD 4–6 TEL 354 422 549 FAX 354 422 546

Brief description of hotel — In an excellent location on the main square, the Hvězda is the best place to stay in Cheb.

Hotel facilities & credit card details — 90 P All credit cards

Town or area name — DOMAŽLICE, 34401

Restaurant name & price range — CHODSKY HRAD $

Address & telephone number — CHODSKÉ NÁMĚSTÍ 96 TEL 379 776 010

Brief description of restaurant — This lively restaurant adjoining the castle serves Czech dishes.

Restaurant facilities & credit card details — 100 Closed Sun. D All credit cards

Hotel & restaurant prices

An explanation of the price ranges used in entries is given in the Hotels & Restaurants section (beginning on p. 302).

PRAGUE AREA MAPS

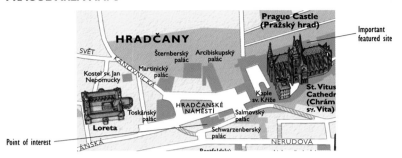

- A locator map accompanies each area map and shows the location of that area in the city.

WALKING TOURS

- An information box gives the starting and finishing points, time and length of walk, and places not to be missed along the route.

REGIONAL MAPS

- A locator map accompanies each regional map and shows the location of that region in the country.
- Adjacent regions are shown, each with a page reference.

NATIONAL GEOGRAPHIC

TRAVELER
Prague
& the Czech Republic

About the author

Stephen Brook first visited Prague in the mid-1980s, and it was one of the central European cities featured in his book *The Double Eagle* (1988). When he returned in 1991, the days of communist rule were over, and the city was enjoying a new lease on life, as reflected in his next book about the city, *Prague* (1992).

Stephen grew up in London, studied at Cambridge, and worked as a publisher's editor in the United States and in London before becoming a full-time writer in 1982. Since then he has written 30 books on a wide range of subjects including travel, wine, opera, dreams, and infidelity. He has also contributed numerous articles to *Vogue, The Times, Cigar Aficionado, Condé Nast Traveller, Decanter,* and other publications.

Now living in London with his wife, Stephen takes every opportunity to travel and explore the world. He retains a special affection for Prague, where some of his forebears lived, as there are few other cities that combine such dramatic beauty with such a vigorous cultural life.

History & culture

A statue of St. Wenceslas mimics the more traditional one in Wenceslas Square.

Prague & the
Czech Republic today

POISED AT THE HEART OF EUROPE, WHERE DIVERSE CULTURES HAVE COL-
lided for centuries, the City of a Thousand Spires has endured conflict after conflict—
dynastic, religious, political, racial. In the process, the fairy-tale city has been built and
rebuilt, collecting diverse artistic styles from far and wide, so that today's visitor may sip
beer in a Romanesque cellar, gaze at baroque and Gothic church spires, admire grand
baroque and rococo palaces, and seek out art nouveau and cubist examples of architecture. More than a decade has passed since the fall of communism, and the city—and surrounding country—has come alive with a new devotion to architecture, music, art, and
literature. The city is on the move again.

THE "NEW" CZECH REPUBLIC

Bohemia and Moravia have been through so
many transformations over the past century
that their inhabitants could be forgiven for feeling perplexed about their identity. Now firmly
ensconced within democratic Europe, the country is still weighed down to some extent by the
consequences of more than four decades under
a totalitarian regime. Essentially Slav in language and culture, its gaze is nonetheless set
firmly westward, and the Czechs long to be
accepted within the European Union as soon as
it is economically feasible. Despite the country's
newly regained independence, there is a bit of
unease among the Czechs, some of whom see
their republic as freshly colonized by external
investors on the one hand and by criminal
fraternities on the other.

The Czech Republic has adapted swiftly to
its liberation from Communist rule in 1989.
Yet that adaptation has been uneven, and any
visitor is bound to notice the discrepancies.
Cities such as Prague and Brno have become
dynamic business centers, with bright new
office buildings, hotels, and supermarkets. The
Trabants and Ladas of old, consigned to the
country lanes, have been replaced by new-
model Škodas (built by Volkswagen) and
Audis. Czechs who have invested wisely or
benefited from the burgeoning tourist
industry or latched on to the right high-tech
industry at the right moment have done very
well for themselves. Foreign investment, most
notably from Germany and Austria, has
focused on the cities, where high-tech industries are sprouting, and a sophisticated cultural and gastronomic way of life thrive.

Prague in particular has become a truly
cosmopolitan city once again. A large
expatriate community, drawn by business and
professional opportunities and by a low cost
of living, has enlivened the city. There are
Internet cafés, bagel emporia, restaurants
offering eclectic cuisines, foreign language
bookshops, and all the other support
services that help prop up an international
population while also offering new vistas to
the indigenous population.

The countryside is a different story. The
small towns and villages of Bohemia and
Moravia have tremendous charm, but many
of the residents are living on restricted
incomes, without the social services structures—free schools, health care, and subsi-
dized accommodations—that were among the
few benefits of Communist rule. Basic services
are still provided, but a bill comes attached to
many others. Salaries are not high, and for
those on low incomes it is a struggle to
maintain a decent standard of living.

In the depressed industrial heartlands,
crime is common and prostitution rife; close
to the borders with Germany and Austria,
local populations work hard to take euros
from the wealthy visitors, by fair means or
foul. The discrepancy between earnings in
countries such as Germany and Austria and
those within the Czech Republic are so great
that the country has become a paradise for

**The Bohemian form of plasterwork
decoration called sgraffito has been a
popular method of decorating houses
for centuries.**

bargain hunters. Food and drink, especially, are extremely cheap to "western" visitors.

TRADITIONS

The Czech Republic has not abandoned its traditions. The quality of its glassware and semiprecious jewelry, especially garnets, has been lauded for centuries. You can still find beautiful handcrafted pieces as well as a huge range of glassware. You can buy such items in major towns throughout the country, but be sure to shop around, as quality and prices may vary greatly.

Western Bohemia is rich in spa towns, those health resorts beloved by overindulged Europeans. Originally founded to offer treatments involving bathing in or drinking the supposedly healthful mineral waters bubbling from springs, they quickly became social centers, offering smart hotels with casinos, restaurants, coffee houses, and tea shops. The two biggest ones in the Czech Republic are Karlovy Vary and Mariánské Lázně, which used to be better known by their German names of Karlsbad and Marienbad. They became run-down during the Communist era, but since have been revived and restored and now are extremely popular with visitors, some of whom come for treatments, though many come as tourists to enjoy the scenery and walks, the coffeehouses and restaurants.

In the past it was not easy to get to know the locals. During Communist rule, contacts with foreign visitors were more or less forbidden, so attempts at conversation often led nowhere. Even today, the older generation of Czechs can seem reserved to visitors, but you'll find the younger generation far more open and welcoming. In the past German was often the second language, but today many people are eager to study English and welcome an opportunity to practice their skills.

THE COUNTRYSIDE

While Prague is the Czech Republic's heartbeat, the countryside possesses its own charms. Vast tracts of land remain relatively undeveloped, places that are rich in natural beauty and cultural interest as well.

Nearly every town of any size in the Czech Republic has something to offer the visitor. Most are laid out with a large central square,

often used as a marketplace, overlooked by the main church and the often brightly decorated town hall. Away from the main square, lanes lead to other churches and, often, to a castle.

The Czech Republic is very conscious of its rich cultural heritage. Almost all of its fortresses, castles, and country mansions are open to the public and contain historical exhibits and, sometimes, art collections as well. Even a small town may have a little museum full of local—sometimes dusty—artifacts.

With music and gusto, a two-man band in a Prague pub honors the Czech antihero character in *The Good Soldier Švejk,* created by author Jaroslav Hašek to poke fun at Austrian control over the Czechs.

The landscape is varied. In the north, mountains rise above the landscape, covered in pretty woods and spangled with resorts beloved by hikers and skiers, depending on the season. In the southern parts of Bohemia and Moravia, the terrain is gentler: There are hilly regions, but also flatter areas dotted with lakes that have for centuries been used to farm fish. Here, too, you'll find the country's best vineyards.

The Bohemian countryside in particular is a hiker's paradise. National parks and nature reserves, such as the Český ráj and the Šumava mountains, are crisscrossed by trails. These parks are filled with rare and bizarre geological formations, ruined castles, fast-moving rivers, deep gorges, and stands of primeval

forest. The Czechs are enthusiastic when it comes to outdoor recreation, so activities such as mountain biking, hiking, and canoeing are all readily available. In winter, the focus turns to skiing, skating, and snowboarding.

VISITING THE CZECH REPUBLIC

Getting around the country is fairly easy, thanks to a well-developed and inexpensive public transportation system. The drawback is that such transportation caters overwhelmingly to the local population, not to visitors, so schedules can seem odd, with many services early in the day and late in the afternoon, and very little in between. There's no doubt that the easiest way to explore the country is by car. The major cities and towns are home to numerous car rental agencies, and some of the locally based ones offer more attractive rates than the international chains. Outside the towns, the roads are fairly empty, although

Centuries-old bridges and golden spires provide a graceful backdrop for the cultural renaissance that has been underway in Prague since the fall of communism in 1989.

slow-moving trucks and tractors can impede your journey. A few freeways radiating from Prague allow swift access from the capital to different parts of the country.

For the visitor, the Czech Republic is a kind of paradise. There is no shortage of hotels and restaurants and other tourist facilities; there are a wealth of cultural attractions to visit and plenty of events to attend. The country as a whole—with uncrowded roads, countless charming towns and renovated spas, and a castle on just about every crag—is a joy to explore. The cuisine may not be the most exciting in Europe, but it's inexpensive and wholesome. The beer is wonderful and the wine increasingly enjoyable. And, except in Prague, prices will come as a pleasant surprise. ■

Food & drink

CZECHS HAVE HEARTY APPETITES. RICH SOUPS, LARGE PORTIONS OF MEAT and dumplings, and heavy desserts are mainstays of their diet, all washed down with what many consider to be the best beer in the world. Nourishing and full-flavored, Czech cuisine is heavily meat based, with beef and, above all, pork taking center stage. Vegetarians may have a tough time here!

Polévky (soups)—hearty and satisfying—can always be recommended, especially at lunchtime. Smoked meat, such as *uzené* (pork) and *šunka* (boiled Prague ham), or *vejce* (eggs) are often used as starters. The principal fish *(ryby)* are *pstruh* (trout) and *kapr* (carp), which can be excellent—it is advisable to order them only in specialist restaurants or at lakeside inns, where they are likely to be fresh.

Main courses are usually served with *knedlíky* (dumplings) or some kind of potato dish. Dumplings are much maligned by those who find them dull and heavy on the stomach. Made from flour, bread, or potatoes, they are served in slices hacked off a large dumpling roll. Their main function is to mop up the rich sauces ladled over most dishes, and this they do admirably.

Svíčková, a Bohemian specialty, consists of thin slices of beef served with dumplings to absorb an abundant white creamy sauce. In winter look for game dishes such as *husa* (goose) and *bažant* (pheasant). When in doubt, choose *vepřové* (pork), which is usually reliable; *vepřový řízek* (schnitzel) is universally available. *Kuře* (chicken) and *kachna* (duck) are also popular.

Traditionally, Czechs didn't bother too much about vegetables, except for *zelí* (cabbage) and *žampiony* (mushrooms). Main courses are usually garnished with *obloha*, a small pile of pickled cabbage, carrot, beets, and lettuce. Sometimes *špenát* (spinach) or an uninspiring salad might make an appearance. Restaurants in major cities and at tourist attractions make more of an effort to provide vegetables or salads, but don't expect it in most eating places.

For vegetarians, a useful, if somewhat stodgy, standby is *smažený sýr* (fried cheese). Pizza parlors and a handful of vegetarian restaurants have made life a little easier for those who prefer a meat-free diet.

In cities some places feature international menus, though the dishes may not be very accomplished. Of course, in Prague and Brno you will find sophisticated restaurants with a standard of cooking as high as most European cities, with prices to match.

DESSERTS

Desserts tend to be filling but often lack variety. *Palačinky* (pancakes) are a good bet. They are usually filled with chocolate sauce, ice cream, or fruit, then topped with whipped cream. *Kompot* (stewed fruits) can be good, too, and fruit dumplings, usually stuffed with plums, apricots, strawberries, or blueberries, are delicious if filling. *Sýr* (cheese) will seem tasteless to visitors more used to French or Italian varieties. The best places to satisfy a sweet tooth are streetside stands, which sell *zmrzlina* (ice cream), or a *cukrárna*, the Czech equivalent of the German or Austrian *konditorei*, where you can usually find excellent *presso* (espresso) and delicious pastries and cakes.

DRINK

The best drink to accompany rich Czech food is undoubtedly *pivo* (beer; see pp. 184–185). Bohemia has been famous since medieval times for the quality of its hops, and almost every town in the republic has its own brewery. The local brew is usually worth trying; otherwise, stick to major brands, such as Budvar, Pilsner, and Staropramen.

Wine (see pp. 270–271) can be very good, though only in wine regions and in top restaurants will you be offered any information about what is in the glass other than the variety of grape. Opinions are mixed on *Becherovka*, a liqueur made from a secret formula blending 20 different herbs. Fruit brandies such as *slivovice* (plum) can be delicious. ∎

Prague's oldest and largest pub, U Fleků boasts seating for 1,200 in its many rooms.

Land & landscape

THE CZECH LANDSCAPE IS A GENTLE ONE FOR THE MOST PART—ROLLING hills, often extensive forested plains, with, on the northern borders, some fairly serious mountains. The landlocked Czech Republic encompasses an area of 30,449 square miles (78,703 sq km) and straddles central Europe, poking deep into Germany to the west and meeting Slovakia to the east. It also shares borders with Austria and Poland.

The Carpathian Mountains rise to the north and east of the country. The development of coal mines, steel works, and other heavy industries has led to conurbations in various parts of the republic, but most notably along the northern border with Poland and Germany. The population is dispersed, partly as a consequence of the placing of new industries and workshops throughout the former Czechoslovakia during the Communist years, in effect transforming hitherto rural areas into industrial centers. Prague is easily the largest city, with a population of 1.2 million, followed by Brno in Moravia.

RIVERS

The Vltava is the best known of Bohemia's rivers and, thanks to its musical and artistic associations, has a special place in the hearts of the people. The region's main river, the Labe (better known in German as the Elbe), has its source in the Krkonoše (Giant Mountains), then flows south, west, and north through Bohemia. Many important towns were

**The Český ráj nature reserve is full
of bizarre rock formations such as the
sandstone Prachov crags.**

founded on its banks, and close to the German
border inland ports such as Ústí nad Labem
and Děčín edge its shores. From here barges
and boats carry cargo downriver through
Germany toward Hamburg and the North Sea.

The Vltava begins in the Šumava mountains
of southern Bohemia. Many picturesque castles
are perched above its banks as it winds northward toward Prague, but the Vltava valley is
not especially fertile. Stretches of the river have
been dammed and converted into artificial
lakes for recreational purposes. These include
the Lipno and, nearer Prague, Slapy reservoirs.
From the capital, the Vltava continues to flow
north until it joins the Labe at Mělník. The
rivers Jizera and Ohře are tributaries of the
mighty Labe, and the Sázava, which winds

through castle-strewn country southeast of
Prague, is a tributary of the Vltava. Another
important river, the Morava, a tributary of the
Danube to the south, rises in the Jeseníky
mountains to flow south through Olomouc
and eastern Moravia.

The republic is richly supplied with
medicinal springs credited with great benefits
to health. Some were prized by the Celtic tribes
that once inhabited the region, but they were
developed commercially only in the 18th
and 19th centuries. This led to the creation
of many spas, notably Karlovy Vary and
Mariánské Lázně, which became fashionable
social and medical centers.

MOUNTAINS & KARST

Much of Bohemia's wealth derived from the
extraction of minerals from the Krušné hory
(Ore Mountains), which straddle the German
border northwest of Prague. The area was settled
by Saxon miners in medieval times, but after a
few centuries the mines were exhausted.
Uranium was once mined at Jáchymov, now better known for its radioactive medicinal springs.

The other important range within Bohemia
is the Krkonoše, which are shared with Poland
along the border northeast of Prague. These
mountains form a region of Alpine pastures
and extensive forests, and industrial towns were
established lower in the glacial valleys that
descend toward the south. The less dramatic
Jizerské hory (Jizera Mountains) adjoin the
Krkonoše to the west; to the southeast, within
Moravia, the Jeseníky range reaches 4,892 feet
(1,491 m).

In southern Bohemia, the rolling Šumava
(Bohemian Forest) encompasses a large nature
reserve of great beauty. Many Bohemian hills
feature strange rock formations, including free-
standing pillars, labyrinths, and natural arches.
These are found in the crag country, known as
the Adršpach–Teplice rocks, and in the Český
ráj (Bohemian Paradise), which is famous for
its "rock towns," a series of bizarre formations
created principally by erosion.

Within Moravia, the most fascinating
geologic feature is the Moravský kras
(Moravian Karst; see pp. 266–267), a Devonian
limestone region of ravines and gullies northeast of Brno. It is celebrated for its caves,
chasms, grottoes, and underground rivers. ■

History of Prague & the Czech Republic

THE EARLY HISTORY OF THE CZECH REPUBLIC IS EXCEEDINGLY COMPLICATED. Mammoth hunters inhabited the region in Paleolithic times, but nothing is known about them. Bronze Age burial sites have revealed that Celtic peoples settled among the more fertile river valleys. One of these tribes, the Boii, arrived in about 400 B.C. from present-day Germany and gave its name to Bohemia. Three hundred years later, the Celts were driven out by German tribes, notably the Marcomanni, who, many years later, drove the Romans from the area.

EARLY HISTORY

Slav tribes began to invade the region that is now the Czech Republic by the sixth century, and toward the end of the century they were in effective control of Bohemia and Moravia. One of these tribes was the Czechs, named after their legendary ancestor Čech. The Slavs were dominated by the Avars, an Asiatic people who controlled what is now Hungary and required tribute from the neighboring Slavs. At the end of the eighth and beginning of the ninth centuries, Charlemagne, the first Holy Roman Emperor, made inroads into Bohemia, even converting a few nobles to Christianity, and his forces helped to expel the Avars from the region.

At about the same time, Mojmír I had established to the east what later became known as the Great Moravian Empire, which lived up to its grandiose name by pushing eastward and conquering parts of Slovakia and Hungary. (Some excavations dating from this time can be visited at Uherské Hradiště in southern Moravia; see p. 276.)

In 846 Mojmír was succeeded by his nephew Rastislav, who converted to Christianity. He requested the Byzantine emperor Michael III to authorize a religious mission to Moravia. Accordingly, the emperor dispatched two Greek brothers, Cyril and Methodius, to Moravia in 863. Here they converted some of the populace, although pagan elements remained for centuries, and Methodius became the first archbishop of Greater Moravia. The Great Moravian Empire was short-lived. Rastislav was deposed by his pro-Germanic nephew Svatopluk in 870, and in 907 Moravian troops were overcome by the Magyar tribes, who had settled in what is present-day Hungary.

THE PŘEMYSLID DYNASTY

Meanwhile, Bohemia, with its forests and pastures and kinder climate, was prospering. In the early ninth century, legend has it, Princess Libuše of Bohemia married a plowman by the name of Přemysl, thus founding the first Czech dynasty, which lasted for four centuries. Prague was the Přemyslid capital, and its castle became the seat of a bishopric in 973. Prince Spytihněv I placed Bohemia under Frankish protection in 895, and Moravia and Bohemia were united during the reign of Prince Břetislav I in 1019.

There was considerable tension between the aspirations of the Přemyslid dynasty and the German rulers who held sway over much of central Europe. Prince Václav I was pro-German, but he paid for his alliance with his life when he was murdered in 935 by his brother Boleslav I. Much revered, Václav I was none other than the "Good King Wenceslas" every carol singer knows about; he was also declared the patron saint of Bohemia. Vratislav II became the first Bohemian king in 1085 and was crowned with the blessing of the German Holy Roman Emperor Henry IV. Henceforth, Bohemia was part of the Holy Roman Empire, a vast confederation of European nations.

Přemysl Otakar I (R.1197–1230) invited German settlers, principally from Saxony, to Bohemia and Moravia to establish towns that soon became important mining or trading centers. Art and architecture flourished under the patronage of a wealthy merchant class.

In 1990 Soviet forces long stationed in the old Czechoslovakia finally took leave of the country for good.

Přemysl Otakar II (*R*.1253–1278), backed by the wealth derived from mining, extended the Bohemian domains from Silesia to Austria, what is today Slovenia and the shores of the Adriatic. Unfortunately for Otakar, the German-based Habsburg dynasty was also consolidating its power, and he was unable to prevent Habsburg encroachment. At the Battle of Moravské pole (Moravian Field) in 1278, Otakar was killed. He was succeeded by his son Václav II (*R*.1283–1305), who conquered parts of Poland. The Přemyslid dynasty came to a sudden end in 1306, when Václav III (*R*.1305–1306) made an abortive attempt to seize the crown of Poland and was murdered.

CHARLES IV

There followed a period of chaos and hostility between Czechs and Germans. In 1311 an arranged marriage between John of Luxembourg (*R*.1310–1346), the son of the Holy Roman Emperor, and Václav II's daughter Eliška brought a measure of stability, and John remained king until his death in battle. John was succeeded by Charles IV (*R*.1346–1378), who was subsequently elected Holy Roman Emperor. It was Charles who made Bohemia into a mighty European power and developed Prague into a major capital city.

Few rulers have left so lasting a mark on a single city as Charles IV did on Prague. Born in the city on May 14, 1316, he was educated at the court of France and the University of Paris, which may account for his cosmopolitan outlook. Although christened Václav, he changed his name to Charles after his uncle, Charles IV. Intelligent and competent, Charles was not on good terms with his father, King John of Luxembourg. As a result, he spent part of his youth in Italy until he was appointed governor of Moravia in 1334 and co-governor of Bohemia seven years later in 1341.

At the remarkably young age of 13, Charles married the sister of the future King Philippe

Prague in 1750—already centuries old—was a flourishing capital city.

VI of France, Blanche of Valois, but three more wives were to follow. He became king of Bohemia in 1346, after the death of his father, and was elected Holy Roman Emperor in 1355. This, as well as his four dynastic marriages, helped him to consolidate his domains, adding parts of modern-day Germany and Poland. Legal and constitutional reforms made Bohemia one of the most advanced medieval states in Europe.

Despite his international vision and aspirations, Charles did not neglect his capital, and Prague soon became the intellectual and cultural center of his empire. On his initiative the Cathedral of St. Vitus (Chrám sv. Víta) and Charles Bridge (Karlův most) were constructed, and the castle, which had been severely damaged by fire in 1304, was renovated. In 1348 a whole new district of the city, the New Town

(Nové Město) with its many churches, was designed as a model of sophisticated town planning. Such remarkable churches as the Karlov and St. Mary of the Snows (Kostel Panny Maria Sněžná) were begun at his command, and, outside Prague, the glittering castle at Karlštejn was his creation, too. The Rivers Vltava and Labe were cleared to make them fully navigable, and vineyards were established on the outskirts of the city.

Charles won the support of Pope Clement VI, his former tutor in Paris, to elevate Prague from a bishopric to an archbishopric in 1344, which in effect put the Bohemian church under his control. Charles also founded Prague University, the first in central Europe. Scholars and artists from Germany, France, Italy, and elsewhere were invited to Prague and contributed to its cultural splendor.

Charles succeeded in elevating Bohemia to one of the most sophisticated of European states, but the country's flourishing condition

Emperor Charles IV was the great ruler who transformed medieval Prague into one of Europe's most important cities.

proved short-lived. After his death from pneumonia on November 29, 1378, the domains were divided among his three sons, and Bohemia's most glorious period was over. Charles's true memorial, however, is the city of Prague. Despite all later additions and changes, it retains the major monuments and urban structure he imposed on it.

The dissolute Václav IV (R.1378–1419) succeeded Charles. Václav unwittingly created a martyr when he had a priest called John of Nepomuk murdered for refusing to reveal a secret disclosed to him in the confessional. John was canonized in 1729, and statues of the saint can be found all over Bohemia.

Václav enjoyed a long reign, but eventually the nobility wearied of him, and he was deposed. By this time there was considerable resentment against the abuses of the Catholic Church, which was in a state of disarray throughout Europe. This led to the rise of the reformist Hussite movement: Influenced by the English preacher John Wycliffe, it had a political as well as religious agenda, seeking to diminish the control of the Catholic nobility over the affairs of the country. The movement was named after the preacher and university rector Jan Hus (ca 1372–1415). He was excommunicated in 1410 and expelled from the university with his followers a year later. In 1414 he was summoned to the Council of Constance to defend his heretical views, but although assured of safe conduct, he was arrested en route. He was tried for heresy, condemned, and burned at the stake in 1415.

Václav IV's anti-Hussite line led to the First Defenestration in 1419, when the populist preacher Jan Želivský marched on the New Town Hall building. There Želivský's followers threw Catholic officials to their deaths from the windows, starting a Prague tradition in dealing with one's opponents. Václav himself died two weeks later and chaos broke out. His brother Sigismund had himself crowned in 1420, but hardly anyone accepted his legitimacy. The Hussite warrior Jan Žižka, eventually blinded in both eyes in separate battles, took up arms against the German and Catholic forces, and his troops conducted a violent anticlerical campaign across the length and breadth of the land.

By 1423 the Hussites had split into two factions: the moderate Utraquists and the more radical Taborites, who were already warring among themselves. Žižka led the Taborites to victory over the Utraquists twice in 1823 and again in 1824. He subdued them, but after his death from the plague in 1424 the divisions led to further fighting. A settlement was finally negotiated by the Catholic Church with the Utraquists in 1433 at Basel in Switzerland, but the rebellious Taborites fought on for a year until they were soundly defeated by the Utraquists at Lipany, to the east of Prague. The Hussite wars were finally over, but the poor, who had been championed by the Taborites, remained destitute and the idealism of the radicals remained unrealized. Nonetheless the Hussite movement, backed by the lesser nobility and the burghers, had won considerable gains, although the great aristocratic landowners, some of whom were also Hussites, remained in overall control.

HUSSITES & JAGIELLONS

Power now came into the hands of the Utraquists, who were led by Jiříz Poděbřad (George of Poděbrady; R.1458–1471); he was elected to the throne in 1458 after many years as regent to the heir to the Bohemian throne, Ladislav. The rise to power of this gifted and tolerant ruler proved unacceptable to the pope, who persuaded the Hungarian king and ruler of Moravia, Matthias Corvinus, to attack Bohemia. George averted this potential threat, but died in 1471. Numerous claimants to the Bohemian throne pressed their case. The successful candidate, elected king by the Bohemian Estates (in effect the Czech parliament), was Prince Vladislav Jagiellon (Vladislav II; R.1471–1516), the son of King Casimir IV of Poland and descended on his maternal side from the Přemyslid dynasty.

He immediately found himself engaged in a power struggle with Matthias Corvinus. In 1490 Matthias died, and Vladislav inherited the crown of Hungary. The following year the Catholic Vladislav, whose daughter Anne had married into the Habsburg family, agreed that the succession to Bohemia and Hungary would pass to the Austrian rulers. There was still no stability in the kingdom: Religious strife between Hussite reformers and traditional Catholics continued unabated, if less bloodily than before. The Czech lands, already enfeebled by decades of war, stagnated under the rule of Vladislav and his son Ludvík.

THE HABSBURGS

After the death of the childless Ludvík in 1526, his brother-in-law Ferdinand of Habsburg claimed the throne of Bohemia. Ferdinand (R.1526–1564) was no more Czech than the Jagiellons had been, but at least he was a firm ruler, with the powerful backing of his brother Emperor Charles V. When Ferdinand invited the Jesuits to Bohemia in 1556, he initiated a new era of Catholic power, although he did his best not to alienate the Protestants, who by this time constituted 85 percent of the population. Ferdinand was succeeded in 1564 by the tolerant Maximilian II (R.1564–1576), who accepted the Bohemian Confession of 1575,

which guaranteed religious freedom—in theory at least.

In 1576 Rudolph II (R.1576–1611) came to the throne and made Prague his principal residence. When Rudolph was elected Holy Roman Emperor, Prague became an imperial capital and a flourishing center of intellectual life and culture. Scientists such as the Danish

Refusing to recant his radical views, theologian Jan Hus was led to a meadow outside Prague's walls in 1415 and burned alive.

astronomer Tycho Brahe, as well as less reputable alchemists like Edward Kelley, were particularly welcome at Rudolph's court.

All the while conflict between Catholic and Protestant was growing, as the Catholic establishment consolidated its grip on power. Rudolph himself was more interested in intellectual and mystical matters than affairs of state. Other members of the Habsburg dynasty were well aware of this and were keen to oust him from power. He tried to shore up his support by wooing the Bohemian nobility. Their price for support was a declaration known as the *Letter of Majesty* of 1609, which guaranteed religious freedom and imposed limits on his powers as a ruler. As a stratagem for survival it didn't work, and in 1611 Rudolph, who was increasingly ill, was forced

to abdicate. His brother Matthias (*R*.1611–19) succeeded him.

Tension has to be diffused or something snaps. In the case of Bohemia, it snapped. In May 1618, Czech Protestant nobles gathered in Prague to form a Diet (or parliament) to express their views. On May 23, a mob, convinced that the regime was ignoring the *Letter of Majesty*, threw three court officials from the castle windows (they were unharmed but humiliated), an act commemorated as the Second Defenestration. This proved to be the starting signal for the Thirty Years War. The Protestant forces took up arms against the Habsburgs and initially scored a number of successes, including the capture of Plzeň.

Matthias died in 1619 and was succeeded by Ferdinand II (*R*.1619–1637). He was soon deposed by the Bohemian Estates, who felt they had the right to elect the king of Bohemia. Their choice was Frederick V, ruler of the Palatinate in Germany, and brother-in-

Fearing the growing power of his top general, Wallenstein, Emperor Ferdinand ordered his murder in Cheb in 1634.

law of the future Charles I of England. But he proved ineffectual, especially against the clever Ferdinand, who persuaded the Catholic Bavarians to make common cause with the Habsburg forces. The amiable Frederick had no stomach for the fight. At the Battle of White Mountain just outside Prague on November 8, 1620, the Protestant forces were routed in just a few hours. Frederick made a run for it, and Ferdinand returned to Prague in triumph and resumed control of the Czech lands. He persecuted the abject Protestant nobility, confiscating their estates and executing their leaders. Thirty thousand Protestant families fled as the Counter-Reformation grew in strength. Their lands were appropriated either by Ferdinand's supporters, such as the imperial commander Albrecht z Valdštejn

(Wallenstein), or by foreign nobility. Bohemia and Moravia were now, in effect, dependencies of the Habsburg Empire.

Wallenstein

Wallenstein sowed the seeds of his own destruction by succeeding so brilliantly as a soldier that he appeared to pose a threat to the emperor. Indeed, for a few decades, a large part of northern Bohemia was run virtually as a separate country under Wallenstein's rule. An aristocrat and soldier, he was born in eastern Bohemia in 1583. In 1606 he converted to Catholicism and supported the imperial cause before and during the Battle of White Mountain. Emperor Ferdinand II, suitably impressed by Wallenstein's military prowess, made him a count in 1617 after a successful campaign against the Venetian Republic. Wallenstein prospered, and his wealth grew by marriage to the very rich Isabella von Harrach.

After the Battle of White Mountain,

Wallenstein rapidly acquired estates such as Frýdlant and Jičín, many of them expropriated from Protestant noblemen who had backed the wrong side. Before long he was the owner of 24 estates and castles, and a colossal château in Malá Strana. The grateful emperor made him Duke of Frýdlant in 1625.

Because his estates included mines and other sources of wealth, Wallenstein became ever richer and more powerful. By putting his own troops at the disposal of Ferdinand II as mercenaries, he became indispensable to the emperor and was appointed supreme commander of the imperial forces in 1625. However, political pressure against the ambitious general led to his dismissal in 1630, but two years later he was reappointed. He soon justified the emperor's confidence in him by defeating and slaying King Gustavus Adolphus II of Sweden at the Battle of Lutzen, in November 1632.

Unfortunately for Wallenstein, Emperor Ferdinand felt increasingly threatened by his commander's independence and by negotiations he had initiated with the Swedes. Wallenstein had raised his own armies, which served the emperor but also made him uneasy. When Wallenstein demanded that his officers swear an oath of personal loyalty to him, the emperor suspected treachery. On February 22, 1634, Ferdinand denounced Wallenstein as a traitor and ordered him captured dead or alive. Three days later, Wallenstein and some of his generals were assassinated by officers loyal to the emperor in Cheb in western Bohemia. His estates were soon distributed, projects such as the planned university at Jičín never came to pass, and the duchy of Frýdlant was no more. To this day it remains unclear whether Wallenstein's negotiations with the enemy were a sincere attempt to bring peace to the war-wracked Habsburg domains, or whether he really was conspiring against the emperor hoping to enrich himself further and even perhaps seize the Bohemian throne.

HABSBURGS TRIUMPHANT

The repeated Swedish invasions of Bohemia and Moravia caused tremendous devastation; not even Prague was immune. The Thirty Years War dragged on, causing unspeakable misery to the civilian population, until in

1648 the Peace of Westphalia was negotiated. Ferdinand died in 1637 and was succeeded by Ferdinand III (*R.*1637–1657). Reactionary Habsburg rule was imposed with a vengeance in an unholy alliance between the Counter-Reformation and Germanization. What is more, the peace treaty insisted that those Bohemians who had fought on the Swedish side should not be allowed to return to their country. One of those exiled was the leading intellectual and educationalist Jan Komenský (Comenius; 1592–1670), whose name is still revered in the Czech lands today.

The Habsburgs ruled from afar, oppressing the impoverished Czech peasantry with punishing rates of taxation. Outbreaks of plague swept towns already devastated by war, adding to the suffering of the people. It was not until the mid-18th century that a measure of prosperity and economic development began to return to these exhausted and depopulated lands. The Czech language, which had flowered under the Hussites, was in danger of becoming no more than a peasant dialect.

Maria Theresa & Joseph II

Under Empress Maria Theresa (*R.*1740–1780) and her son Joseph II (*R.*1780–1790), Bohemia and Moravia were divided into two separate provinces that gained in importance after the Habsburgs lost Silesia in 1745. All political control was exercised from Vienna, and Czech national aspirations were ignored or suppressed, although the Empress created a royal residence at Prague castle. Mines, glassworks, and other factories were beginning to bring prosperity to Bohemia and Moravia, and the population was increasing steadily. Conflict returned to Bohemia in 1756 when Frederick II of Prussia waged war against Maria Theresa. The Prussian troops reached Prague itself in 1757 but were defeated at the Battle of Kolín.

Emperor Joseph introduced religious toleration and allowed Czech culture to develop, even though he confirmed his Habsburg credentials by making German the official language. Serfdom was abolished in 1781. A Czech grammar book, compiled by Josef Dobrovský, was published in 1809. Perhaps it was the introduction of sensible reforms by Joseph that kept the Czechs relatively loyal to

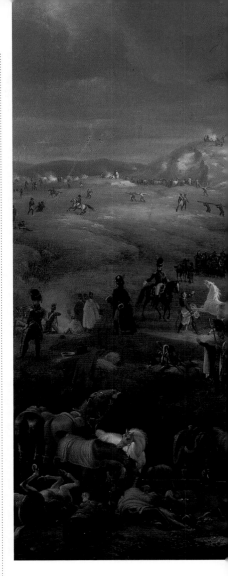

the Habsburgs and far less troublesome than the more volatile Hungarians.

NINETEENTH CENTURY

Those great upheavals of the early 19th century, the Napoleonic wars, had little impact on Bohemia and Moravia, even though the major Battle of Austerlitz was fought close to Brno. Napoleon inflicted a severe defeat on the combined armies of Russia and Austria. Throughout the 19th century Bohemia and

Louis Lejeune's 19th-century painting portrays Napoleon and his troops on the eve of the Battle of Austerlitz in December 1805.

Moravia became increasingly industrialized, especially in the north.

Lip service was paid to national aspirations by the Habsburgs after the revolutionary movements of 1848, but little would change without the Czechs themselves taking the initiative.

Compared with the turbulence in Vienna in 1848, which led to the flight of the emperor to Moravia, the Bohemia uprisings were mild and easily repressed, partly due to the lack of common ground between the German and Czech elements in the population. Some German speakers favored merging with German states.

Political assertion, as well as cultural expression, became increasingly divided along linguistic lines, with Czech and Slovak newspapers and theaters coexisting alongside

their German and Hungarian counterparts; even Charles University was split in this way in 1882. Composers such as Dvořák and Smetana captured the spirit of Czech culture, especially folk culture, in their music.

Political movements, predominantly liberal as well as nationalistic, made slow progress against the stately inertia of the Habsburgs. The establishment of the dual monarchy of Austria and Hungary in 1867, a concession to the national aspirations of the Magyars, only accelerated the pace of Magyarization in the Slovak provinces. It did not lead to comparable concessions to the Czechs, who felt sidelined by the compact between Austria and Hungary. Czech deputies, representing the region at the assembly in Vienna, were increasingly divided into two factions, of which the more radical were known as the Young Czechs. Compared with the Hungarians, their tangible successes were few; nonetheless, the Czechs benefited from reforms such as universal suffrage, which was granted by the Habsburgs in 1907 (women were not enfranchised until 1919).

END OF THE HABSBURGS

When war broke out in 1914, the Czechs were required to fight alongside their Austrian oppressors, but about 100,000 defected and joined the Czechoslovak Legions on the Eastern Front, in France, and in Italy. Defeat in World War I led to the swift collapse of the Habsburg empire. The architects of the Czechoslovak state were Tomáš Garrigue Masaryk (1850–1937), Edvard Beneš (1884–1948), and Milan Ratislav Štefánik, who had formed the Czechoslovak National Council in 1917. Masaryk and Beneš later became president and foreign minister, respectively, in the new government established after the Czechoslovak republic was declared on October 28, 1918. The new republic was composed not only of Bohemia, Moravia, and Slovakia, but also Ruthenia. It was a formula that helped to dismember the Austro-Hungarian Empire, and one that led to grave problems later in the century.

An 1880 engraving catches the lively street life in the heart of the Jewish quarter.

Tomáš Garrigue Masaryk devoted his long life to the creation of an independent Czechoslovak republic and became its first president in 1918.

THE ROAD TO INDEPENDENCE

Tomáš Garrigue Masaryk was born in Hodonín in southern Moravia in 1850; his father was an ill-educated Slovak coachman, his mother a German-Moravian. At first Masaryk seemed destined to make his living as a village craftsman, but his quest for education took him in very different directions. The German School at Brno was followed by university studies in Vienna. He then spent a year studying for a doctorate in Leipzig, where he met his future wife, an American music student, Charlotte Garrigue. After their marriage in New York in 1878, he added her name to his. Masaryk became a classic liberal political leader, and he was appointed a philosophy professor at Charles University in

1882. In 1891 he was elected a member of the Reichsrat assembly based in Vienna.

His many academic works of cultural and political history developed his vision of the kind of state the new Czech nation should be. Although his views were strongly anticlerical, Masaryk was a nationalist in the broadest sense. He began by envisaging Czech nationhood as existing within the prevailing Habsburg monarchy rather than as a breakaway movement. However, the unflagging imperialism of the Austro-Hungarian Empire, especially in the Balkans, angered him deeply, and he turned increasingly toward the idea of Czech independence without embracing Slav nationalism.

At the beginning of World War I, Masaryk moved abroad and initiated the negotiations that would result four years later in the founding of Czechoslovakia. In Paris he, Beneš, and Štefánik established the Czechoslavak National Council. The Czechoslovak Legions, a fighting

Adolf Hitler, having annexed part of the country in 1938, makes his triumphant entry into Prague in March 1939.

force composed of former prisoners and emigrés who fought with Allied troops against Germany and Austria, ensured Allied support for Czech nationalist ambitions.

THE FORMING OF CZECHOSLOVAKIA

In May 1918 Masaryk negotiated the Pittsburgh Agreement, which laid the foundations for the merging of Bohemia, Moravia, and Slovakia into a single state. This was accepted by the Allied powers. A provisional government was established in October 1918, and a month later the National Assembly elected Masaryk as the first president of Czechoslovakia. He was repeatedly reelected until he retired in 1935. As president of the fledgling republic, Masaryk was able to put

along historical rather than ethnic principles—essentially they incorporated the country's heavy industry and manufacturing bases—and his guidelines were accepted at the postwar peace conferences.

The German, Hungarian, and Ruthenian minorities who remained within the borders were not pleased at all, but it was the German population—about three million in number—who complained the loudest. Dissatisfied with the Czech nationalist agenda, Konrad Henlein (1898–1948) spearheaded a movement to initiate change under the banner of the Sudeten German Party. Urged on by Hitler, Henlein made more and more vociferous demands for German autonomy and attracted overwhelming support from Sudeten Germans in elections held in May 1938. Thereafter the demands changed: The Germans wished to be incorporated within Hitler's Reich, a proposal the Czechs understandably found threatening as well as unacceptable.

GERMAN INVASION

Hitler stepped up the pressure and, thanks to the prevailing policy of appeasement, secured the support of the British and French governments. The Czech authorities were adamant in opposing the change. On October 1, 1938, German troops invaded the Sudetenland, the entire external border of Bohemia and Moravia, with the exception of a small part of northern Moravia that was occupied by Poland. Czechoslovakia had lost its industrial heartland. Four days later, Beneš resigned.

On March 15, 1939, Hitler invaded Bohemia and Moravia, which were designated a "protectorate" of the German Reich. For the next few years, the Nazis exploited Czech industrial strength to bolster their war effort. German oppression was constant. The Jews were persecuted, forced to live in ghettos or deported to camps; intellectuals, artists, Gypsies (Roma), and other "undesirable elements" were also imprisoned or murdered. Universities were closed. On May 27, 1942, Czech agents assassinated the brutal Nazi official Reinhard Heydrich. The consequences were fearsome: The village of Lidice, just outside Prague, was destroyed and its population either murdered or deported.

his liberal ideas into practice, making Czechoslovakia one of Europe's most democratic and secular nations. Remaining aloof from the excitements of party politics, he was perceived as the dignified symbol of the nation and guardian of its integrity. He died at the château of Lány in 1937.

New nations are often founded in unpromising circumstances after decades of colonial exploitation, but the new state of Czechoslovakia got off to a good start. It had not suffered excessively during World War I, and there had been no prolonged struggle against its former masters, the Habsburgs of Austria-Hungary. Moreover, Bohemia in particular was strongly industrialized and had excellent natural resources on which a modern prosperous state could be based.

The only stumbling block was the reluctance of the German-speaking corners of the new nation to remain within its borders. President Masaryk had established the borders

This war crime only increased Czech antagonism to German occupation.

SOVIET INVASION

On May 5, 1945, a bloody uprising in Prague spelled the end of German occupation, and four days later Soviet troops entered the city. The end of the war brought bitter consequences for the three million Sudeten Germans, who were briskly expelled. Beneš returned to Prague as president of the republic.

Sharing a common Slavic culture as well as a hatred of fascism, the liberated population was well disposed to the Soviets and their ideology. In 1946 the Communist Party won more votes than any other. Although it was not a clear majority, it nevertheless led to the appointment of the Communist leader Klement Gottwald (1896–1953) as prime minister. The Communists consolidated their hold on power in 1948, and 12 non-Communist ministers resigned their posts, not all of which were filled by Communists. Foreign Minister Jan Masaryk (1886–1948), the son of the former president, did not resign; he was found dead two weeks later, on March 10, in the courtyard of his ministry. It was long suspected that he had been murdered by defenestration in the traditional Prague fashion, but this theory is increasingly regarded as doubtful. Beneš also resigned and was replaced as president by Gottwald. Rigged elections secured an overwhelming majority for the Communists.

THE COMMUNIST YEARS

Czechoslovakia was swiftly transformed into a Stalinist state, and all opposition, even from within the ranks of the Communists, was crushed. Show trials were held, leading to more than 200 executions in the early 1950s. Just ten years after most of the Czech and Slovak Jews had been deported to death camps, anti-Semitism again became a feature of Czechoslovak ideology and propaganda, and a disproportionate number of those executed after the trials were Jewish. The government embarked on a policy of further industrialization, introducing heavy industry into rural Slovakia and elsewhere, with, in some places, disastrous long-term effects on the environment.

Gottwald died just nine days after Stalin in 1953. By the 1960s the Stalinist grip on the country had softened slightly, and a reformist group within the party was able to assert itself, egged on by many of the country's writers and intellectuals. In 1968 the leader of this faction, Slovak Alexander Dubček (1921–1992), became party leader, and the movement was popularly dubbed "socialism with a human face." The Prague Spring (see pp. 120–121) was enormously popular with the Czech and Slovak people, as the regime not only implemented economic reforms but permitted greater personal liberty and lifted much of the repressive censorship. The arts and intellectual life flourished after decades of suppression.

The Prague Spring would prove short-lived, however. Fearing that the movement would lead to secession from the Soviet bloc, the Soviets and their Warsaw Pact allies launched an invasion of Czechoslovakia in August. There was much heroic resistance in

RESTAURACE

To the horror of most of Prague's citizenry, Soviet and Warsaw Pact troops swept into the very heart of the city in August 1968.

the streets of Prague, and in January 1969 a student named Jan Palach set fire to himself in Wenceslas Square (Václavské náměstí) in protest. (His grave, never identified during the communist years, is now a place of pilgrimage at the Olšany cemetery in Vinohrady district.)

Homemade Czech weaponry and sacrificial gestures were no match for Soviet tanks, and might prevailed. Reforms were annulled, and a new hard-line leader, Gustáv Husák, was installed in power, even though he had initially supported the Prague Spring. The new regime was less murderous than Gottwald's, but dissent was stamped upon.

The Czechs, refusing to give up their quest for liberty, were heartened by the Helsinki Declaration on Human Rights. In 1977 a few thousand intellectuals, artists,

journalists, academics, priests, and others from all walks of life signed Charter 77, which affirmed the values of the declaration and argued for the dismantling of the totalitarian state in Czechoslovakia. Not surprisingly, the Communist regime took exception to Charter 77 and persecuted many of its signatories, who lost their jobs, were forced into exile, or were even imprisoned on trumped-up charges. For the Communists, any reminder of human liberties was anathema. The historical museums of Czechoslovakia made only fleeting references to Tomáš Garrigue Masaryk, without whom there probably would have been no Czechoslovakia; while the statues and monuments honoring him in nearly every village and town were torn down.

VELVET REVOLUTION
While Mikhail Gorbachev instigated his drastic economic, political, and social changes of *perestroika* in the Soviet Union, loyalists and

dissidents alike in Czechoslovakia, with their anti-Soviet feelings, looked on with skepticism. As Soviet dogmatism shifted more and more, however, it became clear that the Czech government would have to introduce some modest reforms. The dissident movement took heart and gathered strength, and it was further bolstered by the demolition of the Berlin Wall on November 9, 1989. Street demonstrations became larger and more vocal, as religious groups joined the support-ers of Charter 77. The violent suppression of a demonstration on November 17 marked the beginning of the end for the increasingly dis-credited regime, which had lost what little moral authority it ever had.

On November 20 a vast crowd, estimated at 200,000, gathered to demand the government's dissolution. Dissident groups formed the Civic Forum coalition, demanding the resignation of the communist leadership and an amnesty for political prisoners. Another, even larger

People crammed Old Town Square in a communist-style celebration in 1978.

demonstration took place on November 24 in Wenceslas Square, when the crowds were addressed not only by the playwright and political theorist Václav Havel but by Alexander Dubček, who had languished in obscurity after being deposed by the Soviets.

The Communists began making concessions, but it was too late. The Civic Forum stood firm, and the government fell from power a few weeks later. The old regime, which had long lost any vestige of credibility, succumbed to its own inertia; there was not a person in the land, party members included, who was not aware that the regime was living a lie.

On December 29 an event took place that would have been dismissed as fantasy just six months earlier: Havel, the most prominent and internationally renowned of the Chartists, was elected unanimously as the new head of

During the communist years, annual May Day celebrations were staged in order to demonstrate people's loyalty to the regime.

state. Dissident intellectuals, who under the Communists had been forced to eke out a living as window cleaners or stokers, suddenly found themselves running ministries or embassies. Elections were organized for the following June, and reformist parties, including Civic Forum and the Slovak party People Against Violence, received the most votes. Alexander Dubček was appointed speaker of the new parliament. The Velvet Revolution, so-called at the time because little blood was spilled during the transition from communism to democracy, was complete.

For some years after the Velvet Revolution, it was possible to see, daubed on the walls of Prague, the fading words HAVEL NA HRAD: Havel to the Castle. This was the battle cry for the entire nation in the final weeks of 1989.

Václav Havel

To many it seemed incongruous that this scruffy, chain-smoking, quiet-mannered writer and intellectual should be elevated to the highest office in the land. Havel, however, had for at least two decades been deeply immersed in political and moral issues. His writings and petitions had earned him the constant attention of the secret police and numerous spells in prison, but none of this deterred him from his pursuit of the truth.

After the Soviet invasion, Havel's officially sanctioned career as an artist came to an end, and he was obliged to pursue a new one as a brewery worker. Nothing could suppress his artistic integrity, however, fueled as it was by his profound understanding of the lies and deceptions on which the communist state was founded. In a series of underground publications, he expressed his revulsion at totalitarianism and appealed to the nation's leaders to pursue more truthful and liberating policies. Such appeals not only fell on deaf ears but also led to frequent imprisonment. In 1977 Havel cofounded Charter 77 and was subsequently incarcerated for four years.

When it became clear in the autumn of 1989 that the old communist regime was about to crumble, it was natural for freedom-loving Czechs to turn to Havel. He was a leading figure in Civic Forum, where he demonstrated political savoir faire as well as the moral authority that emanated from his essays and letters, many of which had been written to his wife from his prison cell.

THE NEW CZECH REPUBLIC

The esteem in which Havel was held remained constant, despite the initial confusions that characterized Czechoslovakia's return to democracy. Finance Minister Václav Klaus, who would ascend the ranks to become prime minister of the newly formed Czech Republic in 1993, steered through monetarist policies based on those pursued by British Prime Minister Margaret Thatcher. Czechoslovakia rapidly developed a full-fledged market economy based on the privatization of state resources, and it benefited from proximity to Germany, a country that began to invest heavily in Czech enterprises. Some Sudeten Germans expelled after the war began to press for the return of their former property, but Havel and the government showed no sympathy for their cases. In 1997, amid revelations of corruption within the Civic Democratic Party (ODS), Klaus resigned as prime minister. He staged a comeback in 2003, however, when Havel's term for president ended and Klaus, facing enormous opposition, won the seat in an extremely close, unexpected victory.

Social divisions, bigotry, nationalism, and racism had been suppressed under the Communists, but the restoration of liberty allowed the fears and prejudices of the people to be expressed. The Vietnamese and Roma minorities suffered from attacks and discrimination. Crime, never a serious problem (apart from corruption) under the Communists, was on the increase. Grave social and economic problems affecting the whole population

In 1989 the country was almost unanimous: Václav Havel must go to the castle to become the republic's new president.

seemed no nearer solution.

Nationalism also revived and culminated in demands for independence by Slovak politicians. Following the slim victory of the leading nationalist party under Vladimír Mečiar in the June 1992 elections, the country divided in two in January 1993. To many Czechs this seemed senseless, since Slovakia had always benefited from the industrial prosperity of the Czech lands from which it was now separated.

There is little reason for concern about the country's long-term future. Its economic base is strong, the standard of living acceptable. It benefits from its proximity Germany and Austria, encouraging tourism as well as investment, and its government is in responsible hands. Its democratic traditions are well rooted. ∎

The arts

AFTER 40 YEARS OF COMMUNIST RULE, THE "NEW" PRAGUE IS EXPERIENC-
ing a revival in the the arts and theater, as young playwrights, musicians, writers, and artists
flourish at their work. But Czech artistry dates far back into the country's past—indeed,
few countries are as richly endowed with such a great legacy of art and architecture.

For most visitors, the earliest examples of artistry
will be the three rotunda churches found
beneath street level in Prague, dating from the
11th and 12th centuries, followed by Gothic
buildings from the mid-13th century, among
them Cathedral St. Vitus and St. Agnes Convent.
But that's just scratching the surface. Palaces and
churches abound throughout the Czech Republic
from every period following—Renaissance,
baroque, art nouveau, and cubist foremost
among them. Painting and sculpture thrived in
these same periods, starring such artists as Karel
Skreta and Cosmas Asam. Beginning in the 19th
century, literature and music took front stage,
culminating in perhaps the country's best known
prodigy—Franz Kafka. As the 20th century pro-
gressed, Czechs were quick to adopt new art
forms such as film and mime.

ARCHITECTURE & ART
Romanesque: 11th–13th centuries
Little in the way of ancient artifacts exists,
other than the scant remains from the Great
Moravian Empire at Uherské Hradiště. Some of
the earliest buildings still standing were constructed in the Romanesque style between the
11th and early 13th centuries. This style, which
spread throughout Europe in the 11th century,
was characterized by sturdy columns topped
with rounded arches: a solid, robust, imposing
style of great nobility. The round churches and
St. George's Basilica (Bazilika sv. Jiří) in Prague
belong to this period, but more impressive
survivals are found in Olomouc, and at Porta
Coeli abbey and Třebíč, both in southern
Moravia.

Gothic: 14th–15th centuries
The Gothic style arrived from France in the
early 14th century. The invention of new
vaulting techniques allowed the weight of
large buildings such as cathedrals to be more
evenly distributed. This meant that the solid
masonry characteristic of Romanesque archi-

tecture was replaced by a lighter, more exalted
style with large traceried windows and lofty
vaulted aisles and naves. Charles IV brought
French architects such as Matthew of Arras to
embellish Prague with the new style, notably
St. Vitus's Cathedral (Chrám sv. Víta).
Schwabian architect Peter Parler (1332–1399),
associated with continuing work on the
cathedral, also built superb churches in other
parts of Bohemia. Prague's Old and New
Towns are filled with Gothic churches, mostly
commissioned by Charles IV, and many other
towns boast stately Gothic churches, sometimes enriched with glorious altarpieces,
tabernacles, and paintings. Many castles were
also built, at least partially, in a Gothic style.
Karlštejn is one of the best known examples,
but there are many other medieval fortresses
with substantial Gothic elements, including
Loket, Pernštejn, and Zvíkov. A few outstanding Gothic bridges also survive: The Charles
Bridge (Karlův most) in Prague is the best
known, but the one at Písek is even older.

At the end of the 15th century, Bohemian
architect Benedikt Ried developed a personal
style marked by complex and daring vaulting.
The most spectacular example is the Vladislav
Hall in Prague Castle, but the church of St.
Barbara at Kutná Hora is almost as impressive.

Much Bohemian Gothic painting has
survived. It varies in accomplishment, but the
best of it bears comparison with contemporary
paintings from Italy and Germany. Very little is
known about the identity of the painters, but
one, who at least had a name of sorts—Master
Theodoric—decorated the Holy Cross Chapel
at Karlštejn Chapel with an enormous series of
paintings, a commission from Charles IV. Many
masterpieces of Gothic art from Bohemia and
Moravia are gathered in the Convent of St.
Agnes (Anežský klášter) in Prague.

**Prague's most eccentric modern building,
Frank Gehry's "Fred and Ginger" house**

One of the finest Romanesque doorways is found at the Cistercian abbey of Porta Coeli, near Tišnov in southern Moravia.

Renaissance: 16th–17th centuries

Renaissance architecture—a rebirth of the ancient classical style, replete with forms and ornaments such as columns, round arches, tunnel vaults, and domes—came from Italy but soon took on a distinctly Czech flavor, best demonstrated by the many castles with gabled battlements and three-tiered courtyards. Litomyšl in eastern Bohemia is an outstanding example. It is decorated, like so many similar edifices, with lofty gables and "sgraffito" decoration—a technique of removing an outer layer of plaster to outline the black mortar below. Many mansions were constructed, or reconstructed, in this style, notably the Schwarzenberg Palace (Schwarzenberský palác) in Prague. Two of the loveliest Renaissance buildings in the Czech Republic are the Belvedere, close to Prague Castle (Pražský hrad), and Star Castle (Letohrádek hvězda) on White Mountain, both built in Italianate style in the 1550s.

Baroque: 17th–18th centuries

Artistic development ground to a halt after the civil disorders initiated by the Battle of White Mountain in 1620. The Thirty Years War (1618–1648) allowed no time or leisure for such matters. Indeed, as during the period of the Hussite wars in the 15th century (see p. 24), a substantial proportion of the architectural and artistic heritage of the Czech lands was destroyed. Once the dust had settled, the Catholic victors had the confidence and the wealth to construct town houses and vast country mansions in a full-blown baroque style. This was the style adopted throughout the Habsburg empire, and leading Austrian architects such as Johann Bernard Fischer von Erlach (1656–1723) were also

employed in Bohemia and elsewhere.

Far removed from the harmonious and balanced proportions of the Renaissance, the baroque style was theatrical, delighting in tricks of perspective and light. Walls were not required to be flat: They could be concave or convex, bulging assertively or retreating modestly, according to the whim of the architect. All the resources of the visual arts were put to the service of the baroque architect, providing employment for battalions of sculptors, painters, and plasterers. The Wallenstein Palace (Valdštejnský palác) in Prague is probably the earliest substantial example.

The building boom after the Battle of White Mountain encouraged architects, sculptors, and painters to descend on Bohemia in search of work. Nor were commissions lacking. Many of the masters of the baroque were French (Jean-Baptiste Mathey) and Italian (Francesco Caratti, Carlo Lurago). A distinctive Bohemian style developed in the 18th

The Gothic buttresses of Prague's St. Vitus's Cathedral overlook the Romanesque towers of the Convent of St. George.

century thanks to the genius of Christoph Dientzenhofer and his son Kilián Ignác.

Christoph Dientzenhofer (1655–1722) grew up in Upper Bavaria and together with his four brothers came to Prague to study architecture with Carlo Lurago. The brothers returned to Germany, but Christoph stayed on in Prague and spent his life building churches and other edifices all over Bohemia. Major commissions include the abbey at Teplá in western Bohemia and the church at Břevnov Monastery (Břevnovský klášter) on the outskirts of Prague. But his masterpiece is the Church of St. Nicholas (Kostel sv. Mikuláše) on Prague's Malá Strana Square (Malostranské náměstí), with its broad nave, lofty dome, mighty pillars, and grandiose statuary.

In this project Christoph was aided by his

Christoph Dientzenhofer's design for the Břevnov Monastery near Prague characterizes the baroque style found in his churches throughout Bohemia.

son Kilián Ignác (1689–1751), who designed the dome and choir. Kilián was arguably even more gifted than his father. His dense designs radiate a tremendous power and mastery of space. Among his superlative buildings in Prague are the twin-towered Church of St. John on the Rock (Kostel sv. Jana na Skalce), the facade of the Loreto (Loreta), Church of St. Thomas (Kostel sv. Tomáše) in Malá Strana, the elegant Sylva-Taroucca Palace (Palác Sylva-Taroucca) on Na Příkopě, and the Vila Amerika, now the Dvořák Museum (Muzeum A. Dvořáka).

His works in other parts of Bohemia include the oval Church of St. Mary Magdalene (Kostel sv. Máří Magdalény) in Karlovy Vary and the elegant Ursuline convent (Voršilský klášter) in Kutná Hora.

Baroque architects worked hand in hand with painters and sculptors, whose works decorated the many churches and palaces. From the workshops of artists such as Karel Škréta (1610–1674) and Petr Brandl (1668–1735) came huge numbers of altarpieces. Ferdinand Brokoff (1688–1731), Jan Bendl, and the great Matthias Braun (1684–1738) produced a wealth of dramatic sculpture; much of it is in Prague, but splendid examples are at Kuks in eastern Bohemia. Baroque painting is perhaps harder

to appreciate. Gifted artists such as Škréta and Brandl were prolific, and there is inevitably a certain uniformity to their works. The same is true of famed fresco painters, including Václav Reiner and Austrian Franz Anton Maulbertsch.

Baroque art in Bohemia and Moravia is not confined to museums. Most major churches are decorated with altarpieces by baroque masters, and facades are often rich in carvings by the likes of Brokoff and Braun. Plague columns, a feature of central European town squares, were erected to give thanks for the end of an epidemic; these, too, are often richly decorated by the most famous baroque sculptors.

Vernacular

A vernacular tradition that probably originated in medieval times also continued, especially in isolated rural areas in northeastern Moravia. Wooden farmhouses with distinctive decoration, as well as the lovely wooden churches found in eastern Moravia, were built in a solid yet unchanging style. Many structures, from churches to huts and schoolhouses, are now in *skansens,* open-air museums, of which the largest is at Rožnov pod Radhoštěm in northern Moravia (see p. 284).

A characteristic Alfons Mucha design for the stained glass in St. Vitus's Cathedral in Prague

Rococo

The grandeur of baroque gradually gave way in the mid-18th century to the charm and delicacy of rococo, with its swooping, curvaceous lines and playful elegance. Prague's Goltz-Kinský Palace (palác Goltz-Kinských) is a stylish example. Early in the 19th century neoclassicism was briefly in vogue, and a few country mansions, notably Kačina, were built in this grand but slightly monotonous style, which is marked by regular colonnades and pavilions. However, rather than employ a faded neoclassic style, most 19th-century architects in Bohemia and Moravia, as elsewhere in Europe, opted for eclecticism, selecting elements from a variety of styles. This gave rise to a proliferation of pseudo-baroque mansions and neo-medieval castles such as Bouzov. Typical of this reaching for grandeur are institutional buildings—the National Museum and National Theater in Prague are excellent examples.

Painters, too, adopted eclectic styles, and the works of Josef Mánes (1820–1871) and Karel Purkyně (1834–1868) are stylistically wide ranging. Josef Navrátil (1798–1865) was among the most versatile and gifted of the 19th-century painters. The best of their work can be seen to good advantage in the Trade Fair Palace (Veletržní palác) in Prague, in itself a constructivist masterpiece of the 1920s.

Secession & cubism

At the turn of the 20th century, the branch of art nouveau known as secession, marked by exuberant surface decoration and inventive ironwork, made its way to Bohemia from Vienna. You can see examples in Josefov in Prague and in many smaller towns, such as Pardubice in eastern Bohemia and Karlovy Vary.

Another movement in modern design, cubism, also caught on in Bohemia, and some striking structures, notably Josef Gočár's House at the Black Madonna (Dům U černé Matky Boží) on Celetná in Prague and now a museum of Czech cubist art (closed for renovation), were built in this style.

The architectural regeneration of the early 20th century had its counterpart in the fine arts, especially in the paintings of art nouveau artists such as Alfons Mucha (1860–1939). Innovative painters, including Emil Filla, Bohumil Kubišta, and František Kupka, showed both originality and energy working in cubist, expressionist, and other styles. Mucha's best works, his celebrated posters, were done in Paris, and after his return to

Karel Prager added the striking New Theater to the National Theater in Prague.

Bohemia in 1910, he gave way to Slav nationalism with his overblown "Slav Epic" cycle of the 1920s and other pieces.

Communist times

The communist years, with a dreary insistence on socialist realism as the only acceptable style, were dark ones for architecture and art, despite a brief flowering in the 1960s. Grimly functional buildings, often erected with no sensitivity for their urban context, scarred town centers. Since the Velvet Revolution, the works of modern Czech and Slovak artists, whose paintings could not be shown under the previous regime, are being rediscovered and exhibited. Perhaps the best known is artist and poet Jiří Kolář (1914–2002), who specialized in collages.

Many new buildings are going up in major cities, most notably Prague, but it is too soon to say whether modern architecture will find a distinctive Czech tone. So far the office blocks and hotels could have been airlifted in from Frankfurt or Vienna, and only Prague's most characterful modern building—a joint venture between the Californian architect Frank Gehry and the Yugoslav Vlado Milunič—known as the Dancing House or "Fred and Ginger" building, stands out as truly original.

LITERATURE

Czech developed as a written language only in the 13th century. Before then the languages used were German, Latin, and Old Slavonic, a church dialect brought to the Czech lands by Bishops Cyril and Methodius in 863 (see p. 20). The earliest known works are biographies of saints and historical chronicles.

Even in medieval times, there was a tension between the Czech and German cultures, a tension that by the mid-19th century led to separate cultural institutions for the Czech- and German-speaking populations. Nonetheless, medieval Bohemia and Moravia were essentially bilingual. The religious reformer Jan Hus (see p. 24), who gave his name to the Hussite movement founded after his death, preached only in the vernacular, and thus transformed Czech into a language of literary importance. Hus himself reformed Czech orthography to make this possible. The Czech language continued to be employed principally for theological and philosophical works in the centuries after his death. The Protestant teacher and preacher Comenius (Jan Komenský; 1592–1670) became one of the most revered figures in Czech literary history. His writings brought him renown as an advocate of universal education for children and of greater unity within the Christian faith.

Under the Habsburgs the Czech language was eclipsed by German. The revival of Czech took place under the prompting of Josef Dobrovský (1753–1829), who wrote a definitive history of the Czech language and compiled a German-Czech dictionary. As Czech speakers gained in confidence through the 19th century, combining nationalist, artistic, and political aspirations, so their literary outpourings gained in sophistication and influence. Poets such as Karel Hynek Mácha (1810–1836) and playwrights such as Josef Kajetán Tyl (1808–1859) and Václav Klicpera (1792–1852) proved popular and influential. Easily the best known Czech writer of the 19th century was Jan Neruda (1834–1891), who achieved rapid fame in a variety of literary forms, including essays, vignettes, and short stories, mostly set in Prague (see p. 127).

Despite the resurgence in the Czech language, much important literature continued to be written in German. For many ambitious writers, Bohemia and Moravia constituted too small an arena, and they moved abroad where they hoped to make a greater impact. This was true of the poet, playwright, and novelist Franz Werfel (1890–1945) and of the poet Rainer Maria Rilke (1875–1926), who was a native of Prague.

Yet many writers remained in Prague. The most famous was novelist Franz Kafka

(1883–1924), whose bleak fables include *The Trial*. Hard-hitting journalist Egon Erwin Kisch (1885–1948) traveled the world but returned to his native Prague in 1945.

The declaration of the republic in 1918 gave a new burst of energy to the literary scene. Dramatist Karel Čapek (1890–1938) entertained the Czechs with his satirical plays

The genius of Franz Kafka was unrecognized during his own lifetime (1883–1924).

and travel books, many of which conveyed his underlying message that humankind's wish to dominate and control nature could be destructive to humanity itself. His best known plays are *R.U.R.* (1920), which introduced the word "robot" to the world and was widely translated, and *The Macropoulos Case* (1922), later set as an opera by Leoš Janáček.

The country's most famous modern poet was Jaroslav Seifert (1901–1986), probably best known for the poems he wrote about Prague during the Nazi occupation. He was a signatory of Charter 77 (see p. 35) in 1977, and was awarded the Nobel Prize for literature in 1984. By far the most popular writer in the Czech language of the interwar period, however, was Jaroslav Hašek (1883–1923), who managed, despite a penchant for the bottle, to produce a classic novel that has been translated into numerous languages, *The Good Soldier Švejk.*

Important Jewish writers who left searing accounts of life under Nazi occupation and persecution were Jiří Weil (1900–1959), most famous for his *Life With a Star,* and Arnošt Lustig (1926–), a filmmaker and novelist who settled in the United States. Most of Lustig's fiction is set during World War II, a period he spent in Nazi death camps.

Literature was no more likely to flourish under the Communists than under the Germans. The Nazis had murdered many intellectuals and literary figures, while the Communists tried to compel them to write works of "Socialist Realism" extolling the class struggle. Until the 1960s Czechoslovakia was a literary desert. Only a few publishing houses were authorized, and the state-controlled Czechoslovak Writers' Association defined the narrow limits of acceptability. The years leading up to the Prague Spring (see pp. 120–121) were more liberating, and a number of authors made their reputations during this period, among them Arnošt Lustig, Josef Škvorecký, Milan Kundera, and Ivan Klíma.

After 1968 serious literature went underground, and writers who remained in Czechoslovakia were either silent or published clandestinely, circulating photocopied editions within a small circle of subscribers. A handful of good writers avoided sensitive or controversial topics and and published their works despite communist censorship. They include Miroslav Holub (1923–1998) and Bohumil Hrabal (1914–1997). Hrabal wrote the delightful and touching *Closely Observed Trains* (1965) and the fantastical comic novel *I Served the King of England.*

Among the many writers who left the country was Josef Škvorecký (1924–), who was brought up in Náchod. Some of his novels, such as *The Cowards,* are set in this Silesian region. He immigrated to Canada in 1968, where in addition to writing more novels, he founded 68 Publishers, a publishing house that kept the Czech literary flame alive. Much contemporary Czech fiction is very serious, but Škvorecký has always written with a light and often bawdy touch.

The most famous of the novelists who went into exile is Milan Kundera (1929–).

He left for France in 1975 to teach at the university in Rennes and was subsequently stripped of his citizenship by the Czechoslovak government. His sophisticated, occasionally arch novels have met with great international success; among his best known works are *The Book of Laughter and Forgetting* and *The Unbearable Lightness of Being.* His earliest novels include *The Joke,* originally published in Prague in 1967, which probes into the absurdities of life under communism.

Among the writers who remained in Czechoslovakia were Ludvík Vaculík, the author of *A Cup of Coffee With My Interrogator,* and Václav Havel, whose plays, such as *The Garden Party* and *Audience,* were more frequently performed in London or Paris than in his native Prague. Havel, as a supporter of Charter 77, was repeatedly arrested during the 1970s and '80s, so many of his eloquent essays were penned in his prison cell; one of his best known books collects the letters he wrote from prison to his then wife, Olga. Ivan Klíma (1931–), who published in secret before the Velvet Revolution, has a well-deserved international reputation. His works explore his childhood in Terezín (see pp. 208–211) and the perplexities of love in a communist state. The novels *Love and Garbage* and *Judge on Trial* are among his finest works.

A new generation of Czech writers—Michal Ajvaz (1949–), Jáchym Topol (1962–), and the science-fiction author Eva Hauserová (1954–)—are carving reputations for themselves inside the Czech Republic, but they are as yet little known in other countries.

MUSIC

Bohemia and Moravia have a powerful musical tradition, but the region was late to join the mainstream of European classical music. It took musical giants such as Bedřich Smetana (1824–1884) and Antonín Dvořák (1841–1904) to bring folk music into the more formal embrace of chamber and orchestral music. But from the early Middle Ages there was a tradition of church music, usually set to Slavic texts, and Hussite hymns in the Czech language that emphasized congregational singing; these undoubtedly had an influence on the Lutheran chorales that became so important in Germany. A more sophisticated strand of baroque music flourished in

This frontispiece for a collection of piano pieces reflects Smetana's love of Czech folk music.

Bohemia. Musical education formed part of the school curriculum, and many country houses had their own orchestras.

This native tradition of baroque composition did not establish deep roots. The most successful Czech composers—violin virtuoso František Benda (1709–1786), Johann Stamitz (1717–1757), and Jan Ladislav Dusík (1760–1812)—all preferred to work either in Germany or Vienna, where the profusion of courts offered musicians ample employment.

Mozart, Smetana, & Dvořák

Wolfgang Amadeus Mozart (see pp. 98–99) was deeply appreciated in Prague and spent a great deal of time there, visiting his friends the Dušeks. At their home, the Vila Bertramka, he completed *Don Giovanni*, which was first performed in Prague in 1787.

Smetana (see pp. 228–229) was the first Czech composer who clearly identified himself with the national aspirations of his people. He is best known for his six-part symphonic poem *Má vlast*, celebrating the natural beauties of Bohemia, and every child in the Czech Republic can whistle the principal theme of the movement that depicts the River Vltava.

Dvořák, who played the viola in orchestras under Smetana's baton, was an ardent admirer of the elder composer's work, and by the end of the 19th century his international reputation had eclipsed that of his mentor. Although Dvořák composed 11 operas, he is better known as a symphonic and chamber music composer, and he often used folk melodies of great beauty and singularity within his compositions.

Other Czech composers include Dvořák's son-in-law Josef Suk (1874–1935), who adopted a rich romantic style. Gustav Mahler (1860–1911), a great conductor and symphonic composer, is not often considered to be Czech, but he was Moravian by birth, from the town of Jihlava.

Leoš Janáček (1854–1928) delved deeply into the country's earlier musical traditions, incorporating them into his own work. Born in Hukvaldy, he studied in Prague and spent most of his working life in Brno. His late works—the operas *Katja Kabanova, The Cunning Little Vixen,* and *Jenůfa*—now have a permanent place in the established repertoire, but pieces such as the remarkable *Glagolitic Mass* allude most obviously to the traditions of Czech music.

Bohuslav Martinů (1890–1959) was very prolific, and during his life completed more than 400 works, including operas, ballets, and chamber works of varying quality.

Puppetry and imaginative puppet theater are enduring folk traditions throughout the Czech Republic.

Czechoslovakia has produced many performers of exceptional talent, including the sopranos Ema Destinnová and Eva Randová. The Czech Philharmonic Orchestra, under its conductors Karel Ančerl and Václav Neumann, has long been one of Europe's outstanding orchestras. Leading violin virtuoso Josef Suk is just one of the soloists with an international reputation.

The Czechs have long been devoted to jazz, which attracted enormous disapproval from the communist authorities. In the 1980s the punk movement was adopted with fervor by young Czechs. The leading band was Plastic People of the Universe, whose penchant for bad language landed them in court in 1976. Punk has since been displaced by many other strands of popular music and rock.

THEATER & MIME

Czech theater, mainly a vehicle for national aspirations in the 19th century, was given a new lease on life by Karel Čapek and the avant-garde director E. F. Burian in the inter-war years. In the 1920s the Liberated Theater (Osvobozené divadlo) in Prague became a major European center for the presentation of surrealist plays by the likes of André Breton (1896–1966) and Jean Cocteau (1889–1963). After World War II there was another revival, and in the 1960s a number of excellent small theater companies sprang up in Prague, Brno, and other towns. Some of these, including the Theater on the Balustrade (Divadlo Na Zábradlí) in Prague, had a high quality of direction and performance. They were show-cases for the most talented of the new Czech writers and for the fashionable avant-garde playwrights, among them Samuel Beckett.

Alfred Radok invented the Laterna Magika Theater, now part of the National Theater (Národní divadlo), in 1958, a deft marriage between cinema and theater. This technically brilliant device combines song, ballet and mime, film projections, movable walls, and drama; all these disparate elements work together to pre-sent a breathtaking theatrical illusion.

Mime is a long-standing Czech tradition, and its supreme exponents were Ladislav Fialka (1931–1991) and Bolek Polívka (1949–). Another success is puppet theater, an art that has its roots in the 17th century. In those times puppetry was an itinerant art, but today it is a sophisticated form employing satire, fantasy, music, and humor. Dozens of puppet companies are scattered across the republic, and at Chrudim there is a museum and festival of puppetry (see p. 240).

FILM

There has been a tradition of fine filmmaking since the 1930s, when directors such as Martin Frič (1902–1968) produced films that gained the republic an international reputation for the medium. Zlín, in Moravia, was rebuilt as an avant-garde company town by shoe manufacturer Tomáš Baťa and became a center for film animation under his patronage. Director Karel Zeman (1910–1989) made his reputation here.

The war years and the early years of Stalinist rule virtually froze cinematic devel-opment, but after 1956 there was a gradual thaw. Earlier films, such as Jiří Weiss's (1913–) *The Last Shot* (1950), had already adopted novel ideas, including the use of amateur actors. There was a revival in the 1960s, but works like Jan Němec's political parable *Report on the Party and the Guests* (1966), with its

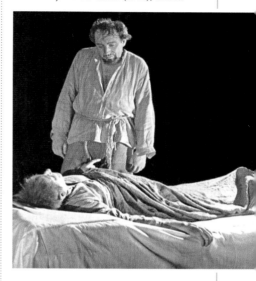

A scene from Janáček's opera *From the House of the Dead,* from a performance in Brno in 1958.

play on the word "party" in its two senses of political organization and festivity, were soon banned. Other outstanding directors were Miloš Forman (1932–), whose best known works include the comedies *A Blonde in Love* (1965) and *The Firemen's Ball* (1967)—both set in provincial Czech towns—and Jiří Menzel (1938–), who made an exquis-ite version of Hrabal's *Closely Observed Trains* (1966).

Czech cinema has never recovered the verve of its accomplishment during the 1960s. The only film to have enjoyed international recognition since the Velvet Revolution has been Jan Svěrák's *Kolja* (1996), a charming tale of a Prague musician and a small Russian boy. Perhaps its success will help stimulate a revival in the Czech film industry. ■

Prague

Prague

VIRTUALLY UNTOUCHED BY WORLD WAR II, AND HAVING ESCAPED Stalinist-style changes during communist rule, Prague's historic center remains intact, its layout fundamentally the same as when first built. No wonder few people fail to succumb to the charms of this beautiful historic city.

Released from oppression by the Velvet Revolution in 1989 (see p. 36), Prague has flourished. Once dilapidated palaces boast renovated facades; entire districts—including Josefov—bustle with boutiques, bars, and restaurants; new shopping malls catering to the newly affluent sprawl on the outskirts. In some respects, Prague is like any other busy old city, combining ancient glories with modern consumerism, but it remains a very special place, essentially unspoiled and a joy to visit and revisit.

Prague was founded, according to legend, when Princess Libuše stood at Vyšehrad and foresaw the greatness of the city that would arise here. She married a plowman named Přemysl, heralding the beginning of the Přemyslid dynasty. Two Slav fortresses were built on either side of the River Vltava, at Vyšehrad and Hradčany, and Bohemia's first monastery was founded nearby at Břevnov in 993. The city expanded swiftly into what is now Old Town (Staré Město), and Vyšehrad's importance faded in favor of the area surrounding Prague Castle (Hradčany). King Přemysl Otakar II created the Little Quarter (Malá Strana) on the slopes beneath the castle in 1257. With the expansion of the Bohemian domains to the Adriatic shores, Prague became an important capital, a status consolidated under Charles IV, who thought and built in international terms. He added a fourth district to the city, the carefully planned New Town (Nové Město).

Prague remains a city of tremendous cultural richness. Charles Bridge (Karlův most) and St. Vitus's Cathedral (Chrám sv. Víta) testify to the ambition of Charles IV and other medieval rulers, and more fragmentary remains at Vyšehrad and the castle recall the very foundations of the city. The defeat of the Protestants at White Mountain (Bílá Hora) in 1620 inaugurated a period of Habsburg despotism, but it also ushered in a new era of architectural splendor, as the nobility came here from throughout the Habsburg empire to build new palaces.

Renaissance architects such as Benedikt Ried devised a uniquely Bohemian style visible in the castle and churches close to the city. The 17th-century Counter-Reformation brought full-blown baroque to Prague, and great architects such as Jean-Baptiste Mathey, Francesco Caratti, and Kilián Ignác Dientzenhofer made remarkable individual contributions. The passion for building on a grand scale continued until the end of the 18th century.

Prague's prosperity continued into the 19th century, and many handsome apartment houses from that period still exist. Under the republic, too, Prague architects became adventurous, building in the cubist style. Yet the city, throughout its history, was a two-culture town: German and Czech. Its theaters, university, and opera houses were all divided along linguistic lines. Czech nationalism doomed German culture in Prague after World War II, yet it remains the city of Franz Kafka as well as Jaroslav Hašek, of Mozart as well as Smetana. Since the Velvet Revolution, Prague has enjoyed a new lease on life, attracting foreign investment and development schemes, many catering to the millions of tourists who visit the city each year. ∎

Visitor information

The Prague Information Service (www.prague-info.cz) has three main visitor centers:

- ✉ Staroměstská radnice (Old Town Hall)
- ✉ Na Příkopě 20
- ✉ Hlavní nádraží (Main railway station)
- ☎ 12 444

Pages 52–53: The broad expanses of Prague's castle are best viewed from the opposite bank of the River Vltava.

On the slopes beneath Prague's spectacular castle and cathedral lies one of Europe's best preserved baroque cities, with its unrivaled collection of palaces and gardens.

Castle District & Little Quarter

One of the many statues of St. John of Nepomuk found throughout Prague

Castle District & Little Quarter

WHEN A FORTIFIED CASTLE *(HRAD)* WAS BUILT HIGH ABOVE THE RIVER Vltava in the ninth century, settlements soon began to grow up around this, the first Prague Castle. The area surrounding and next to the castle became known as Hradčany (Castle District), whereas the district between the castle and the river was called Malá Strana (Little Quarter). By the 12th century a bridge linked the two sides of the river, and churches and houses were built close to the shore on both sides.

Malá Strana formally became a town in 1257. During the 14th century it was enclosed by fortifications, but these provided little protection during the Hussite wars of the 15th century, which inflicted grave damage on the town. It

was rebuilt, only to be ravaged by a great fire in 1541. From this point Malá Strana enjoyed a new period of prosperity, as

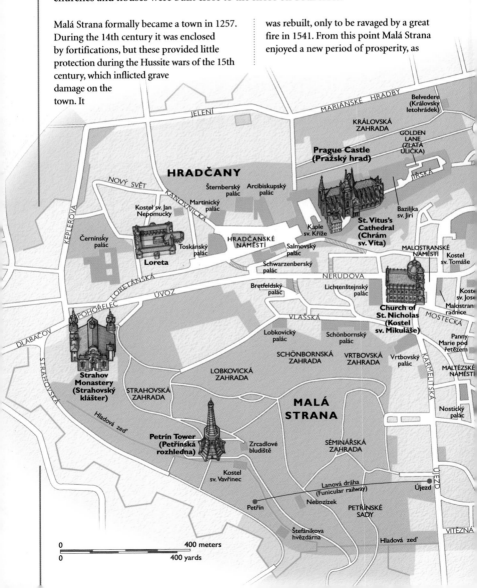

JELENÍ

MARIÁNSKÉ HRADBY

KRÁLOVSKÁ ZAHRADA

Belvedere (Královský letohrádek)

GOLDEN LANE (ZLATÁ ULIČKA)

Prague Castle (Pražský hrad)

JIŘSKÁ

HRADČANY

NOVÝ SVĚT

KANOVNICKÁ

Šternberský palác

Arcibiskupský palác

Martinický palác

Kostel sv. Jan Nepomucky

Bazilika sv. Jiří

KEPLEROVA

Černínský palác

Toskánský palác

HRADČANSKÉ NÁMĚSTÍ

Kaple sv. Kříže

St. Vitus's Cathedral (Chrám sv. Víta)

Loreta

Salmovský palác

Schwarzenberský palác

MALOSTRANSKÉ NÁMĚSTÍ

Kostel sv. Tomáše

LORETÁNSKÁ

ÚVOZ

NERUDOVA

Bretfeldský palác

Lichtenštejnský palác

Koste sv. Jose

POHOŘELEC

VLAŠSKÁ

Malostran radnice

MOSTECKÁ

DLABAČOV

STRAHOVSKÁ

Lobkovický palác

Schönbornský palác

Church of St. Nicholas (Kostel sv. Mikuláše)

Panny Marie pod řetězem

SCHÖNBORNSKÁ ZAHRADA

VRTBOVSKÁ ZAHRADA

Vrtbovský palác

MALTÉZSKÉ NÁMĚSTÍ

Strahov Monastery (Strahovský klášter)

STRAHOVSKÁ ZAHRADA

LOBKOVICKÁ ZAHRADA

MALÁ STRANA

KARMELITSKÁ

Nostický palác

Hladová zeď

Petrín Tower (Petřínská rozhledna)

Zrcadlové bludiště

SÉMINÁŘSKÁ ZAHRADA

Kostel sv. Vavřinec

Lanová dráha (Funicular railway)

Újezd

ÚJEZD

Petřín

Nebozízek

PETŘÍNSKÉ SADY

VITĚZNÁ

Štefánikova hvězdárna

Hladová zeď

0 — 400 meters
0 — 400 yards

Italian architects were hired by the aristocracy to construct their mansions and palaces.

Building accelerated after the Battle of White Mountain in 1620, when the Habsburg nobility consolidated its presence in Prague. By the beginning of the 19th century, New Town (Nové Město) and other districts across the river began to gain in importance, and Malá Strana became something of a backwater, helping to conserve its unique character. Few European cities have retained so many centuries-old palaces and mansions, as well as their baroque gardens.

Although commercialism has invaded the main squares and streets of both Malá Strana and Hradčany, it is surprising how many tranquil streets and gardens remain. Tour guides tend to lead their groups along the main routes and up to the castle and down again, ignoring entire tracts of this ancient quarter. But the details make this side of the city so exquisite: the ancient house signs, the terraced gardens climbing the slopes, the pubs tucked away in narrow cobbled lanes. It can be explored only on foot, and the steepness of the streets can make this a tiring, yet always rewarding, experience. With few permanent residents compared with the bustling districts across the river and the suburbs, Malá Strana is particularly enchanting at night, when the visitors have gone and there is nothing in the townscape to spoil the illusion that you have stepped back three centuries. ■

CHOTKOVY SADY

HOTKOVA   U BRUSKÝCH KASÁREN

KLÁROV   NÁBŘEŽÍ EDVARDA BENEŠE

ALDŠTEJNSKÁ

Valdštejnský palác   ● Malostranská

LETENSKÁ

MÁNESŮV MOST

VOJANOVY SADY

CHARLES BRIDGE (KARLŮV MOST)

Čertovka   Vltava

KAMPA ISLAND

Vltava

Area of map detail

STŘELECKÝ OSTROV

MOST LEGIÍ

The Convent of St. George within the castle now houses a major national collection of baroque art.

Prague Castle

SEEN FROM BELOW, PRAGUE CASTLE (PRAŽSKÝ HRAD) LOOKS
monolithic and forbidding, but once within the castle gates you find
yourself in a town within a town. Scattered among the precinct's
many courtyards and picturesque lanes are not just the royal palace
and the cathedral, but many other palaces and a Romanesque basilica,
as well as fortifications. Allow plenty of time to visit the castle, as
many of its buildings are museums, and both the cathedral and the
royal palace are among the highlights of any visit to Prague.

Founded in the ninth century as a
Přemysl fortress, the castle has
often been the seat of political
power in the Czech lands. There
were extensive building programs
during the reigns of Charles IV
(R.1346–1378) and Vladislav
Jagiellon II (R.1471–1516), and
again under the Habsburgs. Since
1918 the castle has been the official
residence of the president of the
Czech Republic, and guards dressed
in uniforms created by the Oscar-
winning costume designer for the
film *Amadeus* (1984) parade in the
First Courtyard (První nádvoří) to
protect the state rooms.

Within the Second Courtyard
(Druhé nádvoří), entered through
the impressive baroque Matthias

Prague by night: Floodlights bathe the castle, the Charles Bridge, and the Church of St. Nicholas.

Tram: 12, 22, 23 (Malostranské náměstí); 22, 23 (Pražský hrad); 1, 2, 8, 18 (Prašný most). Metro: Malostranská, Hradčanské

Gate (Matyášova brána) of 1614, is the boxy **Holy Cross Chapel** (Kaple sv. Kříže), with its charming gilt and frescoed interior. Access is from the *bureau de change* (exchange office) that occupies part of the building. The chapel, designed by Nikolaus Pacassidates, dates from the mid-18th century. In the opposite corner of this courtyard is the entrance to the **Castle Gallery** (Obrazárna Pražského hradu), located in the former stables. The contents are based on Emperor Rudolph II's collection, but have been expanded. There are fine paintings by Titian, Veronese, Tintoretto, and Rubens, and Czech baroque masters such as Petr Brandl. Near the gallery is the entrance to the immense **Spanish Hall** (Španělský sál), built in the early 17th century but not accessible to the public.

Arched passageways lead from the second courtyard to the square beside the cathedral. Tucked against the west end is the **Old Provost's House** (Staré Proboštsví), a dignified 17th-century building on the site of the former bishop's palace. Just beyond the house, right in the middle of the courtyard, stands a rare copy of a Gothic, 14th-century equestrian sculpture of St. George and the Dragon by the brothers Jiří and Martin of Cluj.

Straight ahead is the entrance to the **Old Royal Palace** (Starý královský palác), which dates from the 12th century and is built on a number of levels. Just beyond the entrance hall is the large **Vladislav Hall** (Vladislavský sál), designed by Benedikt Ried in the late 15th century. Lit by the enormous Renaissance windows, this hall has brilliant vaulting, one of Ried's hallmarks. A passage on the right leads to the **Bohemian Chancellery** (Česká kancelář), another Renaissance chamber; it

was from here that Prague's Second Defenestration took place in 1618 (see p. 26). Protestant nobles, indignant at the loss of privileges under Matthias, confronted two Catholic governors and ejected them from the windows along with their secretary (they survived).

Various other rooms can be reached from the Vladislav Hall: **Diet Hall,** the former throne room, saw the deliberations of the Bohemian nobility; a spiral staircase leads to the New Appeal Court of 1558 and its adjoining repository of land rolls, which documented the property rights of the Bohemian Estates. The ceilings of these rooms are beautifully decorated with colored crests. A doorway from Vladislav Hall leads to Ried's astonishing staircase, with its knotty rib vaults; the staircase is broad enough to accommodate mounted horsemen riding to participate in the tournaments that were held in the hall.

The staircase leads down to **St. George's Square** (Jiřské náměstí), which is close to both the Basilica of St. George and the Convent of St. George. Vikářská, a lane alongside the cathedral choir, leads to one of the castle towers on the right, the Mihulka or **Powder Tower** of 1494, rebuilt in the 16th century. There used to be alchemists' workshops within the tower, and exhibits here relate to alchemy.

During its restoration, the **Basilica of St. George** (Bazilika sv. Jiří) was stripped of most of its baroque encrustations and returned to its pristine Romanesque form. A church has stood on this spot since around 920, making it older than St. Vitus, although the present basilica, with its distinctive twin towers, dates from 1142; the somber facade was constructed in the 1670s. In front of the choir are the painted wooden tomb of Vlatislav I, who died in 921, and a tomb slab, possibly belong to Duke Boleslav II, who died in 999. Ludmila, the wife of the ninth-century ruler Duke Bořivoj, is buried in the basilica, too; she is venerated as the first female Czech martyr and saint.

Adjacent to the basilica is the **Convent of St. George** (Klašter sv. Jiří). During the reign of Joseph II (1780–1790), the convent was secularized and used for some time as a barracks. It was only in the 1950s that the buildings were renovated and converted into the present gallery. For many years it was home to the republic's finest medieval art, which has now been rehoused in the Convent of St. Agnes (Anežský klášter; see pp. 106–109). St. George's has retained its collections of mannerist and baroque art. Whereas medieval art is comparatively rare in the churches and galleries of the republic, 17th-century paintings and altarpieces are encountered everywhere.

St. George's has many dark canvases by Karel Škréta (1610–1674), and Jan Kryštof Liška (1650–1712), along with striking canvases such as the self-portrait by Jan Kupecký (1667–1740). His many portraits of old men show Petr Brandl to be a great painter; included is his study of one of the Apostles. Also worthwhile are the baroque sculptures by such masters as Ferdinand Brokoff and Matthias Braun.

Continue past the basilica along Jiřská. On the left is **Golden Lane** (Zlatá ulička; see pp. 68–69), a street of artisans' cottages in sharp contrast to the palatial splendors all around. The tower at the end of the lane is the **Dalibor Tower** (Daliborka), named after a violin-playing knight who was imprisoned here; his story was later the subject of an opera by Smetana.

PRAGUE CASTLE

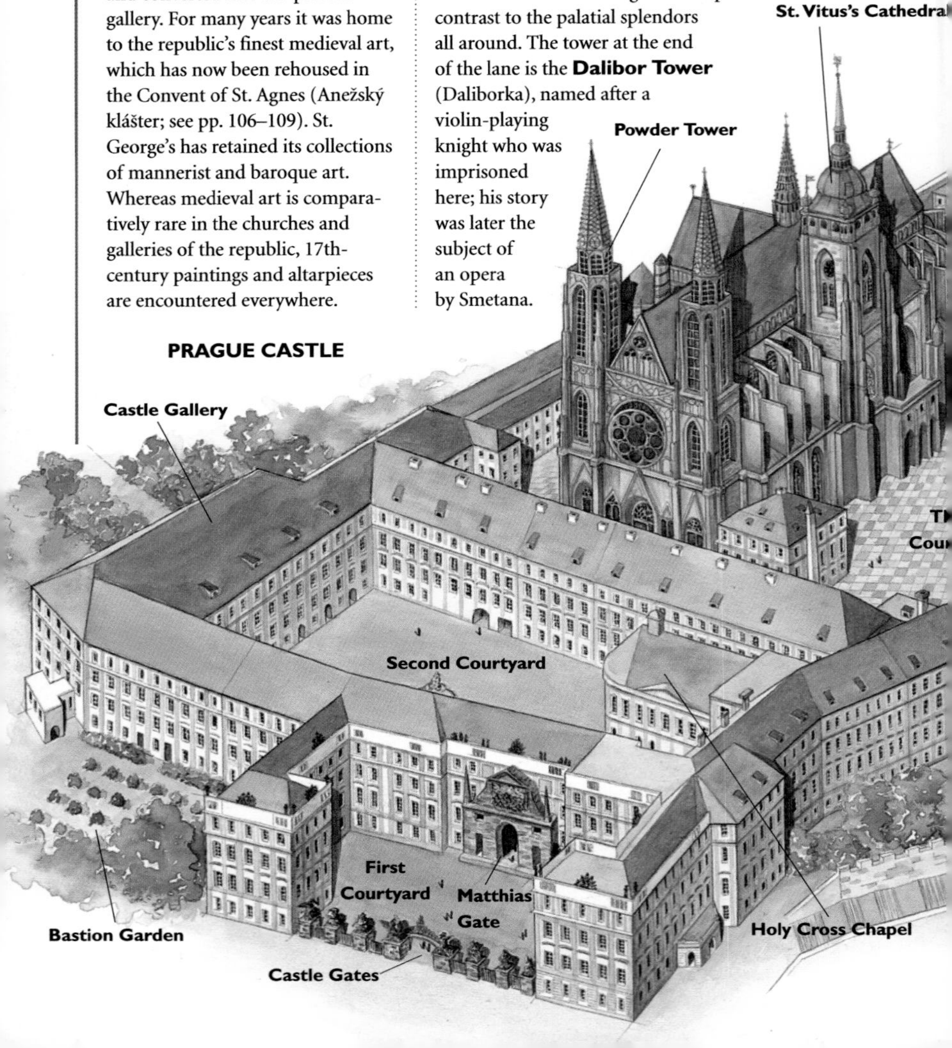

St. Vitus's Cathedral

Powder Tower

Castle Gallery

Second Courtyard

First Courtyard

Matthias Gate

Bastion Garden

Castle Gates

Holy Cross Chapel

Returning from Golden Lane to Jiřská, you come to an imposing mansion, the **Lobkowicz Palace** (Lobkovický palác). Now a historical museum, the palace was rebuilt by Carlo Lurago in the 17th century for the Lobkowicz family. The palace today houses the historical collections of the National Museum (Národní muzeum). Note particularly the charter with which Charles IV established Charles University in 1348 (Room 2); Rudolph II's *Letter of Majesty* of 1609, decisively torn by Ferdinand II to nullify it (Room 8); and the executioner's sword used for the decapitation of the Czech nobles in Old Town Square (Staroměstské náměstí) in 1621 (Room 10). The museum gives a strong impression of Czech culture, while almost completely neglecting the German culture that flourished alongside it.

Opposite the palace is the 16th-century **Burgrave's House** (Nejvyšší purkrabství), which in communist times was converted into one of the world's largest toy museums and a children's center. At the far end of Jiřská stands the grim **Black Tower** (Černá věž), the castle's eastern gate, built in the 12th century and rebuilt during Renaissance times. From here the Old Castle Steps (Staré zámecké schody) lead to the Malostranská metro station. ■

Convent of
St. George

Dalibor Tower

Golden Lane

White Tower

Black Tower

Lobkowicz
Palace

Basilica of
St. George

Old Royal Palace

Ramparts Gardens

Steps
leading to
the Little
Quarter

Benedikt Ried created a unique system of vaulting to decorate the vast **Vladislav Hall** within the castle, completed in 1502.

St. Vitus's Cathedral

ONE OF THE GREAT GOTHIC CATHEDRALS OF EUROPE, ST. Vitus's Cathedral (Chrám sv. Víta) occupies a magnificent perch high above the River Vltava. It stands in the third courtyard of Prague Castle (Pražský hrad) on the site of a rotunda church of 929. When Prague became an archbishopric in 1344, King John of Luxembourg (R.1310–1346) decided to build a larger church worthy of the city, but it took 600 years to complete.

St. Vitus's Cathedral

🔼 Map p. 56

✉ Pražský hrad

💲 **$$$.** Visits to the choir included in castle admission

🚌 Bus: 22, 23. Metro: Malostranská

Charles IV (R.1346–1378) continued with these ambitious schemes, calling on the services of the French architect Matthias of Arras. When Matthias died in 1352, only parts of the choir and its radiating chapels and the ambulatory had been completed. He was succeeded in 1356 by the Swabian architect Peter Parler, who built the superb choir and the glorious south porch known as the Golden Gate. The tower was added by Parler's sons after his death in 1399.

The Hussite wars in the 15th century halted construction, but work was resumed in the mid-16th century. Bonifác Wohlmut is credited with topping the unfinished **Great Tower,** which was further capped by a cupola designed by Nikolaus Pacassi in 1770. The total height of the tower is 317 feet (96.5 m). Work continued on the west front in the 1870s, but the cathedral was not finally completed until 1929. Despite such a protracted history, the neo-Gothic west end blends well with the original Gothic structure, and the interior manages to be thoroughly French in its elegance.

Before the west front was built, the **Golden Gate** (Zlatá brána) was the main entrance into the cathedral. This radiant expression of imperial pride portrays Charles IV and Elisabeth of Pomerania kneeling beneath Christ in Majesty in glass mosaics, which consist of more than a million colored pieces. On either side is a Last Judgment.

The huge window above the gate was added in 1908, but it blends in well enough with the Gothic structure. The Parlers' choir is equally masterly, an exuberant jungle of flying buttresses and gargoyles.

As you enter the cathedral, the first impression of the interior is one of harmony, which is surprising given its prolonged construction history. Look up and along the gallery above the nave. You may just be able to glimpse a series of busts of the royal family and other dignitaries, carved by the Parler workshop, but you will need binoculars to see them properly.

Opposite: A view of the spires of St. Vitus's Cathedral from the lanes of Hradčany Below: The dazzling silver tomb of St. John of Nepomuk, by Joseph Emanuel Fischer von Erlach, is one of the highlights of the cathedral interior.

In the center of the choir is the immense **imperial mausoleum,** completed in 1589 for the tombs of Ferdinand I, his wife, Anna Jagiellon, and their son Maximilian II. It is surrounded by a beautiful, wrought-iron grille by J. Schmidthammer. The tombs were created by the Dutch sculptor Alexander Collin between 1571 and 1589. Three effigies lie in repose on top of the tombs, but they are too high to be seen.

Return to the west end of the cathedral to look at the numerous side chapels. The first ones on the north side contain late Gothic altarpieces

Renaissance Bell Tower

Twin West Towers

West Front

Main Entrance

Triforium

ST. VITUS'S CATHEDRAL

Nave

Old Provost's House

The noble Gothic nave of St. Vitus's Cathedral, the work of Peter Parler and his sons

Chancel

Chapel of St. Wenceslas

reat Tower

and paintings, as well as monumental heraldic tomb slabs. In the third chapel there is brightly colored stained glass by Alfons Mucha (1860–1939). A modern Gothic-style extravaganza frames the spiral staircase that leads up to the gallery. Just beyond the organ gallery another chapel houses tombs from the Renaissance and baroque periods.

Within the **choir,** on the right, you come to the first of a series of wooden reliefs carved in 1623 by Caspar Bechteller, including a vivid depiction of the flight of Frederick V of the Palatinate after the Battle of White Mountain. Others give a vivid impression of Prague just before the baroque period. Note that Charles Bridge (Karlův most) has been carved without its statues. Close by is a far more modern work, the bronze statue of Cardinal Bedřich Schwarzenberg at prayer by Josef Myslbek (1895).

Several chapels in the north ambulatory contain tombs of the 11th- and 12th-century Přemyslid kings, produced by the Parler workshop in the 1370s. In the reliquary chapel, these include tombs for Otakar I and Otakar II. Between the Virgin Mary Chapel and the high altar is the tomb of St. Vitus, a surprisingly modest 19th-century repository for his relics.

The medieval royal tombs in the side chapels and the Habsburg tombs in the burial vaults are overshadowed by the glorious silver **tomb of St. John of Nepomuk.** Wenceslas (Václav) IV ordered John to be thrown into the Vltava in 1393, and in doing so created a Czech martyr (see p. 24). After John was murdered, his body was recovered, and a cult developed around him, resulting in his canonization in 1729. Johann Bernhard Fischer von Erlach's son Joseph Emanuelhis designed the spectacular tomb in 1736, using two tons of silver in the process. The saint kneels on his canopied tomb, which is supported by angels and enclosed within a marble balustrade.

Neighboring chapels are filled with riches: four silver half-figures of saints in **St. Adalbert's Chapel,** dating from the late 1690s; a monumental tomb slab in the **Waldstein Chapel** bearing the features of Peter Parler; and, facing the chapel, another carved panel by Bechteller depicting the destruction of the Cathedral of Sts. Vitus, Václav, and Adalbert by the Hussites on December 21, 1619. Next to the Waldstein Chapel is the rather grotesque **Vladislav Oratory,** created by Benedikt Ried in 1493 with tracery in the form of twigs and branches. Look for the polychrome figure by Matthias Braun portraying a miner leaping forward and bearing a lamp.

The entrance to the royal burial vault is in the next chapel, the **Holy Cross Chapel,** where you will find a silver altar and a faded 14th-century fresco of the patron saints of Bohemia. The passage down to the vault leads through some of the Romanesque remains of the former rotunda. Many of Bohemia's rulers are buried here, though mostly in modern tombs from the 1930s: Charles IV, George of Poděbrady, Václav IV, and Rudolph II.

As you emerge from the vault, return to the ambulatory. To the right of the Holy Cross Chapel is the **Martinitz Chapel** with its Renaissance tombs. Jaroslav von Martinitz was a fanatical Catholic who survived the Second Defenestration of 1618 (see p. 26) and lived on for more than 30 years. Opposite the chapel is a finely carved monument to the distinguished military commander Count Schlick by Joseph Emanuel Fischer von Erlach and František Kaňka.

The last chapel in the ambulatory is the most splendid of them all: the **Chapel of St. Wenceslas** (Kaple sv. Václava), built by Peter Parler between 1362 and 1367 above the saint's burial place. The shrine, built early in the

St. Wenceslas & the door knocker

St. Wenceslas (Václav) was cut down by assassins as he was reaching for a church door knocker in 929 or 935—the victim of a power struggle with his brother Boleslav. According to legend, Wenceslas remained standing even after he had been killed. This explains why the knocker in the chapel is attached to the door near the ambulatory. The knocker, however, dates from the 14th century. ∎

20th century, is embellished with a silver bust of the saint. Some 1,300 semiprecious stones—mostly jasper, amethyst, and chrysoprase—are embedded in the walls, which are painted with fresco cycles from the 1370s. The lower cycle shows scenes from the Passion, executed by Master Oswald of Prague, court painter to Charles IV. The upper cycle is by one of Bohemia's great medieval painters, the Master of Litoměřice; illustrating scenes from the life of Wenceslas, these date from the 1500s. A panel to the right of the 14th-century statue of Wenceslas, by Jíndřich Parler, depicts the moment when the saint was brutally murdered (see box this page). With so much decoration within the chapel, it is easy to overlook the powerful bronze candelabrum of 1532 by Hans Vischer of Nuremberg.

Before leaving the cathedral, take a look at some of the modern stained glass. In addition to the work of Alfons Mucha, there is the rose window in the west front by Josef Klasak, based on designs by František Kysela from the 1920s. In the south transept, an immense window by Max Švabinský, completed in 1934, depicts the Last Judgment.

Golden Lane & alchemy

Tucked against the castle walls, Golden Lane (Zlatá ulička) is framed on either side by the White Tower (Bílá věž) and Dalibor Tower (Daliborka). This now charming little street, with its brightly painted cottages, was the haunt of alchemists during the reign of Rudolph II (1576–1611). The lane was originally inhabited by members of the imperial entourage, but it took its name from the goldsmiths who lived here in the late 17th century rather than from the alchemists who preceded them.

Emperor Rudolph was greatly interested in alchemy, and in the 16th century English magicians such as John Dee and Edward Kelley found a welcome at the Bohemian court, where the emperor became a devotee of the mystical arts. Rudolph, a profoundly

troubled man given to spells of insanity, was fascinated by the theories of alchemists and other quasi-scientists who claimed the keys to the secrets of the universe. Alchemy was essentially the application of scientific principles, as then understood, to magic. Its principal goals were to find the elixir of eternal life and to transform base metals into gold, but there was a strong mystical component in its experiments. Although many alchemists were quacks, the subject was taken seriously, and in the 17th century mathematician Sir Isaac Newton conducted alchemical investigations.

Golden Lane was greatly improved when Empress Maria Theresa (R.1740–1780) required that the shabby wooden houses

Right: Tourists amble the much restored Golden Lane to visit its shops.

An engraving from around 1600 shows the Emperor Rudolph inspecting the achievements of the alchemists he encouraged.

should be rebuilt from more solid materials such as brick. The street became fashionable as an artists' quarter in the late 19th century. Franz Kafka and his sister lived at No. 22 for a short while in 1917, and the Nobel Prize-winning poet Jaroslav Seifert was a resident a decade later, but his house no longer exists.

In the 1950s, the residents were moved out and the present-day color scheme was devised. Thus over the centuries a slum was converted into a picturesque lane dedicated to selling souvenirs. The somewhat folksy appearance of Golden Lane itself is in stark contrast to that of its two towers, which were used as prisons until the 18th century.

For an overview of the subject of alchemy, visit the Powder Tower (Mihulka) on Vikářská (see p. 59). ■

Around Prague Castle

Castle District
- Map p. 56

Sternberg Palace
- ✉ Hradčanské náměstí 15
- ☎ 233 090 570
- 🕐 Closed Mon.
- 💲 $$
- 🚋 Tram: 22, 23 (Pražský hrad)

Loreto Church
- ✉ Loretánské náměstí
- 🕐 Closed Mon.
- 💲 $

HRADČANY (CASTLE DISTRICT), AN AREA ALONGSIDE THE castle, occupies a spur above Malá Strana. It was originally a residential neighborhood for the employees of the castle. Some of the streets around Nový Svět retain that artisanal atmosphere, but much of Hradčany is today occupied by immense palaces and gardens.

For his wife, Anna, Ferdinand I commissioned Paolo della Stella of Genoa and Bonifác Wohlmut in the 16th century to design **Belvedere** (Královsky letohrádek), the exquisite Renaissance pleasure palace set within the **Royal Gardens** (Královská zahrada). Stately arcades transform the first floor into a shady loggia, and the copper roof resembles an inverted ship's hull. In front of the building is the Singing Fountain of 1568, though it requires considerable imagination to discern the song created by the water falling into the bronze bowl. Since the Belvedere is now used as an art gallery, you can visit it only when special exhibitions are held.

Also in the Royal Garden is Wohlmut's **Ball Game Hall** (Míčovna), built in 1569. The original structure was destroyed during World War II, and what you see today, including the sgraffito decoration, is a modern reconstruction. Once a tennis court, the building was converted into a stable block in 1723. The former baroque **Riding School** (Jrdzárna), designed by Jean-Baptiste Mathey, now houses an exhibition gallery.

Hradcany Square (Hradčanské náměstí), with Ferdinand Brokoff's plague column of 1726, faces the entrance to the castle. On the left is the 19th-century **Salm Palace** (Salmovský palác) and the Renaissance bulk of the gabled **Schwarzenberg Palace** (Schwarzenberský palác), its surfaces entirely covered with the best sgraffito designs in Prague. Originally built for the Lobkowicz family, it was bought by the Schwarzenbergs in 1719. Inside is a military museum, closed indefinitely for reconstruction.

Across the square stands the elegant **Archbishop's Palace** (Arcibiskupský palác), with its delightful rococo facade. The palace was designed by Wohlmut for Ferdinand I, who wanted a suitably impressive headquarters for a Catholic archbishop. It has been much altered and renovated, but the final outcome is very satisfying. The stucco decoration on the facade dates from the 1760s.

A passage alongside the Archbishop's Palace leads to the **Sternberg Palace** (Šternberský palác), designed by Giovanni Alliprandi and since 1949 the home of the National Gallery's (Národní galerie's) fine collection of European art. The collection was begun by Count František Josef Šternberk in 1796, and it was rapidly expanded by gifts from other families. It includes Byzantine icons and exceptional Renaissance bronzes. One of the finest medieval works is the eloquent "Lamentation of Christ" by Lorenzo Monaco (1408). Among the other highlights are the confident and complex "Feast of the Rosary" (1506) by Albrecht Dürer, part of Rudolph II's personal collection; the sensuous 1530s "Adam and Eve" by Lucas

Above: An honor guard parades within the castle courtyards.

Left: The first courtyard of the castle leads to the presidential quarters, where official receptions are often held.

Nový Svět is the most picturesque and tranquil lane in Hradčany.

Cranach the Elder, as well as three other works by the same artist; the wonderfully sulky portrait of Eleanor of Toledo by Agnolo Bronzino; a luminous head of Christ by El Greco; a Rembrandt painting depicting a scholar in his study (1634); the rugged portrait of Don Miguel de Lardizábal by Goya; and works by Tintoretto, Hals, and Rubens. On the second floor is the

Chinese Cabinet, a finely restored room with black lacquered walls where the Šternberks exhibited their Oriental porcelain collection.

At the far end of the square you will find the heavy Roman baroque **Tuscany Palace** (Toskánský palác), at one time the property of the Grand Dukes of Tuscany. Close to the palace, the Renaissance **Martinitz Palace** (Martinický palác), at No. 8, belonged to one of the imperial counselors defenestrated in 1618 (see p. 26). The house at No. 6 still belongs to the Mucha family. Once a museum created by Alfons's son Jiří, in the 1990s it was replaced by the Mucha Museum in the New Town (see pp. 134–135).

Beyond the Tuscany Palace, Loretánská leads past the former town hall (Hradčanská radnice) of 1603 and some 18th-century palaces. It then enters a square dominated by the enormous **Černín Palace** (Černínský palác), completed in 1697 for the imperial ambassador to Venice. Francesco Caratti was the principal architect, and the interior decorations are by František Kaňka. In 1851 the Černín family, who could no longer afford to maintain such a vast residence, sold it to the state. Since 1929 it has served as the Foreign Ministry and is closed to visitors, although concerts are sometimes held in its gardens.

Facing the palace, a ramp leads down to the **Loreto Church** (Loreta) of 1626, with a facade from the 1720s by Kilián Ignác Dientzenhofer. This extraordinary pilgrimage complex was commissioned by Kateřina of Lobkowicz, who was obsessed by the Santa Casa of Loreto, Italy. This was supposedly the home of the Holy Family until transported to Italy by angels in the 13th century. Kateřina's Santa Casa was not the only reproduction to be built in Europe; in the Czech lands alone there were about 50 of them, but this is by far the most important. Here the house is surrounded by elaborate frescoed cloisters. The Loreto Church has great baroque charm, if your taste extends to an abundance of cherubs. The Santa Casa is a brick, barrel-vaulted structure in a boxlike Renaissance-style casing enriched with statuary. Piety apart, the main reason to come here

is to see the extraordinary treasury. The most dazzling exhibit is the gilded silver sunburst monstrance studded with 6,222 diamonds. Other exhibits are embellished with pearls and amethysts.

Continue down the ramp, past the modest Capuchin church of 1602, to reach a cobbled lane called **New World** (Nový Svět). With its modest houses, dating mostly from the 17th and 18th centuries, this used to be the poorest quarter of Hradčany; it is in complete contrast to the palatial splendor of the rest of the district. The artisans and servants departed long ago, and today Nový Svět is the trendy location of galleries and restaurants, although it has lost none of its charm. Despite its new chic status, Nový Svět remains a relatively isolated and tranquil corner of the city. The lane leads to another fine Dientzenhofer church, **St. John of Nepomuk** (Kostel sv. Jan Nepomucký), completed in 1729. The interior is adorned with frescoes by Václav Reiner. From here you can follow Kanovnická back to Hradčany Square. ∎

An 18th-century fresco of the Virgin Mary decorates the Loreto Church.

A walk around Little Quarter

This walk will take you through all the main streets and lanes of the Little Quarter (Malá Strana). Huddled around the castle are baroque palaces and mansions, while lower and closer to the river are more palaces as well as some of Prague's most lavish and interesting churches and squares.

Start this walk from **Malá Strana Square** (Malostranské náměstí), which is easily reached by tram 12 or 22. You will be back here later on this walk to look at the square in detail, but begin by walking up **Nerudova 1**, which is one of the best preserved baroque streets in the city, to get a general feel of Malá Strana. At the top, Nerudova becomes Úvoz, a cobbled lane lined with charming baroque houses that leads to the **Strahov Monastery** (see pp. 81–82). Now turn around and walk down Nerudova. The street takes its name from poet Jan Neruda, who once lived at No. 47. It has a glorious collection of facades and carved signs that identified the houses before numbering became the norm. Larger buildings include the 1765 Bretfeld Palace (Bretfeldský palác, No. 33), with its baroque

railings. The 1720s Thun-Hohenstein Palace (Thun-Hohenštejnský palác, No. 20), now the Italian Embassy, has striking Renaissance gables at the rear and a principal doorway guarded by

> See area map pp. 56–57
> Malá Strana Square
> 3 miles (5 km)
> 4 hours, plus time for lunch
> Vojanovy Garden

NOT TO BE MISSED
- Church of St. Nicholas
- Lobkowicz Palace
- Vrtba Gardens
- Kampa Island
- Wallenstein Gardens

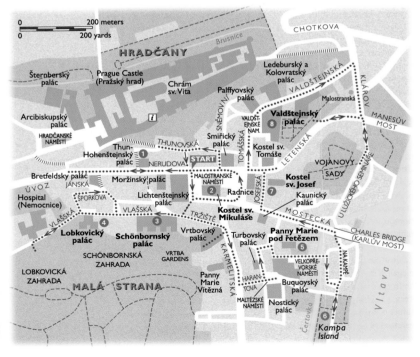

The exquisite baroque Vrtba Gardens are concealed behind a house on Karmelitská.

two eagles carved by Matthias Braun. Number 5, the Moržin Palace (Moržinský palác), is adorned with stooped figures of Moors. Number 12 has a charming sign in the form of three fiddles; a family of violinmakers, the Edlingers, once lived here. At the foot of Nerudova you can quench your thirst at the excellent beer hall, U Kocoura (At the Cat), after tackling the hills of Hradčany.

The hub of Malá Strana is **Malá Strana Square** ②. In the center stands the **Church of St. Nicholas** (Kostel sv. Mikuláše) and, facing it, at the top of the square, rise the majestic plague column of 1715 and the vast **Liechtenstein Palace** (Lichtenštejnský palác) of 1791 at No. 13. The church is one of the masterpieces by the Dientzenhofers, father and son. Its facade, completed in 1710, is curvaceous and eloquent; the interior is broad, richly painted, and crowded with fine statues by Ignác Platzer the Elder. The curves of the facade are reflected inside, too, with undulating galleries. Walk down the aisle to admire the trompe l'oeil paintings in the dome, the green and pink marble piers, the four massive statues of the Church Fathers by Platzer beneath the dome, and the enormous pulpit by Richard and Peter Prachner. The exquisite

gilt organ was played by Mozart during his visit to Prague in 1787.

Now walk to the bottom of the square. Number 21 is the former district **town hall** (Malostranská radnice), completed in 1622 in Renaissance style; today it holds a restaurant, snack bar, and music club. Facing the parking lot at No. 18 is the arcaded, turreted **Smirickych Palace** (Smiřický palác), built in the 17th century and modified a century later.

Sněmovní, the lane alongside Smirickych Palace, leads to more baroque palaces, some now used as the offices of the Czech parliament. After a short distance you reach Thunovská. Turn left and you come first to the British Embassy and then to steps that lead up to the castle. From Thunovská you can see the rear of some of the palaces along Nerudova, many of them Renaissance in origin. The lane called Zámecká brings you back to Malá Strana Square.

Walk to No. 12 at the top of the square. From here a passage leads to Tržiště and Vlašská. Many of the palaces along both lanes are now embassies. Turn right up Vlašská. On the left at No. 15, the **Schönborn Palace** (Schönbornský palác) ③, with its carved wooden doors and splendid gardens, is now the U.S. Embassy. Continue up Vlašská to the spectacularly pedimented **Lobkowicz Palace** (Lobkovický palác) ④, now the

German Embassy. It was here in late 1989 that thousands of East Europeans invaded the gardens and began the exodus that led to the collapse of the communist regimes of Eastern Europe. Continue past the Lobkowicz Palace; opposite the entrance to the hospital on Vlašská is a gate on the left that leads to a small park that overlooks the palace.

Opposite the Lobkowicz Palace, Sporkova leads to a small square; on the corner with Jánská is a charming sgraffitoed house. This is an unusually tranquil corner of Malá Strana. Cross the square and bear right until you reach Vlašská again. Walk down past the U.S. Embassy and past the Irish pub on the left, until you reach Karmelitská. On the corner of Karmelitská at No. 25 is the **Vrtba Palace** (Vrtbovský palác), where the artist Mikolás Ales once lived.

A passage beneath the palace leads to the lovely terraced **Vrtba Gardens** (Vrtbovská zahrada; *closed Nov.–March),* on the slopes behind the palace. Walking past, you would never suspect there are baroque gardens behind the house, which makes their presence all the more delightful. There is no more tranquil spot in Malá Strana in which to stop for a rest in the midst of intense sightseeing. About

330 feet (100 m) down Karmelitská on the right you'll see the early baroque **Church of Our Lady Victorious** (Panny Marie Vítězná). This Carmelite church houses the venerated doll-like statue, "Infant Jesus of Prague" (Pražské Jezulátko), on the right. Visitors come here from all over the world to pray to the statue and to leave gifts.

From Karmelitská turn left down Harantova to Maltézské náměstí, a peaceful rectangular square dominated by the **Nostitz Palace** (Nostický palác) and Ferdinand Brokoff's complex statue of St. John the Baptist. At No. 6, the lovely rococo 18th-century **Turba Palace** (Turbovský palác) houses the Japanese Embassy. Behind the French restaurant U Malířů is the **Church of St. Mary Under the Chain** (Panny Marie pod řetězem) ❺, the oldest church in Malá Strana, dating from 1169. Romanesque arcades and two squat Gothic towers survive, while the interior is a delightful baroque design by Carlo Lurago (1640).

To the left of the church are several baroque mansions, including the former hotel at No. 11 where Mozart and Beethoven once stayed. To the right, at No. 2, the former palace of the Grand Priory (Velkopřevorský palác), and residence of the Grand Prior of the Knights of Malta, used to be an excellent museum of musical instruments, but it has been returned to its original owners. Around the corner, on peaceful Velkopřevorské náměstí, are the two Buquoy palaces, both belonging to the French Embassy, and from here it is a few paces to **Kampa Island** ❻.

The Čertovka stream divides the island from the main shore. Three mills line the stream, the largest of which has been restored. Until the 16th century the island was filled with private gardens belonging to the Malá Strana palaces, especially the Nostický palác. The park was created in the 1940s, and it remains a tranquil corner of the city. Leave the park in the direction of Charles Bridge (Karlův most) to the large square called Na Kampě, the former pottery market. Na Kampě adjoins Charles Bridge. Climb the steps to the bridge and turn left along bustling Mostecká.

The Renaissance Sala Terrena dominates the formal gardens of the Wallenstein Palace.

It's all too easy to become absorbed in the glittering shopfronts here and to ignore the older buildings above. The finest is the **Kaunicky Palace** (Kaunický palác) of 1775, with its rococo facade.

The street opposite is Josefská, which leads to the baroque **Church of St. Joseph** (Kostel sv. Josef)  on the right (with a simple domed interior and a painting of the Holy Family by Petr Brandl on the main altar). The **Church of St. Thomas** (Kostel sv. Tomáše), straight ahead, is another powerful masterpiece by Kilián Ignác Dientzenhofer. Frescoes set in stucco frames adorn the ceiling and dome, and the pews are richly carved.

Behind St. Thomas's Church on Letenská is the famous, if touristy, **St. Thomas's Beer Hall** (pivovar U sv. Tomáše), which has been brewing since the mid-14th century and now serves excellent Braník beer. Return past the church to the square where Tomášská, yet another street with fine baroque houses, links Malá Strana Square with Wallenstein Square (Valdštejnské náměstí). A statue of St. Hubert and a stag adorn the portal at No. 4, a celebrated baroque house. At No. 14 is the large **Palffy Palace** (Palffyovský palác), partly the Prague conservatory, partly a restaurant.

Wallenstein Square (Valdštejnské náměstí) is dominated by the magnificent early baroque **Wallenstein Palace** (Valdštejnský palác) , the city residence of the ambitious warrior Albrecht von Wallenstein (see p. 27). Twenty-three houses and three gardens had to be destroyed to make room for this vast palace. In its heyday it employed 700 servants and had its own riding school and the most sumptuous gardens in Malá Strana.

Unlike the palace itself, now used as the Czech Senate, the gardens are open to the public. Before visiting them, follow the curve of Valdštejnská, where two palaces—the **Ledebur** (Ledeburský palác) at No. 3 opposite the Wallenstein Palace, and the **Kolowrat** at Valdštejnská 10 (Kolovratský palác)—have charming terraced gardens clambering up the slopes behind them. These former gardens of the nobility have now been linked by staircases and passages to create a series of terraces, pavilions, and loggias on a variety of levels *($$)*. Continue past the sumptuous palaces and gardens

The stunning dome of the Church of St. Nicholas, a masterpiece by the Dientzenhofers, in Malá Strana Square

that are now home to the Polish and Indian embassies.

To reach the gorgeous **gardens** of the Wallenstein Palace, bear right at the end of the street; cut through the metro station and take a right on Letenská. The entrance, several doors down at No. 10, is clearly marked but not actually numbered. The gardens are dominated by the magnificent loggia known as the **Sala Terrena** (1627), and they are spacious enough to accommodate an aviary and a chestnut grove dotted with splendid statuary. Another formal garden, the **Vojanovy Garden** (Vojanovy sady), along U lužického semináře, between here and Charles Bridge, is usually less crowded. From here you can return past Letenská on the left to the Malostranská metro. ■

Petřín Hill

Petřín Tower
🅰 Map p. 56
🕐 Closed Mon.–Fri.
Nov.–March
💲 $

Mirror Maze
🕐 Closed Mon.–Fri.
Nov.–Feb.
💲 $

Observatory
🕐 Closed Fri.
April–Oct., & Fri.–
Sun. Nov.–March
💲 $

ADJACENT TO HRADČANY AND THE CASTLE IS A LARGE
open expanse of parkland known as the Petřín Hill (Petřínské sady).
Largely unspoiled and in places still quite wild, it is the largest green
space within the city boundaries.

In early medieval times, this area was part of the large forest fringing the town, and vineyards grew on the sheltered southern slopes. Over time gardens and orchards replaced most of the vineyards, and many fruit trees survive, creating an enchanting sight especially in spring when they blossom. Not surprisingly, the meandering paths that crisscross the hill are popular with courting couples; high-energy children love them too.

You can reach the hill from various spots. There are entrances from Úvoz and Vlašská in Malá Strana and from the Strahov Monastery, and closer to the river short streets connect the park to main thoroughfares such as Karmelitská and Újezd. From Újezd, it's quite a climb to the top of the hill, which is 1,043 feet high (318 m).

The easiest way to reach the summit is by the **Funicular Railway** (Lanová dráha), which leaves from near Újezd. It operates every ten minutes from 9:15 a.m. until 8:30 p.m. daily. The railway was built in 1891 and has two stops, the first of which leads to the expensive Nebozízek restaurant, which takes its name from the vineyard originally here.

Once at the top, you can bear right toward the **Petřín Tower** (Petřínská rozhledna)—you can't miss it, this miniature version of the Eiffel Tower. Built just two years after the original was completed in Paris, for the 1891 Prague Exposition, it demonstrates the close cultural ties

between the two capital cities in the late 19th century. It was moved to this spot on Petřín Hill in the 1930s. It's quite a steep climb to the viewing platform—almost 300 steps—but you'll be rewarded with breathtaking views over the city and far beyond. There's a handy café at the foot of the tower.

Between the funicular station and the tower you'll pass the **Mirror Maze** (Zrcadlové bludiště). This neo-Gothic castle-like structure, modeled on one of the old gates at Vyšehrad, was built at the same time as the funicular, in 1891. The maze is a major draw for children in particular, who delight both in the maze itself as well as in the rooms filled with distorting mirrors.

Behind the tower and the maze you'll see the **Hunger Wall** (Hladová zed'), the surviving part of the great fortifications constructed in the 1360s by Charles IV as a public works project for the starving unemployed. The remains are quite substantial: They stretch for nearly a mile (1,200 m) and are 23 feet high (8 m), linking Újezd to the Strahov Monastery. Indeed, there are many paths on the Petřín Hill that lead directly to the monastery.

Alongside the wall, just a few paces from the Mirror Maze, stands the **Church of St. Lawrence** (Kostel sv. Vavřinec), with its distinctive onion-shaped towers. The church, designed by Ignác Palliardi, was completed in the mid-1770s on the

site of an earlier Romanesque chapel, for which it is named.

You can reach the **Observatory** (Štefánikova hvězdárna) in the park by taking the path in the opposite direction from the one that leads to the tower. It's open to the public, and you can try out some of the remarkably powerful telescopes. There's a small historical exhibition of astronomical devices, many of which, like the telescopes, are intended to excite the curiosity of children.

Close to the observatory is the **Rose Garden** (Růžový sad), where you can rest before descending back to the city. ■

Left: A smaller version of Paris's famous landmark stands atop Petřín Hill.
Below: A panoramic view of the whole city spreads out beneath Petřín Hill.

Strahov Monastery

THE STRAHOV MONASTERY (STRAHOVSKÝ KLÁŠTER), NEAR Pohořelec, lies along the hilltop to the west of Prague Castle (Pražský hrad). Founded in the 1140s by Duke Vladislav II, it was burned down in 1258, and subsequent reconstruction has given the complex an overwhelmingly baroque appearance. Until it was closed by the Communists in 1950, the monastery was in the hands of Premonstratensian monks, a reforming order named after the first abbey at Prémontré in northern France. In its heyday, the order ran 2,000 monasteries across Europe, and Strahov, one of the wealthiest, was their first foundation in Bohemia.

Strahov Monastery
www.strahovmonastery.cz
🅰 Map p. 56
✉ Strahovské nádvoří
☎ 220 517 278
(gallery);
220 516 671
ext. 410 (library)
🕐 Gallery: closed Mon.
💲 $
🚋 Tram: 22, 23
(Pohořelec)

You enter the monastery complex through a substantial baroque gateway designed by Anselmo Lurago in 1742; the statue on top depicts St. Norbert, the founder of the Premonstratensian order. Straight ahead is the entrance to the abbey church, dedicated to the **Church of the Assumption of Our Lady** (Nanebezvetí Panny Marie), and on the left is the soaring former **Church of St. Roch** (Kostel sv. Rocha), built on the orders of Rudolph II in 1612; it is now used for art exhibitions. Within the spacious courtyard the monks, who returned here after 1989, run a restaurant and beer garden.

The facade of the abbey church is another of Lurago's designs, embellished with statues by Johann Anton Quittainer (1709–1765), who also carved the statues above the gateway. Step into the nave and you will be treated to the ravishing sight of this glorious—and

wonderfully restored—church, with its symmetrical altarpieces marking the eye's passage toward the lofty, exuberant main altar. Look upward and admire the stunning rococo frescoed ceiling. The furnishings richly reconstructed in the 18th century—pulpit, pews, organ, railings—are dark and sumptuous. Mozart improvised on the organ up in the west gallery when he visited Strahov in 1787; the monks transcribed his impromptu composition.

The former monastic buildings now house two of the most beautiful baroque libraries in Europe. The first one is the lofty, galleried **Philosophical Library** (Filosofický sál). Its magnificent bookcases and other wooden furnishings were brought here after the monastery at Louka in southern Moravia was dissolved in the 1780s. So important was the Louka library that the Strahov monks had no qualms about altering the dimensions of their own library to accommodate the Moravian furnishings and collections.

The monks further embellished the library by commissioning the great Austrian artist Franz Anton Maulbertsch (1724–1796) to paint the ceiling; he chose the theme of Enlightenment, charting the progress of humankind to knowledge under divine guidance.

Strahov's gardens

A door in the east wall of the monastery leads to Strahov's gardens and orchards (Strahovská zahrada), which stretch down the hill in the direction of Malá Strana. There are excellent views from this point. ∎

Opposite: Anselmo Lurago's dignified gateway leads into the Strahov Monastery.

The Theological Library, one of two libraries at the Strahov Monastery, is one of the loveliest baroque rooms in central Europe.

The Roman busts are a recent contribution from a private collector in 1965.

A corridor leads to the **Theological Library** (Teologický sál), the older of the two libraries. It was built in 1671 by Giovanni Orsi and enlarged in the 1720s. The bookcases are older than the library itself. Its intimate atmosphere is enhanced by its low ceiling, adorned with frescoes painted by the Strahov monk Siard Nosecký and placed within elaborate stucco frames. These paintings include a self-portrait and depictions of other illustrious members of Nosecký's monastic order. Six antique globes and wooden lecterns help furnish the library.

Most of the collections in the libraries were donations, and it's hard to imagine a finer setting for about 3,000 manuscripts and more than 1,500 incunabula (rare volumes printed before 1500). The oldest manuscript is a ninth-century lectionary, the **Strahov Gospel,** with a richly bejeweled cover; a facsimile is on display near the entrance to the Theological Library. Other rare missals, miniature books, manuscripts—including a ninth-century manuscript with tenth-century illuminations of the Evangelists—and a 14th-century astronomical atlas are on display close to the bookshop.

The cloisters beyond the east end of the church used to house a museum of Czech literature, established here in the 1950s after the monastery was closed by the Communists. Now it has been replaced by a **gallery** exhibiting about one-tenth of the monastery's own art collection of a thousand items. Highlights include a magnificent anguished Crucifixion from Jihlava (1330s); panels by the Master of Litoměřice; works by Karel Škréta, Franz Palko, Václav Reiner, and Petr Brandl; and rococo panels by Maulbertsch. The gallery also displays some of the treasury of bejeweled crosses and monstrances. As in the National Gallery (Národní galerie; see pp. 71–72), Brandl is represented by a series of dark portraits of elderly saints, and a fine self-portrait. ■

Old Town Square (Staroměstské náměstí) is the hub of this maze of medieval streets, studded with palaces, squares, and churches. Here, too, is the Jewish quarter (Josefov), its ancient cemetery crowded with gravestones.

Old Town

A heraldic mosaic embellishes the Old Town Hall.

Old Town

OLD TOWN (STARÉ MĚSTO), PRAGUE'S HISTORIC HUB, HAS MAINTAINED ITS medieval layout, centered on the Old Town Square (Staroměstské náměstí). All around the square, and along the lanes that connect it with the bank of the River Vltava, stand old houses with foundations dating back to the 11th and 12th centuries. Another two centuries would go by before the district was given the privileges due an independent township, and the Old Town Hall (Staroměstská radnice), today the central adornment of the square, was founded as late as 1338.

Despite the comparatively small area of Old Town, it contains a huge amount of cultural, religious, and educational activity. There are numerous churches, both medieval and baroque; the remains of the original medieval university, the Karolinum, and its Jesuit successor, the Klementinum; and the major concert hall, the Rudolfinum, standing along the river. In addition to the vast Old Town Square, there are the more intimate squares and marketplaces such as Betlémské náměstí and Uhelný trh. Old Town features fewer aristocratic palaces than Malá Strana, as the nobility preferred to have their residences as close to the royal palace as possible; nonetheless, buildings such as the Clam-Gallas and Goltz-Kinský palaces are as impressive as anything found on the other side of the river.

Just north of Old Town Square is the former Jewish ghetto of Josefov, best known for its ancient cemetery (Starý židovský hřbitov) crowded with thousands of gravestones. It is known as Josefov in honor of Emperor Joseph II, who showed tolerance to the Jews in the late 18th century. In 1850 it became a municipal district within the city of Prague. Overcrowding and unsanitary conditions blighted the ghetto, which was razed toward the end of the 19th century. Its tenements were replaced by tall, imaginatively designed blocks with art nouveau flourishes. Today the streets of Josefov house not only the fascinating remnants of the Jewish quarter but some of the most fashionable shopping streets of the city, filled with designer boutiques and expensive restaurants and bars.

On the northeast edge of Josefov you will find the Convent of St. Agnes (Anežský klášter), with its two churches now used for concerts. St. Agnes is also notable for its display of the National Gallery's medieval art. ∎

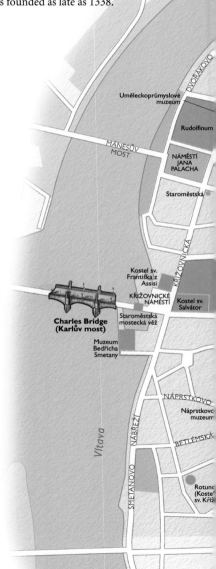

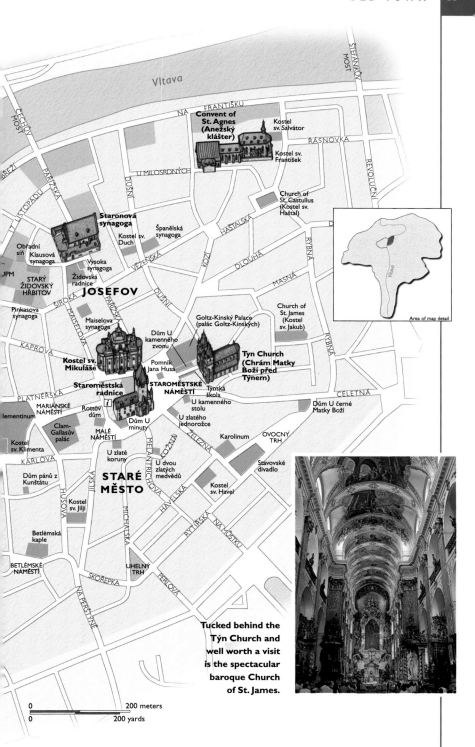

Vltava

NA FRANTIŠKU

Convent of St. Agnes (Anežský klášter)

Kostel sv. Salvátor

RÁSNOVKA

U MILOSRDNÝCH

Kostel sv. František

Church of St. Castullus (Kostel sv. Haštal)

Staronová synagoga

Španělská synagoga

Kostel sv. Duch

Obřadní síň Klausová synagoga

Vysoka synagoga

JPM

STARÝ ŽIDOVSKÝ HŘBITOV

Židovská radnice

JOSEFOV

Pinkasova synagoga

Maiselova synagoga

Church of St. James (Kostel sv. Jakub)

Goltz-Kinský Palace (palác Goltz-Kinských)

Dům U kamenného zvonu

KAPROVA

Kostel sv. Mikuláše

Tyn Church (Chrám Matky Boží před Týnem)

Pomník Jana Husa

Staroměstská radnice

STAROMĚSTSKÉ NÁMĚSTÍ

Týnská škola

CELETNÁ

PLATNÉŘSKÁ

MARIÁNSKÉ NÁMĚSTÍ

Rottův dům

U kamenného stolu

Dům U černé Matky Boží

lementinum

Clam-Gallasův palác

Dům U minuty

U zlatého jednorožce

MALÉ NÁMĚSTÍ

Kostel sv. Klimenta

KARLOVA

U zlaté koruny

U dvou zlatých medvědů

Karolinum

OVOCNÝ TRH

Stávovské divadlo

Dům pánů z Kunštátu

STARÉ MĚSTO

Kostel sv. Jiljí

Kostel sv. Havel

Betlémská kaple

BETLÉMSKÉ NÁMĚSTÍ

UHELNÝ TRH

SKOŘEPKA

PERLOVA

Area of map detail

Tucked behind the
Týn Church and
well worth a visit
is the spectacular
baroque Church
of St. James.

0 ———— 200 meters
0 ———— 200 yards

Old Town Square

Old Town Square

⬛ Map p. 85

🚇 Metro: Staroměstská

Old Town Hall

§ $

HOUSE NAMES

Old houses in Prague have a variety of descriptive names. Sometimes these refer to the owner or builder, sometimes to carvings on the facade or to house signs that once identified the building in the days before addresses.

Opposite: Restaurants and cafés now occupy many of the Old Town Square's arcaded houses.

PRAGUE'S OLD TOWN SQUARE (STAROMĚSTSKÉ NÁMĚSTÍ) IS the very heart of the city, an immense urban space surrounded by mansions, palaces, and churches. The houses facing the square are often Romanesque in origin, but the facades are mostly baroque. Since medieval times the square has been the social core of the city and home to the mightiest merchant families. It has witnessed executions and street battles, and in February 1948, Klement Gottwald proclaimed the establishment of the Communist state from the balcony of the rococo Goltz-Kinský Palace (palác Goltz-Kinských).

The palace faces the vast **Hus Monument** of 1915, designed by Ladislav Šaloun in commemoration of the execution of the great radical reformer 500 years earlier. The monument is more than a statue; it's an impassioned drama: Hussite soldiers and Protestants are portrayed being driven into exile, while the figure of a young mother signifies national revival. The palace houses the National Gallery's (Národní galerie's) collection of prints and drawings, unfortunately not open to the public; it is also used for temporary art exhibitions.

To the right of the Goltz-Kinský Palace stands the Gothic **House at the Stone Bell** (Dům U kamenného zvonu). You can see in old photographs that until the 1980s this structure had a baroque facade. The restorers decided, controversially, to remove the baroque mask and reveal the original Gothic windows and tracery that adorned the 14th-century house; in doing so they created a charming pastel-tinted scene.

Next to the house, on the other side of Týnská lane, you will find the former **Týn School** (Týnská škola), which functioned from the 14th to 19th centuries. An early Gothic, round-gabled structure, the windows suggest an Italianate makeover in the 16th century.

The distinctive twin towers of the **Týn Church** (Chrám Matky Boží před Týnem), a Prague landmark, loom over the square behind the school. You reach the entrance to the church through the arcades of the school. Building started on the church in 1365 and, despite much alteration since, the structure retains its Gothic atmosphere. Work began on the towers in 1402 but was interrupted by the Hussite wars; the spires were not completed until 1511.

The vaulting of the lofty interior is baroque, replacing the Gothic roof destroyed in a fire in 1679. However, the original arcades and aisle windows remain. So do various Gothic furnishings: a winged tabernacle depicting the Annunciation, Nativity, Baptism; the 1414 pewter font, the oldest in the city; an early 15th-century crucifix in the north aisle flanked by the figures of Mary and St. John; and a large seated Madonna and Child, also early 15th century. The baroque furnishings, notably the high altar of 1649, include paintings by Karel Škréta. Given the importance of this church, it is strange that access is limited to a few minutes before and after services.

Just east of the pulpit you will find the church's most interesting monument, the **tomb** of the great Danish astronomer Tycho Brahe (1546–1601), who was invited to Prague by Rudolph II in 1599, but died two years later. Brahe was a remarkable figure, especially as an

The Town Hall's famous medieval Astronomical Clock is a popular attraction when the hour strikes, on the hour every hour, and figures parade across the clockface.

inventor of astronomical instruments. He formulated a theory to appease the church that the planets revolved around the sun, yet died convinced the universe revolved around the Earth!

Return to the square to take a look at some of the houses here. On the south side, No. 17 has a hefty 16th-century portal beneath a bay window, adorned with a contemporary carving of a ram. Next to it is No. 18, **At the Stone Table** (U kamenného stolu); this is a pretty baroque house with delicate stucco decoration. At No. 20, **At the Golden Unicorn** (U zlatého jednorožce), the composer Smetana ran a music school.

Opposite these Gothic arcades stands the **Dům U minuty,** with its 17th-century sgraffito decorations and a carving of a lion and shield. The house is now part of the **Old Town Hall** (Staroměstská radnice) complex, a jumble of buildings. The citizens of Old Town successfully petitioned to establish their own town hall in 1338. The main entrance is a splendid ogee-arched Gothic doorway carved by Matthias Rejsek, and one of the Renaissance buildings has a beautiful gilt window surmounted by the coats of arms of the Old Town. The town hall's most famous feature is the **Astronomical Clock** (Orloj), designed by Mikuláš of Kadaň and constructed in 1410. It's the oldest of its kind in Europe and, not surprisingly, draws immense crowds when it strikes the hour; figures of the 12 Apostles appear in procession and others portraying Human Vanity, Miserliness, Death, and a Turk begin their gesticulations. The clock has often been renovated, most recently after it was damaged by German troops in 1945, when the figures of the Apostles were replaced.

The interior of the town hall, entered through the tourist

information office, is well worth visiting. The building is no longer an administrative center, but it is still used for ceremonial occasions. Art exhibitions are held here, and attractive doorways and painted ceiling beams enliven some rooms. Peter Parler built the chapel in the Old Town Hall in 1381, and the walls are decorated with heraldic frescoes; the glass was destroyed in 1945 and has been replaced with some garish modern equivalent. It is sometimes possible to visit the Romanesque basement of the town hall; the former prison was here, beneath the tower.

On the ground between the town hall and the Týn School, you can see the **memorial** to the 27 Protestant noblemen executed here after the Battle of White

Mountain (see p. 26): 27 white crosses, dated June 21, 1621.

Walk behind the town hall to the sumptuous **Church of St. Nicholas** (Kostel sv. Mikuláše), built by Kilián Ignác Dientzenhofer in the 1730s. In a city crammed with fine baroque church interiors, this has to be one of the finest, its broad facade decorated with statues and busts by Antonín Braun, nephew of the celebrated Matthias Braun. The church is essentially cruciform, topped by a squarish dome. Lavish stucco work by Bernardo Spinetti decorates the inside. The iron railings along the gallery are particularly attractive.

Return to Dům U minuty and follow the passageway into **Little Square** (Malé náměstí), which in former times was the city's fruit market. The square is focused around the Renaissance fountain, with its exquisite 1560 grille, and contains many delightful houses. Number 2, **At the White Lion** (U bílého lva), is an engaging blend of Gothic and rococo. Number 13, **At the Golden Crown** (U zlaté koruny), contains an exceptionally beautiful old pharmacy, with Empire-style furnishings. The **Rott House** (Rottův dům), at No. 3, dates back to Romanesque times, although the facade has paintings by the ever popular Mikuláš Aleš. This 19th-century artist's decorative work may look dated to many visitors, but his work is hard to avoid in Prague, where his frescoes and mosaics adorn many of the city's banks and public buildings. ∎

The Old Town Square, with the Old Town Hall on the left and the Týn Church spires in the background, has always been at the heart of Czech identity.

A walk around Old Town

This walk takes you through the twisting lanes of Old Town, more or less encircling Old Town Square (Staroměstské náměstí). It's a fascinating jumble of mansions, churches, palaces, and museums, as well as the old part of Charles University.

Begin at the Old Town (Staré Město) end of **Charles Bridge** (Karlův most; see pp. 94–97). Bear right and continue through the covered shopping arcade until you come to a promenade that juts into the river. You'll pass the upscale Mlýnec restaurant and a pleasant wine bar, the Three Graces (Tři Grácie), before reaching the **Smetana Museum** (Muzeum Bedřicha Smetany) ❶ *(closed Tues., $).* Founded in 1926, the museum houses a collection of original scores, as well as portraits, letters, and some of the composer's personal possessions. Smetana is revered by the Czechs both as a composer and as an ardent nationalist (see pp. 228–229).

Return to the square that leads to Charles Bridge. Next to the **Church of the Holy Savior** (Kostel sv. Salvátor) is an entrance to

the bulky **Klementinum** ❷, the former Jesuit college founded by the Habsburgs in 1556 to promote the Counter-Reformation and provide an alternative institution to Charles University. This is the largest building complex in the city apart from the castle. As the Klementinum is now part of Charles University, some areas are closed to visitors, but you can gain access to the 170-foot-high (52 m) **Astronomical Tower** (Hvězdárenská věž; *closed Mon.–Fri., $$),* the immense 17th-century reading room with its stucco decorations, the sumptuous **Baroque Hall Library** of 1727, and the heavily decorated and gilt chapel, known as the **Chapel of Mirrors** (Zrcadlová kaple; *closed except for concerts, $).* Mozart played one of the baroque organs here, and the hall is now used for concerts and exhibitions.

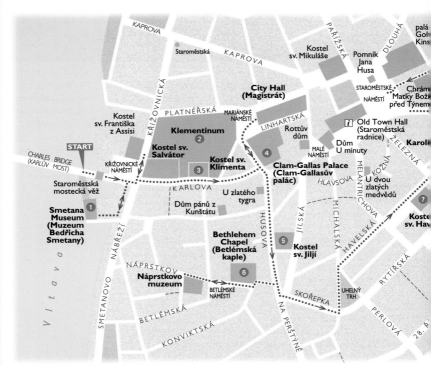

The road linking the Charles Bridge with Old Town Square is **Karlova.** Number 2 is the baroque Colloredo-Mansfeld Palace (palác Colloredo-Mansfeldský); No. 3, At the Golden Well (U zlaté studny), has a fine baroque facade; and No. 4 is the house where the great German astronomer Johannes Kepler lived from 1607 to 1612. Karlova is lined with other baroque mansions with Romanesque foundations, as well as pubs, restaurants, a marionette museum, and upscale stores. In medieval times, this was part of the royal route through the town; today it is the main thoroughfare used by thousands of tourists passing from Charles Bridge to Old Town Square. On the way you pass the **Church of St. Clement** (Kostel sv. Klimenta) ❸; it has a ravishing interior filled with statuary by Matthias Braun, but it is rarely open to visitors. The best time to gain access is in the late afternoon just before services begin.

Continue down Karlova, then turn left onto Husova, where you can hardly miss the immense **Clam-Gallas Palace**

Town houses, such as At the Golden Well on Karlova, were often embellished with statuary, both as decoration and as a means of identification.

(Clam-Gallasův palác) ❹, now the city archives. The palace has one of the finest facades in Prague, designed in the early 18th century by the great Austrian architect Fischer von Erlach. Though it is closed to visitors, you can walk through the public areas; the magnificent stone staircase with its frescoed ceiling is worth seeking out.

On leaving the palace, turn right into Mariánské náměstí, where you can see the mass of the **City Hall** (Magistrát), designed in a secession style by Osvald Polívka in

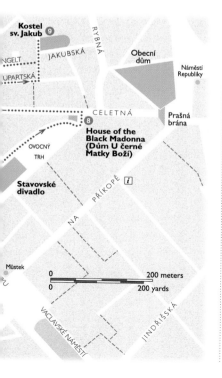

- See area map pp. 84–85
- Old Town end of Charles Bridge
- 2 miles (3.2 km)
- About 4 hours
- Old Town Square

NOT TO BE MISSED
- Baroque Hall Library, Klementinum
- Celetná
- Church of St. James
- Ungelt

1906–1911. Return to Husova and continue down the street, which has some exceptionally pretty rococo facades on the left. Opposite the famous U zlatého tygra pub is Cream & Dream at No. 12, with its delicious Italian ice creams. On the left you will pass the Dominican **Church of St. Giles** (Kostel sv. Jiljí) ⑤. Although the exterior dates from the early 14th century, the high interior was renovated in the baroque style and adorned with frescoes (1734) by Václav Reiner, who is buried in the nave.

Turn right onto Betlémské náměstí to see the **Bethlehem Chapel** (Betlémská kaple) ⑥ *($)*, a somber hall church dating from the late 14th century and reconstructed in the 1950s. It was here that the reformer Jan Hus preached in Czech; he lived in the house to the right of the chapel. On the corner of Náprstkova an 18th-century house now contains the **Náprstek Museum** (Náprstkovo muzeum; *closed Mon., $)*. Founded by Vojtěch Náprstek (1826–1894), this ethnographic museum contains a major collection of 95,000 objects from all over the world, including masks, statues, and weaponry. Its greatest strength lies in the artifacts from early American civilizations.

Walk back toward Husova and continue into Skořepka to Uhelný trh. From this market square three parallel streets lead toward the Karolinum and Estates Theater. Walk along Havelská, its center crowded with market stalls, to the **Church of St. Gall** (Kostel sv. Havel) ⑦, which was founded in 1280 but renovated in the 18th century by Giovanni Santini. Beyond is the green and cream bulk of the **Estates Theater** (Stavovské divadlo) and the **Karolinum,** original home of Prague University, one of Europe's earliest universities, founded by Charles IV in 1348. It still forms part of the university, which has expanded throughout the city. Few of the old buildings of the Karolinum survive. The theater was originally built in 1781 but has been much altered and renovated. It was here that two of Mozart's greatest operas, *Don Giovanni* and *La Clemenza di Tito,* received their premieres.

Take Ovocný trh between the Karolinum and the theater, which brings you to **Celetná,**

Right: The museum devoted to the life and work of beloved composer Bedřich Smetana is located near the Charles Bridge.

a major thoroughfare. On the corner is the unmistakable **House of the Black Madonna** (Dům U černé Matky Boží) ⑧ *(closed for renovation),* one of the finest cubist houses, designed by Josef Gočár. Many of the facades along Celetná are baroque, but most of the houses are far older in origin; others date back to early medieval times. Franz Kafka lived at No. 3 from 1896 to 1907.

Retrace your footsteps a short distance, take the left fork along Štupartská, then the second left along Malá Štupartská to the **Church of St. James** (Kostel sv. Jakub) ⑨. This late 17th-century church, with its

Right: The House of the Black Madonna, designed by Josef Gočár in 1912, is the best known cubist house in the city.

immensely long nave and theatrical double-galleried choir, has some of the finest baroque ornamentation in Prague. In the left aisle is the tomb of Count Vratislav of Mitrovice, a masterwork of 1716 by Fischer von Erlach and Brokoff. Just inside the church entrance on the right is a mummified arm said to belong to a thief who tried to steal the jewels from the statue of the Madonna on the altar four centuries ago; the Virgin seized his arm so hard, it had to be cut off in order to free the thief.

Opposite the church is the **Týn courtyard,** or Ungelt, a warehousing and merchants' center until the 18th century. In the 1980s the courtyard was almost derelict, but today it bustles with shops, cafés, and restaurants. Leave through the Týn Church arcade, which will take you back to Old Town Square. ■

Charles Bridge

MALÁ STRANA IS LINKED TO OLD TOWN BY ONE OF THE most spectacular bridges in Europe, a medieval masterpiece, the 1,700-foot-long (500 m), 16-arched Charles Bridge (Karlův most). Begun by Peter Parler on the orders of Charles IV in 1357, it was not completed until 1402. It replaced the nearby Judith Bridge, which was destroyed in the floods of 1342. For 500 years Karlův most, called simply the Prague bridge until the 19th century, was the only bridge uniting the two halves of the city. But it's not just the bridge that is enthralling; the views from it are superb. Halfway along, looking in either direction, you can enjoy fabulous roofscapes of baroque domes, Gothic spires, medieval towers, Renaissance gables, and the broad expanses of the palaces of the nobility.

Charles Bridge
Map p. 84
Tram: 17, 18
(Staroměstská)

Close to the Malá Strana end is the famous old Three Ostriches (U tří pštrosů) inn. Its name comes from the fresco depicting ostriches, a reference to Jan Fux's feather business, a vital fashion accessory in Renaissance times. In 1714, it's thought, Prague's first coffeehouse opened its doors here.

Charles Bridge's finest feature, sometimes obscured by the crowds of peddlers, entertainers, and tourists, is the series of baroque religious statues lining the balustrades; some of them, however, are 19th-century replacements of carvings damaged in floods, the originals of which can be seen in the Lapidarium of the National Museum. The statues are the work of such Bohemian masters as Ferdinand Brokoff and Matthias Braun. The marriage between the Gothic bridge and its baroque adornments

Opposite: The most famous medieval bridge in central Europe, the Charles Bridge has linked the two sides of the city since 1402. Below: Visitors walking along the Charles Bridge admire its statuary and enjoy the street musicians.

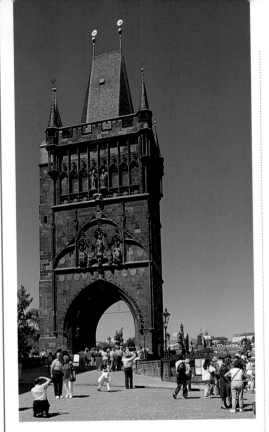

Above: The workshop of Peter Parler produced much of the medieval statuary that decorates the Old Town Bridge Tower.

Opposite: The Charles Bridge can be seen as a gallery of masterworks by Bohemia's most renowned baroque sculptors.

works perfectly. Not all the statues have artistic merit, but the following are among the highlights, beginning at the Malá Strana end.

Brokoff designed two magnificent groups of statuary in 1714. One of them, the second group on the left, depicts **St. Vitus** atop a rocky peak, seemingly unfazed by the snakes and wild animals just beneath him; the other, directly opposite, shows the Saints John of Matha, Felix of Valois, and Ivo.

The next figure along, St. Adalbert, is a copy of a Brokoff statue. Opposite you will see the only marble statue, depicting St. Philip Benizi. The saint standing in front of a putti-encrusted obelisk is St. Cajetan, also by Brokoff. Opposite is another splendid group: the blind **St. Luitgarde** by

Matthias Braun. Farther along on the right, Brokoff also contributed statues of Saints Vincent Ferrer and Procopius (1712), standing on a pedestal that shows the dead arising from their opened coffins.

No group of Prague statuary would be complete without one of **St. John of Nepomuk,** who is represented toward the middle of the bridge on the left by a fine bronze by Matthias Rauchmüller and Jan Brokoff (1683); the pedestal shows the martyrdom of the saint as he was thrown into the Vltava.

Back on the right side of the bridge, Brokoff again indulged in exoticism with his statue of **St. Francis Xavier** (a copy), who is accompanied by a pigtailed Chinese, a Turk, and an Indian chieftain, alluding to the saint's missionary activities. Farther along on the left, a fine 17th-century **Crucifixion** replaces a medieval cross that once stood here. Beyond, on the right, is a surprisingly staid representation of Saints Margaret, Elizabeth, and Barbara, also by Brokoff. The final pair on the bridge are copies: on the left, Jäckel's Virgin with St. Bernard (1709) and, opposite, the figure of St. Ivo (1711) by Matthias Braun.

After such an excess of baroque statuary, it's tempting to race under the Old Town Bridge Tower onto terra firma, but the tower is worth a closer look. The best facade is that facing Old Town; the coats of arms depict the territories of the Holy Roman Empire during the reign of Charles IV, who is shown above, with Václav (Wenceslas) IV wearing an imperial crown. You can climb the tower and survey the city (*$*).

Two churches near the bridge end are worth a visit: on the left, the domed **Church of St. Francis** (Kostel sv. Františka z Assisi) and ahead, the **Church of St. Salvator** (Kostel sv. Salvátor). ■

Mozart in Prague

Wolfgang Amadeus Mozart (1756–1791) first visited Prague in January 1787, when he came to conduct a performance of *The Marriage of Figaro,* which was received with great acclaim by the people of Prague. He was then commissioned to write a new opera that would be given its first performance here: *Don Giovanni.*

Mozart returned to Prague in October to complete work on the new opera. At first he lodged at the Three Golden Lions (Dum U tří zlatých lvů) in Uhelný trh, which belonged to the composer and pianist František Dušek (1731–1799). Mozart had

met Dušek and his wife, Josefina, a renowned singer, in Vienna and Salzburg, and they invited him to stay at their home, Vila Bertramka (see p. 136). This villa stood among the vineyards in Smíchov district. Their hospitality offered Mozart tranquility and congenial company, and here he completed *Don Giovanni,* writing the overture only the night before the premiere on October 29, 1787.

It is said that Josefina, anxious to have Mozart complete a concert aria for her, locked the composer in a pavilion until he had finished it. The result was one of his masterpieces in this form, *Bella Mia Fiamma.*

Mozart returned to Prague many times, usually staying with the Dušeks. He also played on some of the most renowned keyboards in the city—on an organ in the Chapel of Mirrors in the Klementinum and at the Church of St. Nicholas (Kostel sv. Mikuláše) in Malá Straná Square. And there's a story that he improvised a sonata on the organ in the church of the Strahov Monastery (see p. 81).

His last visit was in 1791, when he was commissioned to write another opera, this time to celebrate the coronation of Emperor Leopold II as king of Bohemia. Mozart wrote at astonishing speed in the Vila Bertramka. By this time he was ill, and he was unable to remain in Prague to see the opera, *La Clemenza di Tito,* performed at the Estates Theater.

When he died three months later, he was remembered with Requiem Mass sung by Josefina and attended by thousands of mourners at the Church of St. Nicholas. ■

Left: A contemporary engraving depicts mourners making their way to the Church of St. Nicholas for Requiem Mass after Mozart's death in 1791.
Below: The interior of the Vila Bertramka is now a museum focused on Mozart.

Josefov
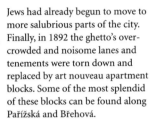 Map p. 85

Jewish Museum
www.jewishmuseum.cz

✉ U Staré školy 1

☎ 224 819 456

🕐 Closed Sat. & Jewish holidays

💲 $$$$

Ⓜ Metro: Staroměstská

The neo-Moorish Jubilee Synagogue, built in 1905, stands on Jeruzalemska outside the traditional ghetto area of Josefov.

Josefov

LIKE MANY BOHEMIAN AND MORAVIAN TOWNS, PRAGUE had a Jewish community from the early Middle Ages onward. Although their presence was tolerated, their lives were often dogged by insecurity. They were tolerated because Bohemian rulers depended on their skills as moneylenders, but for that very reason they were also resented and often persecuted. The original Jewish quarter was near the castle, and it first spread across the river in the 12th century. A walled ghetto until 1848, the Josefov developed an invigorating mixture of thriving business establishments, overcrowded tenements, and ancient synagogues. The area was named after Joseph II, during whose reign laws restricting Jewish activities were relaxed.

In 1850 Josefov was designated a separate district of Prague, but it remained a slum with a completely inadequate water supply. Wealthier

Jews had already begun to move to more salubrious parts of the city. Finally, in 1892 the ghetto's overcrowded and noisome lanes and tenements were torn down and replaced by art nouveau apartment blocks. Some of the most splendid of these blocks can be found along Pařížská and Břehová.

The Jewish quarter is easily approached up Pařížská from Old Town Square. After a couple of blocks you will see on your left the gabled brick structure of the **Old-New Synagogue** (Staronová synagoga). This ancient building dates from about 1275 and resembles a medieval chapel; it's also the oldest synagogue in regular use in Europe. Originally known as the New School to differentiate it from an even older synagogue, it changed its name to the Old-New after other houses of worship sprang up in the district. The brick gables are part of the original medieval structure.

Because the street level has been raised since it was built, and the synagogue is partly underground, the interior is gloomy. The dark rib-vaulted interior, with its 15th-century wrought-iron grille and ancient chandeliers and banners and pews, has remained unchanged for centuries.

The tall pew to the right of the Ark was the seat occupied by the famous Rabbi Judah Loew ben Bezalel (1520–1609). He was a leading figure in Jewish intellectual circles in the late 16th and early 17th centuries. The legend of the Golem (see pp. 104–105) is associated with him. The banner that hangs over the bima (the raised portion of the synagogue from which services are conducted) is that of the Jewish community, which was granted the right to its own flag by Charles IV in 1357. Damaged and renewed, the present banner dates from 1716.

On leaving the synagogue, bear left down Maiselova. On the left you will see the imposing **Jewish Town Hall** (Židovská radnice). It was established in 1541 but after a fire in 1764 was rebuilt. Its most remarkable feature is the clock whose hands move counterclockwise, reflecting the right-to-left movement of Hebrew script. The privilege of building a clock tower was granted to the community in recognition of the role played by Jewish residents in the defense of Charles Bridge against Swedish forces in 1648. The building still houses the Czech Jewish community's governing body.

Turn right onto Široká. On the right lies the entrance to the **Old Jewish Cemetery** (Starý židovský hřbitov). First you come to the 16th-century **Pinkas Synagogue** (Pinkasova synagoga). Frequently rebuilt, it now serves as a poignant monument to the 77,297 Jewish victims of the Holocaust from Bohemia and Moravia. All the names of those who perished are individually recorded on the interior walls. As a crude anti-Israeli gesture, the Communist regime painted over them in 1975, but the names have since been painstakingly restored.

For many visitors the Old Jewish Cemetery is the prime attraction in the area. The last burial here took place in 1787, after which Joseph II prohibited further internments within the city walls. Since then the walled compound seems scarcely to have been disturbed. Many of the ancient gravestones are leaning and worn, but that adds to the dignified calm of the cemetery. The oldest grave, that of **Avigdor Karo,** dates from 1439. A celebrated mayor of the Jewish town, **Mordechai Maisel** (1528–1601) is buried between the Klaus Synagogue (Klausová synagoga) and the Museum of Decorative Arts (Uměleckoprůmyslové muzeum; see p. 110). Close to the museum wall is another unusually ornate tombstone, that of **Hendela**

Old-New Synagogue

🕐 Closed Sat. & Jewish holidays

💲 $$$$

Souvenir stalls near the Old Jewish Cemetery hope to attract the hundreds of visitors who come here.

Above: The tranquil oasis of the Old Jewish Cemetery still contains thousands of tightly packed gravestones.

Opposite: The opulent Spanish Synagogue in Josefov, with its elaborate stucco decorations inspired by those at the Alhambra in Grenada, hosts many an elegant wedding.

Bassevi (1628), whose husband was raised to the nobility. Over the centuries up to 100,000 bodies were buried here, and 12,000 gravestones remain. A shortage of space meant that earth was piled on top of existing graves to permit fresh burials; this explains the undulating terrain of the cemetery.

The old stones are covered with Hebrew inscriptions commemorating the dead and their virtues. They are often adorned with symbolic carvings of pine cones, pitchers, and grapes, which denote values such as fertility and the historic tribe of Israel to which the deceased belonged. Jewish visitors still observe the custom of placing pebbles on gravestones as a mark of respect. No tomb contains more stones than that of Rabbi Loew (see pp. 104–105), which lies close to the Museum of Decorative Arts.

You emerge from the cemetery by a gate right next to the neo-Romanesque **Ceremonial Hall** (Obřadní síň). For many years this housed drawings and paintings produced by children incarcerated in the ghetto at Terezín in the early 1940s (see pp. 208–211), but these exhibits have now been appropriately removed to Terezín itself. Today the hall is a museum containing objects associated with Jewish rituals and customs.

The Ceremonial Hall is one of several buildings close to the cemetery that make up the Jewish Museum. Ironically, it was the Nazis who, by collecting Jewish artifacts from Czechoslovakia in order to demonstrate Jewish "degeneracy," inadvertently helped preserve their history. As you leave the hall, you will see the entrance to the 1694 **Klausová synagoga** to the right. It has an ornate barrel-vaulted interior and displays ancient Hebrew manuscripts and books reflecting the history of the Jewish printed book in Prague. Other exhibits are related to the Sabbath and Jewish festivals, and there are embroidered Torah curtains and silver finials and shields used to decorate the scrolls of the law. Other displays show objects associated with Jewish rituals.

From here, return to the Jewish Town Hall and turn right down Maiselova. Cross Široká and, on the left at No. 10, you come to the **Maisel Synagogue** (Maiselova synagoga). It contains what is, from the artistic point of view, the most absorbing of all the exhibitions in the Jewish Museum: Jewish silverware from all over Bohemia and Moravia, manuscripts, and Torah mantles, some dating back to the 17th century. Other exhibits give an idea of daily life in the ghetto.

The last synagogue is the **Spanish Synagogue** (Španělská synagoga). To reach it, turn right on emerging from the Maisel Synagogue, then right again on Široká. After a block and a half you come to the Church of the Holy Ghost (Kostel sv. Duch) and, just beyond it, the 1868 Spanish Synagogue, which catered to the Sephardic community of Prague. The domed interior is magnificent, with every inch of its surface patterned and painted in a neo-Moorish style. It was kept closed for many years, but it has been beautifully renovated and now serves as a hall illustrating the life of the city's Jewish community in the 19th century. Up in the gallery there are fascinating old photos of Jewish life throughout Bohemia and Moravia; others give a vivid idea of how the old ghetto must have looked before its demolition. Documents and photographs illustrate the deportations of 1941–45 that brought the once vibrant Jewish community of Prague to the point of extinction. ■

Rabbi Loew & the Golem

In the Old Jewish Cemetery in Prague is the gravestone of the revered Jehuda Loew ben Bezabel ben Chaim, Rabbi Loew (1520–1609), who persuaded Rudolph II in 1592 to offer greater protection to the city's Jews. The rabbi was also a friend of the famous astronomer Tycho Brahe and had a reputation as an expert in the natural sciences as well as in the Jewish mystical writings known as the cabbala. Loew was credited with fashioning a creature called the Golem from mud and clay but imbued by the rabbi with a life of its own.

The legend of the Golem has been a source of inspiration to many writers and dramatists.

story goes, after Loew uttered the word "Shem," which is the unknown name of God. Other versions tell how the rabbi placed a piece of paper or stone with the holy word written upon it into the creature's mouth or walked around the Golem seven times counterclockwise. Once given life, the Golem became hard to control. In some tales the rabbi forgot to remove the paper from the Golem's mouth, so the creature went on the rampage, inflicting damage and terrifying the ghetto's inhabitants.

Elaborations of the legend depict the Golem as a heroic creature whose adventures are part sinister, part playful, riding to the rescue when Jewish values or lives were under threat. In an age when Jews felt chronically insecure after centuries of persecution, exile, and false accusations, it must have been reassuring to think that a supernatural creature was on hand with the powers to defend them. The only way to render the Golem lifeless was to remove the breath of life from it, whereupon it would return to its original state. Eventually, according to legend, the inert Golem was deposited out of harm's way beneath the roof of the Old-New Synagogue.

It is not surprising that this fantastical legend emerged from Prague. In Renaissance times, under the patronage of Emperor Rudolph II, the city was the leading European center of alchemy and magic. Although Loew is credited with creating the Golem, such legends were not new. The word, meaning "unformed substance," appears in the Psalms. Medieval cabbalistic texts described a creature whose role was to act as a dependable servant and protector of the Jews. But Rabbi Loew invested his Golem with an anarchic energy of its own.

The best known version of the legend tells how Loew, alerted to unspecified but terrible danger, raced to the banks of the Vltava with his acolytes. Their spells conjured the creature into existence from mud and clay, involving the four elements—earth, fire, air, and water. The Golem became a living creature, so the

Rabbi Loew was the immensely respected leader of the Jewish community in 16th-century Prague.

The story of the Golem has been popularized by frequent retellings, most notably in a novel of the same name by Gustav Meyrink in the early 20th century. In 1920, the tale was the subject of a silent film by Paul Wegener, and other sound versions followed. The legend is clearly related to the Frankenstein story, in which a man-made monster, initially benign, acts in ways beyond the control of its creator. ■

Convent of St. Agnes

THE 13TH-CENTURY CONVENT OF ST. AGNES (ANEŽSKÝ klášter), on the northeast edge of Josefov, fell into decay in the early 19th century, but today its two restored churches are used for concerts. The galleries in and near the cloisters are now the home of the superb collection of medieval art belonging to the National Gallery (Národní galerie).

Convent of St. Agnes

- Map p. 85
- U Milosrdných 17
- 221 879 111
- Closed Mon.
- $$
- Tram: 5, 8, 14 (Dlouhá). Metro: Náměstí Republiky

This royal convent was founded in the 1230s by Agnes, the daughter of Otakar I, and construction continued until 1280. The monastic complex thrived until the Hussite wars (1419–1434) interrupted devotions. Various monastic orders occupied the convent until 1782, when it was secularized by Joseph II. The convent's two churches—**Church of the Holy Savior** (Kostel sv. Salvátor) and **Church of St. Francis of Assisi** (Kostel sv. František)—were semiruinous after years of misuse as storehouses, but they have been well restored, the cloisters have been rebuilt, and excavations have unearthed the tombs of Václav and other Přemyslid rulers. The choirs of the two churches, both dating from the mid-13th century, lie side by side. In 1986 the Church of St. Francis was adapted as a concert hall, and much

of the rest of the convent has been turned into an art gallery.

MEDIEVAL ART

For many years the medieval collections of the National Gallery were housed in the Convent of St. George within Prague Castle. Reorganization of the collections has moved the medieval section to the Convent of St. Agnes, where it is beautifully displayed. This is one of the great collections of medieval central Europe: panel paintings, carved Madonnas, winged altar-pieces, and entire cycles of paintings. Although their styles are very distinctive, the identities of many of the medieval painters represented here are unknown, and they are simply referred to as Masters of the towns where they worked, such as Vyšší Brod and Třeboň.

The collections

The first room contains enthroned Madonnas from the 12th and 13th centuries, and the influence of French art is evident. There is a painted Madonna and Child from Vyšehrad Church (1350s); an unusual silver-gilt *herma,* a covering that encased the skull of St. Ludmila, the grandmother of St. Wenceslas; and Madonnas by the Master of Vyšší Brod.

In the second room a cycle of nine paintings depicts scenes from the life of Christ by the same artist, commissioned in the 1350s. These are devotional panels of considerable charm, but not of outstanding quality, as the artist seems to have had difficulty matching the heads he painted with the bodies to which they were attached. However, the panels showing the Nativity, Christ on the Mount of Olives, the Crucifixion, and the Resurrection are of much better quality. It's not clear whether all the panels were painted by the Master, and it is

A painting of St. Elizabeth of Hungary by Master Theodoric

probable that some were completed by his assistants.

The third room displays works by the painter known only as **Master Theodoric.** He is best known for the 128 paintings he produced for the chapel at Karlštejn Castle (Hrad Karlštejn) in the 1350s and 1360s. Six of them are here, and whether you share the Bohemian admiration for these works is a subjective matter. They are painted in what became known as the "soft style," a self-explanatory term once you see the overly fleshy portrayals.

The next room delivers a blow to the senses with a Crucifixion, graphic in its immediacy and realism, that once belonged to the Emmaus Monastery (Klášter Na Slovanech; see p. 123). There are also rare stained-glass panels from Kolín, 22 miles (35 km) east of Prague, and elegant carvings of the Madonna and Child, as well as a moving carved Pietà from Lásenice.

The following room contains one

of the highlights of the entire collection: panels by the **Master of Třeboň,** all that remains from a winged altarpiece painted about 1380. These are wonderful works, showing the precision and restrained emotion that are so lacking from the Vyšší Brod panels. There is also a moving Crucifixion by the same artist. One of his masterworks is the "Madonna of Roudnice" from the 1380s, a tender depiction of the familiar scene.

Bear right into the next hall, with its succession of Madonnas, painted and carved, and the "Capuchin Cycle" of the early 15th century, consisting of 14 vivid portrait panels. In the same room you will see a resplendent monstrance of about 1400 from Sedlec near Kutná Hora. Highlights of the following room are the early 15th-century "Roudnice Altarpiece" and a Gothic masterpiece: a variant of the carved "Madonna of Český Krumlov."

A panel painting of three female saints by the Master of Třeboň

Retrace your steps past the "Capuchin Cycle" to descend into a large hall. Here the displays include six very decorative panels by the **Master of Rajhrad** and his workshop from Moravia (ca 1430). There is an exceptionally vivid and grimly realistic triptych known as the "Reininghaus Altarpiece,"gory, dense, and high in emotion; a tender "Assumption" from Deštná, highly formal and beautifully detailed; and the "St. George Altarpiece," realistic and accomplished, with beautifully rendered draperies. From Austria comes the "Virgin Mary With the Garlands," an elegant work from the 1480s. The impeccably preserved winged "Velhartice Altarpiece" is a complex work in painted reliefs flanking a statue of the Madonna and Child. There are more panels, beautifully colored, from the workshop of the **Master of Litoměřice,** and the Master's exceptionally dignified triptych of the Holy Trinity.

The next room holds a sumptuous reliquary bust of St. Adalbert (ca 1490), while the following room houses some superb wooden carvings by the I. P. monogrammist (1520–1540), an anonymous artist identified only by his inititals, which, with clear influence from Dürer (1471–1528) and Mantegna (1431–1506), are more international in style than some of the earlier sculptures in the collection. Paintings by Lucas Cranach the Elder and his workshop signal the end of the medieval period and of the collections. An admirable feature of the gallery is that developments in Czech medieval art are placed in a European context. ■

Cloisters

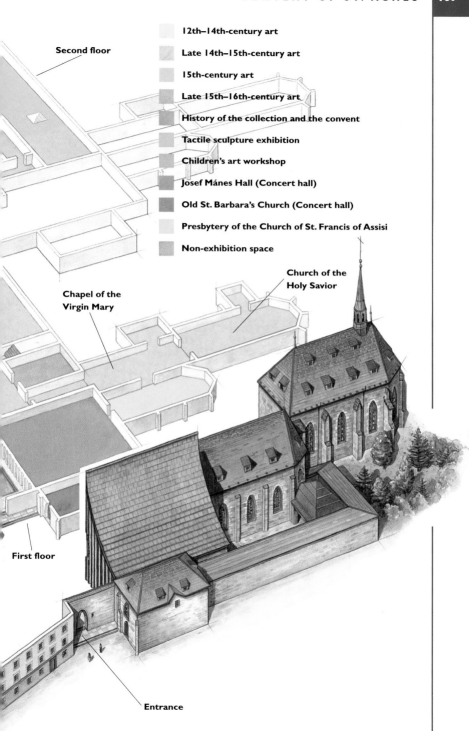

Second floor

12th–14th-century art

Late 14th–15th-century art

15th-century art

Late 15th–16th-century art

History of the collection and the convent

Tactile sculpture exhibition

Children's art workshop

Josef Mánes Hall (Concert hall)

Old St. Barbara's Church (Concert hall)

Presbytery of the Church of St. Francis of Assisi

Non-exhibition space

Church of the Holy Savior

Chapel of the Virgin Mary

First floor

Entrance

More places to visit in Old Town

AT THE TWO GOLDEN BEARS
The fine Renaissance house called At the Two Golden Bears (U dvou zlatých medvědů) stands along Melantrichova, the lane opposite the entrance to the Old Town Hall (Staroměstská radnice), on the corner with Kožná. The carved stone doorway of 1590 topped, as its name suggests, by carvings of two bears, is by Bonifác Wohlmut. If the door is open, you can walk through to the beautiful courtyard with its Renaissance loggia.
🅰 Map p. 85 ✉ Kožná 1 🚇 Metro: Staroměstská

CHURCH OF ST. CASTULLUS
Located in a small square, close to the Convent of St. Agnes, is the fine Gothic Church of St. Castullus (Kostel sv. Haštal). Originally built in the 1230s, the present building dates from the late 14th century. The sacristy contains the

The majestic Rudolfinum is Prague's largest concert hall and the headquarters of the Czech Philharmonic Orchestra.

remnants of Gothic frescoes depicting the Apostles, and there is a notable Calvary sculpture by Ferdinand Brokoff.
🅰 Map p. 85 ✉ Haštalské náměstí

MUSEUM OF DECORATIVE ARTS
The fascinating Museum of Decorative Arts (Uměleckoprůmyslové muzeum or UPM), founded in 1885, lies opposite the Rudolfinum concert hall. Although its exhibits range from the Middle Ages to the 20th century and include superb clocks, porcelain, and furnishings, the main attraction is the magnificent collection of art nouveau and art deco objects.
🅰 Map p. 85 ✉ 17, Listopadu 2 ☎ 251 093 111 🕐 Closed Mon. 💲 $$ 🚋 Tram: 17. Metro: Staroměstská

PALACE OF THE LORDS OF KUNŠTÁT AND PODĚBRADY
Not far from the Church of St. Giles (Kostel sv. Jiljí) is the Palace of the Lords of Kunštát (Dům pánů z Kunštátu), the house where George of Poděbrady lived before he ascended the throne in 1458. It's also worth visiting to see the Romanesque basement, one of the best preserved in the city. Many houses in the Old Town have basements and undercrofts of this period, but few of them are open to the public.
🅰 Map p. 85 ✉ Retězová 3 ☎ 224 212 299 🕐 Closed Mon. & Oct.–May 💲 $ 🚇 Metro: Staroměstská

ROTUNDA
The tiny 11th-century rotunda church (sv. Kříž), one of three surviving Romanesque round churches in Prague, stands on the corner of Konviktská and Karoliny Světlé. Inside are fragments of 14th-century wall paintings, but it's rarely open to the public.
🅰 Map p. 84 ✉ Karoliny Světlé 🚋 Tram: 17. Metro: Národní třida

RUDOLFINUM
Near the Old Town end of Charles Bridge the neo-Renaissance Rudolfinum, named after Crown Prince Rupert of Austria, spreads along the riverbank. It is the home of the Czech Philharmonic Orchestra and also the headquarters of the annual spring music festival known as Prague Spring, which runs from May 12 (Smetana's birthday) to June 3. Tickets go on sale one month before the festival opens. www.festival.cz 🅰 Map p. 84 ✉ Alšovo nábřeží 12 ☎ 224 893 238 (box office), 227 059 346 (gallery), 257 312 547 (box office at Hellichova 18) 🚋 Tram: 17. Metro: Staroměstská ■

Although called the New Town, this district was founded in the 14th century and has its fair share of medieval churches and vast squares. Wenceslas Square (Václavské náměstí) is Prague's most popular gathering place.

New Town & the suburbs

A Madonna and Child from the Church of Our Lady of the Snows on Jungmannova

The quirky gables of the New Town Hall overlook Charles Square.

New Town & the suburbs

ONE OF PRAGUE'S CHARMS IS THE FACT THAT MOST OF ITS SIGHTS CONCEN-
trate within a small area. Because of this, it's tempting to ignore the many attractions elsewhere in the city. The New Town and the suburbs, however, contain a good number of
sights worth seeking out; all of them are easily accessible by the city's efficient public
transportation system.

New Town (Nové Město) is simply an extension of Old Town (Staré Město) that became
necessary as the city grew. It was established by
Charles IV in 1348 and designed on an ambitious scale in a remarkable and forward-look-
ing feat of town planning. Charles created
large open spaces as marketplaces and constructed broad thoroughfares, all in complete
contrast to the tortuous lanes, irregular squares,
and confined spaces of both Malá Strana and
Old Town. The centerpieces of the project were
three enormous squares, two of which survive
in much their original form: Wenceslas Square
(Václavské náměstí) and Charles Square
(Karlovo náměstí). Larger in area than Old
Town, New Town was protected by fortifications
some 2.5 miles (4 km) in length.

As a district, Nové Město has far less character than Malá Strana or Staré Město. Not as
compact as the older parts of town, it was easier

to rebuild and develop in the 19th and 20th
centuries. But among the apartment blocks,
hospitals, schools, office developments, and
other large buildings, there are some gems.
These include the Vila Amerika, now a
museum devoted to the life and work of
Antonín Dvořák; the Karlov church, another
legacy of Charles IV; and, at the other end of
the historical band, the Dancing House,
designed by the modern architect Frank
Gehry. Its unusual sculptural form is sugges-
tive of two dancers, and it is affectionately
known as the "Fred and Ginger" building.

This chapter includes Vyšehrad and other
districts of Prague that don't belong to any
of the ancient townships within the city.
It takes you to remarkable sites on the city's
outskirts, including the magnificent castle of
Troja, the fascinating technical museum, and
the ancient monastic foundation at Břevnov. ■

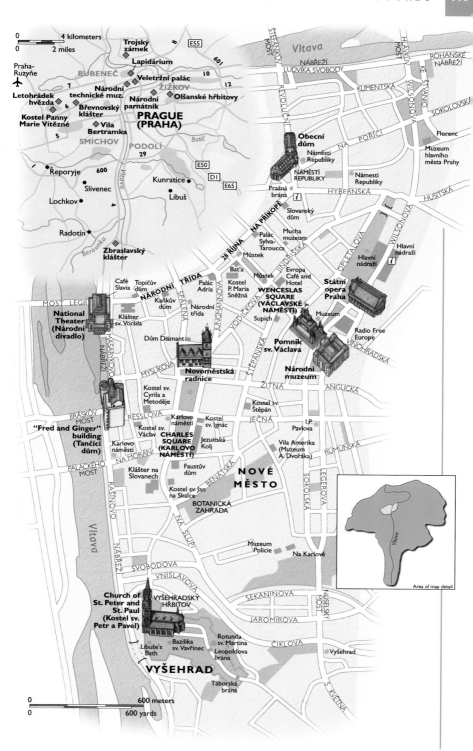

0 | 4 kilometers
0 | 2 miles

Praha-Ruzyně ✈

Trojský zámek

Lapidárium

E55

Veletržní palác

BUBENEČ

ŽIŽKOV

601

Národní technické muz.

Olšanské hřbitovy

Letohrádek hvězda

Břevnovský klášter

Kostel Panny Marie Vítězné

Národní parnátník

PRAGUE (PRAHA)

Vila Bertramka

SMÍCHOV

PODOLÍ

Botič

29

Řeporyje

600

Vltava

Kunratice

E50

D1

E65

Libuš

Lochkov

Berounka

Slivenec

Radotín

Zbraslavský klášter

Vltava

ŠTĚFÁNIKŮV MOST

NÁBŘEŽÍ LUDVÍKA SVOBODY

REVOLUČNÍ

HLÁVKŮV MOST

KE ŠTVANICI

ROHANSKÉ NÁBŘEŽÍ

KLIMENTSKÁ

WILSONOVA

SOKOLOVSKÁ

NA POŘÍČÍ

Obecní dům

Náměstí Republiky

NÁMĚSTÍ REPUBLIKY

Náměstí Republiky

Florenc

Muzeum hlavního města Prahy

Prašná brána ℹ

HYBERNSKÁ

HUSITSKÁ

Slovanský dům

NA PŘÍKOPĚ

Mucha muzeum

Palác Sylva-Taroucca

OBJELETALOVA

WILSONOVA

Hlavní nádraží

28 ŘÍJNA

Müstek

JINDŘIŠSKÁ

Hlavní nádraží ℹ

Bať a

Müstek

Evropa Café and Hotel

NÁRODNÍ TŘÍDA

Café Slavia

Topičův dům

Kaňkův dům

Palác Adria

Kostel P. Maria Sněžná

WENCESLAS SQUARE (VÁCLAVSKÉ NÁMĚSTÍ)

Státní opera Praha

MOST LEGIÍ

National Theater (Národní divadlo)

Klášter sv. Voršila

SPÁLENÁ

Národní třída

JUNGMANNOVA

VODIČKOVA

Supich

Muzeum

Radio Free Europe

MASARYKOVO NÁBŘEŽÍ

Dům Diamant

ŠTĚPÁNSKÁ

Pomník sv. Václava

VINOHRADSKÁ

Novoměstská radnice

Národní muzeum

JIRÁSKŮV MOST

"Fred and Ginger" building (Tančící dům)

RESSLOVA

Kostel sv. Cyrila a Metoděje

MYSLÍKOVA

Karlovo náměstí

Kostel sv. Ignác

ŽITNÁ

Kostel sv. Štěpán

ANGLICKÁ

JEČNÁ

I.P. Pavlova

Kostel sv. Václav

CHARLES SQUARE (KARLOVO NÁMĚSTÍ)

Karlovo náměstí

Jezuitská Kolj

Vila Amerika (Muzeum A. Dvořáka)

RUMUNSKÁ

PALACKÉHO MOST

NA MORÁNÍ

Kostel sv. Jan na Skalce

Faustův dům

BENÁTSKÁ

NOVÉ MĚSTO

SOKOLSKÁ

EGEROVA

Kostel na Slovanech

BOTANICKÁ ZAHRADA

Vltava

RAŠÍNOVO

NA SLUPI

Muzeum Policie

Na Karlově

NÁBŘEŽÍ

SVOBODOVA

VNISLAVOVA

Vltava

Church of St. Peter and St. Paul (Kostel sv. Petr a Pavel)

VYŠEHRADSKÝ HŘBITOV

SEKANINOVA

NUSELSKÝ MOST

Libuše's Bath

Bazilika sv. Vavřinec

Rotunda sv. Martina

JAROMÍROVA

VYŠEHRAD

Leopoldova brána

Vyšehrad

ČIKLOVA

S. KVĚTNA

Táborská brána

0 | 600 meters
0 | 600 yards

Area of map detail

The steps of the National Museum offer the best view of the expanse of Wenceslas Square.

Wenceslas Square

SEEN FROM THE MŮSTEK PLAZA, WENCESLAS SQUARE (Václavské náměstí) unfurls before you in a long sweep, barred at the far end by the portico and domes of the National Museum (Národní muzeum). This is the commercial and political heart of the city, the place everyone flocks to in times of national jubilation or dismay.

Wenceslas Square

Map p. 113

National Museum

Václavské náměstí 68

224 497 111

Closed first Tues. of month

$; free entry first Mon. of month

Tram: 3, 9, 14, 24. Metro: Můstek, Muzeum

Originally a horse market established by Charles IV in the late 1340s, the square assumed greater importance in the mid-19th century, when houses, apartment blocks, and commercial buildings were erected. Then in 1885 the Horses' Gate, part of the city fortifications at the far end of the square, was replaced by the National Museum. The museum has become a city landmark, thanks to its imposing cupola.

WENCESLAS MONUMENT

The square's most celebrated monument, the statue of St. Wenceslas (Pomník sv. Václava), stands in front of the National Museum. There had been a statue of the patron saint in the square since the 17th century, but it was moved to Vyšehrad in 1879. The Czech sculptor Josef Václav Myslbek was commissioned to design a replacement, and the work was finally completed in 1924. The monument is surrounded by

statues of four other patron saints of Bohemia: Ludmila, Procopius, Vojtěch, and Agnes.

The statue soon became the focal point for patriotic demonstrations, which often spilled over into the entire square. In 1918 the Czechs clamored here for their independence from the defunct Austro-Hungarian Empire, and in 1968 thousands came here to protest against the Soviet invasion of the country (see p. 34). Nearby, on January 16, 1969, student Jan Palach set fire to himself in protest against this invasion. Inevitably, when the Velvet Revolution began in 1989, Wenceslas Square again attracted huge crowds, who were addressed by Václav Havel and the hero of the Prague Spring, Alexander Dubček.

THE BUILDINGS

The buildings lining the square mostly lack architectural merit, but there are exceptions. The best known is the art nouveau extravaganza of the **Evropa Café and Hotel,** built in 1906. Close to No. 6 is the **Bat'a Building,** with its plate glass windows, still untarnished and stylish after 70 years. Next door, at No. 8, is the Adam Pharmacy (Adamova lékárna), tall and narrow, with figures over the entrance portraying Adam and Eve, each draped with a snake. Number 12 is a good example of Prague secession style. On the corner of Štěpánská stands the **Supich Building** (Nos. 38–40), constructed between 1913 and 1916 by Matěj Blecha in a brutal secessionist style.

National symbol: Josef Myslbek's statue of St. Wenceslas, Bohemia's patron saint

The interior is an impressive example of monumental design. From the lobby you climb the massive staircase beneath its glass roof, your path lit by globe lamps on brass candelabra. It leads up to a square galleried hall beneath a cupola known as the **Pantheon.** This hall commemorates major figures of Czech intellectual and scientific achievement.

One half of the first floor houses a comprehensive series of prehistory displays; national medals, mostly 19th century; and theater costumes. The other half contains the mineralogy collections. On the second floor you'll find the zoological collections. Though the captions on both floors are in Czech only, most visitors find much here to appreciate.

Other buildings

To the left of the museum on Wilsonova is the former **Federal Assembly Building,** which currently houses Radio Free Europe. The original 1930s building is surmounted, rather daringly, by a modern stone-and-glass structure by Karel Prager. A few paces farther along Wilsonova you come to the **Prague State Opera (Státní opera Praha).** This handsome building with a grand neoclassic portico is now Prague's principal opera house. Its charming interior in red and gold was modeled on the Vienna State Opera, though it is considerably smaller in scale. ■

The art nouveau Grand Hotel Evropa in Wenceslas Square

Jan Palach memorial shrine

National Museum

The vast National Museum (Národní muzeum) was built in the 1880s at the top of Wenceslas Square to house the museum that had been established in 1818. There was a nationalist as well as scientific motive behind its founding, a purpose furthered by its construction in such a prominent position.

Palach memorials

In front of the Wenceslas Monument is a small shrine dedicated to Jan Palach, the 21-year-old student who set himself on fire on the square to protest the Soviet invasion, and for other "victims of communism."

Red Army Square was renamed náměstí Jana Palacha after the Velvet Revolution of 1989. On the facade of the philosophy building where he was a student, on the east side of the square, is a small bronze death mask of Jan, by Olbran Zoubek. ■

Na Příkopě & Národní třída

THE CITY'S BEST-KNOWN COMMERCIAL AND SHOPPING districts run in a more or less straight line from Republic Square (náměstí Republiky), along Na Příkopě, past Můstek at the bottom of Wenceslas Square, and then along Národní třída to the River Vltava. The Czech and German populations divided the area between them in the 19th century, with the Germans preferring Na Příkopě and the Czechs congregating along Národní třída farther south.

Na Příkopě & Národní třída

🗺 Map p. 113

🚇 Metro: Můstek, Náměstí Republiky, Národní třída

Starting from Republic Square, you can scarcely miss the art nouveau bulk of the **Municipal House** (Obecní dům), which was built in the first decade of the 20th century as a cultural center and concert hall. This prestigious project was thrown open to competition, and the winners were Antonín Balšánek, who designed the exterior, and Osvald Polívka, who was responsible for the essentially art nouveau interior. But all the leading artists of the day made their contributions to the decor, including Alfons Mucha, who added striking murals. The main hall is the glass-domed **Smetana Hall,** used for concerts. There are occasional guided tours of the complex, but a quicker way to enjoy the opulent decor is to visit the coffeehouse on the left of the entrance lobby. If you are in an extravagant mood, lunch at the expensive Francouzská restaurant on the other side of the lobby.

NA PŘÍKOPĚ
To the left of Obecní Dům rises the **Powder Gate** (Prašná brána), a former city gate and gunpowder store constructed and reconstructed from the 15th to the 19th centuries; its purpose was as much ornamental as defensive. The gate marks the beginning of Celetná street, but pass by it to reach the broad street of **Na Příkopě.** This was originally a moat alongside the ramparts of Old Town, but in 1760 it was filled in. By the middle of the 19th century

Na Příkopě had become a fashionable street, lined with restaurants, hotels, and mansions; it was also home to many of the city's banks.

At No. 22 is the **Slav House** (Slovanský dům), of baroque and neoclassic origin; today it is filled with upscale stores and offices. Number 20 is the former Commerce and Craft Industry Bank (Živnostenská banka), a heavy-handed structure linked by bridges to another bank building at No. 18. Yet another turn-of-the-20th-century bank is the State Bank, at Nos. 3–5, topped by Babylonian-style copper reliefs and statuary.

The shops of the New Town cater to city dwellers and tourists alike.

A few older buildings survive, of which the finest is No. 10, the **Sylva-Taroucca Palace** (Palác Sylva-Taroucca), built in the 1740s by Kilián Ignác Dientzenhofer. The facade is essentially rococo, but today the palace has been occupied by McDonald's, a theater, and a Moroccan restaurant.

Celetná opens on to Můstek, at the head of Wenceslas Square. Můstek means "little bridge," referring to the bridge that crossed the moat here in medieval times; some of its spans can be seen behind a glass wall in the metro station.

Walking from Můstek toward Národní třída, you pass on your left the **Church of Our Lady of the Snows** (Kostel Panny Maria Sněžná), founded by Charles IV in 1347 as his coronation church. It was an ambitious project, but only the very tall chancel, soaring to a height of 108 feet (33 m), was finished; the Hussite wars of the early 15th century interrupted work. Near the tympanum-topped entrance gate *(closed)* to the churchyard is a strange-looking column; on closer inspection it turns out to be a 1912 lamppost in the cubist style.

NÁRODNÍ TŘÍDA

The square (Jungmannovo náměstí) at the Národní end of the churchyard is named after the linguist Josef

Below: The Municipal House, showcase of early 20th-century design and decoration

Jungmann (1773–1847), who helped establish the historical foundations of the Czech language; there's a monument to him in the square. Beyond the square, Národní třída stretches toward the river; like Na Příkopě, it was constructed when the moat dividing Old Town from New Town was filled in during the 1760s.

The enormous and top-heavy building straight ahead on Národní třída is the **Adria Palace** (palác Adria) by Pavel Janák and Joseph Zasche. The original home of the Laterna Magicka (see p. 51), it was named after an Italian insurance company that was located here. Today it houses offices, restaurants, and the Divadlo Bez zábradlí theater. On the right, at No. 37, is the neoclassic Platyz, with a large shop-filled courtyard behind it. Just beyond the Tesco supermarket is the famous Reduta jazz club, where President Bill Clinton played his saxophone in January 1994. Farther along, beneath the arcades of the **Kaňka House** (Kaňkův dům) at No. 16, you'll find a plaque commemorating a large demonstration held nearby on November 17, 1989.

Much of the next block is filled by the **Ursuline convent** (Klášter sv. Voršila), designed by Marc Antonio Canevale in 1704, and its wine bar and restaurant, the Klášterní vinárna. Across the street are two remarkable secession designs. At No. 7 is the former Praha Insurance Company building, and at No. 9 is the **Topič House** (Topičův dům). Both date from 1903–1906.

National Theater

The convent adjoins the National Theater (Národní divadlo), a building of great cultural importance to the Czechs, who were keen to present plays and operas in their own language. Josef Zítek (1832–1909), who also designed the Rudolfinum (see p. 110), was the

chosen architect, but the theater was open only briefly before it burned down in 1881. It was replaced in 1883 by a massive structure designed by Josef Schulz (1840–1917) and decorated in part by Mikoláš Aleš. The main entrance and portico lie along Národní třída, but the bulk of the structure, with a roof that echoes the design of the Belvedere, faces the river. The operas of Smetana and Janáček were often first performed here and remain in the repertoire alongside those of Dvořák. The relatively small interior is exuberantly decorated with gilt and statuary.

The 19th-century theater is now part of a complex that mounts a program of theater, opera, and ballet, and it remains the flagship of Czech performing arts. The New Theater (Nová scéna), completed in 1983, is a glass structure by Karel Prager. The Laterna Magika theater is also based here.

Opposite the theater is one of the city's best known coffeehouses, Café Slavia. It must have been convenient for Smetana, who lived in the apartment block above. ■

Top left: Art nouveau apartment blocks line the banks of the River Vltava. Above: The interior of the National Theater is decorated in typically opulent 19th-century style.

Prague Spring

The Prague Spring describes the spring-like sense of renewal that seemed to launch Czechoslovakia into a freer era in 1968.

In January 1968, Slovak Alexander Dubček replaced the hard-line Antonín Novotný as First Secretary of the Communist Party. He was known to be a reformist, but his radical ideas must have taken the Soviets' breath away. Like other party leaders before him, he had risen through the ranks of the party system, so it was astonishing that his ideas came close to

One cartoonist's sardonic comment on the Soviet invasion of 1968

suggesting that Czechoslovakia should evolve into a social-democratic state incorporating such liberal ideas as freedom of assembly and the abolition of censorship. Dubček even proposed the democratization of parliament.

It was clear that despite huge popular support for this new policy of "socialism with a human face," it was not going to go down well with the hard-liners, whether within his own party or in Moscow. The Czechs and Slovaks responded quickly to his unexpected loosening of the shackles; the arts flourished; ideas circulated, and anti-Soviet articles, previously a sure path to imprisonment, were published in newspapers. The party leadership often attacked such dangerous ideas but did not prevent them from being raised. The sweet air of freedom was actually wafting through the country, and in the heady atmosphere of the 1960s no one believed it would end.

But it did. By August the Soviet regime had had enough. The challenging of party rule in Czechoslovakia was not only undesirable in itself, but it was setting a deplorable precedent for other countries within the Eastern bloc. On August 21, 1968, the Soviets invaded Czechoslovakia, supported by 500,000 troops from other Warsaw Pact nations (except

Romania). Tanks took up positions in Wenceslas Square (Václavské náměstí). Courageous men and women confronted the invading forces directly; others occupied the steps of the St. Wenceslas statue, which, then as in the past, had become a symbol of national independence.

There was considerable bloodshed. Dubček and other members of his leadership team protested against the invasion but were flown off to Moscow, where they were browbeaten into something like submission before returning home. Dubček remained nominally in charge of the Czechoslovak government, but power lay elsewhere. Protests continued, and, on January 16, 1969, the resistance to Soviet occupation reached a new level of intensity and despair when a student named Jan Palach set fire to himself in front of the Wenceslas statue (see box p. 116). He died three days later from his burns.

Finally, in April 1969, the broken and humiliated Dubček was replaced by Gustáv Husák, who had supported the Prague Spring until he saw which way the wind from Moscow was blowing. With his appointment, spring turned to winter. Many Czech artists and intellectuals were among the 150,000 who emigrated before the borders were sealed, and the country lost such talents as Miloš Forman, Milan Kundera, and Josef Škvorecký.

Husák instituted a thorough purge of the party, reasserted centralized control, and boosted the powers of the secret police. The Czechs and Slovaks were encouraged to make the following pact: In exchange for their conformity to the neo-Stalinist orthodoxies of the new regime, they would be guaranteed a decent standard of living. It worked for 20 years until, in 1989, the regime collapsed as the Velvet Revolution got under way (see p. 36). ∎

Alexander Dubček greets well-wishers during the Prague Spring (above), which was to come to an abrupt halt after tanks rolled into Wenceslas Square (below) in August 1968.

Charles Square

Charles Square
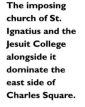
Map p. 113
Tram: 4, 6, 10, 16, 18, 22, 23. Metro: Karlovo náměstí

NEW TOWN HAS LARGELY LOST ITS MEDIEVAL CHARACTER, but it retains the spacious Charles Square (Karlovo náměstí) and many fine churches as planned by Charles IV in 1348. The New Town gradually developed into the commercial center of Prague. In the mid-19th century the gardens in Charles Square were laid out, offering welcome shade and tranquility in this busy part of town.

On the north side, the proud tower of the **New Town Hall** (Novoměstská radnice) overlooks the square. Originally built in the 1360s, and the setting for the First Defenestration in Prague (see p. 24), the hall today is used for cultural events and weddings.

Enthusiasts for Czech cubist architecture should go behind the town hall to the very individual **Diamond House** (Dům Diamant), completed in 1912. Its texture—pebble against concrete—is raw, but its decorative forms are bold and angular.

Between the square and the River Vlatava, along Resslova, is Kilián Ignác Dientzenhofer's baroque

The imposing church of St. Ignatius and the Jesuit College alongside it dominate the east side of Charles Square.

Church of St. Cyril and St. Methodius (Kostel sv. Cyrila a Metoděje), the spiritual home of the Czech Orthodox Church in Prague since 1935. In May 1942 Nazi governor of Bohemia and Moravia Reinhard Heydrich was assassinated by Czech paratroopers, who took refuge here. They died when their hideaway was betrayed to the Nazis. A memorial plaque on the church's facade commemorates these events, and bullet holes from German machine guns still pockmark the walls. Opposite is the small Gothic **Church of St. Wenceslas** (Kostel sv. Václav), containing fragmentary Gothic frescoes. On Resslova, by the river, is the

celebrated **"Fred and Ginger" building** (Tančící dům; see p. 134).

Along the square's east side stands the large Jesuit **Church of St. Ignatius** (Kostel sv. Ignác), which was mostly completed by 1671. The nobly proportioned interior has sumptuous baroque decor and furnishings. Your eye is drawn down the tall pink-and-white barrel-vaulted nave to the dramatic, pillared high altar. Alongside the church, the immense **Jesuit College** (Jezuitská Kolj) fills the entire side of the square between Ječná and U Nemocnice Streets. The college later became a teaching hospital.

At the foot of the square you will find **Faust House** (Faustův dům), once thought of as the residence of Dr. Faustus. It is more certain that it was the home of Edward Kelley,

the Elizabethan adventurer who convinced Rudolph II that he could create the "philosopher's stone" and turn lead and other base metals into gold (see p. 68). Kelley made such slow progress that the exasperated emperor had him imprisoned.

Go south on Vysehradská and you'll come to the **Emmaus Monastery** (Klášter na Slovanech) on the right. Charles IV founded it in 1347 in an attempt to bridge the Eastern and Western branches of Christianity. In 1880 German Benedictines rebuilt much of it in neo-Gothic style. The striking roof of 1967 by František Černý replaced the roof damaged during World War II. Inside, Gothic frescoes survive, although in poor condition, in the cloisters. The monastery is now undergoing restoration. ∎

The Emmaus Monastery is of medieval origin, but its daring roof is a modern addition of 1967.

Church of St. Cyril & St. Methodius
✉ Resslova 9

Church of St. Wenceslas
✉ Resslova & Dittrichova

Emmaus Monastery
✉ Vyšehradská 49

Prague pubs

Prague pubs, easily identified by the word *pivnice* or *hospoda,* vary considerably in style, but few offer much in the way of creature comforts other than tables, benches, and hard chairs. People go to their favorite pubs to drink beer (see p. 184), to meet their friends, and to read the newspaper. Such is the quality of the beer from the city's breweries—including Staropramen, Pražan, and Braník—you can be sure of a decent drink wherever you go.

The best known of all Prague pubs is **U Fleků** at Křemencova 11 *(tel 224 934 019),* between the New Town Hall and the river. This enormous pub, named for the Flek family, is known for its wood-paneled halls and large courtyard, its moderately priced Czech food, and strong dark beer, brewed on the premises since 1499 and known as "Flekovský ležák." It's very much on the tourist circuit and must be one of the

few pubs anywhere with a cabaret show.

Almost as well known is **U kalicha (At the Chalice)** at Na bojišti 14 *(tel 224 912 557)* in New Town, near the Vila Amerika. It's the setting of much of Jaroslav Hašek's novel *The Good Soldier Švejk* (see p. 47), since the hero is a committed beer drinker. Inevitably it has become a mecca for tourists, even those who have no familiarity with the novel. These days it's more of a restaurant than a pub.

LITTLE QUARTER

There are few authentic pubs in the exclusive Little Quarter (Malá Strana) district, but the following are all worth a visit:

U Hrocha (At the Hippo)

This is the genuine article, beneath the castle *(Thunovská 10).* The interior has plain wooden tables and chairs—and good beer.

U Kocoura (At the Cat)

You can quench your thirst here after tackling the hills of Hradčany *(Nerudova 2).* Try the inexpensive dumplings with red cabbage or the cold food platters to accompany the Pilsen or dark Regent beers.

U sv. Tomáše (At St. Thomas)

Behind the church on Letenská is the famous St. Thomas's Beer Hall (see p. 77), which began as a brewery in the 1350s. In the 1950s the brewery closed, and today this large basement pub serves excellent Braník and other beers. In summer you can drink in the garden; there's brass-band music in the evenings.

OLD TOWN

Many pubs have disappeared from Old Town

There is hardly a street in Prague without a cozy, sometimes smoky pub.

(Staré Město) to make way for boutiques and restaurants. But some searching will unearth several unequivocally authentic examples.

U Krále Jiřího (At King George)
Attached to the hotel of the same name, this is a comfortable and reasonably upscale pub, serving several different Czech beers. Also on the premises *(Liliova 10)* is the Blues sklep, with regular jazz nights, and next door is the James Joyce Irish pub.

U Rotundy (At the Rotunda)
If you are feeling intrepid and want to try the real thing, this rough pub with its battered sign is just across from the rotunda church *(Karoliný Svetle)*. The interior is classic: thick with cigarette smoke and frequented by men in overalls.

U zlatého tygra (At the Golden Tiger)
This crowded literary pub is still authentic despite its proximity to touristy Karlova

Prague's pubs are a good place to enjoy a hearty lunch, washed down with beer.

(Husova 17). Although many tourists visit the pub, where the novelist Bohumil Hrabal held court until his death in 1997, there is still a loyal local clientele.

NEW TOWN
There are two microbreweries in New Town (Nové Město), both serving excellent beer. The first is the **Novoměstský pivovar** *(Vodickova 20, tel 222 232 448)*, a basement warren off Wenceslas Square. This busy, often crowded place also serves standard but flavorsome Czech dishes. The other is the airier **Pivovarský dům** *(tel 296 216 666)* on the corner of Ječná and Lípová, near Charles Square. The beers are delicious, especially the regular beers and the wheat beer. Both also produce coffee, banana, and sour cherry varieties. The food is simple Czech fare. ■

Vyšehrad

Vyšehrad
- Map p. 113
- Metro: Vyšehrad

Church of St. Peter and St. Paul
- Closed Tues. & Fri. p.m.

VYŠEHRAD IS BOTH THE STUFF OF LEGENDS AND A REAL place. It was long believed that this was the original fortress of what would become the future capital of Bohemia, but recent archaeological research suggests the castle at Hradčany was established earlier. Whatever the truth of the matter, Vyšehrad existed by the mid-tenth century, situated on a crag high above the Vltava. The site was large enough to construct a sprawling fortress and relatively easy to defend.

The rugged cliffs of Vyšehrad offer a fine view of the river and city.

Legend recounts how Vyšehrad was founded. Libuše was a Czech princess, a daughter of chieftain Krok. When he died, she needed a husband in order to legitimize her rule. She chose a plowman called Přemysl, thus creating the Přemyslid dynasty, and promptly founded first Vyšehrad and then Prague Castle. There is no evidence to back this story, which nonetheless has a tenacious hold on the Czech imagination and its folkloric tradition. Although Vyšehrad later became the royal residence of Vratislav II, it gradually lost influence to Hradčany castle on the other side of the river, and by 1140 had been supplanted by it.

Vyšehrad's location, protected by craggy cliffs, is best appreciated from the other side of the Vltava. Under Charles IV its defenses were improved, linking them to other walls around the city. Charles also decreed that the coronation route for Bohemian rulers would begin at Vyšehrad and terminate at Hradčany. The Hussites occupied the fortress for some years in the 15th century, making additions of their own, but the only significant alterations occurred when further fortifications were added in the 17th century. By the 19th century Vyšehrad had outlived its usefulness and many of the buildings were dismantled, although the gates and some walls were left intact.

Despite all these changes, there are some genuinely ancient corners of Vyšehrad. Inside the fortress the **Rotunda of St. Martin** (Rotunda sv. Martina), a Romanesque round church from the late 11th century, is one of three such churches still in existence in Prague, and some of Charles IV's fortifications survive. Excavations are continuing to ascertain the archaeological history and legacy of the site. The gateways into the fortress, the **Tábor Gate** (Táborská brána) and the **Leopold Gate** (Leopoldova brána), both date from the mid-17th century. The Tábor Gate was the main entrance to the fortress, but to enter the citadel you must also pass through the impressively rusticated baroque Leopold Gate. Its pediment is topped by battered stone lions and an eagle. On either side of the gate are the mighty brick walls of the 1740s.

Just beyond the rotunda, turn left on K Rotundě. The lane leads to the remains of the **Basilica of St. Lawrence** (Bazilika sv. Vavřinec; *closed Tues. & Fri. p.m.*), then continues to an esplanade high above the walls from which there's an impressive view onto the river. Bear right and follow the path to other viewpoints. From these you can see the Gothic ruins on a crag known as **Libuše's Bath,** and over to the Castle and Petřín Hill.

You are now close to the **Church of St. Peter and St. Paul** (Kostel sv. Petr a Pavel). The original church was a Romanesque structure, but today it's essentially neo-Gothic. This handsome building, with its two tall spires built in 1902, is visible from miles around.

The lane near the west front of the church offers excellent and unusual views of the city. Nearby is a copy of Jan Jiří Bendl's statue of St. Wenceslas, and a restaurant opposite the church entrance has a terrace. The park to the south of the church contains four enormous statues by Josef Myslbek (1848–1922).

Vyšehrad is also the site of Prague's most revered cemetery, **Vyšehradský hřbitov.** An existing burial ground was expanded in 1875 and Renaissance-style arcades added. It became a resting ground for the major figures of the Czech national revival, including composers Dvořák and Smetana, opera singer Ema Destinnová, poet Jan Neruda (see box this page), writer Karel Čapek, and artists Mikoláš Aleš, Josef Myslbek, and Alfons Mucha. Competitive zeal among the bereaved has resulted in an abundance of extravagant tombstones with busts and portrait reliefs. Dvořák's tomb is one of the grandest, topped with a conventional bust of the composer, who is identified in gilt lettering. Close to Dvořák's grave is the brightly gilt secession monument to one Josefina Brdlíková, and at the end of the cemetery is the grandiose Slavín monument, a memorial to 53 famous Czech artists. ■

Above: Antonín Dvořák is one of many national heroes buried in the Vyšehrad cemetery.

Below: Bohemia's best known 19th-century poet, Jan Neruda, also has a memorial at Vyšehrad.

Jan Neruda

Jan Neruda, the son of a tobacconist, was born in Malá Strana in 1834 and spent much of his life in the house known as The Two Suns (Nerudova 47). After a spell as a teacher, he earned his living from 1865 as an essayist and critic for the leading daily newspaper of Prague, but he was best known as a poet and as a writer of short stories, notably his *Tales of the Malá Strana* (1878). His radical views were best expressed in his essays, which often focused on social problems. His reputation was not restricted to the streets of his hometown. The Nobel Prize-winning Chilean poet Pablo Neruda adopted his name as a pseudonym out of admiration for his work and his political stance. Jan Neruda died in 1891. ■

Trade Fair Palace

THE STRIKING TRADE FAIR PALACE (VELETRŽNÍ PALÁC) near the Stromovka Park was built in the 1920s as an exhibition hall for Czech industry, but after a fire in 1974 it was virtually abandoned. In the 1990s reconstruction turned it into a showcase for 2,000 items from the National Gallery's (Národní galerie's) collections of modern and contemporary art. It is also the new home for the modern art collection formerly in the Sternberg Palace (Šternberský palác)— notably paintings by Henri Rousseau, Gustav Klimt, Pablo Picasso, and other modern masters, as well as works of Czech art.

The Trade Fair Palace has been imaginatively converted into the republic's finest gallery of modern Czech art.

The conversion of the building has been brilliantly executed. The principal galleries are laid out on the main floors, with subsidiary exhibits in the galleries around the main atrium. The result is spacious and airy, and the clean lines of the building never distract from the exhibits themselves, which are informatively displayed. If you want

to visit the galleries in chronological order, start on the fourth floor and work your way downward.

FOURTH FLOOR

The earliest exhibits are the collections of 19th-century art. Josef Myslbek, whose grandiose sculptures adorn much of the city, is represented by various busts. The paintings are varied. Antonín Machek (1775–1849) was an accomplished portraitist, as were Josef Manes (1820–1871) and Karel Purkyne (1834–1868), but you may be more intrigued by the Prague interiors of Ludvik Kohl (1746–1821). There are gentle landscapes by F. X. Procházka (1746–1815) and Josef Navrátil

Marc Chagall

(1798–1865), as well as inflated historical and genre paintings by the revered Mikoláš Aleš (1852–1913). Aleš's work is found all over Prague; he decorated the Storch house in Old Town Square and contributed murals to the National Theater, so his work is revered by the Czechs, but it may seem too highly colored and overblown to less partisan observers. A painting by Gabriel Max (1840–1915) depicting the "Crucifixion of St. Julia" caused a stir in 1865, when the saint was portrayed as a buxom peasant girl. There are symbolic wood carvings by František Bílek (1872–1941) and a few fine works by Austrians Gustav Klimt (1862–1918) and Egon Schiele (1890–1918). Galleries devoted to applied arts supplement this core collection, a pattern repeated on the other floors.

THIRD FLOOR

The third floor focuses on the years from 1900 to 1930. There are garish paintings, including some boisterous

Trade Fair Palace
www.ngprague.cz
🗺 See map inset p. 113
✉ Dukelských hrdinů 47
☎ 224 301 111
🕐 Closed Mon.
💲 $$$$. Free first Fri. of the month
🚊 Tram: 5, 12, 17. Metro: Nádraží Holešovice

Modernist works once banned by the Communist regime are now freely displayed in the gallery.

Above: 19th-century Czech artists excelled at portraiture.

Below: A Picasso cubist painting

nudes, by František Kupka (1871–1957), and later, purely abstract work. Fine Czech cubist paintings confirm the stature of artists such as Emil Filla (1883–1953), Antonín Procházka (1882–1945), and Bohumil Kubišta

(1884–1918). Watch for the cubist furniture, too: It looks uncomfortable, but the design is remarkably original. A fine collection of French art has come here from the Sternberg Palace (see p. 71). This is a substantial array of paintings by Delacroix and Daumie, busts by Rodin, a rare self-portrait (1890) by Henri Rousseau, and Impressionist and Post-Impressionist works by van Gogh and others. The Picasso collection is exceptional in its quality and quantity.

SECOND FLOOR

Here you will find eclectic examples of Czech art from 1930 onward. Some are derivative—Daliesque paintings by František Janoušek (1890–1943), Bonnard-influenced Václav Bartovský (1903–1961)—while others are typical of various art movements, from abstraction to modish installations. The lower floors are used for temporary exhibitions. ■

Right: The atrium and galleries of the Trade Fair Palace were renovated in the 1990s.

Around Prague

ON THE EDGES OF PRAGUE ARE A NUMBER OF CHURCHES and châteaus well worth visiting. Most of them are easy to reach by public transportation. The Star Castle is quite unlike any other castle in Bohemia, and Brevnov Monastery is an excellent example of a moribund institution given a new lease on life when the monks returned here after the Velvet Revolution.

Brevnov Monastery

🅰 See map inset p. 113

✉ Markétská 1

☎ 220 406 111

🕐 Closed Mon.–Fri.

💲 $

🚋 Tram: 8, 22. Metro: Malostranská

Church of Our Lady of Victory at White Mountain

🅰 See map inset p. 113

✉ Karmelitská

🚋 Tram: 8, 22

Star Castle

🅰 See map inset p. 113

☎ 220 612 230

🕐 Closed Mon.

💲 $

🚋 Metro: Hradcanská, then tram 1 or 18 to the terminus

Troja Castle

🅰 See map inset p. 113

✉ U Trojského zámku 1

☎ 233 540 739

🕐 Closed Mon. April–Oct., Mon.–Fri. Nov.–March

💲 $$$

🚋 Metro to Nádraží Holešovice, then bus 112 to end of line

BREVNOV MONASTERY

The original Brevnov Monastery (Břevnovský klášter) was founded in 993 by Prince Boleslav II and St. Adalbert, bishop of Prague, as the very first monastic institution in Bohemia. In the 18th century, the Dientzenhofers (see p. 43) built a complex of baroque buildings. The grandest is the slightly austere **Church of St. Margaret** (Kostel sv. Markéta), which comes into view as you enter the monastery gateway. Despite its size, the interior has no aisles and is, compared with most of Prague's other baroque churches, restrained in its decor. There's a fine organ gallery, crowded with white putti, choir stalls, and altarpieces by Petr Brandl (1668–1735). In the crypt you can see remains of the 11th-century church, excavated in the 1960s. Gradual restoration of the other sumptuous buildings is under way. The Benedictine monks returned to the monastery in 1990, just three years before its millennial anniversary.

CHURCH OF OUR LADY OF VICTORY AT WHITE MOUNTAIN

Soon after the decisive battle near here in 1620 (see p. 26) a chapel dedicated to St. Wenceslas was built, but a few years later, on the orders of Ferdinand II, it was replaced by a monastery and new chapel. The arcades surrounding the Church of Our Lady of Victory at White Mountain (Kostel Panny Marie Vítězné) are reminiscent of those at the Loreto Church in Hradčany (see p. 73), and the interior is richly frescoed. The church lies close to the tram terminus at Bílá Hora.

STAR CASTLE

The remarkable Star Castle (Letohrádek hvězda), in the shape of a six-pointed star, stands within a former game reserve founded in 1530 by Ferdinand I. A number of avenues traverse the park, all leading to the castle on the top of White Mountain. It was built in the 1550s as a hunting lodge for the son of Ferdinand I, Archduke Ferdinand of Tyrol. Used as a barracks and military store until 1874, the castle was not properly restored until the 1950s. The interior's most exciting features are the exquisite Renaissance stucco decorations, depicting mythological scenes, as well as medallions and purely ornamental plasterwork. Today the castle is a museum dedicated to the lives and works of writer Alois Jirásek (1851–1930) and artist Mikoláš Aleš (1852–1913). In the basement is an exhibit about the Battle of White Mountain (see p. 26).

TROJA CASTLE

Count Václav Vojtěch Šternberk built Troja Castle (Trojský zámek) in the 1680s as a summer residence just outside the city, easily accessible from Hradčany. The first building was designed by Gian Domenico Orsi, but the handsome if boxlike building you see today, with whitewashed walls and rust-red

The strange and aptly named **Star Castle** stands in parkland on the fringes of Prague.

stonework, is Jean-Baptiste Mathey's Bohemian version of a Roman villa. Boldly gesticulating statues of deities adorn its grand and magnificent exterior double staircase. The most imposing room is the lavishly frescoed banqueting hall; the murals mostly portray the Habsburgs' achievements and Leopold I's victories over the Ottoman Turks in the 17th century. A permanent exhibition of Czech paintings from the late 19th and early 20th centuries, notably works by Václav Brožík, is housed in the villa. The terraced gardens were laid out in the early 18th century.

ZBRASLAV MONESTERY

Zbraslav Monastery (Zbraslavský klášter) was founded 8 miles (12 km) south of the city in 1292 as a burial place for the Bohemian kings, though only Václav II and Václav IV were actually laid to rest here. Subsequent wars left the monastery in ruins, until it was rebuilt as a château in the early 18th century. Since 1998 the interior has housed the National Gallery's fine collection of Asian and Islamic art, beautifully laid out and clearly labeled. First-floor exhibits, mostly devoted to Japanese art, include enamelware, Buddhist sculpture, and lively figurative paintings. Upstairs, the first Chinese room is filled with bronze ritual objects up to 3,200 years old, as well as funerary figurines, ceramics, and examples of Buddhist art. There are smaller collections of Tibetan, Indian, and Islamic art on the same floor. ■

Zbraslav Monestery

🗺 See map inset p. 113

✉ Bartoňova 2, Prague 5-zbraslav cp. 2

☎ 257 921 638

🕐 Closed Mon.

💲 $$

🚇 Metro: Smíchovské nádraží, then bus 241, 243, or 129 to Zbraslavské náměstí

More places to visit in New Town & the suburbs

BOTANICAL GARDENS
The hilly open spaces of Prague's Botanical Gardens (Botanická zahrada) are welcome in a district crowded with institutions and apartment blocks. Originally located in Smíchov, south of Malá Strana, the gardens were moved here in 1897. The giant water lily is the most popular attraction.

🗺 Map p. 113 ✉ Na Slupi 16 💲 $
🚇 Metro: Karlovo náměstí

CHURCH OF ST. JOHN ON THE ROCK
The delightful Kostel sv. Jan na Skalce, designed in the 1730s by Kilián Ignác Dientzenhofer, is remarkable for its magnificent exterior staircase, which was designed later by another architect, Anton Schmidt. The church is dramatically located on top of a crag above street level, facing the Emmaus Monastery along Vyšehradská (see p. 123); its towers are set at a jaunty angle on either side of the facade. St. John is open only during Mass, via the entrance on Charles Square (Karlovo náměstí).

🗺 Map p. 113 🚊 Tram: 18, 24. Metro: Karlovo náměstí

CHURCH OF ST. STEPHEN
Tucked between Žitná and Ječná, the Gothic Church of St. Stephen (Kostel sv. Štěpán) houses the tomb of Matthias Braun, one of Bohemia's greatest and most prolific baroque sculptors. It contains a fine 15th-century pulpit and paintings by baroque masters such as Karel Škréta, as well as a Gothic painting of the Madonna (1472).

🗺 Map p. 113 ✉ Štěpánská 🚊 Tram: 4, 6, 10, 16, 22, 23. Metro: Karlovo náměstí, I. P. Pavlova

"FRED AND GINGER" BUILDING
It comes as a welcome surprise in historic Prague to see this funky, jazzy building by the brilliant, if quirky, Californian architect Frank Gehry. It is affectionately called the Dancing House (Tančící dům) for its resemblance to two dancers. The new office building sprang up along the riverbank next to a building owned by Václav Havel's family, and he played a large part in encouraging an unconventional approach to this prime site. Its most striking feature is the curvaceous glass tower, topped by the Perle de Prague restaurant.

🗺 Map p. 113 ✉ Corner of Resslova and Rašínovo nábřeží 🚊 Tram: 3, 7, 16, 17, 21. Metro: Karlovo náměstí

KARLOV CHURCH
Although slightly off the beaten track, Karlov Church (Na Karlově) is one of the most remarkable buildings established by Charles IV, in 1350. Its highly unusual octagonal design is an architectural tribute to Charlemagne's imperial chapel in Aachen in Germany. The church was modified in 1575 by Bonifác Wohlmut, who built the extraordinary vaulting and cupola. František Kaňka helped renovate the church in the 1730s and is largely responsible for the interior's appearance. This must be one of the most theatrical baroque churches in the republic, with polychrome figures portraying the Visitation, flanked by sculptured onlookers leaning out of windows to see what is going on.

🗺 Map p. 113 ✉ Ke Karlovu/Horská
🕐 Open Sun. & holidays p.m. 🚌 Bus: 504, 505, 511. Metro: I. P. Pavlova

LAPIDÁRIUM
Stromovka Park is filled with exhibition buildings, and the pavilion on the right is the Lapidárium of the National Museum, a resting place for often fragile and weathered original statues dating from the 11th to the 19th centuries. The Lapidárium was established in 1905 and is a treasure house of sculptural art. Among the highlights are many of the original carvings from the Old Town Bridge Tower, the Charles Bridge, and the beautiful Krocín fountain that stood in Old Town Square until 1864.

🗺 Inset map p. 113 ✉ Výstaviště 🕐 Closed Mon. 💲 $ 🚇 Metro: Nádraží Holešovice, then tram 5, 12, or 17 to Stromovka Park

MUCHA MUSEUM
This museum, dedicated to the work of one of Bohemia's best known art nouveau artists, is housed in the 18th-century Kaunicky palác, which opened in 1998. Exhibits include paintings, drawings, and sculptures, as well as

Alfons Mucha is best known for his art nouveau posters, including the *Salon des Cent* of 1896.

memorabilia of Alfons Mucha (1860–1939). His posters have become familiar images—fey girls with swirling draperies, all in art nouveau borders with stylish floral embellishments. After Mucha's return from Paris in 1910, his work became more nationalistic, with poses reminiscent of socialist realism.
⚠ Map p. 113 ✉ Panská 7 ☎ 224 215 409 💲 $$$ 🚋 Tram: 3, 9, 14, 24. Metro: Můstek

NATIONAL TECHNICAL MUSEUM
For those interested in the history of technology and industry, few museums in Europe match Prague's National Technical Museum (Národní technické muzeum). Founded in 1908, it houses exhibits related to timekeeping and transportation—an excuse to assemble a huge collection of locomotives, old motorcars, biplanes, penny farthings, motorcycles, cameras, and a hot-air balloon.

In the basement is a realistic mock-up of a coal mine that can be visited only on a guided tour (45 minutes).
www.ntm.cz ⚠ See map inset p. 113
✉ Kostelní 42 ☎ 220 399 111 🕐 Closed Mon. 💲 $$ 🚇 Metro: Vltavská, then tram 1, 8, 25, or 26

OLŠANY CEMETERY
Since 1784 Olšany Cemetery (Olšanské hřbitovy), the large burial ground along Vinohradská, has been the city's main cemetery. It is divided into a number of sections. Many visitors come to the Jewish cemetery, on the other side of Jana Želivského street, to visit the grave of Franz Kafka *(clearly indicated)*. This melancholy cemetery is a reminder of the size of Prague's Jewish community before World War II. Just inside the gates of the main Christian cemetery on the right is the grave of

Jan Palach (see p. 116). His body was removed by the authorities in 1973, but in 1990 his coffin was returned to its original grave.

See map inset p. 113 Vinohradská 153 Tram: 5, 10, 11, 16. Metro: Flora (Christian cemetery), Želivského (Jewish cemetery)

POLICE MUSEUM

The Police Museum (Muzeum Policie) can be found in the former cloisters adjoining the Karlov church (see p. 134). The present-day museum ignores the distasteful role of the police before 1989 and focuses on uniforms, weaponry, and equipment. There are rooms devoted to road safety, showing videos of spectacular car accidents, and the crime and detection exhibits have some very gruesome photographs. For light relief there is a section on safe-breaking.

Map p. 113 Ke Karlovu 453/1 224 922 183 Closed Mon. $ Bus: 504, 505, 511. Metro: I. P. Pavlova

Veteran car enthusiasts will have a field day at the National Technical Museum.

PRAGUE MUNICIPAL MUSEUM

A few yards from the Florenc metro station, the Prague Municipal Museum (Muzeum hlavního města Prahy) tells the story of the city and exhibits paintings, furniture, and sculptures from Prague's towers and churches. The most popular exhibit is the model of the city constructed from wood and paper by

Antonín Langweil in the 1830s. This laborious work depicts 2,000 buildings. It provides firm evidence of the appearance of Kampa Island before it became a park and of the Jewish ghetto before its demolition.

Map p. 113 Na Poříčí 52 224 816 772 Closed Mon. $ Tram: 8, 25. Metro: Florenc

VILA AMERIKA

This exquisite, if boxlike, villa was built by the ubiquitous Kilián Ignác Dientzenhofer as a summer residence for Count Michna in 1720. The house became dilapidated during the 19th century, but it was saved from ruin and is now the Dvořák Museum (Muzeum A. Dvořáka). The displays, which include a small collection of the great composer's scores, possessions, and musical instruments, document his career and life. Concerts take place between April and October in the small frescoed recital hall.

Map p. 113 Ke Karlovu 20 224 918 013 Closed Mon. $ Metro: I. P. Pavlova

VILA BERTRAMKA

The Dušek family lived in this charming villa in Smíchov, often playing host to Mozart during his visits to Prague between 1787 and 1791 (see pp. 98–99). It became a museum honoring the composer in the 1920s and has often been renovated. Exhibits include a harpsichord once played by Mozart, though many exhibits are facsimiles. Concerts are frequently held at the villa or in the lovely setting of the gardens.

See map inset p. 113 Mozartova 169 257 318 461 $$ Metro: Anděl

ŽIŽKOV

The hilltop suburb of Žižkov is named after the Hussite hero Jan Žižka (ca 1360–1424). On top of the hill, site of a great Hussite victory in 1420, stands a vast monument (1929–1932) known as the National Memorial (Národní památník). Frescoes illustrate triumphant moments in Bohemia's history, and the colossal 1950s equestrian statue of the general by Bohumil Kafka is, according to UNESCO, the world's largest bronze equestrian statue.

See map inset p. 113 Metro: Florenc ■

A number of fascinating castles and interesting towns surround Prague, the highlight of which is Charles IV's summer castle of Karlštejn, with its chapel sparkling with precious jewels.

Day trips from Prague

The bejeweled chapel at Karlštejn Castle

Day trips from Prague

UNLIKE MOST EUROPEAN CAPITALS, Prague remains a small city. Heading out of the city, before long you will find yourself in open countryside. The country around Prague contains a surprising number of castles and châteaus, almost all of which are well worth visiting.

The best known castle is Karlštejn, the summer residence of Charles IV. It is also the most visited one in the country, apart from Prague Castle. But there are other medieval castles to see, such as Český Šternberk, Kokořín, and Křivoklát. Another popular excursion is to the château of Konopiště, which was rebuilt by Archduke Franz Ferdinand in the 1890s and is still packed with family memorabilia.

Two châteaus belonging to the Lobkowiczs, one of many Bohemian families who built up their fortunes under the Habsburgs, are open to the public. One is at Mělník, the best known of Bohemia's wine regions; the other is at Nelahozeves, the village where Antonín Dvořák was born. The château here is filled with some of the Lobkowicz family's art treasures.

Of the many small towns within easy reach of Prague, the most absorbing is Kutná Hora, a former rich mining town that is lavishly endowed with magnificent buildings. Nearby you will find one of Europe's largest charnel houses. Kolín has a mighty medieval church, Mladá Boleslav is home to a Škoda Museum that motoring enthusiasts will find enthralling, and Poděbrady is famed for its spas.

Although none of these is very far from the capital, some are quite hard to reach without a car. Prague does not have a ring road, so driving from one town to the next can take time; plan your excursions to take this into account. ■

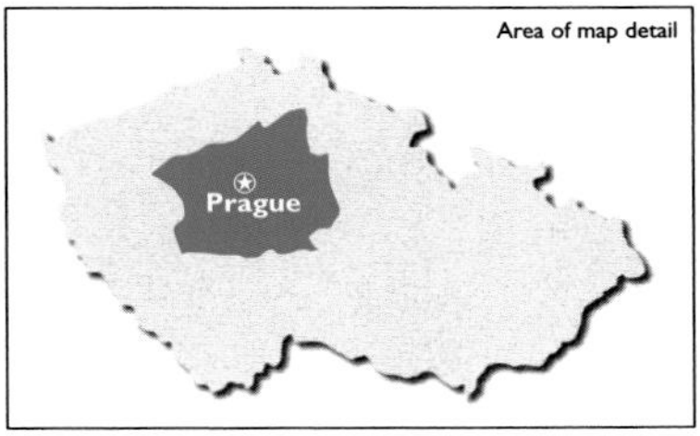
Area of map detail
Prague

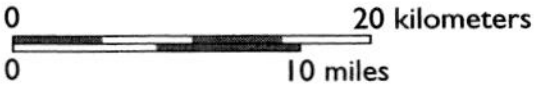
0
20 kilometers
0
10 miles

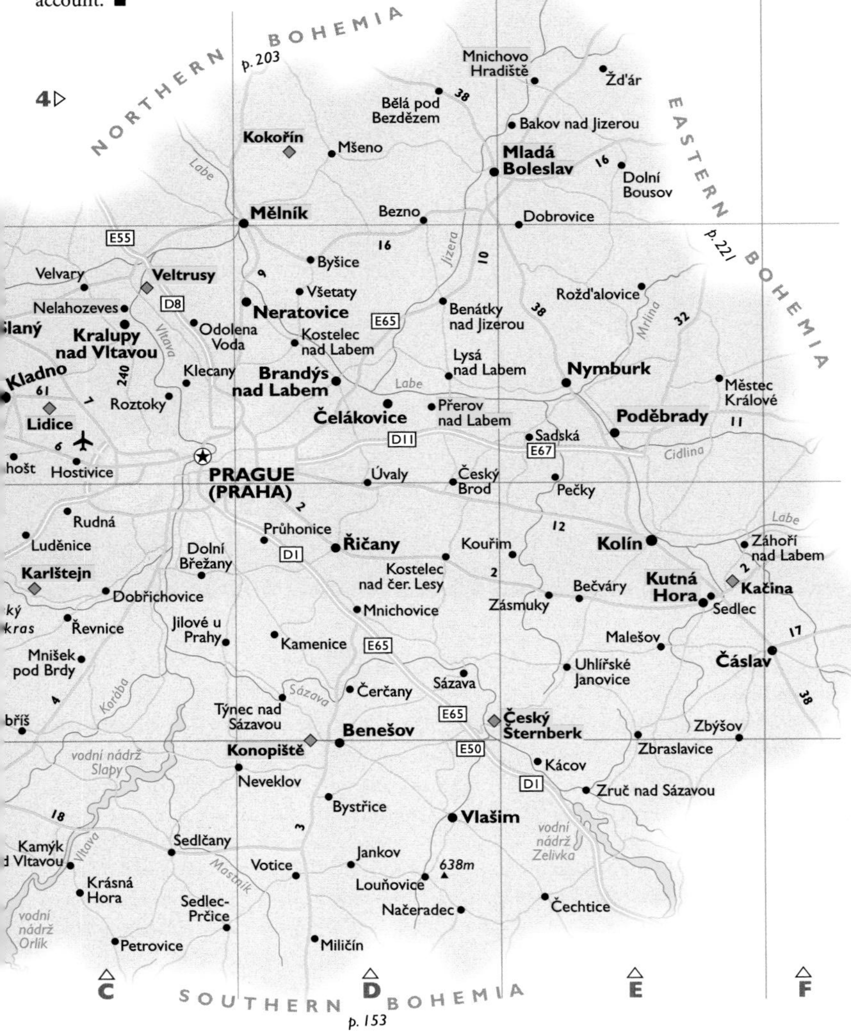
NORTHERN BOHEMIA
p. 203
4▷
EASTERN BOHEMIA
p. 221
SOUTHERN BOHEMIA
p. 153
Mnichovo Hradiště
Žďár
Bělá pod Bezdězem
Bakov nad Jizerou
Kokořín
Mšeno
Mladá Boleslav
Dolní Bousov
Mělník
Bezno
Dobrovice
E55
Byšice
Velvary
Veltrusy
Všetaty
Rožďalovice
Nelahozeves
D8
Neratovice
E65
Benátky nad Jizerou
Slaný
Kralupy nad Vltavou
Odolena Voda
Kostelec nad Labem
Lysá nad Labem
Nymburk
Městec Králové
Kladno
Klecany
Brandýs nad Labem
Roztoky
Lidice
Čelákovice
Přerov nad Labem
Poděbrady
D11
Sadská
E67
Hostivice
PRAGUE (PRAHA)
Úvaly
Český Brod
Pečky
Rudná
Průhonice
Luděnice
Dolní Břežany
D1
Říčany
Kouřim
Kolín
Záhoří nad Labem
Karlštejn
Kostelec nad čer. Lesy
Kutná Hora
Kačina
Dobřichovice
Bečváry
Zásmuky
Sedlec
Mnichovice
Řevnice
Jílové u Prahy
Kamenice
E65
Malešov
Mníšek pod Brdy
Uhlířské Janovice
Čáslav
Čerčany
Sázava
Týnec nad Sázavou
Český Šternberk
Zbýšov
Benešov
Konopiště
E50
Zbraslavice
vodní nádrž Slapy
Kácov
Neveklov
D1
Zruč nad Sázavou
Bystřice
Vlašim
vodní nádrž Zelivka
Kamýk nad Vltavou
Sedlčany
Jankov
Votice
638m
Krásná Hora
Louňovice
Sedlec-Prčice
Načeradec
Čechtice
vodní nádrž Orlík
Petrovice
Miličín
Labe
Vltava
Jizera
Mrlina
Cidlina
Sázava
Kocába
Mastník
C
D
E
F

Karlštejn

Karlštejn was both a fortress and a summer residence of Charles IV.

THE WALLED FORTRESS OF KARLŠTEJN, SET IN THE MIDDLE of the Český kras region, sprawls up a steep hillside above the Berounka River. It was built as a royal castle for Charles IV by the Frenchman Matthias of Arras, who also worked on St. Vitus's Cathedral. Work began in 1348 to create a fortress that would function both as a summer palace for the king and a safe place for his art treasures and the crown jewels. One of the peculiarities of Charles's tenure was his refusal to allow women to enter the walls of Karlštejn.

Bohemian karst

The Bohemian karst (Český kras), the limestone plateau into which the Berounka River has cut its winding course, is a protected area, rich in rare flora such as orchids. Here gorges, sinkholes, potholes, and caves have been created over time by water dripping through the limestone. ∎

Despite partial reconstruction during the Renaissance and heavy-handed restoration in the late 19th century, Karlštejn's impregnable walls and towers—especially the 88-foot-high (27 m) keep or Great Tower—remain an impressive sight. The interior, although bare, is worth a visit. Here you can see the emperor's apartments, including his bedroom, and two remarkable chapels. The first is the **Chapel of St. Mary** (Mariánská kaple), decorated with faded 14th-century frescoes depicting the founding of the castle. Of more interest is the **Chapel of St. Catherine** (Kaple sv. Kateřiny), the emperor's private place of prayer. Richly decorated with medieval frescoes and plaques of semiprecious gems set into the wall, it includes a fine portrait of Charles IV with his third consort, Anne of Svídnik.

The heart of the castle is the **keep tower,** where the most precious jewels and relics were kept. Within the tower is the astonishing **Chapel of the Holy Cross** (Kaple sv. Kříže), gilded and richly embellished with 2,200 precious gems and a huge 14th-century cycle of paintings depicting the saints by Master Theodoric of Prague. This chapel was built to house irreplaceable religious relics as well as the Habsburg imperial jewels and insignia now displayed in Vienna and Prague. Until recently the chapel

was closed to visitors in order to preserve its artistic treasures, although some of Theodoric's panels can be seen in the Convent of St. Agnes (Anežský klášter) in Prague (see pp. 106–109). There are occasional tours, however. They are limited to 12 people and expensive, but it is worthwhile asking about them. They must be pre-booked.

Such is Karlštejn's popularity with tourists that the approach to the castle is lined with souvenir stalls and snack bars. It's a good idea to get there early, before the castle is overrun with bus tours. Trains leave Prague's Smíchov station hourly for Karlštejn. It's then a 15-minute hike to the castle entrance, and in summer carriages are available, for a price, to haul you most of the way there. ∎

One of the priceless medieval panels by Master Theodoric at Karlštejn

Karlštejn

🗺 139 C2

✉ 17 miles (28 km) SW of Prague

☎ 274 008 154 (to book tours)

🕐 Closed Mon.

💲 $$–$$$$. Tours: $$$$

🚊 Train from Prague's Smíchov station

Kutná Hora & around

Above: The vast Jesuit College almost dominates the Cathedral of St. Barbara. Opposite: The superb vaults at the Cathedral of St. Barbara in Kutná Hora

IN THE MIDDLE AGES, KUTNÁ HORA WAS ONE OF THE MOST important towns of central Europe; in Bohemia, only Prague was larger. Silver mining, using German settlers as the main workforce, was the foundation of its prosperity, and the establishment of the royal mint in about 1300, employing Italian workers, added to its cosmopolitanism. After three centuries the mines were exhausted and the town went into a decline. In addition to the ravages inflicted by the Hussite wars in the 15th century and the Thirty Years War in the 17th century, there was a very destructive fire in 1770.

Husova street mounts the long ridge on which Kutná Hora is built and leads onto a small square set around the plague column dating from 1715. A lane called Lierova, on the right, brings you to **Stone House** (Kamenný dům), a lively Gothic house, inventively carved, and now a local museum. Farther up Husova is the lovely 1750 baroque facade of the **Church of St. John of Nepomuk** (kostel sv. Jana Nepomuckého) by František Kaňka. Husova emerges onto Rejskovo náměstí, whose massive 1495 Gothic fountain dominates the center.

To the left lies náměstí Narodního odboje, a larger and more tranquil grassy square. The massive 17th-century **Jesuit College** (Jezuitská kolej) designed by Domenico Orsi stands at the far end. By following the side of the college to the end and then bearing right, you can enjoy the wonderful approach to the fabulous **Cathedral of St. Barbara** (Chrám sv. Barbory), heralded by 13 large baroque statues opposite the facade of the college. From the balustrade there are fine views onto the Vrchlice Valley.

St. Barbara is the patron saint of miners, and it was the town's miners who financed the construction of the cathedral. It resembles a great

Kutná Hora

🗺 139 E2

✉ 40 miles (65 km) E of Prague

🚆 Trains from Hlavní nádraží via Sedlec. Bus from Florenc in Prague

Visitor information

✉ Palackého náměstí 377
e-mail infocentrum@ kutnohorsko.cz

☎ 327 512 378

The charnel house at Sedlec presents a surprisingly artistic assembly of bones and skulls.

Stone House
- ✉ Václavské náměstí 183
- ⊕ Closed Mon.
- 💲 $

Cathedral of St. Barbara
- ⊕ Closed Mon.
- 💲 $

Italian Court
- ✉ Havlíčkovo náměstí
- 💲 $

Small fort
- ✉ Barborská 28
- ☎ 327 512 159
- ⊕ Closed Mon. & Nov.–March
- 💲 $$$

Charnel house
- ✉ Zámecká, Sedlec
- ☎ 327 561 143
- 💲 $

ship, its flying buttresses like a galleon's oars, its roof like wind-puffed sails. The cathedral was begun in 1388 by Peter Parler and his son Jan, and continued by Benedikt Ried and Matthias Rejsek. They devised the marvelous geometric rib vaulting inside in the late 15th and early 16th centuries, but the cathedral was not completed until the 19th century. Remarkable 15th-century frescoes in the chapels of the south aisle and the choir depict miners at work.

Just south of Palackého náměstí, the main square, the tall tower of the Gothic **Church of St. James** (Kostel sv. Jakuba) looms up. This is Kutná Hora's oldest church, and its elegant interior has paintings by Petr Brandl, who is buried in the town, and Karel Škréta. Next to it is the **Italian Court** (Vlašský dvůr), the former mint until it was closed in 1726; it was also used as a royal residence by Václav IV in the early 14th century. The medieval oriel window of the chapel survives, adding a graceful note to the otherwise coarsely restored courtyard. Inside you can see a display of some

of the silver coins minted here until production ceased in 1547. Between the Italian court and the cathedral is the Hrádek, or **Small fort,** a 15th-century building that now houses a museum of minting and coinage. Visit an abandoned medieval mine beneath its foundations on a guided tour.

North of the main square, on Jiřiho z Poděbrad, you come to the **Ursuline convent** (Voršilský klášter), designed by Kilián Ignác Dientzenhofer. This palatial convent would be hugely admired elsewhere, but in this architecturally rich town it is easily overlooked.

SEDLEC

Sedlec, 2 miles (3.2 km) northeast of Kutná Hora (reached by buses 1 or 4), has a remarkable early church by Giovanni Santini, **Church of the Assumption of the Virgin Mary** (Kostel Nanebevzetí Panna Marie), with highly original stucco vaulting (*$*). Next to the church, the former Cistercian monastery is now, incongruously, a tobacco factory.

Across the road, signs lead to the monastery cemetery, where, in the crypt of the Gothic chapel, you'll find an extraordinary **charnel house.** The cemetery was the fashionable burying place of the Bohemian nobility, but it was soon overcrowded. In 1870 František Rint was commissioned to use the bones for artistic purposes. He came up with the bizarre idea of fashioning bells, chalices, candelabra, and even a coat of arms out of them.

KAČINA

At Kačina, 4 miles (7 km) northeast of Kutná Hora, is a magnificent neoclassic pedimented château begun in 1802 linked to pavilions by elegant colonnades. This languorous cream-colored expanse of building rejoices in a large park, laid out in English style. ■

CATHEDRAL OF ST. BARBARA

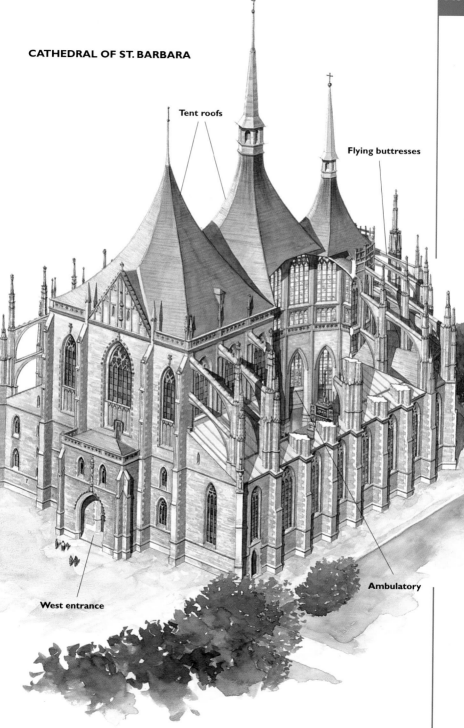

Tent roofs

Flying buttresses

West entrance

Ambulatory

More places to visit as day trips from Prague

ČESKÝ ŠTERNBERK

Much of the terrain around Prague is flat, but southeast of the city is the winding Sázava Valley, which penetrates the surrounding hills. High above it sits one of Bohemia's most sinister-looking castles: Český Šternberk. It spreads along the top of a crag, one side overlooking the village, the other the Sázava River. Originally a medieval castle stood here, but Český Šternberk has been often rebuilt and added to, so that today's appearance is a scruffy Renaissance style. The castle was in the hands of the Šternberk family, apart from a few decades, from the 13th century until 1948. Confiscated by the Communists, the castle was restored to the family in the 1990s. Highlights of the interior include a graphic art collection from the time of the Thirty Years War.
🗺 139 D2 ✉ 28 miles (45 km) SE of Prague via E50 from Prague, direction Brno ☎ 317 855 101 🕐 Closed Mon. May–Sept., & all Nov.–March 💲 $–$$$

KOKOŘÍN

Northeast of Mělník is a picturesque region of wooded hills and dells called the Kokořínsko. It is a popular destination for day-trippers from Prague, because the pretty valleys and unusual rock formations make this attractive and relatively undemanding hiking country. The village of Kokořín is the dramatic setting for a 14th-century castle. The exterior is fun to explore, though the interior has little to offer.
🗺 139 D4 ✉ 12 miles (20 km) NE of Mělník (see p. 147) via route 273

KOLÍN

Kolín is an old industrial town on the banks of the Labe. In the main square stands the richly sgraffitoed and gabled town hall, brilliantly decorated in 1887. Up the slope is the great 13th-century **Church of St. Bartholomew** (Kostel sv. Bartoloměje), with the belfry of 1504 attached by an arch to the church's towers. Built from coarse stone, the church is austere, though the sheer height of the choir and its flying buttresses, added to the existing church by Peter Parler, give it tremendous flair. In the interior the elegance of the choir contrasts with the robust simplicity of the nave.
🗺 139 E2 ✉ 38 miles (58 km) E of Prague on route 12 🚆 Train from Hlavní nádraží station in Prague

KONOPIŠTĚ

The château of Konopiště is set in a splendid park with a famous rose garden. It belonged to Habsburg Archduke Franz Ferdinand d'Este from 1887 until his assassination in Sarajevo in 1914. In the 1890s he more or less rebuilt the castle, while retaining its medieval towers and a fine baroque gateway by František Kaňka. Three guided tours are needed to see the entire interior. The first tours the state rooms, the second takes in the Este family's collection of arms and armor, and the third (limited to eight people) visits the private apartments of the archduke and his family. The corridors, lined with hunting trophies, reflect Franz Ferdinand's passion for hunting.
🗺 139 D1 ✉ 25 miles (40 km) S of Prague via E50, then S on route 3 ☎ 317 721 366; fax: 317 724 271 🕐 Closed Mon.–Fri. Nov.; & all Dec.–March 💲 $$–$$$$$ 🚆 Train from Hlavní nádraží in Prague to Benešov. Bus from Florenc terminal in Prague

KŘIVOKLÁT CASTLE

Křivoklát Castle (Zámek Křivoklát) overlooks the Křivoklátsko nature reserve, a forested craggy region. The castle was built in the 13th century as a hunting lodge for the Přemyslid kings. It was subsequently the childhood home of the future Charles IV. In the 1650s the Habsburgs sold Křivoklát, and from 1685 the Fürstenberg family, the new owners, reconstructed it. The 80-minute guided tour includes the elegant Gothic chapel and the Knights' Hall, with late Gothic sculpture.
🗺 138 B2 ✉ 28 miles (45 km) W of Prague via route 6, then route 201 ☎ 313 558 120 🕐 Closed Mon. April–June & Sept.–Oct.; Mon.–Fri. March; & Nov.–Feb. 💲 $$–$$$ 🚆 Train from Hlavní nádraží in Prague; change at Beroun for Křivoklát

LÁNY

The château of Lány, dating from the 14th century, was the summer residence of the presidents of Czechoslovakia and is still that of

The Šternberk family has owned Český Šternberk for more than 700 years.

the Czech president. Only the gardens and deer park are open to the public. Czechs visit Lány to pay homage to the founder of Czech democracy, President Masaryk, who is buried here.  138 B3 25 miles (40 km) W of Prague on route 7, then left on route 236 Closed Mon.–Tues. April–Oct., & Nov.–Dec.

LIDICE

Few sites match the stark horror of Lidice, just northwest of Prague. On June 4, 1942, Nazi Reichsrotektor Reinhard Heydrich was assassinated in Prague, and six days later the Germans took their revenge. Every one of the male inhabitants of the mining village of Lidice was shot, and the women and children were deported to concentration camps. Then the entire village, which had been selected at random, was razed. After the war a new village was built nearby. These dreadful events have been commemorated in a series of stone reliefs beneath concrete arcades. Next to this impressive monument is a small **museum** that narrates the barbaric events of that terrible day, which were filmed by the perpetrators. To the right of the museum, a large park contains more monuments to the dead of Lidice. 139 C3 20 miles (32 km) NW of Prague via 7, then left on 61 toward Kladno **Museum** 10 června 1942 $ Bus from Dejvická metro station

MĚLNÍK

Mělník is the principal town of the Bohemian vineyards. Despite its bucolic associations, it is mainly an industrial town, but standing on the terrace next to the castle and looking out onto the plains, where the Rivers Labe and Vltava meet, it's easy to forget that. The south-facing slopes were first planted with vines imported

The Lobkowicz family owns many castles, but it is their Renaissance château at Nelahozeves that houses their fine art collection.

from Burgundy by Charles IV in 1365. Mostly destroyed by Swedish forces during the Thirty Years War, the **castle** has been largely rebuilt. Acquired by the Lobkowicz family in 1753, it was returned to them after 1989, following confiscation by the Communists. The courtyard boasts medieval elements and sgraffitoed galleries. The restored rooms are filled with baroque furnishings and Czech baroque paintings. You can also visit the castle's wine cellars and taste the wines produced here, or drink them at the wine bar or restaurant (*$$$*). Next to the castle is a Gothic church; in the crypt a macabre **charnel house** is stacked with the bones of plague victims. There's a small viticultural **museum** next to the town hall.

139 D4 20 miles (32 km) N of Prague on route 608, then on route 9 Train from Hlavní nádraží in Prague to Všetaty, change for Mělník. Bus from Florenc or nádraží Holešovice in Prague **Castle** $; Cellar tour: $$–$$$ **Charnel house** Closed Mon. $ **Museum** náměstí Míru 11 315 627 503 Closed weekends Oct.–April

MLADÁ BOLESLAV

In an attempt to brighten up this town long dedicated to motor car production, the art nouveau post office has been painted in lilac and blue, and the Renaissance town hall has been sgraffitoed. Just north of the town center on Václava Klementa is the **Škoda Museum,** where dozens of old cars and motorcycles are displayed. Elegant motorcycles from the turn of the 20th century are especially interesting, as fetching in their way as the grander saloon cars in their bright red and yellow colors.

139 D4 31 miles (50 km) NE of Prague on E65 Train from Hlavní nádraží in Prague **Škoda Museum** Václava Klementa 294 326 831 134 $

MNICHOVO HRADIŠTĚ

Mnichovo Hradiště is the burial place of Albrecht von Wallenstein (Valdštejn). His descendants owned the E-shaped **château** here until 1945. There are three tours on offer. The first takes in the elegantly furnished salons and library, the second showcases the château's still functioning theater, and the third visits Wallenstein's tomb within the grounds. The general was murdered in Cheb in 1634 and buried near Jičín; a century went by before his remains were brought back to the château.

139 E4 31 miles (50 km) NW of Jičín **Château** Closed Mon. May–Sept., & Mon.–Fri. April & Oct. $–$$

NELAHOZEVES

Antonín Dvořák was born in 1841 in the village of Nelahozeves, near Veltrusy. This otherwise unremarkable place is dominated by its massive late Renaissance **château,** owned by the Lobkowicz family since 1623. Its somewhat plain walls have been brightened up by splendid 16th-century sgraffiti. The estate was returned to its original owners following the breakdown of the Communist regime. The family's fine art collection features paintings by Pieter Bruegel the Elder, Rubens, and other masters.

An imposing statue of King George of Poděbrady is the appropriate centerpiece of the town named after him.

🗺 139 C3 ✉ 17 miles (27 km) N of Prague. W on route 7, then N on route 240 🚆 Train from Masarykovo nádraží in Prague to Nelahozeves zastávka **Château** ☎ 315 709 111 🕐 Closed Mon. 💲 $$

PODĚBRADY

Poděbrady is a glassmaking town located along the River Labe. Its main square is dominated not by its sturdy plague column but by the equestrian statue of the first Hussite king, George of Poděbrady, who is believed to have been born here in 1420. Behind the statue rises the formerly moated Renaissance **castle,** now part of Charles University. Mineral springs rich in iron made Poděbrady develop as a spa town in the early 20th century.

🗺 139 E3 ✉ 25 miles (40 km) E of Prague on E67 🚆 Train from Hlavní nádraží **Visitor information** ✉ Jiřího náměstí 20, 29031 ☎ 325 611 090 **Castle** 🕐 Closed Mon. & all Nov.–April

PŘEROV NAD LABEM

Přerov nad Labem is home to a small *skansen* (open-air museum of vernacular buildings). Founded in 1895, it was the first such museum in central Europe. Come here to see these partly timbered buildings if you are not going as far as the bigger skansens (see pp. 284–285).

🗺 139 D3 ✉ 18 miles (30 km) E of Prague via E67 then N on route 272 🕐 Closed Mon. May–Sept.; Mon.–Fri. April & Oct.; & all Nov.– March 💲 $ 🚆 Train from Hlavní nádraží to Čelakovice; change to local bus. Bus from Palmovka station in Prague

PŘÍBRAM

Příbram is an unprepossessing mining town, but on the eastern outskirts is the Marian shrine known as **Holy Mountain** (Svatá Hora), a 17th-century Jesuit creation. A covered stairway leads up to the vast shrine from Dlouhá street. The large **Mining Museum** (Hornické muzeum) shows a miner's cottage, a machine room with steam engine, and mineral collections. The main attraction is a trip down to the former coal face.

🗺 138 B1 ✉ 35 miles (56 km) SW of Prague via route 4 🚆 Bus from Na Knížecí bus station in Prague **Mining Museum** ✉ naměstí Hynka Kličky 293, Příbram IV–Březové Hory, 26102 ☎ 318 626 307 🕐 Closed Mon. April–Oct., Sat.–Mon. Nov.–March 💲 $$

VELTRUSY

Veltrusy is a curious russet-colored, early 18th-century château. It has a highly original star shape with a huge dome at the center, and it sits in a large English-style park, packed with decorative follies. Many of the rooms are decorated in rococo style and filled with porcelain and fine furniture.

🗺 139 C3 ✉ 15 miles (25 km) N of Prague via E55, then N on route 608 🕐 Closed Mon. May–Sept.; Mon.–Fri. March, April, Oct., Nov.; & all Dec.–Feb. 💲 $–$$$ 🚆 Train from Masarykovo nádraží in Prague to Kralupy, then bus ■

Czech
Republic

Czech Republic

AFTER THE BUSTLE OF PRAGUE, A VISIT TO THE REMAINDER OF THE CZECH
Republic can sometimes seem like stepping back in time. The countryside is dotted with
quaint towns focused around elegant arcaded main squares, with castles, sometimes
ruinous, guarding the valleys and old trade routes. Magnificent châteaus take you back to
the time when the Habsburg aristocracy owned vast estates in Bohemia and Moravia.

Bohemia and Moravia are two former
provinces of Czechoslovakia. Both have hilly,
even mountainous northern sectors, heavily
industrialized in places, whereas the south has
gentle landscapes. Bohemia's proximity to
Germany and Austria ensures that it receives
more visitors than Moravia.

In western Bohemia you'll find famous spa
towns that have been successfully revived after
decades of neglect. Plzeň is home to the
famous Pilsner beer, and the equally famous
Budvar comes from České Budějovice in
southern Bohemia. The southern region
contains some splendid castles, such as Český
Krumlov. In southwest Bohemia lie the
Šumava mountains and lakeland, popular

**Pages 150–151: The riverside fortress of
Ledeč nad Sázavou southeast of Prague**

with hikers and water-sports enthusiasts. The
mountains of northern Bohemia are more
dramatic, but air pollution, although now
being addressed, cast a blight on them.

Moravia's capital is Brno, a sprawling town
with an interesting historic center. Olomouc is
equally worthwhile. The industrial cities of
Opava and Ostrava in northern Moravia are
less rewarding. In the south, wine-growing
villages such as Znojmo and Mikulov attract
an increasing number of visitors. Southern
Moravia also has culturally fascinating towns,
especially Kroměříž.

An unusual feature in both southern
Bohemia and Moravia are the fishponds that
dot the land, most of which are the size of small
lakes and have been cultivated as fish farms for
centuries. This watery landscape is best explored
from small towns such as Třeboň. ■

**The Zvíkov castle, with its impressive 13th-century round tower, has belonged to the
Schwarzenberg family, one of the greatest landlords in Bohemia, for 350 years.**

Southern Bohemia is packed with medieval castles and baroque châteaus, as well as such charming towns as Český Krumlov and Písek. The surrounding Šumava mountains and Lake Lipno are fine settings for a laid-back getaway.

Southern Bohemia

A playful detail from the Hall of Masks at Český Krumlov castle

Southern Bohemia

SOUTH BOHEMIA IS THE REGION THAT SHOWS THE PROVINCE AT ITS MOST relaxed and urbane. Largely free of the social and economic problems that blight parts of northern and eastern Bohemia, the south is a land of castles, handsome towns, and a variety of landscapes. The Šumava mountains offer ample opportunities for hiking, boating, and lazing about, while farther east, the Třeboňsko is a delightful watery region of fishponds that were established in the Middle Ages and still raise a large crop of Bohemia's favorite fish, carp, each year.

Česke Budějovice is the principal town of the region, and the home of Budvar beer (see pp. 160–161). The town center is imposing and attractive, though there is little, other than sampling the local brew, to detain most visitors for more than a day or so. The ideal base for excursions has to be the medieval town of Český Krumlov, both fascinating and beautiful in itself, and perfectly located for visiting the many other towns and churches and castles of the region. This is probably the best spot in the republic to sample its varied landscape and rich cultural heritage. It is also filled with castles and mansions. The castles drive (see pp. 162–165) links some of the country's most impressive castles, ranging in style from gauntly medieval to lavish 19th-century pastiche. Many of them overlook the River Vltava, which flows right through the region. Bohemia's northern stretches are popular with people from Prague looking for rural relaxation during warm weekends.

The eastern part of the region, beyond Třeboň, is less picturesque than the Vltava Valley and the Šumava mountains and lakes, but there are interesting towns and castles to visit, such as Jindřichův Hradec and Pelhřimov. Tábor is particularly worthwhile, especially if you have some interest in Bohemia's culture and history—it was a leading Hussite center and retains many vestiges and reminders from that period. ■

Just part of the mighty castle at Český Krumlov above the River Vlatava

Český Krumlov

Český Krumlov

🗺 154 C2

✉ 100 miles (160 km)
S of Prague via
E65, exit S onto
route 3, then right
on route 39

🚆 Train from
Prague via České
Budějovice. Bus
from Prague

THE FASCINATING MEDIEVAL TOWN OF ČESKÝ KRUMLOV IS dominated in a quite spectacular way by its colossal castle, which spreads along a series of crags above a steep loop in the fast-flowing Vltava. So irregular is the rock formation here that one spur pierces the very underbelly of the main castle. From 1302 until 1602 the castle was owned by the Rožmberk family, who extended the fortress into the second largest castle in Bohemia; since 1717 it has been in the hands of the Schwarzenbergs.

THE CASTLE

Bridges link the castle (hrad) with the main part of the Old Town, and galleried houses loom out over the fast-flowing river. A short climb from the town brings you to the castle entrance, reached across a small bridge that crosses over a bear moat. The gorgeously colored castle tower, painted in 1590, overlooks the entrance, which leads to a series of sgraffitoed and frescoed courtyards. A three-tiered viaduct connects the castle from one crag to another, while above the viaduct are three more tiers of corridors.

To visit the castle, you must sign up for one or both of two tours. Most of the interiors are in a baroque or rococo style, and the

Visitor information

✉ Náměstí Svornosti 2, 38101 Český Krumlov
e-mail infocentrum @ckrf.ckrumlov.cz

☎ 380 704 622

Castle & gardens

🕐 Closed Mon. & Nov.–March

$ Tours: $$–$$$ each
Theater: $$–$$$

Left: The huddled town of Český Krumlov, in the shadow of its castle, follows the twists of the River Vltava. Below: One of the cobbled lanes threading through the Old Town of Český Krumlov

collections displayed in some of the castle's 300 rooms include Chinese porcelain and rare tapestries. The ballroom, or Hall of Masks, is painted with charming trompe l'oeil carnival scenes completed in 1748 by Josef Lederer (Tour 1 only).

Walk across a long covered bridge to reach the terraced gardens and the exquisite rococo **Castle Theater** (Zámecké divadlo) of 1767. It retains much of its original scenery and costumes, and its refinement is a considerable relief after the primeval terrors of the castle's labyrinthine cellars.

OLD TOWN

The old town has become very commercialized, and dozens of glass and porcelain shops, as well as tackier souvenir and clothes shops, cafés

and restaurants, cater to the streams of mostly Austrian and German tourists. But the town is well organized, and guided tours are available from the town hall in the main square, náměstí Svornosti. The **town hall**

(radnice) itself has superb Gothic arcades and a rustic cornice. Behind the square is the early 15th-century **Church of St. Vitus** (Kostel sv. Víta), with contemporary frescoes in the north aisle, lofty vaults, and the tomb of William of Rožmberk.

Nearby along Horní street is the

Passage to 5th courtyard

Picture Gallery

Hall of Masks

Cloak Bridge

Chinese Salon

Bedroom

Baldaquin Salon

Great Dining Hall

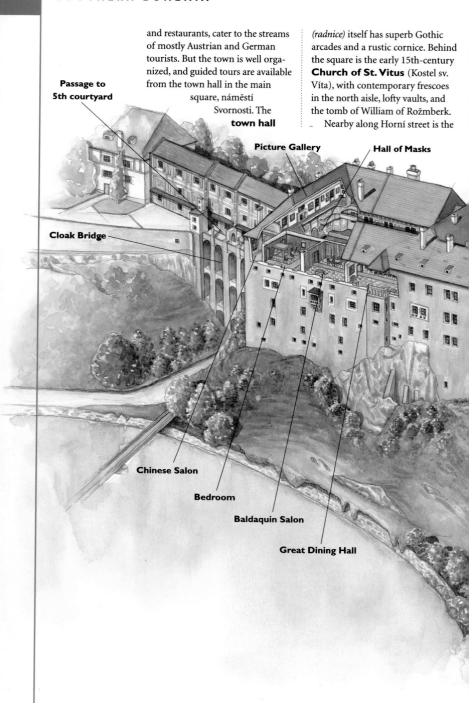

Jesuit College of 1588 (now partly converted into a luxury hotel), with its beautifully sgrafittoed and painted eaves. The Austrian expressionist painter Egon Schiele (1890–1918) came to live in Český Krumlov in 1911, scandalizing the citizenry with his nude models. In the 1990s a former medieval brewery on Široká was converted into a **gallery** with a permanent exhibition of his work, mostly watercolors and drawings. It is a more stimulating place to

visit than the **Regional Museum** (Okresní muzeum) on Horní, whose displays relate to the town's history, weaponry, and furniture. Back on náměstí Svornosti, the main square, is a **Museum of Torture** *($$)*, a sad indication of the village's decline into commercialism.

In summer the town becomes even more crowded than usual during several festivals. The Five-Petaled Rose Festival in June is a two-day jamboree with medieval parades, fireworks, and street fairs. Also held are a chamber music festival in early summer, an ancient music festival in July, and a jazz festival in August. ■

Egon Schiele gallery
- ✉ Široká 70
- 💲 $$

Regional Museum
- ✉ Horní 152
- ☎ 380 711 674
- 🕐 Closed Mon. Oct.–April
- 💲 $

Courtyard

Bear Moat

Castle Tower

St. George's Chapel

České Budějovice

České Budějovice

🗺 154 C2

✉ 88 miles (147 km)
S of Prague via
E65 then S on 3

🚆 Train from Prague

Visitor information

✉ náměstí Přemysla
Otakara II 12,
37001 CB
e-mail infocb@
c-budejovice.cz

☎ 386 359 480

Black Tower

🕐 Closed Mon. &
Nov.–March

💲 $

Museum of South Bohemia

✉ Dukelská 1

🕐 Closed Mon.

💲 $

ČESKÉ BUDĚJOVICE, REGIONAL CAPITAL OF SOUTHERN Bohemia, is located at the point where the Rivers Malše and Vltava meet. Beer lovers around the world are familiar with the town's German name, Budweis. This is the home of Budvar, or Budweiser, and you can sample the mild golden brew in countless beer halls.

Close to the Austrian border, České Budějovice has a distinct air of prosperity. The town originally acquired its wealth from the salt trade and later from silver mining. Přemysl Otakar II gave it its charter in 1265. Although always a staunchly Catholic town, České Budějovice was spared attack during the Hussite wars. It also benefited from Habsburg patronage after the Thirty Years War. A devastating fire in 1641 destroyed much of the town, and decades went by before it regained the level of prosperity it enjoyed in the 16th century. In 1832 the first horse-drawn railway in Europe linked the town with Linz in Austria.

Rivers and canals encircle the city, and in the middle of its medieval grid plan is the immense main square, **náměstí Přemysla Otakara II,** the largest in the Czech Republic. The arcaded square as a whole is a great urban ensemble rather than a collection of buildings of individual quality, and many of its buildings date from the 18th and 19th centuries. Josef Dietrich's grandiose balustraded Samson fountain of 1727 gushes like a geyser in the center of the square. The fine **town hall** (radnice), with its baroque steeples, was rebuilt by Antonio Martinelli in 1730. In the opposite corner of the square stands the imposing 16th-century **Black Tower** (Cerná věž), which rises 235 feet (72 m) and can be climbed by anyone with sufficient stamina to reveal a bird's-eye view over the town. In clear weather you can see Třeboň,

12 miles (19 km) to the east. The tower adjoins the cathedral, which was rebuilt in the baroque style in the 1640s and subsequently over-restored. As a result the interior is somewhat lacking in atmosphere.

Krajinská leads to the former 16th-century butchers' stalls (Masné krámy) on the left, long ago converted into a beer hall and the ideal

place to sample Budvar. From this corner of the square, Piaristická goes to the medieval Dominican monastery, unimaginatively made over in baroque. Next to the church the gabled **salt store** (*solnice*) of 1513 is a rare example of a Renaissance warehouse.

From the town hall, Biskupská takes you past the peach-and-white former bishop's palace in the direction of the River Malše, where some of the medieval fortifications survive, including the prison tower. The **Museum of South Bohemia** (Jihočeské muzeum), close to the river, has extensive historical and natural history collections as well as paintings and special exhibitions.

The **Budvar Brewery,** just north of the city center off the road to Prague, has been modernized. For beer aficionados the one-hour tour is essential (*tel 038 770 5340, $$, book in advance*). The tour explains why traditional Czech beer—Budweiser—has nothing in common with the American Budweiser. Attempts by the powerful American company to take over the Czech original have, up until now, been successfully resisted. Those who find they learn more than they bargained for can console themselves afterward in the brewery's own beer hall and restaurant. ■

No town square in the republic can match that of České Budějovice when it comes to sheer size.

Land of castles drive

Castles in all shapes and sizes scatter across southern Bohemia: strongholds guarding small towns; fortresses buried in the countryside watching over crucial trade routes; rural aristocratic retreats. Follow this drive to some of the most interesting and beautiful examples.

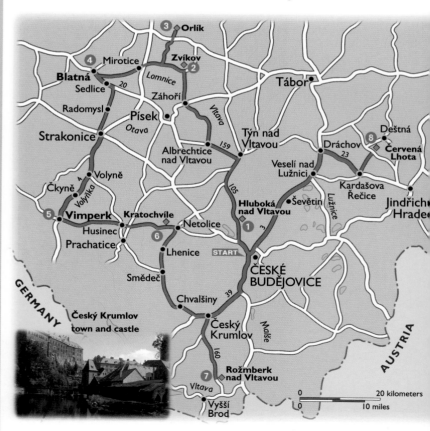

See area map p. 154
► České Budějovice
◄► 233 miles (375 km)
⊕ 2–3 days
► Červená Lhota

NOT TO BE MISSED
- Hluboká nad Vltavou
- Zvíkov
- Rožmberk nad Vltavou
- Červená Lhota

Five miles (8 km) north of České Budějovice on route 105 you come to one of southern Bohemia's most popular attractions: the lofty castle of **Hluboká nad Vltavou** ❶. Standing on a broad crag above the River Vltava, it is one of the Schwarzenberg family's neo-Gothic fantasies *(closed Nov.–March, $$$)*. Originally a medieval royal fortress, it was acquired by the family in 1662, and two centuries later, having decided that Hluboká should be their principal Bohemian residence, they spent a fortune revamping the castle. The Schwarzenbergs also laid out its handsome

The Schwarzenberg family transformed a medieval fortress at Hluboká nad Vltavou into a neo-Gothic castle, using what they imagined to be a Victorian style.

park, which is open even when the castle itself is closed. This building is an enjoyable architectural romp, packed with crenellated towers and fearsome defenses to protect the family against no one. The interior has exceptional woodwork and is sumptuously furnished, containing an armory, a library, tapestries, and a collection of Bohemian paintings. Equally worthwhile is the art collection, in the former riding school (*jízdárna; closed Mon.*), culled from municipal collections throughout southern Bohemia. It ranges from medieval Bohemian panels to 20th-century Czech paintings. There are two guided tours of the castle: One is comprehensive; the other, shorter and less interesting, focuses on the armory.

From here continue north for 15 miles (24 km) on route 105 to Týn nad Vltavou, then bear left toward Písek. At Albrechtice nad Vltavou head north on minor roads to **Zvíkov ②,** a remote castle spread across a wooded promontory overlooking the green waters of the Rivers Vltava and Otava (*closed Mon. May–Sept., Mon.–Fri. April & Oct., & all Nov.–March, $*). Built in the 13th century by the Přemysl rulers, Zvíkov became first a property of the Rožmberks, a powerful feudal family and, in the 17th century, another Schwarzenberg possession. Fortunately the

Schwarzenbergs resisted the temptation to improve this medieval and Renaissance structure, but after the castle was badly damaged during the Thirty Years War, it had to be partly rebuilt. Zvíkov retains a formidable 13th-century round tower, Gothic cloisters, and lovely though heavily restored frescoes from about 1500 in the chapel and bridal chamber.

Head northward up the road that follows the Vltava until you soon come to **Orlík ③,** owned by the ubiquitous Schwarzenbergs since 1719 and reclaimed by the family in 1992, following confiscation by the Communists in the 1940s. The castle (*closed Mon. April–May & Sept.–Oct., & Nov.–March, $–$$$*) was founded in the 13th century and largely rebuilt in the second half of the 19th century as a somewhat preposterous neo-Gothic fantasy. The interior is furnished in an Empire style, with much weaponry and porcelain, as well as displays chronicling the history of the owners. The castle has a lovely setting beside a reservoir. It must have been even more impressive before the river was dammed in the 1950s, when the castle soared high above the flowing waters.

Return south the way you came, then go west through Mirotice to **Blatná ④,** a small town best known for cultivating roses. Its splendid moated castle (*closed Mon. mid-*

May–mid-Sept., Mon.–Fri. April–mid-May & mid-Sept.–Oct., & all Nov.–March, $), along the road to Plzeň, is entered beneath a large machicolated gate tower. The Gothic chapel, with its delicate oriel window, is all that survives from the original 13th-century structure. The Renaissance wing, designed by Benedikt Ried in the 1520s, has curious tiers of windows set at an angle to the main arrowheads. You can visit the interior on a lengthy guided tour; the most bizarre highlight is a set of furniture made from antlers.

From Blatná take the road south to Strakonice, and continue on route 4 to **Vimperk ⑤,** on the edge of the Šumava mountains. The village cowers beneath a crag on which the castle perches *(closed Mon. & all Nov.–April);* it can be reached by a steep path from the main square. Originally built by

The exquisite castle of Červená Lhota seems to float on the surface of a small lake.

Encircled by a large moat, Blatná castle enjoys an idyllic location.

Přemysl Otakar II in the 13th century, the castle was restyled over time by the Schwarzenbergs. The view is terrific; the interior, now the local museum, has a collection of glass objects.

Go east toward České Budějovice for 22 miles (36 km) to the charming Renaissance château of **Kratochvíle** ❻ *(closed Mon. May–Sept., Mon.–Fri. April & Oct., & all Nov.–March, $–$$$)*. Designed and built by Italian architects in the 1580s, it is perfectly symmetrical and neatly surrounded by walls, pavilions, and formal gardens. Founded as a hunting lodge by the Rožmberk family, it is now a museum dedicated to film animation.

Instead of continuing toward České Budějovice, head south to Český Krumlov and keep going to **Rožmberk nad Vltavou** ❼, a village and castle *(closed Mon. May–Sept., Mon.–Fri. April & Oct., & Nov.–March, $–$$)*

named for the Rožmberks. The sgraffitoed building, which overlooks the winding River Vltava, is more like a succession of fortresses built along a ridge. Inside, the finest room is the banqueting hall, covered in 16th-century Italianate frescoes.

Return to Český Krumlov and take route 39 northeast to České Budějovice. Leave the town on route 3 in the direction of Tábor. At Dráchov turn right toward Jindřichův Hradec; then turn north at Kardašova Řečice toward Deštná and watch for signs to **Červená Lhota** ❽. It's a long drive but worth it, as this château *(closed Mon. May–Sept., Mon.–Fri. April & Oct., & all Nov.–March, $–$$)*, buried in remote wooded countryside, is the most exquisite of them all. The rust-red 16th-century building—a manor house that replaced a castle on this site—sits on an islet reached by a cobbled causeway. Seen after some of the more pompous châteaus of Bohemia, this aristocratic retreat is a real gem. ■

Třeboňsko region

SINCE THE 14TH CENTURY, CZECHS HAVE CAPITALIZED ON
the swampy, peat-mossy Třeboňsko region by building fishponds
to raise carp, popular especially during the Christmas holiday.
Much of the area is now a nature reserve, as the bogs and other
wetlands support a precious variety of wildlife—notably the white-
tailed eagle.

The powerful Rožmberk family
turned carp farming into an industry in the 16th century. It was a
complex undertaking, as a system
of canals had to be devised to link
the numerous ponds and lakes and
assist with their drainage. The
Rožmberks constructed these con-
duits, hiring the best engineers of
the time. Their successors at
Třeboň, the Schwarzenbergs, continued to manage this important

resource, which at one time con-
tained 6,000 ponds.

The town of Třeboň is walled,
and it still retains some of its original gateways, which remain the sole
access to its center. Close to the
16th-century Svinenská Gate is the
Regent Brewery, functioning
here since the town was founded by
the Rožmberk family. The last of
the line, Petr Vok, died here in
1611, after a lifetime of intellectual

and hedonistic activity, notably the pursuit of alchemy, then wildly fashionable in Bohemia.

The **castle** dominates the little town. It was built by the Rožmberks soon after Třeboň was founded in the 1370s. In 1660, some years after Petr Vok's death, the castle became the property of the Schwarzenbergs, a Bavarian family that soon got into the habit of acquiring properties from extinct aristocratic Bohemian families. Before long they were the largest landowners in the country, and remained so until their expulsion in 1945.

The sprawling Renaissance castle buildings, with their monotonous expanses of sgraffitoed wall, seem to occupy much of the old town. There's even room within the courtyard for a pizzeria. Approaching from the main square, you pass through elaborate Renaissance portals into tranquil courtyards. The castle itself can be visited only by guided tour. There are three to choose from: The first visits the Renaissance interiors; the second views the private apartments of the Schwarzenbergs, furnished in the 19th century; and the third combines the two. Afterward it's pleasant to stroll in the English-style park.

From the castle, walk the short distance to the elongated **main square.** The arcaded Renaissance and baroque houses look onto a crisply carved Marian column (1780) and a fountain (1569). The town hall's sturdy 17th-century galleried tower can be climbed in summer. The houses are ornamented with a variety of gables, notably the crenellated ones of the 1544 house called the White Pony (Bílý koníček), now a hotel. One block from the square, on Husova, is the 14th-century **Church of St. Giles** (Kostel sv. Jiljí). Frescoes

from the 15th century survive in the elegant church interior.

Třeboň lies beside tree-fringed Lake Svět, and the spa buildings, where you can take a course of therapeutic mud baths, are set back from the shore. Across the lake, a 20-minute walk from the town, is the park called **U Hrobky,** where the Schwarzenbergs built their **mausoleum** in 1877. It's a thrusting neo-Gothic fantasy more appropriate to a Scottish estate than the Bohemian countryside. A guided tour takes you into the burial crypt.

An impressive network of well-marked trails allows you to explore the Třeboňsko, linking some of the bigger ponds situated north of Třeboň. The largest of these is close by: the aptly named Lake Rožmberk, created in the 1580s. Another trail traverses the peat bogs from Červené blato, 10 miles (15 km) to the south of town. The region is in effect an extended nature reserve and a popular destination for bird-watchers. ∎

Castle

🕐 Closed Mon. April–Oct., & all Nov.–March

💲 $–$$$

Schwarzenberg Mausoleum

🕐 Closed Mon. April–Oct., & all Nov.–March

💲 $

A detail from a precious medieval altar-cloth originally displayed at Třeboň, now in the Prague National Gallery

The castle at Jindřichův Hradec is a showcase anthology of Bohemian architectural styles.

Jindřichův Hradec

🅼 155 E3

✉ 80 miles (128 km) SE of Prague via E65, then S on route 3

🚆 Train from Prague, change at Veselí

Visitor information

✉ Panská 136, 33701 e-mail info@jh.cz

☎ 384 363 546

Jindřichův Hradec

EAST OF ČESKÉ BUDĚJOVICE, CLOSE TO THE MORAVIAN border, lies the little-visited town of Jindřichův Hradec. In medieval times the Rožmberk family were Lords of Hradec, one of two families who dominated southern Bohemia, and parts of Moravia. They built the first stronghold here in the early 13th century, and it was added to over the centuries. In the Middle Ages the town, situated on a major trading route, became prosperous, but over the years it gradually lost its eminence and is today a small textile-producing center.

By the time the last member of the Rožmberk family died in 1611, the **castle,** set above Lake Vajgar, had become a hodgepodge of architectural styles. There's a stone-built round keep from the 13th century, an assorted range of Renaissance buildings, and several tiered, arcaded courtyards. A legend tells that it is roamed by the White Lady, the ghost of Berta of Rožmberk, an unhappy chatelaine of the 15th century. She was forced into a loveless marriage but when bidding farewell to the man she loved, Count Šternberk, the couple were caught by her husband and she suffered years of mistreatment thereafter.

Although much of the castle exterior is unappealing, the recently

restored interior is a marvel. To see it all, you are obliged to take three separate 50-minute guided tours: Tour A covers the baroque rooms, Tour B takes in the medieval sections, and Tour C follows the Renaissance portions.

Perhaps the most arresting structure within the castle is the pink-and-white garden "Rondel," or rotunda, with its porthole windows and lovely gilt stucco decoration (the highlight of Tour C). It was designed, like much of the castle, by Italian architects. Baldassare Maggi was the most important, and he worked for the Rožmberks beginning in 1575. The most striking rooms are the austere Gothic chapel and the ceremonial hall, with 14th-century frescoes narrating the life of St. George (Tour B).

With its maze of cobbled lanes and sober but attractive houses, this is an interesting town to explore on foot. Follow the lane that leads from the castle to the main square, **náměstí Míru,** where an 18th-century Marian column tapers up to a resplendent sunburst. Attractive stuccoed merchants' houses and the town hall surround the square, and there are two fine Gothic churches. The **Church of St. John the Baptist** (Kostel sv. Jana Krtitele), unfortunately, is closed to the public. Behind the town hall, the **Church of the Assumption of Our Lady** (Kostel Nanebevzetí Panny Marie) has some uninspiring 17th-century frescoes.

The **District Museum** is situated on Komenského in the former 17th-century Jesuit seminary. A big draw is the mechanical nativity scene, peopled with over a thousand figurines fashioned by Tomáš Krýza (1838–1918), after half a century of toil. It is said to be the largest such scene in the world. Another room is devoted to the composer Bedrich Smetana, who lived near the castle from 1831 to 1835. ∎

The strikingly beautiful garden rotunda within the castle grounds

Castle
- Closed Mon., & all Nov.–March
- Tours: $$–$$$ each; all three $$$–$$$$$

District Museum
- Balbínovo náměstí 19
- Closed Mon. April–May & Oct.; & all Nov.–March
- $

Tábor

Tábor

154 D4

52 miles (84 km)
S of Prague via E65
then route 3

Train and bus from
Prague

Visitor information

Infocentrum, Žižkovo
náměstí 2, 39001
e-mail
infocentrum@
mu.tabor.cz

381 486 230

Hussite Museum

Closed Mon.
Sept.–May

Museum: $
Catacombs: $

Bechyně Gate

Closed Nov.–April

Museum: $. Tower: $

AN EXTREME WING OF THE HUSSITES FOUNDED TABOR IN 1420 in their quest to establish a stronghold in southern Bohemia near where religious reformer Jan Hus had retired six years earlier. They named the settlement after Mount Tabor in Palestine, a name that in turn became associated with this group of radical religious and social reformers—henceforth known as the Taborites (see pp. 172–173). Proclaiming the equality of all peoples, and holding all possessions in common, the Taborites in essence created an early form of commune.

The river flows below the town, while to the west is Lake Jordán, Bohemia's oldest artificial lake, created in 1492 by damming a river. The old city is a remarkably compact maze of narrow streets, hemmed in by the fortifications, some of which survive. Of the medieval castle that stood here before the Hussites arrived, only the round Kotnov tower survives.

The town's splendid main square, **Žižkovo náměstí,** is named after the Hussite general Jan Žižka, whose statue stands here. A Renaissance fountain of 1567 sits in the center of the square. The proudly gabled old town hall, originally built in 1440 but since rebuilt in an essentially Renaissance style, now contains a splendid vaulted council chamber of 1515 and the **Hussite Museum** (Husitské muzeum). Its most intriguing exhibit is a cart fortified by Žižka with cannon, a formidable weapon in its day.

Radiating out from beneath the town hall, a series of tunnels burrows for some 9 miles (14 km). Initially said to be for the purpose of storing beer kegs, they were probably intended as a place of shelter, both from hostile attack and from the fires that frequently roared through the cramped town. A half-mile (0.8 km) stretch of these catacombs can be visited (tours leave from the museum).

On the north side of the main square is the **Church of the Transfiguration** (Kostel Proměnění Páně), built in a late Gothic style in the second half of the 15th century, although the generous gables are clearly Renaissance additions. The rib-vaulted interior is a curious blend of baroque and neo-Gothic. Its very tall **tower** can usually be climbed for a fine view of the town ($). A lane next to the church, Svatošova, leads to the Augustinian priory, with its curvaceous baroque facade. Also leading into the square is the main shopping street **Prazská,** which has more attractive Renaissance houses than the square itself; some of the sgraffito decoration remains in good condition.

From the town hall, Mariánská and then Klokotská lead from the main square to the remains of the medieval **Kotnov Castle** (hrad Kotnov), a section of which, since 1611, has been used as a brewery. Next to the castle is the 15th-century **Bechyně Gate** (Bechyňská brána). The gateway is now a small well-organized museum about medieval society. Exhibits include weapons, armor, and farming implements. It gives access to the castle tower, which can be climbed for views over the town. Half a mile (1 km) west of the old town you'll find the baroque church of Klokoty with its onion domes. ■

Opposite: The River Lužnice glides far below the old town of Tábor, once a Hussite stronghold.

Jan Hus & the Hussites

Jan Hus, the Czech people's first national hero, was born about 1370 in Husinec in southern Bohemia. He studied at Prague University and was influenced by the radical social and theological doctrines of the Oxford theologian John Wycliffe (ca 1330–1384). In 1400 Hus joined the priesthood and, in 1402, he was appointed professor of philosophy at Prague University.

A 16th-century portrayal of the death at the stake of Jan Hus in 1415

The central tenet of Hussitism was the need to take communion *sub utraque specie* (in both kinds), when the congregation would be given both bread and wine, unlike the Catholic practice of the time of giving wine only to the clergy. King Václav allowed Hussite opponents to return to their parishes in 1419, but rioting broke out and ended in the First Defenestration (see p. 24). A few weeks later the pope initiated a crusade against the Hussites.

Adapting Wycliffe's ideas and preaching in Czech rather than in Latin, Hus gave a reformist and nationalist message to the congregations who came to hear him at Prague's Bethlehem Chapel (Betlémská kaple). He opposed indulgences, the self-enrichment of the clergy, and other abuses of church power, and he attacked the often miserable conditions in which the peasantry were compelled to live.

Hus's espousal of the Czech language and literature proved divisive. German-speaking teachers and students, who formed the majority at the university, left Prague to found a new university in Leipzig in 1409. Church authorities soon lost patience with him, and in 1410 he was excommunicated and forbidden to preach. Initially he enjoyed the support of King Václav IV, but by 1413 his condemnation of the sale of indulgences to fund papal wars alarmed the king, who benefited financially from the practice. Hus prudently took refuge in southern Bohemia; here he wrote theological works and spread his ideas throughout the countryside. He was arrested on the way to the Council of Constance under a safe-conduct assurance, and was subsequently burned at the stake on July 6, 1415.

Some of the doctrines most closely associated with Hus were spread only after his death.

The Hussite movement was not a united force. The more moderate supporters were known as Utraquists; they were essentially religious reformers, whereas the radical Taborites linked religious reform with social reform, favoring the abolition of class differences. The Taborites leveled violent attacks against Catholic property and clergy alike, as well as the powerful German merchant classes. At first they enjoyed remarkable success. Under their charismatic leader, Jan Žižka, the Taborites had huge support from the impoverished peasantry of Bohemia and Moravia. The Taborites easily defeated Catholic forces. In 1433 the Vatican agreed with the Utraquists at the Council of Basel to permit communion "in both kinds," but this alone was not acceptable to the Taborites. They fought on, but they could not withstand the combined forces of the Utraquists and the Catholics, and were finally defeated at the Battle of Lipany in 1434.

The modern Hussite Church, formed in 1920, advocates the ordination of women and the right of priests to marry. ■

Right: No one is sure whether this 16th-century portrait is a true likeness of the great reformer.

Šumava

THE GENTLE ROLLING ŠUMAVA MOUNTAINS UNFURL along the border with Austria and Germany, becoming more rugged and sparsely inhabited as you move northwest along the ridges. At the southern end of the range a resort area has been created along the northern shores of Lake Lipno, a narrow reservoir some 25 miles (40 km) in length. The developments are low-keyed, appealing to families in search of a tranquil and inexpensive holiday, while behind the villages the low forested hills offer a peaceful landscape ideal for undemanding hiking.

A few hotels are located at **Loučovice,** not far from Vyšší Brod (see p. 178). If touring rather than boating is your aim, then the best place to stay is **Prachatice,** a former hilltop salt-trading post and a highlight of the Šumava region. Although of medieval origin, with some surviving fortifications, most of the compact little town was rebuilt under the Rožmberk family in the 16th century; the beautifully vaulted Gothic **Church of St. James** (Kostel sv. Jakuba) has been retained. Many of the houses on the main square and the narrow streets of the old town are sgraffitoed, both with geometrical decoration and vivid battle scenes. The town is at its liveliest in mid-June, when a medieval festival, the Gold Trail, with parades, fireworks, and sports contests, takes place.

For a lakeside stay, **Frymburk** is ideal, situated at the end of a peninsula jutting into the lake. From the jetty a ferry links the town to the southern shore, which used to be off-limits as a military zone. The village of **Černá v Pošumaví** is more spread out, with many pensions, holiday cottages, and campsites. The lake's main resort, **Horní Planá,** was the birthplace of the poet and painter Adalbert Stifter (1805–1868), whose house is now a **museum** containing the artist's memorabilia.

Northwest of here the landscape changes as you enter the Bohemian Forest section of the Šumava. The name Šumava derives from the word *šumět,* which means "to murmur" or "to rustle,"as the rustling of trees was the only sound that disturbed the scattering of people, mostly German foresters, who from medieval times inhabited and traveled across the mountains. Little has changed. Empty roads wind through wooded hills and plateaus with few signs of habitation; the large German-speaking proportion of the population was expelled after World War II.

Volary is one of the most convenient towns for exploring the region. Although not exceptional, it retains a handful of

Above: A lonely scene near Kristanov in the Šumava mountains Above left: An environmentalist protest against tree clearances in the Šumava

alpine-style houses that survived a fire in the mid-19th century; this was a fashion imported in the 16th century by Tyrolean and Styrian settlers. The town of **Vimperk,** with its castle (see pp. 164–165), is an increasingly popular year-round resort.

The absence of industrialization means there is little of the pollution that afflicts the mountains of northern Bohemia, and since 1991 much of the region has been designated a national park to preserve its unspoiled character. It may be less well developed than other Czech mountain regions, but the Šumava is slowly regaining its popularity with vacationers and hikers, not least because of its proximity to the German border. Although the highest peak has an elevation of only 4,776 feet (1,456 m), the expanses of the Šumava are surprisingly wild and austere, its forested and stony plateaus punctuated by mountain lakes and treacherous peat bogs such as the Modrava moors. With luck, visitors may even spot the occasional lynx or otter.

Today marked trails guide the hiker through the terrain, but in the past secret paths through the bogs were used by smugglers. The slopes of the peak of Boubín (4,468 feet/1,362 m), easily accessible from Volary or Vimperk, are covered with a primeval forest, maintained as a nature reserve since 1858. Glimpses of ruinous hilltop fortresses are a constant reminder that the Šumava was always a natural frontier between the Germanic west and the Slav east. ∎

Šumava

🅜 154 A2, B1, B2

🚌 Bus from Prague to Prachatice. Train from České Budějovice to Volary

Stifter Museum

✉ Palackého 21, Horní Planá

☎ 380 738 473

🕐 Closed Mon. March–June & Sept.–Oct.; Sun. & Mon. Nov.–mid-Dec.

💲 $

More places to visit in southern Bohemia

BECHYNĚ

Bechyně is a small spa town on the edge of a gorge above the Lužnice River. The Rožmberks' castle here is not open to the public, but the town's other medieval stronghold is now used for local history and art exhibitions. The former Franciscan church has a stunning 16th-century vault; however, the monastery has become a school and access is tricky except during Sunday services. The town's former synagogue on Široká houses the **Museum of Firefighting** (Hasičké muzeum; *closed Mon. & Nov.–April, $*).

154 C3 12 miles (22 km) SW of Tábor on route 137, then W at Sudomerice on route 135 Train from Tábor; bus from Tábor and České Budějovice

HUSINEC

North of Prachatice, on the road to Vimperk, is Husinec, the birthplace of Jan Hus. The unpretentious house in which he was born is now the **Hus Museum** (*closed Mon. & Oct.–April, $*). A festival commemorates his life and achievements every July 5 and 6.

154 B2 25 miles (40 km) NW of České Budějovice on route 20, then W at Cesnovice on 145 Bus from Prachatice

KÁMEN

The 17th-century **château** at Kámen squats above the village on top of a large rock outcrop. It houses, of all things, a **Museum of Motorcycling.** Between the wars, Czechoslovakia built impressive

Kámen château is better known for its collection of old motorcycles than for its architecture.

motorbikes, and aficionados should enjoy this large display.

🏔 155 E4 ✉ 15 miles (24 km) E of Tábor on route 19 🚌 Bus from Pelhřimov and Tábor Museum 🕐 Closed Mon. May–Sept.; Mon.–Fri. April & Oct.; & Nov.–March 💲 $

PELHŘIMOV

The old walled town of Pelhřimov has two surviving gateways, a Gothic church, and gabled Renaissance and baroque houses in its cobbled main square. The **town museum** *(closed Mon., $)* is also here; its most interesting feature is the frescoed music room. Pelhřimov comes to life in June for a beer festival, which coincides with Czechs attempting to set new records of bizarre feats. A special museum, the **Muzeum rekordů a kuriozit** *(closed Mon. June–Aug., & all Sept.–May, $),* located in the Jihlava Gate (Jihlavská brána), features, among other things, a wooden bicycle, a large painting made from pasta, and the world's longest paper chain.

🏔 155 E4 ✉ 22 miles (39 km) E of Tábor on route 19 🚌 Bus from Prague and Brno

The stone bridge at Písek, built in the mid-13th century, is the oldest such structure in the republic.

PÍSEK

Písek straddles the River Otava, which deposited the gold-bearing sand that brought the town prosperity in the Middle Ages. The town boasts the oldest stone bridge (mid-13th century) in the Czech Republic. The scant remains of the medieval **castle** *(closed Mon., $),* which was burned down in 1510, can be seen within the courtyard of the mustard-colored baroque town hall. The surviving wing of the castle contains the town museum (Prácheňské muzeum) and is worth seeing for the Knights' Hall, frescoed in the 1470s, and some gold exhibits. There are also displays relating to the concentration camp at nearby **Lety,** where a quarter of the Gypsies (Roma; see pp. 288–289) who were sent there in 1942 and 1943 died. Within the main square and the neighboring streets are fine Renaissance houses, the delightful **Church of the Holy Cross** (Kostel Povýšení sv. Kříže), and the Gothic **Church of the Birth of the Virgin Mary** (Kostel Narození Panny Marie).

🏔 154 C3 ✉ 28 miles (46 km) W of Tábor via route 19 🚌 Train and bus from Prague; train from České Budějovice **Visitor information** ✉ Heydukova 97; e-mail icpisek@pi.bohem-net.cz ☎ 382 213 592 🕐 Closed Sat.–Sun. Sept.–June

SLAVONICE

Close to the border with Moravia and Austria, Slavonice, founded in the 13th century, prospered because of its proximity to Vienna. After the Thirty Years War in the 17th century that renown faded, but the architectural glories remain. Slavonice is now a UNESCO historic site thanks to its numerous Renaissance houses, many of them sgraffitoed, grouped around two squares, **náměstí Míru** and **Horní náměstí**. The Gothic **church,** with its lofty bell tower of 1549, is especially worth seeing. 155 F2 20 miles (32 km) SE of Jindřichův Hradec. E on route 164, then 151, right on 409 Bus from Prague via Dačice

STRAKONICE

The inhabitants of Strakonice are an enterprising people, as this little town manages to produce fezzes, motorcycles, and even a local version of bagpipes, known as *dudy.* It is the venue for an annual bagpipe festival.

Near the town center is an eclectic **castle,**

A UNESCO historic site, Slavonice is now one of Bohemia's best preserved towns.

the headquarters of the powerful chivalric order of Knights Hospitaller of St. John until 1694. The outer windows of the castle make its 13th-century origins clear, although the overall aspect is Renaissance. Inside the courtyard you can see the elegant Gothic choir of the chapel and the medieval round keep. The castle now houses a museum of bagpipes and

motorbikes. It's a bit ramshackle, but for enthusiasts of either passion it is worth a visit. 154 B3 34 miles (57 km) NW of České Budějovice via route 20 to Vodňany, right on route 22 Train from České Budějovice **Castle** Closed Mon. & Nov.–April $

VYŠŠÍ BROD

South of Český Krumlov in the Vltava Valley is the white Cistercian **monastery** of Vyšší Brod *(closed Mon. & Oct.–April, $–$$),* founded in 1259 by the Rožmberk family. It took a century to complete. Protected by its walled compound, the monastery managed to deter Hussite attacks, but the buildings were damaged in a fire of 1536 and again during the Thirty Years War (1618–1638). The Communists closed the monastery in 1950, but in 1990 the Cistercians returned.

After the demise of the Rožmberk dynasty in 1611, Vyšší Brod came under the patronage of the Schwarzenbergs. The cloisters and 13th-century chapterhouse, its vaults supported on a single central pillar, are impressive. The dark Gothic church itself, despite drastic restoration and alteration, is also worth visiting. But to see the great medieval cycle of paintings by the Master of Vyšší Brod, visit the Convent of St. Agnes (Anežský klášter) in Prague (see pp. 106–109). The surviving monastic buildings contain a fabulous 70,000-volume rococo library with fantastical carved bookcases, painted ceiling, and a **postal museum** *(closed Nov.–March, $).* 154 C1 19 miles (31 km) S of Český Krumlov on route 160, then W on 163 Bus from Český Krumlov

ZLATÁ KORUNA

The walled Cistercian monastery of Zlatá Koruna was founded in 1263 by Přemysl Otakar II. Badly damaged during the Hussite wars, it was later restored. The 13th-century **chapterhouse** is impressively vaulted, and the Gothic **church** is very fine, despite baroque additions. The library is a much later addition, dating from the 1770s, and contains an unmissable confection of gilt and stucco. 154 C2 4 miles (6.5 km) NE of Český Krumlov via route 39 Bus from Český Krumlov Closed Mon. & Nov.–March Guided tour: $$ ■

Western Bohemia is home to the republic's famous and fashionable spas, most notably Karlovy Vary. Plzeň is another major draw, especially for fans of Bohemia's renowned beers.

Western Bohemia

A Klatovy shop sign

Western Bohemia

SINCE WESTERN BOHEMIA BORDERS GERMANY, IT IS HARDLY SURPRISING that the German influence on the region has always been strong. Even today, over half a century since the German population was expelled after its enthusiastic embrace of Hitler's Third Reich (see pp. 33–34), the famous spa towns of western Bohemia are still better known under their old German names of Karlsbad (Karlovy Vary) and Marienbad (Mariánské Lázně).

Germans and Bohemians lived side by side for centuries, not always in harmony, but these days the German half of this old equation is missing, leaving the region as a whole somewhat depleted. Now that the borders are no longer an obstacle, German tourists are returning to the spa towns, which are reverting to their former glory. Karlovy Vary has become a highly commercialized tourist center, though its grandeur and charm remain unimpaired. And the regional capital of Plzeň has certainly retained its importance, since it is the home of major industries like engineering and brewing. Laid out on a grand scale, Plzeň is one of the noblest towns in Bohemia and well worth visiting.

A less welcome feature of the easing of travel restrictions between Germany and former Eastern Europe is the burgeoning of prostitution close to the borders. The proliferation of streetwalkers in towns such as Cheb and along the main highways has brought with it drug dealers and petty criminals. None of this should put you off, though, as such problems rarely impinge on tourists.

The old town center of Cheb is a delightful relic of German Bohemia, although it has become somewhat run-down. The Chodsko region is one of the few that has retained its folkloric traditions, best seen in the town of Domažlice. Western Bohemia doesn't have as many castles and monasteries as other parts of the Czech Republic, but places such as the Teplá monastery are of great interest, and there are quite a few charming old towns, such as Loket and Klatovy. ■

Left: The opulent
design of the main
spa buildings at
Mariánské Lázně
reveals its high
status in history.

Plzeň

Plzeň

⬛ 181 C3

✉ 55 miles (88 km)
SW of Prague on
E50

Visitor information

✉ náměstí Republiky
41, 30116
e-mail infocenter@
mmp.plzen-city.cz

☎ 378 032 750

Brewery Museum

✉ Veleslavínova 6

☎ 377 235 574
(for tours)

$ $$

TO MOST PEOPLE, PLZEŇ, AT LEAST IN ITS GERMAN FORM of Pilsen, means beer. And rightly so. Pilsner Urquell, for many beer lovers, epitomizes lager-style beer. Some of the visitors who flock to Bohemia's second largest city do so to visit its churches and monuments, but it would be safe to say that the majority head straight for the brewery, a short distance from the city center.

You can't miss the famous gateway, the emblem that appears on every label of Plzeňský Prazdroj, to give Urquell its Czech name. The brewery, which was established in 1842, can sometimes be toured, but if a tour is not available, you can console yourself at the Prazdroj restaurant beside the entrance. Northeast of the main square, náměstí Republiky, on Veleslavínova, is a charming old yellow house that is now the excellent **Brewery Museum** (Pivovarské muzeum), with its own beer hall, Na Parkanu.

But there is more to Plzeň than beer (see pp. 184–185). The old town is built on a grand scale and encircled by wide boulevards that isolate it from much of the surrounding industrial city. Founded in 1295 by King Václav II, its location at the confluence of four rivers (Mže, Radbuza, Úhlava, Úslava) helped the city to prosper rapidly, and the original grid plan survives to this day. After a period of decline following the Thirty Years War in the 17th century, Plzeň grew quickly in the 19th century, when both the brewery and the Škoda armaments works were established. This accounts for the high proportion of turn-of-the-20th-century buildings, including ornate apartment houses and the railway station.

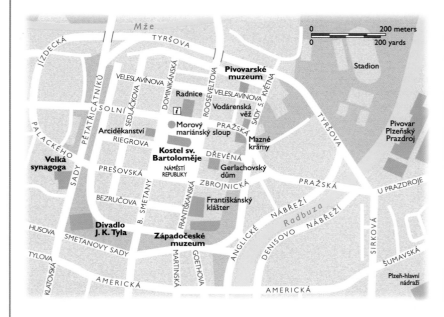

There are more such houses in náměstí Republiky, though they tend to be overshadowed by gabled Renaissance and baroque houses, and, of course, by the lofty **Church of St. Bartholomew** (Kostel sv. Bartoloměje). The bulk of this Gothic sandstone church, placed roughly in the middle of the square, obscures the fact that this is the largest city plaza in Bohemia. You can climb the 335-foot-high (102 m) steeple—the highest in the republic. The other tower was knocked down by lightning in 1525 and never rebuilt. The sober dignity of the church's interior is not enhanced by the lurid stained glass, but there is an exquisite 14th-century Madonna on the high altar.

North of the church is the plague column of 1686, topped by a gilt Madonna, and the dark sgraffitoed Renaissance town hall, with its powerful, gabled, brick upper floors. Just south of the square is the Franciscan friary, which has a lovely Gothic interior despite its baroque facade and trimmings. Behind the friary and facing the boulevards that encircle half the old town stands the **Museum of Western Bohemia** (Západočeské muzeum). Thoroughly restored in 2000, this museum contains, among other exhibits, a comprehensive armory from the 14th century onward. West of the square, down Prešovská, you can visit the huge quasi-Oriental **Great Synagogue** (Velká synagoga); after years of neglect it was restored to use in 1998. One of the largest synagogues in Europe, its Oriental touches inside match the general design. Across the boulevard the neoclassic **Tyl Theater** (Divadlo J. K. Tyla) would not look out of place along Vienna's Ringstrasse. ∎

A dazzling church-top view over part of the main square at Plzeň

Museum of Western Bohemia
- ⊠ Kopeckého sady 2
- 🕐 Closed Mon.
- 💲 $

Great Synagogue
- ⊠ Sady Pětatřicátníků 11
- 🕐 Closed Sat., & mid-Oct.–March
- 💲 $

What's in a name?

Plzeň never patented its name. This proved a grave oversight, since all manner of insipid brews now parade as Pilsner or Pils, just as the bland American Budweiser (fermented partly from rice) has little of the flavor of Bohemian Budweiser or Budvar. Budvar remains the only state-owned brewery, which has protected it from takeover by Western or American rivals. ∎

Pilsner beer

If Bohemia is identified worldwide with one product, then it has to be beer. No village is without its *pivnice*, or pub, in which waiters wade through the crowds dispensing foaming glasses of delicious lager from loaded trays. The Czechs not only make excellent and inexpensive beer, they drink huge quantities of it, too, estimated at about one bottle per day for each member of the population, and that includes babies!

Bohemians are proud of their reputation as champion beer drinkers.

It's not easy to pin down precisely why Bohemian beer has set the standard for the rest of the world, but the crucial element is probably the quality of the hops. These have been grown around Žatec in northern Bohemia since the ninth century; their quality is so outstanding that they are exported worldwide. Since water, as well as hops, is added to the malt before fermentation begins, the quality of the water is important, too. Plzeň's water is especially soft; this quality, combined with the handpicked Žatec "Bohemian Red" hops and sweet top-quality barley, may well account for the rich flavor and texture of the beer brewed in the town.

It's impossible to say when brewing began in Bohemia, but by the 13th century the industry was established in Prague, Plzeň, and České Budějovice, which remain the principal Czech brewing centers. No one knows for certain what medieval beers tasted like, but they were dark and often flavored with herbs and spices.

It was not until the 1840s that a new, cooler method of fermentation—known as bottom fermentation—permitted the production of a stable, translucent, golden lager beer, the style enjoyed today. The Plzeň Brewery was the first to adopt the new method after its foundation in 1842, and

Pilsner Urquell remains the standard-bearer for this popular style of beer: bracing and hoppy in flavor, topped with a thick creamy head.

The strength specified on the label refers to "original gravity" or density rather than alcoholic degree. You are most likely to encounter strengths of 10 degree (about 3.5 percent) and 12 degree (about 4.5 percent). Some special bottled beers are often dark in color (*černé*) and are considerably higher in alcohol. Higher strength beers are undoubtedly fuller, sweeter, and richer, but their power means that they are less well adapted to quenching thirst than their lighter counterparts.

Today there are dozens of breweries in the Czech Republic, and many local brews, rarely encountered outside their production area, can be extremely good. The best of the more celebrated brands include Urquell and Gambrinus from Plzeň, Staropramen and Braník from Prague, the milder Budvar from České Budějovice, Kozel from Velké Popovice, and the exceptionally hoppy Krušovice from Krušovice.

Bohemian beer has always been acclaimed for its purity of flavor, a quality to do not only with the excellent raw materials but also with the absence of chemicals and other additives. Although the beers remain pure, changes that are quite controversial include the growing use of pasteurization of bottled beers, which can diminish the aromas and flatten the flavor, and the injection of carbon dioxide, leading to a thinner, gassier brew.

Drinking beer

In pubs, beer is served in half-liter mugs, but you can always ask for a *malé,* holding a third of a liter. Pubs tend to focus on one or two brands, so do not expect a wide range of products. On the other hand, there is no such thing as poor Bohemian beer. ■

Beer production begins with hop cultivation (below) and ends with a full mug in a pub (above).

Karlovy Vary

Karlovy Vary

181 B5

78 miles (133 km)
W of Prague

Visitor information

Kur-Info, Vřídelní
Colonnade
e-mail kurinfor@
plz.pvtnet.cz

353 224 097

KARLOVY VARY, KARLSBAD, IS THE GRANDEST OF THE Bohemian spas, known for the curative properties of its waters for at least a thousand years. It remains hugely popular with visitors partly because of the grandeur of the spa buildings, and partly because of its dramatic location within a narrow valley. Prettily decorated houses, many in an art nouveau style, line the steep lanes, while the shopping streets close to the springs are always thronged with visitors. The spa was popularized during the reign of Charles IV and continued to enjoy royal patronage. Peter the Great visited at least twice (in 1711 and 1712). Earlier visitors came here to bathe, though by the late 18th century the fashion changed to drinking the waters.

Very few old buildings survive in Karlovy Vary despite its antiquity. Most of the spa buildings, hotels, sanatoria, and mansions date from its boom years in the late 19th and early 20th centuries. Karlovy Vary follows the twists of the River Teplá just before it joins the Ohře, and the narrowness of the forested valley means that the spa is a very elongated place. Traffic is banned from the main streets and parking lots are provided at various locations.

Many of the buildings in the secession style, the Austrian and Czech version of art nouveau, have undergone sparkling renovation, and new hotels are replacing some of the more staid establishments. Serious cure-seekers stay in the various hotel-sanatoria of the resort.

Several popular festivals add to Karlovy Vary's appeal. The film festival held each July attracts a large number of visitors. Others come in May for the jazz festival, and in the autumn for the Dvořák festival. ■

The story of the spas

Since Roman times, if not earlier, Europeans have recognized that waters from mineral springs can have therapeutic qualities. By the late 18th century certain spas had become not only renowned for their curative properties but also fashionable, particularly with the wealthy.

They are still very popular, especially with Germans and central Europeans. Spa visitors stay in a hotel-like sanatorium and follow a medically prescribed program of treatments for some weeks, which could include mud baths and pool treatments as well as the imbibing of mineral waters. Different spas claim to have waters and treatments to ameliorate specific ailments.

Other visitors come to spas for the towns themselves, because they are beautifully located and have many good hotels and restaurants. ■

Above: The swimming pool is the most popular feature of the Thermal Sanatorium in the town center. Left: The spa buildings and hotels of Karlovy Vary lie along the banks of the River Teplá.

A walk around Karlovy Vary

In a few hours you can traverse the whole of Karlovy Vary. It's a very compact place, hemmed in by the steep hills on either side, and almost all the buildings are within a short distance of the springs strung out along the valley floor.

If you come by train or road from Prague, you will end up in the commercial part of the town, where you must leave your car. Head for the broad pedestrianized T. G. Masaryka, which is close to the railroad station. At the

- ⚐ See area map p. 181
- ▶ T. G. Masaryka street
- ↔ 3 miles (4.5 km)
- ⏱ 3 hours
- ▶ Diana Lookout

NOT TO BE MISSED
- Mlýnská kolonáda
- Vřídlo spring
- Church of St. Mary Magdalene
- Grandhotel Pupp

top of the street is the **Jan Becher muzeum** ❶ (*T. G. Masaryka 57, $$*), dedicated to an herbal digestive tonic that you will either adore or loathe. The tonic was invented by Jan Becher at the end of the 18th century and has been produced commercially since 1807. Continue down T. G. Masaryka to the banks of the Teplá and the Poštovní Bridge, where you can hire a horse-drawn carriage, although it's easy enough to explore the spa on foot. The grand impression made by the turn-of-the-20th-century buildings is marred by the modern Thermal Sanitorium, erected here in the 1970s. Behind it is a large open-air swimming pool.

Natural springs, with their bracing curative waters, are encountered all over the town.

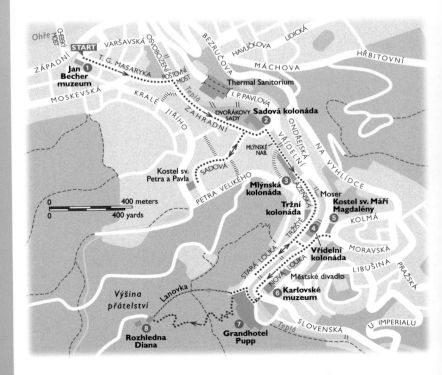

The spa center consists essentially of two streets on either side of the River Teplá, with frequent bridges linking the two sides. Continuing southward you pass the 12 principal springs housed within five colonnades along the river. The first is on the far side of the genteel and flower-filled Dvořák Gardens (Dvořákovy sady), the cream-painted **Sadová kolonáda ❷,** designed by Viennese architects in 1882. The street called Sadová, heading away from the river to the right, climbs to the restored onion-domed Russian Orthodox church (Kostel sv. Petra a Pavla) of 1897. From the colonnade, Mlýnské leads to the splendid 1871 **Mlýnská kolonáda ❸,** the heart of the spa, resembling a Greek marketplace. Four very hot springs bubble beneath its columns. Facing the main portico is a timber-framed building called Petr, where Peter the Great is said to have lodged.

To sample the waters, stop at any of the numerous street stalls and buy a small

The mighty columns of the Mlýnská kolonáda reflect a time when this was the most fashionable spa in Europe.

porcelain beaker shaped like a flattened teapot in order to keep the water from staining your teeth; alternatively, bring your own cup. You can help yourself from any of the warm springs at the various colonnades. Don't smoke anywhere near the springs; the no-smoking police will make a firm approach in your direction.

Immediately after the Mlýnská kolonáda you come to one of the main streets of the spa, Lázeňská, with its secession buildings painted mustard and green, and decorated with ornate ironwork. A major draw for shoppers is the Moser glassware shop at No. 28, a retail outlet for the Moser factory elsewhere in the town. It's clear that many of today's visitors are more interested in spending than curing, and Karlovy Vary is full of shops selling glassware,

A WALK AROUND KARLOVY VARY

Russians used to flock to town in the 19th century, which explains the presence of this flamboyant Russian Orthodox church.

porcelain, jewelry, arts and crafts, and *oplatky* wafers (see p. 196).

Lázeňská bends right past the dainty wooden **Tržní kolonáda** of 1883. Across from it is the principal spring, the **Vřídlo**, housed in the **Vřídelní kolonáda** ❹, which was constructed from glass and marble in 1975. The Vřídlo is the hottest and most vigorous spring in town, surging up with such force that it resembles a geyser.

Continuing south you come to the main shopping street, Stará Louka. Across the Teplá, on a slope overlooking the Vřídelní kolonáda, is the curvaceous blue-gray and white **Church of St. Mary Magdalene** (Kostel sv. Máří Magdalény) ❺, built by Kilián Ignác Dientzenhofer in 1736. Its interior is sensational: a single galleried space beneath a broad dome adorned with richly gilt baroque altars.

On Nová Louka stands the primrose neo-baroque theater (Městské divadlo), where the European premiere of Dvořák's *New World Symphony* was given in 1894; the frescoed interior and curtain were painted by leading secession artists, including Gustav Klimt.

At the end of this stretch of the river is the **Karlovy Vary Museum** (Karlovské muzeum) ❻ *(Nová Louka 23, closed Mon.–Tues., $$),* featuring local ecology and history. At the bend of the river, the **Grandhotel Pupp** ❼ sits among lovely gardens and pine woods; it has a dynamic statue of Beethoven, who patronized the spa. The hotel was founded in the late 18th century, but it has been rebuilt and extended. Today it is a club and casino as well as a luxurious hotel, and it's worth sneaking in to look at the lavish interiors, notably the concert hall.

The hotel is also the starting point for many walking trails. The most popular one leads up to a café and **Diana Lookout** (Rozhledna Diana) ❽, which you can also reach by funicular *(Lanovka).* Especially keen walkers might be tempted by the trail that covers the 10.5-mile (17 km) distance from here to the charming town of Loket, southwest of Karlovy Vary, on the River Ohře (see pp. 201–202). ■

Cheb

Cheb

🅰 181 A4

✉ 107 miles (180 km)
W of Prague

🚆 Train or bus from
Prague, Karlovy Vary,
& Plzeň

Visitor information

✉ Infocentrum, náměstí
Krále Jiřího z
Poděbrad 33
e-mail infocentrum@
cheb-etc.cz

☎ 354 422 705;
fax 354 434 385

MODERN CHEB, KNOWN AS EGER BEFORE WORLD War II, IS an industrial town, but the historic center is well worth exploring. With many half-timbered houses, it looks more like a small German town than a Czech one, which is not surprising, given its history. Cheb is just 3.5 miles (6 km) from the German border. Germans first settled here in the 11th century, and the town quickly became an important trading post between Bavaria and Bohemia. Only in 1322 did it become part of the Czech domains.

Cheb's strategic location meant that it suffered badly during the Thirty Years War, when both sides used it as a base. Industrialization in the 19th century revived the fortunes of the town. Enjoying a good deal of political independence, Cheb, with its German population, fought hard against growing Czech nationalism in the 19th century. Much of the population was also sympathetic to the Nazi cause during World War II, which prompted the government to expel all such sympathizers after the German defeat.

Cheb's arrow-shaped main square (náměstí Krále Jiřího z Poděbrad) is fringed by unusually tall houses, most of them dating from the 17th century and more German than Bohemian in style. Neglected for many years, the square is now lively once again, with many cafés and restaurants. At the top end of the sloping square is the famous **Roland fountain,** and at the bottom is a medieval group of half-timbered houses known as **Špalíček,** once inhabited by Jewish merchants.

The streets across from Špalíček, notably Židovská, occupy the former ghetto; the Jewish community was expelled on many occasions and was exterminated during World War II. The baroque town hall, at the narrow end of the square, now houses a collection of modern Czech art and temporary exhibitions *($)*. Opposite the town hall, Jateční, a lane packed with fine baroque houses, leads to the former Franciscan friary. Here, admire the impressive 14th-century cloister and the 18th-century **Church of St. Clare** (Kostel sv. Kláry), attributed to Kilián Ignác Dientzenhofer.

Opposite Špalíček is a house with ostentatiously steep gables and a fine Gothic doorway, now a gallery. Next door stands the **Gabler House** (Gablerův dům), lavishly decorated with rococo stucco; Goethe used to lodge here. The **Cheb Museum** (Chebské muzeum), also at this end of the square, was where General Albrecht von Wallenstein (Valdštejn) was murdered in 1634 (see p. 27). The museum contains a reconstruction of the room in which the general was assassinated on the order of Ferdinand II. Behind the museum, the **Church of St. Nicholas** (Kostel sv. Mikuláše) is of Romanesque origin but mostly neo-Gothic in style; only the towers of the original structure remain. Nearby is the baroque Dominican church.

Little is left of the town's riverside imperial castle, **Chebský hrad,** apart from its black keep of volcanic stone. The Holy Roman Emperor Frederick Barbarossa had it built in the 12th century as both a stronghold and a royal palace. Climb the keep and enjoy the views, then visit the remarkable two-storied chapel, with Romanesque capitals in the lower story, and more elegant Gothic capitals in the upper. The nearby deconsecrated **Chapel of St. Bartholomew** (Kaple sv. Bartoloměje), with fine vaulting of 1414, displays Gothic statuary. ■

Cheb Museum
- ✉ náměstí Krále Jiřího z Poděbrad 3
- 🕐 Closed Mon.
- $ $–$$

Chebský hrad
- 🕐 Closed Mon. & Nov.–March
- $ $

Tall 17th-century houses edge Cheb's venerable market square.

Spacious parks
and gardens
surround
Mariánské Lázně's
therapeutic
springs.

Mariánské Lázně

MARIÁNSKÉ LÁZNĚ, MARIENBAD, THE MOST CHARMING OF Bohemia's spa towns, is a relative newcomer among spas: It was developed only in the early 19th century by the abbot of the Teplá monastery, some 8 miles (12 km) to the east. Václav Skalník designed the landscaped gardens, and within a few decades this isolated spot in the Bohemian forest was a delightful ensemble of parks and pavilions, grouped around 40 therapeutic springs.

Mariánské Lázně

🅜 181 B4

✉ 117 miles (196 km) W of Prague. SW on E50 past Plzeň, then N on route 21

🚍 Train or bus from Prague, then take trolleybus 4 or 5 to the town center from the station

The spa soon became fashionable, and the great German writer Goethe was a prominent early visitor in the 1820s. Russian writer Nikolai Gogol wrote part of his novel *Dead Souls* while staying here, and Wagner composed *Lohengrin* at Marienbad in 1848. Surpassing these artistic seals of approval was the patronage of royalty, and King Edward VII of England and Emperor Franz Josef of Austria were frequent and celebrated visitors. Today Mariánské Lázně is especially popular with German visitors.

The stately and sometimes pompous buildings have been well restored after decades of gentle decay. The ensemble is better than the individual components, and of all the Czech spas, this is probably the most harmonious and alluring.

The main street, Hlavní, which runs the length of the town, is an almost uninterrupted row of hotels, coffeehouses, and opulent turn-of-the-20th-century apartment houses. Here, too, you'll find the very small **museum** (Dům F. Chopina) dedicated to another famous visitor, Polish composer Frédéric Chopin (1810–1849). He came here in 1836 to pursue the young woman who was to become his fiancée; they never married because of his failing health. During the third week of August, the spa hosts a Chopin festival. All these buildings, many of which have balconies, face onto the spa gardens and to the wooded Slavkov hills in which the town nestles. The buildings are splashy and showy and excessively ornate, yet somehow they retain their dignity.

Behind Hlavní, on Ruská, are the former **Anglican church** (Anglickánský kostelík), now an exhibition hall, and the **Russian Orthodox church** (Kostel sv. Vladimíra) of 1902. It's worth going inside the Russian church to see the lavish iconostasis that is made of porcelain and often claimed to be the largest single piece of porcelain in the world.

Hlavní ends at the Hotel Pacifik, and to the right are the spa buildings, many of which are being over-hauled. The core of the spa, the curving **Kolonáda,** or Colonnade, was built from wrought iron in 1889. Resembling a greenhouse or Victorian railroad station, it is a structure of great charm. People taking the cure at the various springs sheltered by the Kolonáda

Visitor information

✉ Infocentrum, Hlavní 47, 35301

e-mail infocentrum@marianskelazne.cz

☎ 354 622 474

Chopin museum

✉ Hlavní 47

⊕ Closed Mon., Fri., & Sat.

💲 $

More places to visit in western Bohemia

FRANTIŠKOVY LÁZNĚ

The most modest of the major western Bohemian spas, Františkovy Lázně was developed in 1793 and later renamed in honor of the Austrian emperor Franz I. Goethe and Beethoven were among its notable visitors. The town offers acres of gardens and parks but is surrounded by marshes rather than the hills of its better known rivals. Laid out on a strict grid plan, it gives an overall impression that is somewhat prim, and even the Colonnade of 1844 is rigid. With its gardens, outdoor cafés, and neoclassic buildings painted the mustard yellow called *kaisergelb*, it's pleasant enough. In recent years, the immense green-roofed casino has been reconstructed, bringing wealthier visitors from across the German

border and giving the whole spa a new lease on life. The **Glauber Spring** (Glauberův pramen) is the most handsome spa building, but the main source is the **Francis Spring** (Františkův pramen) in a reconstructed rotunda. This is the best place to sample the sulfurous waters. The mud baths here have radioactive qualities believed beneficial in the treatment of cardiac and rheumatic ailments. ⓜ 181 A4 ✉ 4 miles (6 km) NW of Cheb on route 21 **Visitor information** ✉ Četur, Anglická 5 ☎ 354 542 210 🚌 Bus from Prague and Plzeň. Train from Prague, change at Cheb

JÁCHYMOV

Jáchymov is one of Bohemia's more haunting spots. The town was founded in the 16th century when silver deposits were discovered here, and by the 1840s uranium was being mined and used to color glass and crystal. During the 1950s thousands of prisoners, mostly political detainees, were sent to work the mines, with dreadful consequences for their health. The mines were eventually closed in 1960, though at the upper and most shabby part of the town a pithead survives. Amazingly, this scruffy spa still attracts regular visitors who come here to take the treatments at the town's radioactive springs. One of the main centers is called Radium Palace! ⓜ 181 B5 ✉ 10 miles (16 km) N of Karlovy Vary on route 25 🚌 Bus from Prague. Train from Karlovy Vary

KLATOVY

This ancient walled town was founded in 1260 on the edge of the Šumava mountains (see pp. 174–175). In the top corner of its finely proportioned sloping main square, náměstí Míru, is the immense rough-hewn **Black Tower** (Černá věž) of the 1550s with a splendid astronomical clock from 1759. It's pressed up against the 16th-century town hall, which is gabled and decorated with modern sgraffiti in best Bohemian style. From the top of the

The casino, as much as the springs, has become a major draw to visitors at Františkovy Lázně.

Its location above a rocky crag made the 12th-century castle at Loket especially suitable as a prison, from medieval times until as recently as 1947.

tower you look out onto the Šumava mountains. Nearby is Kilián Ignác Dientzenhofer's superb **Jesuit church,** its broad white facade peopled with statuary in niches. The interior, with curvaceous galleries and stucco decoration, contains fine baroque furnishings and remarkable trompe l'oeil frescoes. The ghoulish **crypt** contains some 40 mummified corpses of town worthies exposed in their coffins. They include many Jesuit priests who died between 1676 and 1783. Near the church is a 17th-century pharmacy; since the mid-1960s, this beautifully preserved building, with its neoclassic facade and all the original rococo fittings, has been a **museum.** Take a stroll through the old town to visit what remains of the walls and bastions, passing a Gothic church and the Renaissance **White Tower** (Bílá věž) on the way. Today Klatovy is best

known for its cultivation of carnations after seeds were brought here from France in 1813. 🄰 181 C2 ✉ 25 miles (40 km) S of Plzeň on route 27 🚍 Bus from Prague and Plzeň **Visitor information** ✉ náměstí Míru 63 ☎ 376 313 515 **Black Tower** 🕒 Closed Mon. May–Sept.; Mon.–Fri. April & Oct.; & Nov.–March 🆂 $ **Crypt** 🕒 Closed Mon. April–Sept., & Oct.–March 🆂 $ **Pharmacy Museum** ☎ 376 312 049 🕒 Closed Mon. May–Oct., & Nov.–April 🆂 $$

LOKET

The town of Loket stands on a loop of the River Ohře, beneath a 12th-century royal **castle** that seems to grow vertically from its irregular granite crag. Unlike many medieval castles in Bohemia, the original architectural style is almost intact, with towers, walls, and keeps huddled together. The three-year-old future Charles IV of Bohemia was imprisoned here by his father for some months in the late 1310s to forestall any possible uprising; it became a prison again between 1788 and 1947. The interior is not very interesting, but the watchtower offers attractive views. Much of the town is shabby but slowly being restored to its original charm. Loket, however, has a porcelain factory, and its shops sell fine contemporary examples.

 181 B4 ✉ 9 miles (13 km) SW of Karlovy Vary on route 6 🚌 Bus from Karlovy Vary **Castle** 🕐 Closed Mon. 💲 $$

PLASY

This vast but dilapidated Cistercian monastery was originally constructed in the 12th century but rebuilt by Jean-Baptiste Mathey (1630–1696) and Giovanni Santini (1677–1723). The monastery's finest feature is the sumptuous cloister, with its frescoed side

The huge monastery at Plasy resembles a palace more than a house of prayer.

chapels, which can be visited on a guided tour. The rest of the buildings have been converted into a school and art gallery. In 1826 the recently secularized monastery became the property of the reactionary Austrian chancellor Metternich. The thick heavy structure exudes power rather than spirituality. Metternich had the church in the cemetery

across the main road rebuilt as the family mausoleum in a neoclassic style.

🅰 181 C4 ✉ 16 miles (26 km) N of Plzeň on route 27 🕐 Closed Mon. May–Sept.; Mon.–Fri. April & Oct.; & Nov.–March 💲 $ 🚌 Bus or train from Plzeň

ŠVIHOV

South of Plzeň is the grim castle of Švihov, built in the late 15th century and completed in 1530 by the Rožmberk family as a fortress so formidable that the Habsburgs later demanded its fortifications be demolished. What remains is a somewhat emasculated fortress, an impression enhanced by the presence of sheep in the grassy forecourt and swans on the moat. The hall and Benedikt Ried's Gothic chapel can be visited on a guided tour.

🅰 181 C2 ✉ 18 miles (29 km) S of Plzeň on route 27 🕐 Closed Mon. May–Sept.; Mon.–Fri. April & Oct.; & all Nov.–March 💲 $$ 🚌 Train from Plzeň or Klatovy

TEPLÁ

The once wealthy Premonstratensian abbey of Teplá, founded in the 1190s, is again in the hands of a monastic order, following its closure in 1950 by the Communists. In the 16th century the monks here were the proprietors of Mariánské Lázně and developed the spa in 1808. Following secularization Teplá was used first as a school and then as a barracks, but the returning monks have restored the abbey energetically, adding on a modern restaurant and hotel that blend in well with the mostly 18th-century buildings, designed by the Dientzenhofer family.

The facade of the church retains Romanesque features, but the interior is rich in baroque statuary, with a fine altarpiece. The pride and joy of the abbey is its galleried library: It is the second largest in the Czech Republic, stacked with 80,000 volumes, including many illuminated manuscripts and rare books from the 16th century onward. It was built in the early 20th century, but with all the swagger of neo-rococo opulence.

🅰 181 B4 ✉ 8 miles (12 km) E of Mariánské Lázně. NE on route 230, then SE on route 210 or by signposted back roads 🕐 Closed Mon. & Jan. 💲 $$ 🚌 Train from Karlovy Vary and Mariánské Lázně ∎

Northern Bohemia has lovely old towns such as Litoměřice and Liberec, but it's also a paradise for hikers, who come to explore the "Czech Switzerland" and the Jizerské mountains.

Northern Bohemia

An isolated country shrine

Northern Bohemia

NORTHERN BOHEMIA IS AN ABSORBING CORNER OF THE COUNTRY. ITS cultural identity is German, and towns such as Děčín, Teplice, Liberec, and Ústí nad Labem were predominantly German speaking until 1945, when the Germanic population was expelled and, in some cases, murdered. The cultural vacuum left by their departure has never been filled.

The Czech Republic has always been a rich country, both under the Habsburgs and subsequently as an independent nation. The source of that wealth was heavy industry based on abundant mineral resources. But the drawback to industrialization was pollution, and it is nowhere so apparent as in northern Bohemia. Along the German border you will find a swath of smokestacks and open-cast mines, as well as a pall of toxic chemicals. Entire towns were abandoned or moved to make way for the bulldozers. The pollution has blighted the landscape, damaged the health of both Czechs and Germans, and destroyed much of the surrounding forests. Since 1989 protests from inside and outside the country have become more vocal, and some of the worst excesses have gradually been reduced.

Although much of the countryside is flat farming land, there are hillier stretches near the border and in places such as Klášterec in the Ohře Valley. Indeed, the region called České Švýcarsko (Czech Switzerland) is one of the most charming corners of hill country in the entire republic, and it has long been popular with ramblers.

Along the southern fringes of the region are delightful little towns, including Kadaň, Žatec, Louny, and Litoměřice. The once German-speaking towns of Liberec and Jablonec may be shadows of their former selves, but they still retain some grandeur and civic pride.

Also worthy of a visit, but for very different reasons, is Terezín, a garrison town, fortress, and prison under the Habsburgs. It was later adopted by the Nazi occupiers as the ghetto of Theresienstadt, a staging post for most of its inhabitants on the way to the death camps of Poland. ■

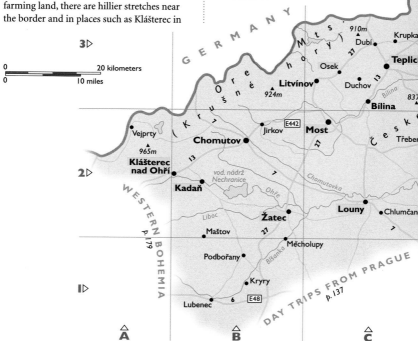

Children and adults alike enjoy the chairlifts within the České Švýcarsko nature reserve.

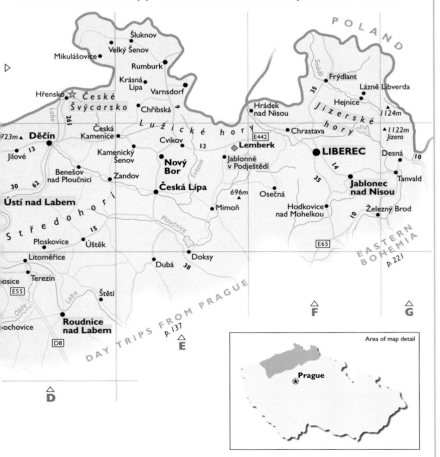

POLAND

Šluknov

Velký Šenov

Mikulášovice

Rumburk

Frýdlant

Lázně Libverda

Krásná
Lípa

Varnsdorf

Smědá

Hejnice

35

Hřensko ☆ Č e s k é
Š v ý c a r s k o

Chřibská

Hrádek
nad Nisou

J i z e r s k é

1124m

Labe

261

L u ž i c k é   h o r y

h o r y

723m▲ **Děčín**

Česká
Kamenice

Cvikov

13

Chrastava

▲1122m
jizera

Jilové

13

Kamenický
Šenov

**Nový
Bor**

Svitava

E442

□ Lemberk

Jablonné
v Podještědí

LIBEREC

Desná

10

Beneŝov
nad Ploučnicí

Zandov

Česká Lípa

14

35

**Jablonec
nad Nisou**

Tanvald

30

62

696m
▲

Osečná

Ústí nad Labem

S t ř e d o h o ř í

15

Ploučnice

Mimoň

Hodkovice
nad Mohelkou

10

Železný Brod

Ploskovice

Úštěk

E65

EASTERN
BOHEMIA

Litoměřice

Doksy

p. 221

osice

Terezín

Dubá

38

△
F

△
G

E55

Labe

Štětí

Ohře

**Roudnice
nad Labem**

D A Y   T R I P S   F R O M   P R A G U E

p. 137

ochovice

D8

△
E

△
D

Area of map detail

⊛ **Prague**

Litoměřice

Litoměřice

🗺 205 D2

✉ 46 miles (74 km) N
of Prague via E55

🚌 Bus from Florenc
bus station in
Prague

Visitor information

✉ Mírové náměstí 15,
41201
e-mail info@
mulitom.cz

☎ 416 732 440

🕐 Closed Sun.
Oct.–April

**North Bohemia
Fine Arts Gallery**

🕐 Closed Mon.

💲 $

THE BEGUILING TOWN OF LITOMĚŘICE LIES IN AN exceptionally fertile agricultural region celebrated for its fruits and flowers. A former Slav fortress founded in the ninth century, it prospered following an influx of German merchants and became one of the richest towns in Bohemia.

That all came to an end when it was wrecked during the Thirty Years War. After the war, Ferdinand III (R.1637–1657) ordered Litoměřice to be rebuilt. The reconstruction was undertaken by local architects, in particular Ottavio Broggio, who was born here in 1668. His stately baroque buildings line the slopes above the River Labe.

The main square, **Mírové náměstí,** has a plague column and fountains that are lost among its vast cobbled expanses. In one corner is Broggio's mostly rebuilt Gothic **Church of All Saints** (Kostel Všech svatých), which incorporates a tower from the medieval fortifications, and extraordinary witch's-hat turrets that line the ridge of the choir. Just down Jezuitská from here is another Broggio design, the **Jesuit church,** with its richly ornamented portal and facade. The **Old Town Hall** (Staroměstské radnice) displays Gothic arcades and a Renaissance main building, topped by a profusion of gables. It

now houses a museum *(closed Mon., $)* of art from nearby churches.

The most conspicuous house on the square is No. 15, **House at the Chalice** (Dům U Kalicha) from 1537, capped by an artichoke-shaped turret representing the Hussite symbol. Close to it, at No. 12, **House at the Black Eagle** (Dům U černého orla), with its chocolate-colored sgraffiti, is now a hotel and restaurant.

At the far end of the square, at Michalská 7, is the **North Bohemia Fine Arts Gallery** (Severočeská galerie vytvarného umení), founded in 1874. The core of the collection is six panels from an altarpiece by the Master of Litoměřice (ca 1500), who worked mostly as a court painter in Prague. His idiosyncratic style depicted heads that were too small and hands that were too large.

North of the square is the over-restored 14th-century **castle,** once a brewery but now a cultural center. At the end of Michalská, turn left. The second street on the right leads to the pink-and-gray **Church of St. Wenceslas** (Kostel sv. Václava) by Broggio. Straight on, you come to náměstí Dómské, the cathedral square. The 11th-century **St. Stephen's Cathedral** (Chrám sv. Štěpána), rebuilt in 1654, contains paintings attributed to Cranach the Elder. ■

**Above: The main square at Litoměřice is a typical Bohemian jumble of architectural styles, spanning five centuries or more.
Right: Ploskovice is home to the exuberant summer palace of the Habsburg Emperor Ferdinand V.**

Summer retreat

Broggio was not only a church architect. At Ploskovice, 4 miles (6 km) northeast of Litoměřice, is a fine country house he built in 1720. In the 1850s Emperor Ferdinand V and his family used this as a summer residence. They commissioned the sparkling neo-rococo interior decoration by Josef Navrátil. A guided tour takes you through the private rooms of the emperor and empress, and a splendid hall decorated with murals by Václav Reiner (1689–1743). This large white mansion, charmingly ornamented and with statues and urns adorning the top balustrades, is set in a walled park. ■

Terezín

Terezín

🅐 205 D2

🚌 Bus from Prague

Ghetto Museum

✉ Komenského, 41155

💲 $$$

A VISIT TO TEREZÍN WILL GIVE YOU DEEP INSIGHT INTO some of World War II's darkest days. The Habsburgs built the town as a fortified garrison and prison in the 1780s, which was dreadful enough. But more atrocious years came with the Nazis, who expelled the residents and converted the place into a ghetto camp. Thousands of Jews from all over Europe were brought here; many died of hunger and disease, many more were shipped to death camps (also see pp. 210–211).

The tranquil main square of Terezín gives no hint of its sobering history.

The town was designed on a formal grid plan surrounded by a double set of immense brick fortifications 2.5 miles long (4 km), linked by underground tunnels, which are still intact. The Small Fortress had long been a state jail for political prisoners. The assassin of Archduke Franz Ferdinand, Gavrilo Princep, was held here until his death in 1918. In June 1940, the German SS took over the Small Fortress. It became a frequent destination for Resistance and political opponents, many of whom were executed here. Tours of the fortress are a vivid reminder of

Nazi criminality, but greater imagination is needed to visualize the streets of the town itself as the vast ghetto it became.

The starting point for any visit should be the **Ghetto Museum** (Muzeum ghetta), founded in 1991 and established in the center of the town on Komenského. It incorporates a memorial to the thousands of children who died here. The drawings made by them are movingly displayed. A video contrasts segments of the Nazi propaganda films that reversed the truth about Terezín, with contemporary drawings portraying the reality of the camp. You can buy a ticket that gives you admission to all the sites, and pick up useful maps that will show you their location.

One of these sites is the **Magdeburg Barracks** (Magdeburská kasárna), a few blocks to the south on Tyršova, in the building where the self-governing council of the ghetto had its offices. Exhibits chronicle the camp's cultural life, and tell of the musicians, artists, and writers who continued to work productively. Other exhibits include a reconstruction of a women's dormitory, and graphic drawings of life within the cramped ghetto. Some of the artists paid to produce them were dispatched to the Small Fortress and executed for having perpetrated "propaganda of horror" with their all too realistic drawings.

The **Small Fortress** (Malá pevnost) stands on the edge of the town on the other side of the River Ohře. Although there had always been a prison here, beginning in 1940 it became a prison operated by the SS. As you approach, you see the large Christian and Jewish cemeteries, with their unmarked gravestones. Within the sprawling fortress, you can visit the cramped cell blocks and solitary confinement cells.

The crematorium, located about half a mile (1 km) south of the main museum, was used to dispose of the bodies of the 2,500 individuals who died or were executed in the fortress and at least 30,000 more who died in the ghetto. Alongside is a Jewish cemetery on the site of mass graves; after the space was full, it became necessary to burn the dead here. ■

A guide shows visitors exhibits culled from the former ghetto and transit camp at Terezín.

The story of Terezín

A stark Jewish memorial in the cemetery at Terezín

Although most Jews of central Europe had since the Middle Ages encountered anti-Semitism as an everyday fact of life, anti-Jewish discrimination and persecution were not a prominent feature of Czech life. Jewish communities had been established for centuries throughout Bohemia and Moravia, and synagogues in Prague, Plzeň, and other cities testify to their prosperity by the mid-19th century. Inevitably the nation could hardly remain untouched by the political upheavals of the 1930s. The rise of Hitler unleashed the desire of the Sudeten Germans to be incorporated within the Third Reich, and encouraged anti-Semitic feelings.

Even after the invasion of Czechoslovakia in 1939, the mass murders that marked Nazi oppression in Poland were uncommon. Instead, the Nazis deported Bohemian and Moravian Jews to the newly created "ghetto" at Terezín (known in German as Theresienstadt).

Beginning in November 1941, the 3,500 people who inhabited Terezín were relocated, and behind its massive fortifications the barracks were converted into a concentration camp. Although this was no extermination camp, conditions were so terrible that some 33,000 of the inmates died of disease and hunger during the war. Despite the overcrowding and prison conditions, the camp was partly self-governing, and the inmates ran schools and cultural activities, largely as a propaganda exercise to show that the Jews were being treated well.

Beginning in October 1942, Terezín was used as a transit camp for 155,000 Jews (105,000 were under the age of 15) from all over Europe. Many of those who survived the privations of Terezín were shipped from 1942 onward to Polish ghettoes such as Lodz or directly to Auschwitz and other extermination camps.

One of the most grotesque features of Terezín was that the Nazis disguised part of it as a show camp. They made a film that depicted the inmates leading a normal life, visiting banks and shops that did not in fact exist, while bands played and tea parties were enjoyed in manicured gardens. It also showed the arrival of Jewish children from Holland and the warm welcome they received from the camp commandant. What this propaganda film did not show was these same children being sent to Auschwitz a few days later.

Scenes of everyday life were staged in June 1944 for the benefit of a Red Cross delegation, which was not shown the barracks where the surviving inmates were housed in squalid conditions. They were shown the Ghetto Elder touring the ghetto in a chauffeur-driven car, but they did not know that the "chauffeur" was an SS officer in disguise. The delegation was fooled and issued a favorable report on the ghetto. When the camp was liberated by Soviet forces on May 8, 1945, there were 17,500 emaciated survivors. Among them were writers Ivan Klíma and Arnoš Lustig, who wrote movingly about the camp and their war experiences. But most of the writers and artists who came to Terezín never left.

Even in this dreadful place, Jews managed to maintain a cultural life: Plays and operas were staged, sporting activities took place, and children drew and painted and wrote poems. So in Terezín there is much to lift the spirits: the unquenchable creativity of people of all ages and from all parts of Europe who knew they would never see their homes again. ■

Above: A colossal star of David reminds visitors to Terezín cemetery that most of those who died here were Jewish inmates of the camp.
Left: It was mainly political prisoners who were confined in these cheerless cells in the Small Fortress at Terezín.

Frýdlant & the Jizerské hory

IN THE EASTERN CORNER OF NORTHERN BOHEMIA, CLOSE to the Polish border, are the Jizerské hory (Jizera Mountains), which in effect are the western extension of the more dramatic Krkonoše (Giant Mountains) of eastern Bohemia (see pp. 232–235). This is lovely countryside with hillsides clad in spruce forests and flower-sprinkled meadows. Unfortunately, it is a landscape considerably marred by the lamentable effects of acid rain on the higher reaches of woodland. Replanting to combat these effects is under way.

Frýdlant
- 205 F4
- 15 miles (23 km) N of Liberec
- Train from Liberec

Frýdlant Castle
- Closed Mon. & Nov.–March
- $$–$$$

Although the mountains don't reach the same heights as those of the Krkonoše, some rise to over 3,600 feet (1,100 m). Visitors flock here, both from the Czech Republic and from parts of Poland and Germany just across the borders. For the best view of the region, drive out of Liberec (see pp. 218–219), a once prosperous manufacturing city not far from the Polish border, and up to the top of Mount Ještěd, where you can eat at the revolving restaurant.

In a valley among the hills north of Liberec is the village of **Frýdlant.** Its melancholy **castle** is believed to have been one of the models for Franz Kafka's novel *Das Schloss (The Castle)*. There's no direct evidence for this, though it is known that Kafka did visit the castle as part of his job when working for an insurance company. It stands on a wooded basalt crag on the edge of town, overlooking the River Smědá.

The castle combines a mixture of elements from several different periods: The 13th-century medieval fortifications and round tower blend in with Renaissance and neo-Gothic buildings. Much of what is visible today is the work of the 16th-century Lombard architect Marco Spazzio. It was owned, as

were most of the castles in the region, by Albrecht von Wallenstein (Valdštejn), who was created Duke of Frýdlant (see p. 27), and subsequently by the Clam-Gallas family, who renovated the buildings.

There has been a museum in the castle since 1801. The mostly neo-Gothic interior is richly furnished. There is a fine collection of paintings by Bohemian baroque masters, but to get inside, you must join a very lengthy guided tour.

It's also worth stopping in the village center to look at the **Church of the Holy Cross** (Kostel Nalezení sv. Kříže), which contains a magnificent Renaissance tomb by the Dutch sculptor Gerhard Heinrich. ■

The Bohemian general Wallenstein was lord of this part of the country, and Frýdlant was one of his castles.

Lázně Libverda

In the heart of the hills, some 8 miles (12 km) east of Frýdlant is the small spa of Lázně Libverda. This seems to be one of the few spas Goethe didn't visit, but Carl Maria von Weber wrote part of his opera *Der Freischutz* here in 1821. The location is charming, though it's very low-key and as a social venue it can hardly compete with the more famous spas of western Bohemia. It offers, however, guest houses, restaurants, springs, and undemanding walks in the hills. It is undeniably tranquil. ■

A drive through the České Švýcarsko

In sharp contrast to much of the industrialized north of Bohemia is the delightful national park known as České Švýcarsko (Czech Switzerland). The region acquired its name not from Czech tourism officials, but from Swiss Romantic artists who visited it in the 1770s. Between Hřensko and Česká Kamenice, the hills are pierced by small valleys packed with well-kept villages of half-timbered cottages.

Numerous guest houses cater to the increasing number of tourists who visit the region. Concealed in the woods are the cliffs and rock pillars and sandstone formations that give the areas around Jetřichovice and Hřensko their drama. When, eons ago, volcanic rock reached the surface, fissures, canyons, and other stunning rock formations were created. Unfortunately, air pollution has hastened the erosion of these natural wonders. The region is also valued as a protected zone for flora and fauna, and it has an outstanding collection of fern species within its boundaries.

The České Švýcarsko is best approached from **Hřensko ❶**, north of Děčín. The village sits in a gorge edged by overhanging rocks where it joins the Labe Valley. Hřensko itself is quite a pretty place, with its half-timbered cottages in Germanic style, but unfortunately not enhanced by the profusion of roadside stalls selling cheap souvenirs to tourists.

The **Pravčická brána** is the largest natural stone bridge in central Europe, some 85 feet across (26 m) and 68 feet high (21 m), deep in the woods east of Hřensko. It can only be reached on foot and is a 3-mile (5 km) hike from the village. You can take a slightly shorter path from Mezní Louka, where you can leave your car; and there is ample parking at Hřensko, too. Mezní Louka has a hotel and

campsite if you wish to stay. A path from the village leads in an easterly direction to another less spectacular stone bridge, the Malá Pravčická brána.

From Mezní Louka you can drive a short distance southwest to the hamlet of **Mezná ❷**, perched above the Kamenice gorge, which can be crossed at this point over a wooden bridge. Hikers often come to Mezná, then return by boat to Hřensko. It's a tranquil

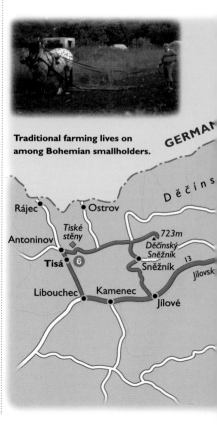

Traditional farming lives on among Bohemian smallholders.

🏔 See area map pp. 204–205
▶ Hřensko
↔ 70 miles (112 km)
🕐 1 day
▶ Děčín

NOT TO BE MISSED
- Pravčická brána
- Mezná
- Panská skála
- Rose Garden (Růžová zahrada)

place, on grassy slopes among the forests. Even in summer it's not crowded, and there are a handful of rustic guest houses and restaurants. Take the main road east from Mezní Louka to **Jetřichovice** , a charming village where some of the old farmhouses have been converted into simple guest houses.

Continue southward to the drab town of **Česká Kamenice** ❹, where there is a fine baroque chapel. Another notable rock formation lies 3 miles (5 km) east of here, just beyond Kamenický Šenov. This is the **Panská skála,** thousands of polygonal basalt columns that resemble organ pipes lined up in a row; they formed when molten basalt cooled.

From Česká Kamenice continue toward Děčín via **Benešov nad Ploučnicí** ❺, with two interesting 16th-century **castles** (*closed Mon. May–Sept.; Mon.–Tues. April & Oct.; &*

The dales and streams of the České Švýcarsko are especially popular with hikers.

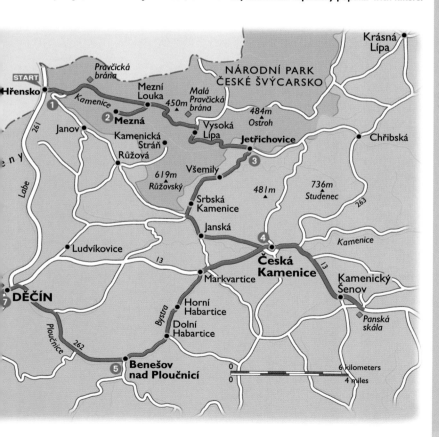

all Nov.–March, $–$$$). The lower of the two has Renaissance interiors and a collection of furniture, armor, and Oriental art. The upper castle offers changing art exhibitions and some empty rooms with splendid painted ceilings.

The České Švýcarsko continues to the west of Děčín, so carry on past the town on route 13 to Libouchec, where a road leads north to **Tisá** ❻ and the border town of Rájec. Tisá has a distinctive landscape of sandstone boulders (Tiské stěny), accessible by footpath from the village. The other point of interest in this area is the table-topped mountain called **Děčínský Sněžník**, between Děčín and Ostrov. Hiking trails from those two towns lead up to it.

Drive to Jilově on Route 13, and then eastward back to **Děčín** ❼. Like Ústí nad Labem (see p. 220), Děčín is a heavily industrialized inland port along the River Labe. Its late 18th-century castle spreads along its crag like a cat on a fence; it is approached through a gateway and by a long ramp. Left derelict after decades of abuse by Czech, German, and Soviet soldiers, the castle is gradually being restored. At the top of the ramp on the right you come to the splendid baroque **Rose Garden** (Růžová zahrada), originally planted in the 1670s by Maximilian Thun-Hohenstein, whose family owned the castle until 1932 (*$*). It's an enchanting spot, perched high above the town and decorated with pavilions, statues, and urns. There is also a small marionette museum *(closed Mon., $).* ■

East of Hřensko is a remarkable stone bridge known as the Pravčická brána, the largest of its kind in central Europe.

Beneath the domed baroque church at Jablonné v Podještědí is a ghoulish crypt laid out with mummified corpses.

More places to visit in northern Bohemia

JABLONEC NAD NISOU

Jablonec nad Nisou was a very prosperous, German-speaking town until 1945. Its turn-of-the-20th-century villas and grand constructivist municipal buildings from the 1920s and '30s testify to the success of its costume jewelry and brass industries. The **Museum of Glass and Jewelry** (Muzeum skla a bižuterie) justifies a visit for its first-rate collections.

 205 F3 8 miles (14 km) E of Liberec on route 14 Tram 11 from Liberec **Visitor information** Mírové náměstí 19, 46751 Jablonec; e-mail icjablonec@jablonec.cz 483 357 335 Closed Sun. **Museum of Glass and Jewelry** U Muzea 4 Closed Mon. and Oct.–May.

JABLONNÉ V PODJEŠTĚDÍ

Dominating the town of Jablonné v Podještědí is its large domed **church** with billowing pink-and-white facade, built by the Austrian baroque architect Johann Lukas von Hildebrandt in 1699. In the crypt you will find the remains of mummified corpses, but to see them you have to sign up for a guided tour of the monastic complex.

Two miles (3 km) east of town lies **Lemberk,** a castle of 13th-century origin remodeled by General Wallenstein (Valdštejn). Its richly furnished rooms can also be visited on a guided tour.

 205 E3 13 miles (22 km) W of Liberec via route 35, then route 13 Bus from Prague's Florenc station, or from Karlovy Vary, and Liberec **Church** Closed Mon. Tour: May–Sept. only **Lemberk Castle** Closed Mon. May–Sept., Mon.–Fri. April & Oct., & Nov.–March $

KADAŇ

The old double-walled town of Kadaň southwest of Chomutov was much damaged during the Thirty Years War. The main square is lined with arcaded houses of various periods, grouped around a tall plague column adorned with statuary. An elegant 15th-century white **tower** looks over the square, outclassing the 18th-century **church.** Across the square from the tower is Katová ulička, the Hangman's Lane, a covered passageway almost too narrow for two people to squeeze by each other. Tyršova leads to the much restored gray-green **castle.**

📍 204 B2 ✉️ 10 miles (15 km) SW of Chomutov on route 13, then left on route 568 🚊 Train from Prague

KLÁŠTEREC NAD OHŘÍ

Klášterec nad Ohří, with its salmon-pink 17th-century **château** occupying a spur above the River Ohře, lies close to Kadaň. Though much altered since it was built, the château contains a large collection of Bohemian porcelain; of equal interest is its park, adorned with statues by the baroque sculptor Jan Brokoff and a collection of rare central European trees.

📍 204 B2 ✉️ 4 miles (6.5 km) W of Kadaň 🚊 Train from Prague **Château** 🕐 Closed Mon.–Fri., & Nov.–March. Guided tours: April–Oct. only 💲 $$

LIBEREC

Before its German population was expelled in 1945, Liberec was an extremely prosperous

It is hard to tell from the pristine interior that in 1975 Most's entire church was shifted far from its original site, which is now a lignite mine.

industrial city, producing mainly textiles. Its fantastical Flemish-style neo-Gothic **town hall** (*Radnice*) of 1893 is undeniably impressive, though hardly typically Bohemian. The style is appropriate, since the town was founded in the Middle Ages by Flemish linen weavers. It was also the hometown of Konrad Henlein, who led the movement for the Sudeten Germans to be united with Nazi Germany.

Liberec's **château** was once owned by the Clam-Gallas family, one of the richest and most powerful in Bohemia. Next to it is the **gallery** of paintings from the collection of Johann Liebig, Liberec's leading textile magnate. The **Museum of Northern Bohemia** (Severočeské muzeum) contains

medieval tapestries and interesting exhibits relating to local industries.

🅐 205 F3 ✉ 63 miles (106 km) N of Prague on E65 **Visitor information** ✉ náměstí Dr. E. Beneše 2/32, 46001 Liberec; e-mail mic@ infolbc.cz ☎ 485 101 709 **Museum of Northern Bohemia** ✉ Masarykova 11 🕐 Closed Mon.

LOUNY
You enter the walled town of Louny through its commanding late Gothic gate, which along with the church tower is the only building to have survived a devastating fire in 1517. The skyline is pierced by the roof of the **Church of St. Nicholas** (Kostel sv. Mikuláše). The rib vaulting inside is typical of Benedikt Ried, who reconstructed the town in the 1520s. There is also sensational carving on the high altar of 1704, resembling a tropical jungle petrified in wood. The main square is unexceptional, except for one Renaissance

house at No. 28 *(tel 0395 652 456);* from its oriel window the authorities would pronounce the death sentence on unlucky (or criminal) citizens in the 16th and 17th centuries.

🅐 204 C2 ✉ 38 miles (63 km) NW of Prague on route 7 🚆 Train from Prague's Masarykovo nádraží

MOST
In 1975 the entire town of Most had to be demolished and relocated to make way for lignite mines. Girdled by steel, the 16th-century **Church of the Assumption** (Kostel Nanebevzetí Panny Marie) was shifted on a specially built railroad line 2,750 feet (840 m) from its original location to another site. It was worth saving, for it has a luminous interior filled with interesting examples of religious art roughly contemporaneous with the church. It was designed by Jakob Heilmann, a pupil of Benedikt Ried's, and has spectacular vaulting.

🅐 204 C2 ✉ 67 miles (112 km) NW of Prague via route 7 to Louny, then N on route 28 🕐 Closed Mon. & Tues. 💲 $ 🚆 Train from Prague

OSEK
West of Teplice stands the resplendent Cistercian monastery at Osek. It retains its 13th-century chapter house and cloister, but the church itself is a baroque masterpiece by Ottavio Broggio. The stuccoed interior is magnificent, if dilapidated; watch for the superb wooden and gilt choir stalls. In the 1990s Cistercian monks returned to Osek, after expulsion by the Communists.

🅐 204 C3 ✉ 7 miles (11 km) W of Teplice via route 27 🕐 Closed Sun. a.m. & all Mon. April–June & Sept.; & all Nov.–March 💲 $ 🚆 Train from Teplice

ROUDNICE NAD LABEM
Near the center of town stands the colossal rust-and-white neoclassic château that once belonged to the Lobkowicz family. It was designed by Francesco Caratti in the 1660s, but, sadly, it has become dilapidated and is closed to the public. The former riding school, outside the château walls, is now a **gallery** containing a major collection of modern Czech art, focused around a collection

by painter Antonín Slavíček.

 205 D2  30 miles (50 km) NW of Prague via E55 **Gallery** Closed Mon. $

TEPLICE

A town of astonishing contrasts, Teplice lies close to the German border. You will find entire streets of derelict buildings, blackened with dirt, left empty when the German population was expelled in 1945. Yet in the core of the town are delightful parks overlooked by elegant spa buildings. It was a spa in the 11th century, if not earlier, but was developed only in the 18th century. Beethoven, Liszt, Wagner, and Ibsen were among its famous visitors. In 1813 the rulers of Austria, Russia, and Prussia met here to sign the "Holy Alliance" against Napoleon. Numerous villas in secession and neoclassic styles testify to the former opulence of the town. On the main square,

Liberec, once a flourishing textile town, is built on a grand urban scale.

Zámecké náměstí, is an enormous plague column of 1718 by Matthias Braun; the neoclassic castle, now the regional **museum;** and the castle's adjoining church. The square's most handsome mansion has become a hotel, the Prince de Ligne (see p. 315). The castle park offers a useful starting point for many walking trails.

204 C3 52 miles (87 km) NW of Prague via E55, then route 8 Train from Prague **Museum** Zamecké náměstí 14 417 537 869 Closed Mon. $

ÚSTÍ NAD LABEM

Ústí nad Labem is the biggest town in northern Bohemia and the largest port on the River Labe, except for distant Hamburg. The ruinous **castle** on a protruding basalt rock is known as Střekov, and this romantic pile gives Ústí a certain drama. Wagner was inspired to write *Tannhäuser* following a visit here.

There is little in this heavily industrial town itself to detain you, other than the **cathedral** dating from the early 16th century, its steeple thrown off balance after a bombing raid during World War II, and a **theater** in secession style. The town's reputation was severely damaged in 1999 when the council constructed a wall to separate the Roma people, otherwise known as Gypsies, from the Czech communities. The building of this wall prompted international protests, and also confirmed the Roma's own long-held view that they were being actively discriminated against by certain Czech authorities. A short while later the wall was taken down.

205 D3 54 miles (90 km) N of Prague via E55 Train from Prague **Střekov Castle** Closed Mon. & Jan.–March $

ŽATEC

Žatec is a faded but dignified little town, surrounded by fields in which the best hops in Bohemia have been grown for centuries (see pp. 184–185). The much renovated town hall heads the main square and looks onto a plague column reminiscent of petrified profiteroles. Behind the town hall is the hefty medieval **Church of the Assumption** (Kostel Nanebevzetí Panny Marie), which is guarded by a row of baroque statuary. To the left of the church stands one of the medieval town gates, and behind it is what is left of the castle (*hrad*), now a brewery.

204 B2 50 miles (83 km) W of Prague via route 7, then left on route 27 Train from Prague ■

The Giant Mountains are Bohemia's winter sports center, and in summer visitors flock to the hills and castles of the Český ráj. There are also alluring towns, such as Náchod and Hradec Králové, and the ghostly baroque spa of Kuks.

Eastern Bohemia

Exhibits at the puppet museum at Chrudim

0 _____ 20 kilometers
0 _____ 10 miles

NORTHERN BOHEMIA p.203

POLAND

6▷

Harrachov
Špindlerův Mlýn
1602m
Sněžka
Pec pod Sněžkou
Žacléř

Jablonec nad Jizerou
Giant Mountains (Krkonoše)
Vrchlabí
Janské Lázně
Mladé Buky

Stěnava

E65 Turnov
Semily
Jilemnice
Lomnice nad Popelkou
14
293
295
Jizera
Labe
Hostinné
Adršpach-Teplice
Trutnov
Teplice nad Metují
Broum
Dřevíč

Hrubá Skála
35
16
Úpice
Červený Kostelec
Hronov
Police nad Metují

5▷ Č e s k ý
r á j
Sobotka
Nová Paka
16
Jičín
Lázně Bělohrad
Dvůr Králové nad Labem
37
Upa

Libáň
Ostroměř
Miletín
Betlém Kuks
Ratibořice
Česká Skalice
Náchod

32
Cidlina
Hořice
E67
vod. nádrž Rozkoš

Kopidlno
Smidary
Jaroměř
Josefov
Nové Město nad Metují

35
33
Smiřice
Dobruška
1115m

4▷ Nový Bydžov
Nechanice
E442
Všestary
Čas Černilov
Opočno
Orl

Karlova Koruna
Bystřice
11
11
HRADEC KRÁLOVÉ
Třebechovice pod Orebem
Solnice
Rychnov nad Kněžnou

Chlumec nad Cidlinou
Opatovice nad Labem
Orlice
Týniště nad Orlicí
Častolovice
Kostelec nad Orlicí
Rokytnic Orlick hor

36
Lázně Bohdaneč
Sezemice
Holice
E442
Vamberk

Chvaletice
Přelouč
2
Pardubice
36
35
Tichá Orlice
Choceň
Žamb

3▷ Labe
Heřmanův Městec
Loučná
17
Letoh
14

17
Chrudim
Hrochův Týnec
Vysoké Mýto
Ústí nad Orlicí

Ronov nad Doubravou
Slatiňany
Chrast
Luže
Česká Třebová

Třemošnice
37
Nasavrky
Skuteč
Dolní Újezd
Litomyšl

Golčův Jeníkov
Železné hory
Chrudimka
Proseč
Opa

Habry
Hlinsko
Svita

2▷ Ledec nad Sázavou
Chotěboř
Ždírec nad Doubravou
Polička
34
Svi

Světlá nad Sázavou
38
34
Bystré

Sázava
150
Havlíčkův Brod
SOUTHERN MORAVIA p.243
Brně

SOUTHERN BOHEMIA p.153
Lipnice nad Sázavou
34
Přibyslav
Slapanka

1▷ E65 D1
Štoky
E50

DAY TRIPS FROM PRAGUE p.137

△ A   △ B   △ C   △ D

Eastern Bohemia

EASTERN BOHEMIA IS THE MOST REMOTE PART OF BOHEMIA AND HAS THE most spectacular scenery anywhere in the republic. The northern frontier with Poland is dominated by the Krkonoše Mountains, which are high enough to be a very popular skiing resort in winter; in summer it's possible to explore the remoter reaches along some of the many hiking trails. Far more gentle in its contours, but equally popular with Czech visitors and tourists alike, is the Český ráj (Czech Paradise) near Turnov, a rolling landscape of ruined castles and strange rock formations. If you travel farther south, however, the countryside is flatter and frankly not very appealing.

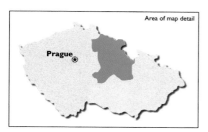

This is made up for by the many interesting towns that flourished here. The main one is Hradec Králové, which has all the usual attractions of a Bohemian town—large main square, churches, museums—but was also a center for Czech cubist architecture, much of which has survived. Here, too, is one of the best Czech modern art museums. Litomyšl is the birthplace of the composer Smetana, and it has an especially lovely Renaissance castle.

There is much to see in eastern Bohemia, and most of it is rewardingly eccentric. Kuks was a large and dramatically sited spa development, a rich man's fancy that evolved into a private resort. But on December 22, 1740, the complex was destroyed overnight by severe floods. Today only part of the spa is intact, yet it remains a haunting place. Josefov is one of those severe Austro-Hungarian garrison towns. Its layout, fortifications, and atmosphere will be familiar to those who have already visited Terezín.

There is no shortage of interesting castles and châteaus to visit in eastern Bohemia. Náchod, Pardubice, Opočno, and Nové Město have much to recommend them, and Karlova Koruna is another masterpiece by that baroque genius Santini. The large château at Častolovice is one of the few stately homes in the republic where it is possible to stay, though this trend is set to continue as more and more country mansions and castles are reinvented by their original owners. ∎

The picturesque main square at Náchod is overlooked by a handsome castle.

Hradec Králové

HRADEC KRÁLOVÉ LIES ALONG THE BANKS OF THE RIVERS Orlice and Labe. It was founded in the 14th century and 500 years later was the second most important town in Bohemia. It offers all the attractions of most Bohemian towns, but an abundance of architecture from the early 20th century and two notable museums make Hradec Králové particularly interesting. It was a Hussite fortress in the 16th century and fully fortified in the 18th century, and, although the fortifications were subsequently demolished, traces of the old walls are still visible.

On one side of the Labe stands the tranquil old town on a long ridge, much of which is occupied by Velké náměstí, the large main square. Across the river is the new town, which became a showcase for the best architects of the early 20th century. A huge 16th-century bell tower, the **White Tower** (Bílá věž), dominates one end of Velké náměstí. The structure dwarfs even the turreted towers of the lofty Gothic brick cathedral next to it and gives a bird's-eye view over the town. The only medieval

furnishings remaining in the cathedral are the tall stone tabernacle of 1497 in the choir and a paneled altarpiece of 1494 in the south aisle. In the north aisle is a painting of St. Anthony by Petr Brandl (about 1730), whose work adorns so many churches in Prague. What makes the main square visually arresting is the sheer variety of buildings, from modest arcaded merchants' houses with shops beneath to the baroque elegance of the bishop's palace of 1716. In the middle of the square is a grandiose plague column of 1717 and a well with a delightfully ornate ironwork grille.

At the other end of the square you'll find the pretty, yellow 17th-century Jesuit church by Carlo Lurago; it also features paintings by Brandl. Standing next to it is the Jesuit college.

The **Gallery of Modern Art** (Galerie moderního umění), opposite the Jesuit College, is housed in a gray secession-style building of 1912 by Osvald Polívka, and has an outstanding collection. There are voluptuous early works by Mucha (1860–1939), which are quite different from the posters for which he became well known. Watch for the arresting portraits and other Cézanne-influenced works by Bohumil Kubišta (1884–1918). Some playful and colorful paintings by Josef Čapek (1887–1945) are thoroughly

Hradec Králové

🗺 222 C4

✉ 62 miles (100 km) E of Prague via E67 to end, then route 11

🚆 Train from Prague & Brno. Bus from Prague

Visitor information

✉ Infocentrum, Gočárova 1225, near bus station
e-mail hk@mic.cz

☎ 495 534 482

Left: One of the gigantic seated statues by Stanislav Sucharda at the entrance to the riverside Kranské Museum

representative of his cubist technique. From the profusion of works in this museum, try not to miss the surreal abstracts by Josef Šíma (1891–1971) and good cubist works by Emil Filla (1883–1953).

The often remodeled town hall is next to the White Tower, and nearby Ke kopečku leads down to the river, passing the Hotel Bystrica, designed by the pioneering architect Jan Kotěra but now more or less derelict.

Down on the embankment, on Eliščino nábřeží, stands the striking **Kranské Museum** of 1912, also designed by Kotěra. It blends secession pretensions—huge seated statues by Stanislav Sucharda, representing History and Industry, flank the entrance—with a geometric strength and originality of its own. Inside there are fine stained-glass windows by František Kysela, but the actual collections are of little interest, except for the model of the town as it appeared in 1865.

Kotěra also designed the main bridge nearby, which leads into the heart of the new town, much of which was laid out by his pupil Josef Gočár. Gočár's work can be seen to best advantage in Masarykovo náměstí, where he employed Czech cubist elements yet retained the proportions and gentle coloring of traditional vernacular Czech architecture. Less appealing is the harsh, functionalist stadium he built on the banks of the River Orlice. Václav Rejchl designed the town's railroad station, with its elegant clock tower. ■

The main square at Hradec Králové, with two churches, a bishop's palace, and an art gallery

White Tower
🕐 Closed Mon. & Nov.–March
💲 $

Gallery of Modern Art
✉ Velké náměstí 139
☎ 495 514 893
🕐 Closed Mon.
💲 $

Kranské Museum
✉ Eliščino nábřeží
🕐 Closed Mon.
💲 $

Litomyšl

The Portmoneum house preserves the colorful artwork that Josef Váchal painted on its walls, ceilings, and furnishings.

LITOMYŠL HAS A KNACK FOR MAKING ITSELF KNOWN. "Smetanov Litomyšl," the international opera festival held in the town each summer, is a long-standing event. Luckily for Litomyšl, seven European presidents chose the town for a summit meeting in 1994, and the authorities were galvanized into restoring the town's rich collection of noteworthy buildings, which are now in impeccable condition.

There was a castle here a thousand years ago, and a town was founded around it in 1259. Litomyšl soon acquired importance as the seat of a bishopric, but that came to an end after the Hussite general Jan Žižka captured the town in 1421.

The main square, Smetanovo náměstí, resembles a long, broad, and curved high street, with arcaded houses of all periods lining both sides. Number 61, **At the Knights** (U rytířů), is the most spectacular: Its flamboyant Renaissance facade dates from 1546, statues of knights flank the heavily decorated stone windows, and there is an impressive coffered ceiling inside.

Behind this house, along Boženy Němcové, which runs parallel to the square, are a number of churches,

including a large yellow one, by Giovanni Alliprandi and František Kaňka, on a rampart reached by covered steps from the little square below. Across from the church is the magnificent sgraffitoed and gabled **château,** one of several owned by the Pernštejns, a noble Moravian family active and powerful from the

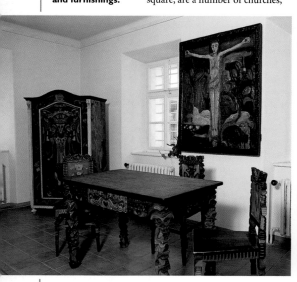

late 13th century. It was built by the Aostali brothers in the 1570s. Along one side is a sundial dated 1728 and—a curious feature—windows that look not into rooms but into the splendid three-tiered, galleried courtyard. The château still has its perfect little theater, constructed in 1797 and complete with original scenery by Josef Platzer.

The guided tour of the château takes you through elegantly furnished rooms and porcelain collections, and it is worth seeing the theater. The former riding school displays casts but not originals of classical antiquities *(closed Mon. & Oct.–April, $)*.

Bedřich Smetana's father managed the castle brewery, across from the castle courtyard's portal, and it was here that the composer was born in 1824. The small **Smetana Museum** commemorates his life.

Litomyšl has more to offer than these rich cultural treasures. With the castle to your left, take the first turn right and walk down to Terézy Novákové 75, an outwardly unremarkable house known as the **Portmoneum** (after its owner). In the 1920s, artist Josef Váchal, nephew of Mikoláš Aleš, decorated the interior. He coated the walls with bizarre murals full of religious and mystical allusions; he designed the furnishings, too. ∎

Smetana Museum
🕐 Closed Mon. May–Sept., Mon.–Fri. April & Oct., & Nov.–March
💲 $

Portmoneum
🕐 Closed Mon., & Oct.–April
💲 $

The château at Litomyšl is one of Bohemia's finest Renaissance palaces, complete with an 18th-century theater.

Bedřich Smetana

Although Antonín Dvořák may enjoy greater international renown, it is Bedřich Smetana who the Czechs hold in even warmer regard as a composer. In large part this is because he reacted to Habsburg cultural domination by passionately espousing Czech nationalism. Consequently, Czech legends and historical episodes feature as the basis for his operas and other works. By doing so, he helped to forge the cultural identity of the Czech people in the late 19th century.

stream to a proud river surging through the Czech heartlands. Almost as popular is his comic opera of 1866, *The Bartered Bride*. Set in a Bohemian village, it tackles the familiar theme of a young lady in love with one suitor, but under parental pressure to marry another, richer young

Bedřich Smetana, even more than Dvořák, is the Czechs' favorite composer, thanks to the nationalist ardor, which is expressed in his music.

Bedřich Smetana was born in 1824 in Litomyšl (see pp. 226–227), where his father was the manager of the local brewery and an enthusiastic amateur musician. German was the official language of Bohemia from 1784 onward, and German was the first language of the Smetana household. As a child Bedřich had a poor knowledge of Czech, which is ironic given his later role as a champion of Czech nationalism. It soon became clear that young Bedřich had inherited his father's gifts to an even greater degree, proving a fine string and piano player. He pursued his musical studies in Prague and became a much admired music teacher. His nationalist views, however, did not endear him to the authorities, and in the late 1850s he moved to Sweden to become conductor of the Gothenburg Philharmonic. Back in Prague four years later, Smetana became a leading advocate of the establishment of a national theater as a showcase for Czech drama and opera, and he later became its principal conductor.

At the same time he was, of course, composing. His best known work is the symphonic poem *Má vlast (My Home)* from 1875, especially its opening movement, which depicts the growth of the River Vltava from a modest

Costumes for an 1866 production of *The Bartered Bride*, Smetana's best-loved opera

man. Smetana seems to have felt some irritation at its enormous success, since he was more proud of his operas on historical and nationalist themes, such as *Dalibor* (1868) and *Libuše* (1881). His operas are regularly performed in Prague and at the music festival held each summer in his native Litomyšl.

Like Beethoven, he was to end his days in total deafness. In the 1870s he began to experience a very high note persistently whistling in one of his ears, a warning of the deafness that was to come. Even the complete inability to hear his own music did not prevent him from composing, and one of his most moving works is the string quartet of 1876 entitled *From My Life,* in which the music is interrupted by a high sustained note on the violin, an echo of the sound that heralded his isolating deafness. There was worse to come: Smetana's

health steadily deteriorated and he suffered a stroke; he descended into madness and in 1884 died of syphilis at the age of 60.

Smetana was buried in the cemetery at Vyšehrad, in recognition of his status as a national hero. Ironically, at his death he was revered more for his work in establishing the National Theater (see p. 119) than for his compositions, only a few of which were regularly performed during his own lifetime. It was Smetana who provided a special composition to be performed at the official opening of the theater in 1883, and when the building was reopened after the site was redesigned in 1983, the occasion was marked, appropriately, with a performance of his opera *Libuše.* The riverfront museum close to Charles Bridge (see p. 90) has become his major memorial in the capital. ■

Kuks

KUKS, NORTHWEST OF JAROMĚŘ, IS A BAROQUE SPA COMPLEX completely different from the better known spas in western Bohemia. It was founded by an aristocrat of German origin, Count Franz Anton von Sporck (1662–1738), who inherited the property and a large fortune at the age of 17. Finding that waters from a spring on his estate were rich in minerals, he resolved to build a spa complex, a project that began in 1694 and lasted for the next 25 years.

Kuks

 222 C5

 13 miles (20 km) N of Hradec Králové via route 33 to Jaroměř, then N on route 37

🚌 Train from Hradec Králové

The resort lacked nothing: As well as the baths, hospital, and château, Sporck provided a theater, maze, and racecourse. The spa was completed in 1724 and became an ultrafashionable resort for central European high society, offering cultural diversions as well as the curative waters. There were pageants on the river, hunts, and concerts by Sporck's private orchestra. Johann

Sebastian Bach was one of the many artistic visitors to Kuks.

There was, however, a major design fault in the original layout: Many of the buildings faced each other across the Labe. They were destroyed by floodwaters in 1740 when the river broke its banks. Worse, the actual spring was found to be beyond repair, so there was no future for the spa. Sporck had died

in 1738, and there was little incentive to restore Kuks. In 1901 much of the château was torn down.

Nonetheless, what remains is still impressive. Overlooking the river from a broad terrace are the former **hospital** buildings, now being restored; the oval chapel by Giovanni Alliprandi; and the burial crypt of the Sporck family. The baroque **pharmacy** retains its original furnishings. But the best feature is the parade of 24 radiant **allegorical statues** (mostly copies; the originals have been taken indoors) by Matthias Braun (1684–1738). These are lined up along the hospital terrace and adorn the dark facades of the buildings. They depict the Vices on one side and the Virtues on the other. Perhaps predictably, the Vices seem more inspired than the Virtues. ■

The formal hospital buildings are the most substantial remnants of the original spa.

Hospital & pharmacy
🕐 Closed Mon. May–Sept., Mon.–Fri. April & Oct., & Nov.–March
💲 $

Betlém

At Betlém, 2 miles (3 km) to the west, Sporck created another park embellished with carvings of biblical scenes, hewn from the rocks by Braun. These were completed in 1733 but are now very eroded. In Sporck's day this was a religious grove, with grottoes and hermitages hollowed out from the rocks on the wooded hillside, but many of the statues and buildings were carted off for use as building materials at Josefov and elsewhere. It's well signposted from Kuks and can be reached by foot from a parking lot after turning left at Žireč and continuing for 2 miles (3 km). Despite the damaged and eroded condition of the surviving carvings, Betlém is a unique and moving experience, a rare fusion of art and nature. ■

Betlém
🅰 222 C5
🕐 Closed Mon. & Nov.–March
💲 $

The Krkonoše mountains cover an immense area of fir-clad slopes and peaks.

Krkonoše

IN THE NORTHERN PART OF EASTERN BOHEMIA, PUSHING up toward the border with Silesia in Poland, rise the highest mountains in Bohemia, the Krkonoše (Giant Mountains). Sněžka, at 5,255 feet (1,602 m), is the highest peak in the Czech Republic. Much of the area has been protected as a national park since 1963.

Krkonoše

 222 B6, C6

67 miles (107 km) NE of Prague via E65 to Mladá Boleslav, E on route 16 to just past Nová Paka, then N on routes 293 & 195 to Vrchlabí

Most of the Krkonoše massif lies within Bohemia, though the 68 square miles (177 sq km) in Poland have also been protected since 1959. The ranges are fringed on the south by the spa of Janské Lázně and the town of Vrchlabí, and to the north by the resorts of Harrachov and Špindlerův Mlýn. Rivers such as the Jizera and the Labe, whose sources lie here, have carved deep valleys through the mountains, which are characterized by rounded summits rather than conical peaks. From November to April enough snow drapes the rounded ridges and crests of the mountains to make them perfect for winter sports.

Come summer, marked paths traverse the mountains for 625 miles (1,000 km), making this ideal territory for walkers as well. These trails are well supplied with huts *(boudy)* providing food and shelter. Dozens of stylized signs help to guide hikers and prevent them from getting lost, even in winter, when snow covers the ground. In summer there can be treacherous fogs and low temperatures at higher elevations, so be sure to take warm clothing and a good map. If you do not want to explore the Krkonoše on foot, view the mountains from the cable cars and chairlifts that glide up to the summits from Pec pod Sněžkou, Špindlerův Mlýn, and Janské Lázně.

One of the most popular walks straddles the ridges that separate Bohemia from Poland. Many visitors cannot resist climbing **Mount Sněžka,** which can easily be done from Pec pod Sněžkou, some 2,733 feet (833 m) below the summit. The climb takes five to six hours both ways. The most spectacular trail is the **Harrach path,** originally laid out by Count Harrach in 1879, but it is open only during the summer months. Many of the trails offer access to some of the fascinating features of the mountains: peat bogs, rock walls, and waterfalls.

Krkonose National Park is of exceptional interest to naturalists, since the mountains are home to 165 species of birds; up near the peat bogs you might encounter black grouse or fan-tailed capercaillies. The 1,300 species of flora found in the park include many rare trees and other plants that thrive in the unusual high peaty pastures characteristic of the Krkonoše. How long they will remain is doubtful, as air pollution and acid rain, in particular, have wreaked appalling damage on the spruce forests. The Krkonoše mountains have the highest rainfall in Bohemia, easing the way for ruinous pollutants.

In medieval times the mountains were far more forbidding than they are today because they were uninhabited. The forests inspired feelings of awe and apprehension that were often reinforced by the experiences of German and Italian prospectors, who began mining operations in the 16th century, and

Visitor information
There are information centers at all the resorts mentioned; they are well supplied with maps and current weather information, and they can usually help find accommodations, which are plentiful. The best centers are at Vrchlabí, on the main road next to the museum (Dobrovského 3, tel 0438 451111), and at Harrachov (Harrachov 150, tel 0432 529600, fax 0432 529425, e-mail mico@harrachov.cz).

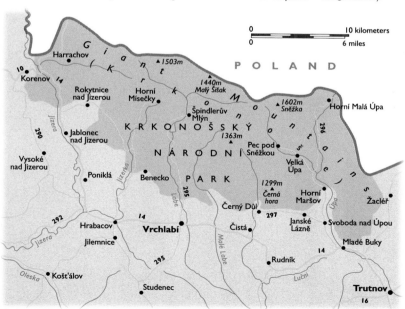

Skiing Museum

✉ Harrachov, 75 miles (126 km) NE of Prague

🕐 Closed Mon.

💲 $

Left: The republic's best winter sports resorts are located in the Krkonoše. Below: Even the keenest hiker would find it hard to walk all of the Krkonoše's 625 miles (1,000 km) of trails.

by farmers who felled some of the woodlands to provide summer pasture for their cattle. The hostile environment of the mountains inspired terror of the unknown. This was personified in the form of a supernatural giant known as Krakonoš, who was said to be responsible for the natural calamities that were part of the struggle for existence in the harsh climate.

Only in the late 18th century did the mountains first attract tourists. In those days you needed to be intrepid, because the only accommodations were in mountain huts. In the following century the resorts that flourish today began to develop on the edges of the mountains. The main and most convenient base for visitors is just outside the park at **Vrchlabí.** Along the main street are attractive wooden arcaded houses, some of which now contain a regional museum focusing on arts and crafts and the history of local tourism *(closed Mon., $).*

Just inside the park boundaries

is the small spa town of **Janské Lázně,** founded in 1677 though not developed until the late 19th century. Compared with the main resorts in the mountains, this is a quiet place. But some may prefer its charms to the raucousness of the other towns.

The road north to Harrachov follows the winding River Jizera, passing through villages with charming wooden houses decorated with white vertical or horizontal lines. These are formed by painting the mortar between the logs or by covering the sides of the building with a delicate white lattice.

Harrachov is more attractive than Vrchlabí. Embedded in the forests, it has been a glassmaking town since 1712 as well as a resort, and it has a festive atmosphere, especially in winter. In bad weather a visit to the **Skiing Museum** here helps while away an hour.

Špindlerův Mlýn and **Pec pod Sněžkou** are among the republic's best ski resorts, though neither is a great beauty spot. ■

Český ráj

THE THICKLY FORESTED ČESKÝ RÁJ, OR CZECH PARADISE,
a nature reserve south of Liberec, is a compact area strewn with
bizarre rock formations and ancient castles. It typifies the astonishing
rapidity with which the landscape can change as you travel through
Bohemia. One moment you are among lush fields in a river valley; the
next you are plunging through narrow gorges or traversing a high
plateau. Throughout the Czech Paradise you will find a variety of
geological wonders—sandstone rock formations, stone bridges, and
crystal formations.

Český ráj

238; 222 A5–B5

50 miles (80 km)
NE of Prague via
E65 to Turnov

Visitor information

náměstí Českého ráje
26, 51101 Turnov
e-mail info@turnov.cz

481 366 255

Valdštejn Castle

Closed Mon.–Fri.
April & Oct., &
Nov.–March

$

The densely wooded hills and steep
slopes of the Český ráj have been a
protected area since 1955. Ancient
hilltop castles and other fine buildings of historic interest mark the
skyline. In summer this small but
spectacular area of sandstone hills
and basalt outcrops is popular with
weekending Prague residents and

other visitors, but it is rarely overcrowded.

Between the northern and
southern sections of the park is the
town of Turnov, which is a handy if
not very appealing base; Jičín, to
the southeast, is more attractive but
slightly less convenient. In both
towns you can easily obtain detailed

maps showing all the hiking trails and major geological attractions in the region. **Turnov** has the **Český ráj muzeum** (*Skálova 71, closed Mon. May–Sept.; Mon.–Fri. Oct. & April; and all Nov.–March, $*), a local museum with extensive mineralogical and archaeological collections. On the outskirts of town, just off the road to the glass-making town of Železný Brod, is the mostly Renaissance château of **Hrubý Rohozec** (*closed Mon. May–Sept.; Mon.–Fri. Oct. & April; and all Nov.–March, $*), a primrose-colored expanse with fine views from its terraces. The interior contains prettily furnished rooms.

From Turnov, a road leads south toward Jičín, forming one of the informal borders of the Český ráj. Just off the road on the right you will come across the restored ruins of the 13th-century **Valdštejn Castle** (Valdštejn hrad), which was partly rebuilt in neo-Gothic style. Its 18th-century stone bridge and statuary have escaped destruction. A few miles farther south is the village of **Hrubá Skála,** and nearby are the most dazzling of the rock formations, often known as "the rock city." There are about 400 of them, some with fanciful names such as "dragon's tooth," and many can be scrambled up and over with ease. Part of the reconstructed **château** of Hrubá Skála above the village has been converted into a hotel.

Trosky Castle (Trosky hrad) was built on two volcanic pillars—one 154 feet high (47 m), the other 187 feet high (57 m)—which had burst through the sandstone. There are two fantastical lookout towers on these basalt rocks—the lower called Baba (grandmother), the higher Panna (maiden). Both offer spectacular views over the country-side. In the early Middle Ages they formed a medieval fortress and were surrounded by triple walls.

After 1620 the castle came into the hands of General Wallenstein (Valdštejn); then it was occupied by Swedish forces in 1648 and burned by the Habsburgs. To reach the castle, go south from Hrubá Skála, then head for Troskovice and leave your car in a parking lot there.

Above: Kost is the best maintained of the Český ráj's ancient castles.

Below: The strange rock formations of the Prachov crags

Trosky Castle
- 🕐 Closed Mon.
  May—Sept.; Mon.—Fri.
  April & Oct.; &
  Nov.—March
- 💲 $

Humprecht hunting lodge
- 🕐 Closed Mon.
  May—Sept.; Mon.—Fri.
  April & Oct.; &
  Nov.—March
- 💲 Guided tour: $

Kost hrad
- 🕐 Closed Mon.
  May—Sept.; Mon.—Fri.
  April & Oct.; &
  Nov.—March
- 💲 $$

In the west of the Český ráj, overlooking the village of Sobotka, is the remarkable **Humprecht hunting lodge** of 1666. A circular building on a hilltop, it resembles a stumpy moon rocket. Inside, the windowless dining room repeats the circular feature. Head north on the same road for 2 miles (3 km) to the 14th-century fortress of **Kost hrad,** perched on a crag alongside the village of Podkost. A large square keep rises up from the bulk of this well-preserved medieval castle, which houses a collection of Gothic art. Around here, and throughout the Český ráj, there are half-timbered cottages, often painted green.

Between Sobotka and Jičín (and reached by bus from Jičín) are the **Prachov crags** (Prachovské skály), the largest of the region's "rock towns." Neolithic people settled in the pillars, tunnels, cliffs, bridges, and grottoes. Easily accessi-

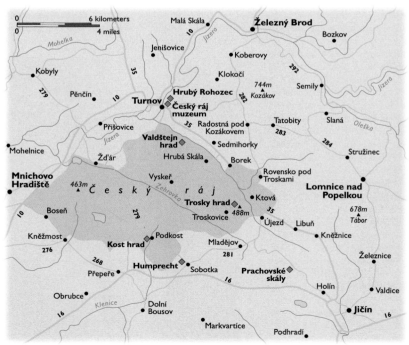

Not a spaceship, but the baroque Humprecht hunting lodge rising from a wooded hilltop

ble, Prachov can get overrun in summer and on weekends, but a visit is still worthwhile.

Southeast of the Český ráj is the town of **Jičín,** which was largely rebuilt by General Wallenstein, who adopted the town as the capital of his duchy of Frýdlant (see p. 213). Here he founded a hospital, college, and mint, but further plans for the town were brought to a halt by his assassination in 1634 (see p. 27). One of his lasting embellishments is the long avenue of over a thousand linden trees, stretching more than a mile (2 km) alongside the road to Semily. The avenue leads to the gardens of Libosad, created by Wallenstein as a summer retreat, but the site has been neglected. Back in the town itself, you enter the main square through the Valdická Bráma, a tower that was built in the 1570s and can be climbed *($)*. The 1627 **Church of St. James** (Kostel sv. Jakuba Většího) is on the left, with its set of sea-green altarpieces.

Wallenstein's squat **château** dominates the arcaded square. Built in the 1620s, its bright yellow facade, two lofty courtyards, and great expanses of windows offer a more cheerful aspect than some of his other castles. It was here in 1813 that Tsar Alexander I of Russia, Emperor Franz I of Austria, and Friedrich Wilhelm III of Prussia formed the Holy Alliance that spelled eventual defeat for Napoleon; the treaty was signed in Teplice. The château now houses a gallery and **museum.** At the end of the square a lane leads to náměstí Svobody and the Gothic **Church of St. Ignatius** (Kostel sv. Ignáce). This pleasant town makes a good base for visiting the Český ráj. ■

Jičín

⛰ 222 B5

✉ 18 miles (27 km) SE of Turnov via route 35

Visitor information

✉ Valdštejnovo náměstí 1

☎ 493 534 390

Jičín museum

🕐 Closed Sat.–Sun.

$ $

More places to visit in eastern Bohemia

ADRŠPACH-TEPLICE
Just northwest of Teplice nad Metují, close to the Polish border, lie the Adršpach-Teplice rocks. This small but dramatic region of some 400 sandstone rock formations is similar to the "rock towns" of the České Švýcarsko and Český ráj (see pp. 214–215 and p. 238).
🅰 222 D5 ✉ 3 miles (5 km) NW of Teplice nad Metují

ČASTOLOVICE
The 13th-century fortress of Častolovice, remodeled in the late 16th century and then twice more at the end of the 19th century, was returned to the Šternberk family in the 1990s, after confiscation by the Communists in the 1940s. Its park looks as though it is straight

from the English countryside. The highlight of the richly furnished interior is the spectacular **Knights' Hall,** with its painted wooden ceiling. Countess Diana Sternbergová-Phipps, the owner, presents the castle as a home rather than a museum, and also rents out rooms.
🅰 222 D4 ✉ 18 miles (30 km) SE of Hradec Králové via route 11 🕑 Closed Mon. May–Sept.; Mon.–Fri. April & Oct.; and Nov.–March 🅢 Guided tour: $$

CHRUDIM
The town of Chrudim has a sinuous baroque plague column and a dark brooding Gothic church. It is best known for its puppet festival, held every July, and its exceptional **Puppet Museum** *(Břetislavova 74, $),* housed in a remarkable 1570s mansion with arcaded galleries. On display you'll find puppets and marionettes from near—Moravia, Bohemia—and far.
🅰 222 C3 ✉ 8 miles (13 km) S of Pardubice via route 37

JOSEFOV
A garrison town on the outskirts of Jaroměř, Josefov was built as a Habsburg fortress in the 1780s on similar lines to those adopted at Terezín (see pp. 208–211). It is a forbidding place, with grim brick fortifications and drab mustard-colored barracks. Military buffs might enjoy a candlelit tour of the fort's underground tunnels that formed part of the communications network connecting different parts of the fortress.
🅰 222 C4 ✉ 12 miles (19 km) NE of Hradec Králové via route 33 🕑 Closed Mon. May–Sept.; Mon.–Fri. April & Oct.; & Nov.–March 🅢 $

KARLOVA KORUNA
The remarkable **château** of Karlova Koruna is located on the outskirts of Chlumec nad Cidlinou. Built in the early 1720s by Giovanni Santini and František Kaňka and set within a large park, the château has been restored to the original owners, the Kinský family. It's a

The Puppet Museum at Chrudim displays traditional puppets from all over the world.

Reconstructed several times since it was built in the 16th century, Nové Mesto nad Metují Castle forms the focus of the main square in this lovely old Czech village.

striking building, vaguely star-shaped, with curved facades and dramatic flights of steps. The interior exhibits a fine collection of Czech baroque art and Kinský family portraits.

▲ 222 B4 ⊠ 18 miles (30 km) W of Hradec Králové via route 11 ⊕ Closed Mon. May–Sept.; Mon.–Fri. April & Oct.; & Nov.–March ⑤ $

LIPNICE NAD SÁZAVOU

The one claim to fame of the otherwise unremarkable village of Lipnice nad Sázavou is that it was home to the novelist Jaroslav Hašek (1883–1923), who wrote *The Good Soldier Švejk*. Lipnice's medieval **castle** has been partly restored, and you can visit the Gothic chapel and other rooms. Hašek's home, at the beginning of the lane that leads to the castle, is now a commemorative **museum** *(open Tues.–Sun. June–Aug., $),* containing the writer's books, photographs, and memorabilia. His grave lies in an obscure corner of the churchyard reserved for those who had not died in a state of grace.

▲ 222 B2 ⊠ 50 miles (80 km) SW of Pardubice via routes 37, 34, 150 and minor roads Castle ⊕ Closed Mon. May–Sept.; Mon.–Fri. April & Oct.; & Nov.–March ⑤ $

MORAVSKÁ TŘEBOVÁ

In Moravská Třebová's spacious central square stands its majestic plague column dating from 1717. The town's **castle,** with its splendid arcaded and galleried courtyard, was once owned by the Liechtenstein family. Its finest feature, best viewed from the courtyard, is the three-tiered gateway, built in 1493 and said to be the earliest Renaissance structure in Moravia. The interior is closed to the public.

▲ 223 E2 ⊠ 51 miles (85 km) SE of Hradec Králové via route 35

NÁCHOD

Close to the Polish border, Náchod cowers beneath a large sgraffitoed castle on a hilltop. In the center of the main square is the 14th-century **Church of St. Lawrence** (Kostel sv. Vavřinec), with its two squat wooden towers and, inside, a charming gallery. The most impressive building is the **Hotel U Beránka,** which has a stylish secession interior. It also serves as the town theater. Náchod's sprawling **castle** is Renaissance and baroque. Ferdinand II gave it to Ottavio Piccolomini of Aragon, Wallenstein's bodyguard, in the 1630s, as a reward for his treachery in his general's assassination. It contains a stuccoed chapel and furnishings, tapestries, and paintings. The Czech novelist Josef Škvorecký was born in Náchod in 1924, and the town appears in his novels under the name Kostelec.

🅰 222 D5 ✉ 24 miles (38 km) NE of Hradec Králové via route 33 🚆 Train from Prague **Visitor information** ✉ Kamenice 144 🕐 Closed Sun. **Castle** 🕐 Closed Mon. May–Sept.; Mon.–Fri. April & Oct.; & Nov.–March 💲 $–$$

NOVÉ MĚSTO NAD METUJÍ

Nové Město nad Metují was once a stronghold of the Pernštejn family. The attractive main square is lined with 16th-century houses, a Gothic church of 1519, a gabled 16th-century town hall, and the Pernštejns' **castle,** a Gothic (1501) building subsequently given many overhauls. Approaching the castle along a bridge that crosses the former moat, you pass a series of statues of dwarves by Matthias Braun. These were acquired by textile tycoon Josef Bartoň, who bought the then run-down castle in 1908, and installed them as part of his extensive renovation. The interior is unusual: One hall is vaulted in leather, and there are cubist furnishings alongside Renaissance ones.

🅰 222 D4 ✉ 5 miles (8 km) S of Náchod via route 14 🚆 Train from Náchod **Castle** 🕐 Closed Mon. 💲 Guided tours: $–$$

OPOČNO

The Renaissance **château** at Opočno sits high above the Polabí plain. A highlight is the fabulous courtyard, with its magnificent Italianate three-storied loggia. Inside you'll find one of Bohemia's finest armories and a succession of handsome rooms containing Italian paintings and other possessions of the Colloredo family, which once owned the castle.

🅰 222 D4 ✉ 8 miles (13 km) S of Nové Město nad Metují on route 14 to Dobruška, then SW on 298 🚌 Bus from Hradec Králové 🕐 Closed Mon. May–Sept.; Mon.–Fri. April & Oct.; & Nov.–March 💲 Guided tours: $–$$

PARDUBICE

Notorious as the production center for the explosive Semtex, Pardubice prefers to be known for the annual steeplechase. The town was rebuilt by the Pernštejn family after a fire of 1507 destroyed it, but the Thirty Years War in the 17th century severely damaged it again. The old town is approached from náměstí Republiky, where a slightly garish art nouveau **theater** of 1909 faces the charming Gothic **Church of St. Bartholomew** (Kostel sv. Bartoloměje), with its gabled roof, delightful Renaissance north door, and needle-thin spire. The former **Grand Hotel** by Josef Gočár is now a commercial center.

Walk into the main square, Pernštejnské náměstí, through the 16th-century **Green Gate** (Zelená brána) topped with wildly asymmetrical turrets. Opposite the gate is the busy shopping street of Míru, with its fine trio of secession houses decorated with colorful ceramics. In the center of the square a Marian column of 1695 has a set of statues grouped around it. Among the many handsome Renaissance houses is **U Jonáše,** the Jonas House, at No. 50, which has a stucco relief of 1797 showing Jonah being ejected from the whale. To the left, Pernštěnská leads to the walled **castle** *(zámek),* separated from the old town by gardens beneath its walls. Its overall style is sgraffitoed Renaissance, but its Gothic origins are visible in the courtyard. Inside you will find a Gothic hall, rooms with Renaissance murals, a **regional museum** focusing on the Pernštejn family, and a permanent collection of Czech art.

🅰 222 C3 ✉ 12 miles (21 km) S of Hradec Králové via route 37 🚆 Train and bus from Hradec Králové; train from Prague **Visitor information** ✉ Třída Míru 60; e-mail info@pardub.cz ☎ 466 612 474 **Green Gate** 🕐 Closed Mon. May–Sept. & Oct.–April 💲 $ **Castle** 🕐 Closed Mon. 💲 $

RATIBOŘICE

The **château** at Ratibořice is an elegant pink building, originally constructed in 1708, with a curious penthouse. Exhibits here are connected with Božena Němcová, a novelist who wrote about this part of Bohemia in the 1850s. The interior contains early 19th-century furnishings. Much of the surrounding countryside, the Úpa Valley, is now a nature reserve crossed by marked hiking trails.

🅰 222 C5 ✉ 6 miles (10 km) W of Náchod via route 33 **Château** 🕐 Closed Mon. May–Sept., Mon.–Fri. April & Oct., & Nov.–March 💲 $ ∎

Arguably the most attractive corner of the country, southern Moravia has a rolling landscape and vineyards, the perfect Renaissance town of Telč, the fascinating city of Brno, and impressive castles and châteaus.

Southern Moravia

Theater and opera abound throughout the republic.

Southern Moravia

SOUTHERN MORAVIA PROBABLY HAS MORE TO TEMPT THE VISITOR THAN any other region in the republic. In a way, it epitomizes everything the Czech Republic has to offer. There is urban sophistication in Brno, but there are grand châteaus at Jaroměřice, Buchlovice, Valtice, Kroměříž, and many other places; eerie castles at Pernštejn; and a significant battlefield at Slavkov, where the Battle of Austerlitz was fought on December 2, 1805.

After Prague, Brno is the most important and most enjoyable city of the republic: urbane, bustling, and rich in culture. On its outskirts is the famous Moravian Karst (Moravský kras), a landscape through which underground rivers have gouged out spectacular caves, some open to the public—and very popular.

At Zlín, to the east, is another expression of urbanism: a town largely created by one man, shoe manufacturer Tomáš Baťa (1876– 1932). And if Zlín is an example of what patronage can achieve, there are precedents elsewhere in the region. At Kroměříž, worldly and ecclesiastical ambitions created a great palace and gardens. In Telč, the visions of a powerful 16th-century lord, Zachariáš of Hradec, extended not just to his own castle but to the entire town. His inspiration produced Telč's expansive main square, lined with exquisite arcaded houses.

There is great architecture throughout southern Moravia, ranging from the Romanesque basilica at Třebíč to the weird and wonderful designs of the most individual master of the Czech baroque, Giovanni Santini, at Žďár nad Sázavou.

Churches and monasteries abound in southern Moravia, as do ancient synagogues. For many years the Jewish history of the Czech Republic was suppressed, but that has all changed. The great synagogue in Brno is once again open, and visitors are rediscovering the plethora of ancient synagogues and cemeteries throughout the region.

The region also possesses most of the country's vineyards. While the wine is not particularly famous, the quality has improved remarkably since the end of communism in 1989. ■

NORTHERN MORAVIA
p. 277

Konice

Kostelec
na Hané
Prostějov

'35m
kalky   150

Plumlov

Jedovnice

Němčice
nad Hanou

E462

Ivanovice
na Hané

Kroměříž
palác   Kroměříž

Hulín   47

Holešov

Bystřice
pod Hostýnem

Hostýnské
vrchy

rtiny   Vyškov

D1

Rousínov

Zdounky   Otrokovice
587m

Fryšták

Zlín   Dřevnice

Vizovice   Klášťov
753m

55

49   492

Slavkov
apanice u Brna   Bučovice   50

E50   Chřiby

Velehrad

Napajedla

490

Valašská
Klobouky

Buchlov
Buchlovice

Luhačovice   Slavičín   57

Brumov-
Bylnice

Klobouky

Kyjov

Uherské
Hradiště

Uherský
Brod   Bojkovice

Uherský
Ostroh   55   50

Bánov

783m
Javorník

ustopeče
D2   Kobylí   Dubňany

Veselí
nad Moravou   54   Strání

White Carpathian Mts
(Bílé Karpaty)

Mutěnice   Rohatec   Strážnice

E65   Hodonín
Podivín   51

SLOVAKIA

ice
40   Břeclav

Valtice

E   F   G   H

Brno

Brno

🏔 244 D3

✉ 117 miles (195 km) SE of Prague

Visitor information

✉ Old Town Hall, Radnická 8
e-mail kic.brno@ brn.pvtnet.cz

☎ 542 211 090

Moravské muzeum

🕐 Closed Mon.–Tues.

$ $

TWO HILLS DOMINATE BRNO: THE CATHEDRAL STANDS ON top of one; atop the other broods the Špilberk fortress. Even today the grim castle can send a shiver down your spine. Although Brno is a sprawling industrial city, the historic center is fascinating.

Celts settled in the Brno area 2,500 years ago. In the ninth century, Slavs built a castle on what today is Petrov Hill, and from the 11th century onward it was the seat of the Margraves of Moravia. In 1641 Brno replaced Olomouc as the Moravian capital, thus inviting the aggressive attentions of the Swedes and Turks, who inflicted great damage on the city although they never captured it. Many of the baroque buildings are the work of Mořic Grimm and his brother, the city's

best known architects. The city walls were demolished by 1861 and replaced by parks and boulevards.

Industrialization, especially textile manufacture, in the 19th century brought great prosperity to Brno, which also gave its name to the Bren gun, originally produced here. By the end of the century it was the second largest city in the country, and its progressive merchant classes, largely Jewish, were keen for the city to showcase the latest industrial and commercial design. In 1928

An industrial city, Brno nevertheless possesses a culturally lively flair all its own.

Capuchin Monastery
💲 Crypt: $

Old Town Hall steeple
🕐 Closed Oct.–March
💲 $

they created the huge trade fair complex, with its innovative architectural styles; it attracts thousands of international visitors each year.

Two hills dominate the old city: Petrov and Špilberk. Petrov is the site of the cathedral, whose spindly spires can be seen for miles around. After Petrov hill was savaged by Swedish forces in 1645, during the Thirty Years War, the **Cathedral of St. Peter and St. Paul** (Dóm sv. Petra a Pavla) was rebuilt in the baroque style by Mořic Grimm. Then the exterior and entire choir were Gothicized in the early 1900s. More recently, Jiří Marek contributed some striking modernist-expressionist "Stations of the Cross." Next to the cathedral is the Renaissance **Archbishop's Palace** (Biskupská palác; not open to the public).

Steps and cobbled lanes lead down from Petrov to one of Brno's two main squares, **Zelný trh,** the bustling vegetable market focused around the Parnassus Fountain of 1695 by Johann Bernard Fischer von Erlach. The main building on the square, the relatively plain 17th-century **Dietrichstein Palace** (Ditrichštejnský palác), is now the **Moravské muzeum.** Dedicated to Moravian history, the museum contains some craft and folklore exhibits. In the prehistoric finds, the prize exhibit is the 25,000-year-old **Venus of Věstonice,** the oldest known statuette representing the human form.

On leaving the palace, turn right and walk through the iron gates into the Bishop's Courtyard, where the less exciting **Biskupský dvůr muzeum** is devoted to Moravian fauna (including a record-breaking collection of cicadas) and coins. Down the slope from here, in Kapucínské náměstí, is the plain **Capuchin Monastery** (Kapucínský klášter), where some

150 mummified corpses (including that of architect Mořic Grimm) were deposited clothed and exposed in the crypt. In 1784 the practice—a gruesome sight, but not unusual in central Europe—was stopped on health grounds. In the last room 24 Capuchin monks are laid out on the bare earth, their heads supported on bricks; some faces are disconcertingly well preserved after 250 years.

Across Zelný trh from here you can see the complex steeple of the **Old Town Hall** (Stará radnice), resembling a series of spiked Ottoman helmets. Anton Pilgram, who later adorned St. Stephen's Cathedral in Vienna with carvings, designed the Gothic portal in 1511, its central pinnacle deliberately skewed as though it were about to topple. Hanging in the arched entryway is the so-called Brno Dragon (Brněnský Drak), instantly recognizable as a mounted alligator; it was presented by a Turkish delegation to Matthias Corvinus. Centuries ago this was a novelty, and the people of Brno have a soft spot for this unusual gift to their city, as well as for the cartwheel hanging on the wall. In 1636 Georg Birk, a carter, wagered that he could fashion the wheel from a log and roll it the 35 miles (50 km) from his village to Brno all in one day. He won his bet.

Just beyond the Old Town Hall is the 1655 Dominican **Church of St. Michael** (Kostel sv. Michala), which has the usual set of baroque altarpieces and statuary, although the carvings above the pulpit look as though a bomb had detonated in heaven. Next to the church is the baroque **New Town Hall** (Nová radnice). This was originally the Dominican monastery, designed by the Grimm brothers in the 1690s.

Opposite the New Town Hall, a short street leads down to the largest square in the old town,

Governor's Palace
- Closed Mon.–Tues.
- $

Pražákův palác
- Husova 18
- Closed Mon.–Tues.
- $

UPM
- Closed Mon.–Tues.
- $

In this early 17th-century print, the city is already dominated by the awesome Špilberk fortress.

náměstí Svobody, which is dissected by tramlines and has a McDonald's. Brno's main street, Masarykova, connects the square to the railway station. Compared with most main squares in Czech cities, náměstí Svobody is nondescript, and even the plague column is a rigid design. From the top of the square, Jánská leads to the **Minorite church** (Kostel sv. Jana), designed by the Grimms, who studded its broad facade with vigorous statues. The richly decorated interior is enlivened by a top-heavy baroque organ festooned with putti playing instruments. Opposite the church, along Minoritská, some fine secession houses and shops have been freshly restored and sparkle with gold leaf. At the other end of Jánská is a glass-paneled department store called **Centrum,** built by shoe tycoon Tomáš Baťa (see pp. 262–263) in 1928.

Continue past Centrum onto Malinovského náměstí, where on the left stands the 19th-century **Mahen Theater** (Mahenovo divadlo). It has pretensions to grandeur, with an impressive drive sweeping up to the entrance porch. The interior is sumptuous, including fine staircases, chandeliers, salons for strolling during the intervals, and, of course, a tiered auditorium that is heavily gilded, luxurious yet intimate. In 1882 it was the first theater in Europe to use electric lighting.

Another street leading out of Svobody—Rašínova—takes you to the large Gothic **Church of St. Jacob** (Kostel sv. Jakuba), Brno's parish church, with its lofty belfry. The aisles are sustained by piers so slender they seem incapable of holding the weight of the enormous structure, even aided by a maze of delicate rib vaults. This Gothic elegance is refreshing after so much baroque in churches elsewhere in Brno. Continue another block along Rašínova to the **Church of St. Thomas** (Kostel sv. Tomáš), a baroque

BRVNN
Vulgo Brinn Marchionatus Morauiæ
Ciuitas insignis.

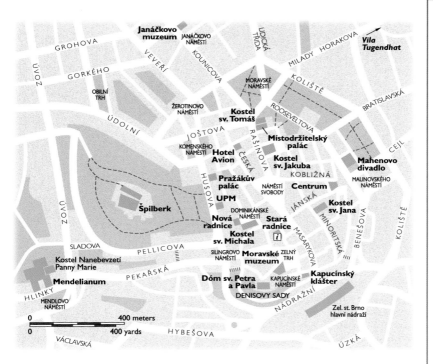

building notable for a triple-decker pulpit.

Adjoining St. Thomas is the former 18th-century **Governor's Palace** (Místodržitelský palác), designed by the Grimms and since 1992 housing part of the Moravian Gallery collections. The Gothic collection is exquisite, with an abundance of wood carvings and paintings, including a 15th-century panel depicting the martyrdom of St. Osvald by a prototype of the guillotine. Rubens's vivid snake-strewn portrait of Medusa's head is here, too. There are also good examples of 18th-century paintings by Daniel Gran, Johann Lucas Kracher, Franz Anton Maulbertsch, and Angelica Kauffmann, and 19th-century portraits by Friedrich Amerling and Hans Makart. Down the road from the palace, on the

corner of Česká, you come to the **Hotel Avion,** designed by Brno's leading 20th-century architect, Bohuslav Fuchs.

Two other branches of the Moravian Gallery are on Husova, near the Špilberk. The modern art museum, housed at Husova 18 in the **Pražákův palác,** has impressive cubist paintings by Emil Filla and Antonín Procházka. It's also worth visiting for the melancholy portraits by Jan Zrzavý.

Across from the palace is the applied arts museum, known as **UPM,** with examples from Gothic times to the present day. The comprehensive collection includes Gothic ivories, 17th-century glass, and early 19th-century Biedermeier furniture. There was then a complete collapse of taste until the secession and the cubist movement breathed

One of Moravia's most important modern buildings is the Tugendhat House, designed by German architect Mies van der Rohe for textile tycoons.

new life into furniture design and restored standards of the most exquisite craftsmanship. Some of the furnishings for Ludwig Mies van der Rohe's Tugendhat House (see p. 251) are displayed here.

Opposite these museums is Špilberk hill. The Bohemian king Přemysl Otakar II built a **fortress** (hrad Špilberk) here in about 1270, and during the Thirty Years War it was converted into a fearsome citadel where political opponents of the Habsburgs were incarcerated in its dungeons. Embarrassed by the prison's notoriety, the Habsburgs closed it in the 1850s. In 1880 it was reopened as a tourist attraction.

During the Nazi occupation,

Špilberk dungeons
Closed Mon. & Nov.–March
$

Janáček Museum
Closed Fri.–Sun.
$

Tugendhat House
Černopolní 45
Closed Mon.–Tues.
Guided tours: $$

Mendelianum
Mendlovo náměstí 1
Closed Sat.–Sun.
$

Gregor Mendel

Southwest of Špilberk is the Augustinian priory where the Austrian monk Gregor Johann Mendel (1822–1884) lived. His studies of the inheritance of qualities in the garden pea and beans led to major discoveries in the laws of heredity and the development of the science of genetics. Mendel published the results of his research in scientific journals, but their full significance was overlooked by contemporary scientists. Disillusioned by the indif- ference with which his work was greeted, he abandoned scientific research to become the abbot of the monastery in 1868, and his true greatness was recognized only after his death. His work led to an understanding of the nature and properties of chromosomes and thus the mechanisms of heredity. A museum, the **Mendelianum,** commemo- rates his achievements, and you can visit the famous priory garden where he conducted his experiments. ∎

museum *($)*. It's quite a climb up the hill to the citadel, but the view from the top is terrific.

Leoš Janáček spent most of his working life as a composer in Brno, and his house is now the **Janáček Museum** (Janáčkovo muzeum). You can reach it from náměstí Svobody by taking Rašinova to the north, then continuing along Kounicova, which leads to the museum.

Beyond the town center are the **fairgrounds,** Výstaviště, originally laid out in 1928 and still in regular use. They provided a showcase for the leading Czech architects, then working in a functionalist style.

An important modern building in Brno, set in the suburb of Černá Pole, is the **Tugendhat House** (Vila Tugendhat) of 1930, designed by Mies van der Rohe. The stark white villa is revolutionary for its radical design of "free floating space." Badly damaged by the Nazis after its owners fled in 1938, the house has since been restored. ■

however, the Gestapo found the fortress ideal for their purposes, and many victims were imprisoned, tortured, and executed here. You can visit the **Špilberk dungeons** and torture chambers, and the west side of the fortress is now the city

Deep beneath the whitewashed walls of the Špilberk fortress burrow dark dungeons once used by both the Habsburgs and the Nazis.

Znojmo

THE ANCIENT HILLTOP TOWN OF ZNOJMO LIES CLOSE TO the Austrian border. Bohemian Prince Břetislav I built a citadel here a thousand years ago to defend an important trading route. The Přemyslid king Otakar II was buried in a monastery near the town in 1278, and in 1437 Emperor Sigismund breathed his last here. Its military usefulness diminished over the centuries, and Znojmo became a tranquil regional center marred by industrial outskirts.

Some of the fortifications have survived, and Znojmo has two principal squares: Horní náměstí is higher up; the larger Masarykovo náměstí is flanked by the town hall. The old town hall was destroyed by the Nazis, but the remarkable pinnacled tower of 1445 has survived. Just off Horní náměstí on Slepičí trh, you can join a 40-minute guided tour to the **underground tunnels** *(podzemí),* used both for defensive and storage purposes. The square was severely damaged during World War II and is now a hodgepodge of buildings, the best being the House of Art (Dům umění) at No. 11. The courtyard is arcaded, and the buildings are used as an art gallery.

From the town hall Mikulášská leads to the tall, elegant Gothic **Church of St. Nicholas** (Kostel sv. Mikuláše), which is furnished with an exuberant baroque pulpit. Behind it, the tiny 16th-century **Chapel of St. Wenceslas** (Orthodox kaple sv. Václava) forms part of the town ramparts. A terrace nearby offers views onto the Dyje River Valley below.

It's a short stroll from here to what's left of the **castle,** which is now a brewery, a very Czech solution to a problem of conservation. Within its precincts stands a small Romanesque **rotunda** that dates from the early 11th century. The precious 12th-century frescoes decorating it are the most complete and best preserved examples from the period in the Czech Republic. The lower tier depicts scenes from the life of the Virgin, while those above illustrate the legendary Libuše and the Přemyslid kings. The Přemyslids themselves commissioned this remarkable cycle in 1134. Also within the castle is the **South Moravian Museum** (Jihomoravské muzeum), with varied archaeological and natural history collections.

There are two worthwhile attractions on the outskirts of town. A mile (2 km) out on the road to Mašovice is the baroque **Church of St. Hippolytus** (Kostel sv. Hypolita); it sits on the site of the original ninth-century Znojmo, which switched to its present hilltop two centuries later. Frescoes in the dome are by Austrian artist Franz Anton Maulbertsch, whose work also adorns Kroměříž (see pp. 264–265). And just south of Znojmo, off the Vienna road, is **Louka,** where the Premonstratensian monastery was founded in the 12th century. The monastery's Philosophical Library was moved, in its entirety, to Strahov monastery in Prague (see pp. 80–82). The baroque buildings, larger than many a palace, were long used as a barracks and are derelict, but the plain church of 1689 has been restored. In the courtyard stands a black cross wreathed in barbed wire, and an inscription honors the "victims of Stalinist Bolshevism 1945–1989." ■

Znojmo
- 244 C1
- 33 miles (56 km) SW of Brno

Visitor information
- Obroková 10 e-mail tic@oknet.cz
- 515 222 552

Town hall tower
- Closed Sun. April & Oct., Sat.–Sun. Nov.–March
- $

Underground tunnels
- Closed Mon. April–Sept., Sat.–Sun. Nov.–March
- $

Rotunda
- Closed Mon. June–Sept.; Mon.–Fri. May & Oct.–April; & all Nov.–March
- Guided tour: $$

South Moravian Museum
- Přemyslovců 6
- Closed Mon. May–Sept., & Mon.–Fri. Oct.–April
- $

Opposite: The Church of St. Nicholas rises above the roofs of Znojmo.

Jewish Moravia

Although the Jewish synagogues and cemeteries of Prague have been attracting visitors for decades, the other Jewish centers of the republic are only now being rediscovered. There was already a substantial Jewish community in the Czech lands in early medieval times, and King Přemysl Otakar II offered royal protection in a charter of 1254. It wasn't always effective, and Jews suffered from the same discrimination and attacks as elsewhere in Europe.

The Jewish cemetery at Třebíč is the largest in the republic.

Despite the expulsions and occasional pogroms, the Jewish culture managed to thrive. By 1938 the Jewish population of Bohemia and Moravia was around 120,000; the sheer scale of the main synagogue in Brno gives some idea of the size and wealth of the local community. World War II and the Holocaust reduced that community to tatters, and well over half the population perished. Many of those who survived emigrated after the war ended, and more went in 1968 when the Soviet invasion extinguished hopes of liberalization. Numbers for the Jewish population today are hard to come by, but one estimate is about 6,000. During the communist years the community kept a low profile, but since 1989 Bohemia and Moravia have taken pride in the remnants of a once vital culture. Most synagogues were destroyed by the Nazis or converted for other uses, but a few survive, as do cemeteries, many of which contain gravestones dating back three centuries. Hardly a town in Moravia is without its Jewish traces, and here are a few highlights:

Boskovice

At Boskovice, north of Brno, there's a cemetery with graves dating back to the 17th century. The graves lie in lines across a wooded slope, a tranquil and haunting spot. (A key

is available from the information center in the town hall.) Plačkova street retains several Jewish houses.

Holešov

In Holešov, north of Zlín, the synagogue *(closed Mon., $)* is on Striční, two blocks behind the information office on the main square, náměstí E. Beneša. This is the Šachova synagóga, named after its most celebrated rabbi. The building dates from 1560, but the lovely interior is essentially 18th century, from the Hebrew inscriptions on the walls to the fine ironwork around the bima. The gallery has been adapted into a small museum. Behind Striční, on Hankého, is the entrance to the Jewish cemetery, a few recent graves a welcome reminder that the Jews of Moravia were not entirely wiped out by 1945. Hundreds of older gravestones, dating back to the 17th century, lie in random order.

Mikulov

There has been a Jewish community in Mikulov, south of Brno close to the Austrian border, since at least 1369, rising to 3,500 in number during the 19th century. Two rare survivals are the 15th-century synagogue at Husova 13 *(closed Mon. & Oct.–April)* and the overgrown Jewish cemetery on Brněnská.

Třebíč

Not far from the basilica of St. Procopius, which stands on a hill overlooking Třebíč, is the former ghetto. Two synagogues—one from 1639 on Tiché náměstí, the other at Bohuslavova 42—still exist, and to the north of the former is the largest Jewish cemetery in the republic, outside Prague, with 3,000 headstones dating back to the 1640s. ∎

Šachova synagóga in Holešov is one of Moravia's most beautiful synagogues.

Valtice & Lednice

Valtice

- 🏔 245 E1
- ✉ 40 miles (64 km) S of Brno via E65, Břeclav exit
- 🚆 Train from Mikulov or Břeclav

Visitor information

- ✉ Náměstí Svobody 4, Valtice
- ☎ 519 352 977

Château

- 🕐 Closed Mon. May–Sept.; Mon.–Fri. April & Oct.; & all Nov.–March
- 💲 $–$$

Valtice cellars

- 🕐 Closed Mon. & Oct.–April

VALTICE AND LEDNICE ARE TWO OF THE VAST MORAVIAN châteaus owned by the Liechtenstein family. Although quite close to each other, they are entirely different in style and atmosphere. Valtice is the more interesting house, but Lednice is set on very beautiful grounds, which can also be visited. The Liechtensteins were one of the most powerful families of the Austro-Hungarian Empire. They owned two enormous palaces in Vienna and dozens of estates in Moravia, where they first became landowners in the 14th century. In 1945, after accusations of collaboration with the Germans, the family fled the country as the Soviets advanced. Their estates were confiscated, and the family is still negotiating with the Czech authorities for the return of their extensive properties.

VALTICE

Valtice is a pompous baroque château festooned with coats of arms, statues, and military emblems. There was a castle here in the 12th century, but it was frequently altered and rebuilt. Its present appearance dates from the early 18th century.

Part of the château is now a hotel, but some state rooms are open to the public. Valtice has a certain grandeur, the opulent high baroque chapel being notable. The wood-paneled Gold Chamber adjoining the princess's bedroom is another exquisitely ornamented room. Many of the rooms are almost bare,

The baroque château of Valtice looks out over formal gardens dotted with statues.

At Lednice the Liechtensteins built a vast neo-Gothic château, adjoining an immense park.

however, because after the château was expropriated in 1945, it was stripped of its furnishings.

Valtice has its own wine estate; the **cellars,** which can be visited, date from the 1430s. In August, a baroque music festival held at Valtice includes open-air performances of both opera and ballet.

LEDNICE

Lednice is quite different. Where Valtice is about power, Lednice's endearing neo-Gothic fantasy is playful, an attempt to dress up in history. The Liechtensteins lost interest in Valtice in the 18th century and concentrated on Lednice. The existing structure was built by Jiří Wingelmüller in 1856, the latest in a succession of rebuildings of the château owned by the family since the mid-13th century. Guided tours of the château show you the brightly colored and heavily paneled interior. It is impressively lavish, if hardly the epitome of good taste.

THE PARK

In the park between the châteaus are three lakes created in the 17th century, as well as a larger natural lake strewn with islets. With so much water around, the park is a haven for waterfowl. Over the centuries pavilions, summerhouses, a mock-ruined castle, and, most curious of all, a huge Turkish-style minaret of 1802 were added. You can walk the 4 miles (7 km) from one château to the other, along an avenue of lime trees. ∎

Lednice
- 245 E1
- 38 miles (61 km) S of Brno
- Train from Břeclav

Visitor information
- Zámecké náměstí 68, 69144 Lednice
  e-mail tic@lednice.cz
- 519 340 986

Château
- Closed Mon. May–Sept.; Mon.–Fri. April & Oct.; & all Nov.–March
- $$–$$$

Strážnice's Folk Festival

Folk festivals, typically held in the summer months, are enormously popular throughout the country. Perhaps the most famous of all is Strážnice's boisterous festival in late June, which draws thousands of visitors each year to this easygoing town, 12 miles (19 km) south of Uherské Hradiště.

It has to be recognized, however, that many so-called "folkloric" events lack authenticity. With religious practice severely discouraged by the Communists, there were fewer outlets for the almost universal desire to enjoy feasts and festivals. In some cases traditional observances were retained without their religious overtones; in others, a somewhat bogus return to national roots was seen as a way of keeping the people entertained while at the same time fostering a national consciousness without nationalist overtones. Traditional costumes and melodies were put at the service of the state during May Day parades and other glorifications of the communist way of life. Books and posters can still give the impression that the countryside in the Czech lands is filled with smiling peasantry in brightly patterned national costumes. In truth, such costumes are rarely glimpsed, except during these festivals.

A new musical tradition was also created, since the puritanical Communist authorities took a dim view of jazz and rock and roll, which were associated with the depravities of the West. In their place were brass bands, folk dance ensembles, and musical

Of the many folk festivals in the republic, none can rival Strážnice in size and diversity.

contests. Naturally, the more wily composers and performers, especially in the field of folk song, turned the situation to their advantage, devising satirical or subversive songs in the guise of traditional music. Membership in folkloric ensembles was often little more than a cover for trips out of the country, a form of travel restricted to the privileged few until 1989.

In Strážnice *(visitor information, Irra, Predmestí 399, tel 578 332 184),* as in other towns with a similar tradition and identity—including Domažlice (see pp. 198–199), in western Bohemia, and Buchlov (see p. 274)—folklore and marketing join hands. Workshops in the town manufacture hand-painted ceramics with folkloric themes, and the castle museum features displays of local folk art.

The town has lost most of its fortifications, although two Renaissance gateways survive.

The castle *(closed Mon. & Nov.–April, $)* was originally built in the 13th century, but the present structure is an 1850s reconstruction in a Renaissance style. An attractive *skansen (closed Mon. & Nov.–April, tour $)*, an open-air museum of folk architecture, is located on the edge of town. Most of the structures here date from the 19th century; they include a winery, smithy, and decorative beehives.

Strážnice's festival, first established in 1946, is spread over three days, and, although billed as international, it focuses mostly on local traditions in music, dance, and costume. The performances take place on the castle grounds, and there are also parades within the town, with a strong emphasis on children participation. Huge quantities of food, wine, and beer are consumed, and the atmosphere is predictably boisterous. ■

Traditional fiddlers strike up a tune in the fields around Strážnice.

Velehrad

SIX MILES (9 KM) NORTHWEST OF UHERSKÉ HRADIŠTĚ, IN pretty hill country, stands the immense monastery of Velehrad. It's not only the 18th-century church with its two tall steeples that is impressive, it's also the whole complex of yellow-and-white monastic buildings surrounding it.

The first Cistercian monastery in Moravia was built here in the early 13th century, but Hussites partly destroyed it in 1421. The monastery lay derelict until the 17th century, when its remains were incinerated in 1681. Plans for reconstruction got under way rapidly in the 1680s, with Giovanni Tencalla as the principal architect. In 1710 the work was completed, and the present church was consecrated in 1735. Beneath the church is a lapidarium, where the **crypt** and some remains of the original church can still be seen, giving an idea of the size of the structure; it was clearly built on a very large scale. There are also vestiges of the Romanesque church in the apses at the west end.

Velehrad is an important pilgrimage church, with tens of thousands of worshipers visiting each year. One reason it attracts so many pilgrims is its dedication to the Apostles of the Slavs, Saints Cyril and

Methodius (see p. 20). Some people therefore conclude, falsely, that it was the site of St. Methodius's bishopric.

The two priests were dispatched as missionaries to Moravia from Constantinople in 863. Here they preached in the vernacular, winning the admiration of the populace. Cyril returned to Rome, where he spent the rest of his life, but Methodius returned to Moravia, enduring hardships and imprisonment, thanks to the jealous interventions of other clergy. He rose to become a bishop. It was once believed that he died here at Velehrad in 885, but this is now thought to be incorrect.

Nevertheless, on July 5, a state and church holiday, pilgrims come here in droves. More than 150,000 worshipers flocked here in 1985 for the 1,100th anniversary of Methodius's death, despite Communist authority disapproval. Even this large number was easily surpassed when, on April 22, 1990, Pope John Paul II paid homage to the two saints at Velehrad; it is estimated that half a million worshipers were present.

The 18th-century building is baroque, but the interior, with its immense length and serene atmosphere, retains its impressive Romanesque proportions. Note the delightful, if faded, trompe l'oeil frescoes, the pink and eggshell-blue paintwork, richly carved choir stalls (1700), and a succession of side altars, each with differing stucco decoration. Keep an eye out, too, for the 1745 organ, festooned with cherubs. ∎

Pope John Paul II visited this holy site and pilgrimage church in 1990.

Zlín

ZLÍN IS A FACTORY TOWN, BUT A FACTORY TOWN WITH A difference. When the Bat'a footwear factory was constructed here, Tomáš Bat'a (1876–1932) built not only his own villa but also an entire company town, providing his workers with accommodations. The company was founded in 1894 and, as it prospered, so Zlín grew, from a small town with just a few thousand people to a city sprawling along a verdant valley with almost 100,000 inhabitants.

Bat'a made his fortune during World War I, when the millions of soldiers in the Austro-Hungarian forces wore the boots he manufactured. The company continued to expand, and when Bat'a died in a plane crash in 1932, his company was the world's largest shoe manufacturer. In 1938 his son, also called

Tomáš, saw there was no future for the Bat'as in Moravia and immigrated, together with a substantial part of his workforce, to Canada, where the company expanded further.

It may be decried as old-fashioned paternalism, but Bat'a wanted to provide his workforce with good housing and prestigious

This early 20th-century company town features its own large hotel (right) and an array of factories and offices (below).

educational and cultural amenities. He brought in the finest architects of the day, including Frenchman Le Corbusier (1877–1965), as well as the Czech Jan Kotěra, who built Baťa's own villa. Le Corbusier's designs for the new town didn't satisfy Baťa, who gave the commission to Kotěra's pupil František Gahura (1891–1958). The principal building was the shoe factory itself; now called the Svít Corporation, it houses a comprehensive **museum** about shoes and their manufacture. The factory's most remarkable feature was a glass elevator that had a dual role as Baťa's mobile office, allowing him to visit and work on each floor of the building. Opposite the factory are a department store, the Moskva Hotel, and a cinema, all part of the original town plan. So is the large square called Masarykovo náměstí, with one of the town schools and the concert hall.

Zlín is not particularly beautiful, but its buildings are functional and well designed, and for the most part they have aged well. Like many grand town-planning schemes, Gahura's was never completed. Moreover, much was destroyed during World War II. The modernized Renaissance **castle,** a heavy square yellow block near the factory, is of interest, less for its architecture than for its excellent museum. The collection features 20th-century Czech art upstairs (with representative paintings by Filla, Kubišta, Josef Čapek, and Antonín Procházka, as well as by contemporary artists), plus exhibits on southeast Moravia.

From 1949 to 1990 the town was called Gottwaldov after Communist leader Klement Gottwald, who died in 1953. Famous natives of Zlín include playwright Tom Stoppard and Ivana Trump, ex-wife of tycoon Donald Trump. The town is also known for film studios specializing in animated films. ∎

Zlín

🗺 245 G3

🚌 Bus from Uherské Hradiště & Brno. Train from Olomouc & Brno

Visitor information

✉ Town hall, Bartošova 12

☎ 577 214 138

Shoe museum

🕐 Closed Mon. April–Oct., Sat.–Sun. Nov.–March

💲 $

Castle

🕐 Closed Mon.

💲 $

The visionary approach of Tomáš Baťa radically transformed Zlín, but his death in 1932 prevented some of his projects from being completed.

Kroměříž Palace

Kroměříž

🅰 245 F3

✉ 40 miles (64 km)
E of Brno

🚆 Train from Brno,
change at Kojetín.
Bus from Brno &
Prague

Visitor information

✉ Velké náměstí 50/45

☎ 573 334 191

🕐 Closed Sun. in winter

THE OLD TOWN OF KROMĚŘÍŽ WAS ALMOST DESTROYED during the Thirty Years War. The prince-bishops of Olumouc reconstructed it, from 1686 onward, on the grandest scale. Not only did they build a palatial residence for themselves, but they laid out elaborate Italian gardens, all of which survive to this day, as does the fine gallery attached to the palace. Even in a country rich in palaces, this one is just about unrivaled in its pomp and opulence.

After the Thirty Years War, only a single tower remained of the Renaissance Bishop's palace, so the present complex, which stands just north of the main square, was almost entirely rebuilt by Prince-Bishop Karl Eusebius von Liechtenstein-Kastelkorn. He appointed the Italian architects Filiberto Lucchese and Giovanni Tencalla to draw up plans for his new palace. They came up with a somewhat intimidating early baroque design. Italian craftsmen, including Baltasare Fontana, decorated the interior and carried out the stuccowork. The prince-bishop also established a court orchestra.

The only way to visit the palace is by guided tour, which takes 90 minutes. There is also a tour that takes you to the top of the lofty

tower, but this is of less interest. The original interior was destroyed by fire in 1752, and the artists commissioned to repair the damage were Franz Anton Maulbertsch and Josef Stern. The colorful style of Stern's frescoes, on the theme of Parnassus, a Greek sacred mountain, contrasts with the austere exterior of the palace. In the 1770s the Diet Hall (Sněmovní sál) was lavishly painted by František von Freenthal.

The stupendous **library** holds more than 50,000 volumes, along with a collection of globes and an extensive musical archive, including scores by Mozart and Haydn. A collection of coins and medals reflects the fact that there was a mint at Kroměříž between 1613 and 1760. On the tour you also visit the Hunting Hall, the Throne Room, the Audience Hall, and the Tsar's Hall, where Emperor Franz Josef I and Tsar Alexander III met in 1885.

You'll need a separate ticket to visit the **picture gallery,** which is housed on the second floor of the palace. You tour the rooms without a guide, so you can take your time. The famous art collection, the largest in the Czech Republic outside Prague, is based on the acquisitions of Karl von Liechtenstein, who astutely bought up private collections. The gallery has masterpieces that include religious works by the Master of Kroměříž and Lucas Cranach the Elder. The Italian paintings include Veronese's fragmentary "Apostles," a cycle by Jacopo Bassano on the story of Noah, and a 1571 masterpiece by Titian: "The Flaying of Marsyas by Apollo," a brooding and unsettling visualization of the gruesome scene. There are also works by Jan and Pieter Breughel, and a tender double portrait by Anthony van Dyck of the English King Charles I and his Queen, Henrietta.

Fountains, small lakes, romantic tree alleys, and small English gardens are just some of the charms of the palace gardens.

Kroměříž Palace
☎ 573 502 011
🕐 Closed Mon.
  May–Sept.; Mon.–Fri.
  April & Oct.; & all
  March–Dec.
💲 $$$. Gallery: $$

Few ecclesiastical palaces in Europe can match that of Kroměříž for grandeur and pomp.

Surrounding the palace, the beautiful **gardens,** extending to the banks of the River Morava, contain many lakes and waterways. Attractions include a Chinese Pavilion, an aviary, and a menagerie.

To visit the rest of Kroměříž, return to the main square (Velk namestí). From here, Jánská leads to the sinuous baroque **Church of St. John the Baptist** (Kostel sv. Jana Křtitele), and Jánska itself contains houses for the church's officials. From the Church of St. John the Baptist, walk up Pilarova to the 13th-century **Cathedral of St. Maurice** (Chrám sv. Mořice); though it's one of the few surviving medieval buildings in town, its interior is disappointing. The Jewish **town hall** (Radnice) at Moravcova 9 is the only surviving example outside Prague.

Don't miss the prince-bishop's other splendid **flower garden** (Kvetná zahrada), west of the town on Svobody. ■

Moravian Karst

Moravian Karst
245 E3
Train from Brno to Blansko, then bus to Skalní Mlýn

Visitor information
Rožmitálova 6, Blansko
516 410 470

SIXTEEN MILES (25 KM) NORTH OF BRNO IS A FASCINATING region of Devonian limestone hills known as the Moravian Karst (Moravský kras). Some 4 miles wide (6 km) and 16 miles long (25 km), it's a forested area of spectacular rock formations and deep ravines, with miles of caves and tunnels. Many of these caves have been carved out by an underground river, the Punkva. Of the thousand or so caves in the region, only four are open to the public, and many are being explored for the first time.

The **Punkevní caves** (Punkevní jeskyně; $$) are the most spectacular and popular, with long lines forming in summer. Arrive early to avoid a tedious wait or a sellout for the rest of the day. Along with the Kateřinská caves, they are best reached by taking the road from Blansko toward **Rock Mill** (Skalní Mlýn) nature reserve *(visitor information, tel 516 413 575).* Here you'll find a parking lot and hotel. From Skalní Mlýn it is a short walk to the Kateřinská caves and a mile-long (2 km) walk to the

Punkevní caves; a small train shuttles back and forth *($)*.

The hour-long tour of Punkevní passes through five large caves, glistening with stalactites and stalagmites formed by the steady drip of rainwater through the limestone, and emerges at the lake at the foot of the Macocha Abyss. This chasm is 453 feet deep (138 m), created when the rock roof of an immense cave collapsed. The abyss is filled with luxuriant vegetation, owing to the exceptionally warm and moist microclimate of the chasm.

If you want to see how the chasm looks from the top, take a cable car *(buy a ticket before entering the caves, $)* to the crest of the abyss,

A ride on the underground Punkva River is just one highlight of the Punkevní cave tour.

where there is a restaurant. You can also get there by road: Take the Ostrov direction from Skalní Mlýn, and turn left after just over a mile (2 km). The tour continues by boat, a 1,640-foot-long (500 m) ride on the underground Punkva River.

Much less crowded are the **Kateřinská caves** (Kateřinská jeskyně). They have a remarkable collection of stick stalagmites in two vast caverns *(30-minute tour)*. In summer, concerts are held in this amazing setting. The **Balcarka caves** (Balcarka jeskyně), east of the Macocha Abyss, are smaller, but they have colorful stalactites and stalagmites *(45-minute tour)*.

Linked by galleries and domed chambers, the **Sloupsko-Šošůvské caves** (Sloupsko-Šošůvské jeskyně), just south of the hamlet of Sloup, are the spookiest. Many fossils have been discovered here, and in 1966 the remains of a Neanderthal man were found nearby, as well as vestigial prehistoric wall paintings.

For a change, the wooded hills of the Moravian Karst are easily explored along walking trails. ■

The gaping maw of the Macocha Abyss falls 450 feet (137 m) from the top.

Kateřinská caves
- 325 yards (300 m) from the Skalní Mlýn parking lot
- Closed Nov.–Jan.
- $

Balcarka caves
- Just over a mile (2 km) from the Skalní Mlýn parking lot
- Closed Nov.–Jan.
- $

Sloupsko-Šošůvské caves
- S of Sloup
- Closed Nov.–Jan.
- $

Pernštejn castle's spacious vaulted library

Pernštejn

OVERLOOKING THE RIVER SVRATKA AND THE LITTLE TOWN of Nedvědice is the amazing castle of Pernštejn. Originally a 13th-century fortress, stronghold of the Pernštejn family, it grew to become one of the largest and best-preserved castles in the country. The oldest sections are the ramparts and the round tower.

Pernštejn

- 244 D3
- 25 miles (40 km) NW of Brno via routes 43 and 387
- Train from Brno to Nedvědice, then 1-mile (1.6 km) walk to castle, or taxi from station
- Closed Mon. May–Sept.; Mon.–Fri. April & Oct.; & Nov.–March
- $$–$$$

Opposite: Sitting astride a craggy spur, Pernštejn was never conquered.

Because the castle was believed, with good reason, to be totally secure, the Pernštejns gradually converted it into a palatial residence as well as a fortress. By 1596, the family had fallen on hard times and were forced to sell the castle. It changed hands several times until it was purchased in 1818 by the Mitrovic family, who owned it until 1945. The most celebrated feature is the wooden bridge, with a perilous drop beneath, that links two of the keeps. There are many defensive machicolations, so the building gets fatter but more angular and more elaborate as it rises. It is baffling to imagine how such a complex structure could have been constructed on this rocky and vertiginous spur. Unsurprisingly, with such a dominant position, the castle was never conquered.

You set off on the 80-minute tour through one set of walls and gateways after another—the outer walls sheltering a restaurant and pub. Gradually the amazing sight of the top-heavy castle comes into full view. The initially Renaissance interior was adapted and decorated in the 18th and 19th centuries, and its staid, and occasionally over-pretty state, comes as a disappointment after the high drama of the exterior. But there are older parts that have not been altered to the same extent—notably the chapel of 1570, the baroque Knights' Hall with its stucco swags, and the library. Some of the later decorations are quite successful, including the low-ceilinged Hall of Conspirators, with its neo-Gothic furnishings and painted coats of arms. ∎

Czech wine

It is understandable that Bohemia became world famous for its beer, as good as it is. But few know about Czech wine. The winemaking tradition dates back to the third century, when Romans grew grapes in the Palava region near Mikolov, in southern Moravia on the Old Amber Trail. Archaeologists know this because a vintner's knife for cutting vines was found at the site of the camp. In 1358 winemaking received royal patronage under Charles IV, who had been educated in the French court. He began importing Burgundy grapes from France, thereby turning Prague into a major viticulture center.

The hops harvest depicted in sgraffito at Klatovy

You'll find vineyards along the Elbe River in Bohemia and along the Danube River in Moravia, though it's the latter region, the larger of the two, that is most lauded. The region around Mikolov especially (see pp. 252–253), with its cool microclimate and warm, south-facing slopes, remains one of the most productive wine regions in the Czech Republic. It's not surprising that the wines here bear a resemblance to their Austrian brethren, grown across the border in a region known as the Weinviertel. As in Austria, white wines are favored—about 75 percent of Czech wines are white—and the grape varieties are similar: Ryzlink Rýnský (Riesling), Ryzlink Vlašský (Welschriesling), Müller-Thurgau, Tramín (Gewürztraminer), Rulandské bílé (Pinot Blanc), and the often excellent Veltlinské zelené (Grüner Veltliner).

The Czech reds can be good to excellent, though different from French or Spanish wines, since many of the grapes used are different. The best reds often come from the Velké Pavlovice region of Moravia. Among the leading varieties, resembling those found in neighboring Austria, are Frankova (Lemberger, Blaufränkisch),

Svatovavřinecké (St. Laurent), and Zweigelt.

Specialty wines such as Ice and Straw are also very popular, as is Muscat wine, which leans toward flowery without being too cloying. A notable quantity of sparkling wine is also produced.

A category of Czech wine known as "Archiv" is popular in restaurants, despite their very high price tags. These are older vintages that have been aged in the bottle for at least two years and sometimes even a decade or more. Many of the wines are made from grape varieties such as Müller-Thurgau, best enjoyed young. Archiv wines not only cost a lot, but they almost certainly prove disappointing. With improvements in quality becoming evident from year to year, it is sensible to select the youngest vintage available, especially for white wines.

Under communist rule, almost all wine production fell into the hands of cooperatives, which valued volume over quality, thereby assuring the downfall of the fine wines once grown in Czechoslovakia. Today many of those cooperatives have become private companies that dominate the market. There are also a number of private producers, including the Lobkowicz family in Mělník in Bohemia, and many smaller growers in Moravia who are aiming for higher quality. Assisted by the Viticultural Law, passed in 1995 to govern and standardize the industry, it's assured that Czech wines are making a strong comeback.

Czech wine producers have followed the Austrian example by instituting a Wine Salon, an annual tasting event that identifies the country's best growers. A bottle bearing the gold sticker of the Salon will usually be worth trying. A complete collection of Salon wines is available for tasting and purchase in the wine cellars at Valtice in Moravia (see pp. 256–257). ■

Above: The harvesting of grapes, carefully
handpicked and gathered, at Mikulov
Left: Overlooking the southern Moravian
vineyards at Mikulov
Below: Hobby winemaking; stirring up the
fermenting grapes in a private cellar

Telč

Telč

🅰 244 B3

✉ 54 miles (87 km)
W of Brno via
route 23

Visitor information

✉ Town hall, náměstí
Zachariáše z Hradce
10
e-mail info@
telc-etc.cz

☎ 567 234 145

Château

🕐 Closed Mon. &
Nov.–March

💲 $$–$$$

THE EXQUISITE TOWN OF TELČ, IN THE WESTERN PART OF
the region, is understandably popular with visitors. Built by the Lords
of Hradec in the 14th century, it relied economically on the fishponds
that dot the surrounding countryside. These large ponds, linked by a
canal that traverses the castle grounds, give the town a shimmering,
aquatic appearance that greatly adds to its charm. A devastating
fire in 1530 destroyed much of Telč, although its Gothic churches survived. In 1992 the town was made a UNESCO World Heritage site.

At the top of the square named
after Zachariáš of Hradec you'll
find the Renaissance **château.** An
existing stronghold was rebuilt for
Zachariáš of Hradec by Antonio
Vlach and Baldassare Maggi in the
1560s and '70s. The lovely gardens,
magnificently decorated halls, and
gorgeous chapel reflect the sumptuous Italianate taste of the family.

The château remained in their
hands until 1712, when it passed to
the Liechtensteins.
Visitors are offered two tours.
Tour A, the better of the two, takes
an hour and gives access to the
beautifully decorated Renaissance-
style rooms, some of which have
delicate sgraffito decoration. In
complete contrast is the African

Hall, where hunting and safari trophies are displayed. The intricately stuccoed chapel was built around 1580 as the burial place of Zachariáš and his wife, Kateřina, who are represented in pious effigies. Attached to the castle is the small **gallery** *(closed Dec.–Feb.)* devoted to the work of the surrealist and landscape painter Jan Zrzavý (1890–1977). Tour B, the shorter of the two tours, visits the rooms decorated after Zachariáš's time.

But it's the main square, **náměstí Zachariáse z Hradce,** that makes Telč so irresistible: Long rows of arcaded gabled houses, hardly any two alike, are painted in delicate pastel colors, and between them is an expanse of cobbles, interrupted only by fountains and a twisting plague column of 1720.

The most delightful house is on the corner of U Masných krámů, with its recently restored sgraffiti and frescoes and Renaissance oriel. A medieval survival is the **Church of St. James** (Kostel sv. Jakuba), across from the castle.

At the other end of the square is the oldest church in Telč, the 13th-century **Church of the Holy Spirit** (Kostel sv. Ducha), whose tower *(closed Sun., $)* can be climbed for views over the town. Down Palackého from the square you will find the town's **Great Gate** (Velká brána), from which you can reach the remaining fortifications. At the far end of the square, take the lane to the right before the gallery to the town's other medieval gateway, the **Little Gate** (Malá brána), leading into the castle's park. ■

The loveliest town square in the republic is surely the gentle span of arcaded houses and shops at Telč.

More places to visit in southern Moravia

BÍTOV

At Bítov, high on a crag along the southern border with Austria, stands a medieval **castle,** much expanded over the centuries. Although impressive from the outside, the mostly neo-Gothic interior is less interesting, with exhibits focusing on the castle's history.

🅼 244 B2   ✉ 24 miles (38 km) NW of Znojmo. NW on route 38 for 3 miles (5 km), then NW on route 408, at Desov S on route 411 🚌 Bus from Znojmo 🕐 Closed Mon. May–Sept.; Mon.–Fri. April & Oct.; & Nov.–March 💲 $$

BUCHLOVICE

The gorgeous, early 18th-century **château** of Buchlovice lies within a beautiful English-style park. Its design is usually attributed to Domenico Martinelli. The château faces an equally majestic pavilion, the curved facade of each building complementing the other, with balustrades, gravel terraces, and parterre gardens separating the two. The cozy rococo interior is beautifully furnished. The whole design is ambitious yet essentially modest: Everything seems perfectly in place.

Continue toward Brno for 3 miles (5 km), and there's a sharp turn to **Buchlov,** a thick-walled and compact 13th-century **castle,** from which there are splendid views.

🅼 245 F2   ✉ 6 miles (10 km) W of Uherské Hradiště via route 50 🚌 Bus from Brno **Buchlovice château** 🕐 Closed Mon. May, June, Sept.; Mon.–Fri. April & Oct.; & Nov.–March 💲 $ **Buchlov castle** 🕐 Closed Mon.–Fri. April & Oct., & Nov.–March 💲 $

BUČOVICE

To the east of Slavkov rises the moated Renaissance château of Bučovice, once owned by the Liechtensteins. It has an unimaginative exterior, but there's a superb galleried court-yard and a beautifully decorated interior designed in the late 16th century. One entire room is bizarrely painted with hares exacting vengeance upon their foes, human and canine.

🅼 245 E2   ✉ 6 miles (10 km) E of Slavkov via route 50 🚌 Train from Brno **Château** 🕐 Closed Mon. May–Sept.; Mon.–Fri. April & Oct.; & Nov.–March 💲 $

JAROMĚŘICE NAD ROKYTNOU

North of Znojmo is the village of Jaroměřice nad Rokytnou, with its vast **château.** Commissioned in 1711 by Count Questenberg, the building took 25 years to complete. The château contains a theater, as the count was a great patron of music: The first Czech opera (O původu Jaroměřic by František Václav Míča) received its premiere here in 1730, and a music festival is still held in summer.

🅼 244 C2   ✉ 22 miles (35 km) N of Znojmo via route 38 🚌 Bus from Brno **Château** 🕐 Closed Mon. May–Sept., Mon.–Fri. April & Oct., & Nov.–March 💲 $–$$

JIHLAVA

North of Telč, the medieval silver-mining town of Jihlava has a sloping main square adorned with a plague column of 1679 and fountains. Next to the **Church of St. Ignatius** (Kostel sv. Ignáce), you can access the so-called **catacombs** (closed Jan., $), underground tunnels used for storage and refuge during the Thirty Years War. At No. 58 two Renaissance houses now contain the town's **museum** (closed Mon., $), which has mostly natural history collections. The building itself is more rewarding. The remaining fortifications lie south of náměstí Masarykovo, the main square, and the **Church of the Assumption** (Kostel Nanebezetí Panny Marie), with its Gothic frescoes, stands 200 yards (180 m) west of it. The composer Gustav Mahler (1860–1911) grew up here. His connections with the town are honored in a **museum** (Kosmákova 9, closed Mon. April–Oct., & all Nov.–March, $), just off the lower main square. For fun, there's a zoo a short walk from the main square, with a good collection of cats, including snow leopards, as well as monkeys and hippos.

🅼 244 B3   ✉ 45 miles (72 km) W of Brno via E65 🚌 Train from Brno **Visitor information** ✉ Masarykovo náměstí 19 ☎ 567 308 034

KŘTINY

The lofty white pilgrimage **church,** designed in the early 18th century by Giovanni Santini, completely dominates the village of Křtiny. The interior is essentially one vast domed

The charming 18th-century château at Buchlovice stands in welcome contrast to the more overblown country houses of Moravia.

expanse, exuberantly frescoed in high baroque style. Rolling woodlands all around make a lovely setting, and opposite is a restaurant.
🅜 245 E3 ✉ 10 miles (16 km) NE of Brno via route 373 🚌 Bus from Brno

LUHAČOVICE

Northeast of Uherské Hradiště, the grand spa of Luhačovice lies among wooded hills. Its briny mineral springs are said to benefit respiratory ailments. Slovak Dušan Jurkovič (1868–1947) designed many of the sanatoria in a folksy secessionist style. There are more impressive spas, but anyone with an interest in European domestic architecture will not be disappointed.
🅜 245 G2 ✉ 18 miles (29 km) NE of Uherské Hradiště. E on route 50 to Uherský Brod, then N on route 492 🚌 Bus from Brno

MIKULOV

Thanks to the Nazis, who blew up the original Dietrichstein castle in 1945, the **castle** *(closed Mon. April–Oct., & all Nov.–March, $)* at Mikulov is essentially a modern reconstruction. The cellars hold a 17th-century cask, probably Europe's largest wine barrel, with

a capacity of 26,680 gallons (101,300 liters). Near the main square stands the 15th-century **Church of St. Wenceslas** (Kostel sv. Václava), with a belfry and enchanting rococo interior. The pompous 1840s facade of the **Church of St. Anna** (Kostel sv. Anny) conceals the church and **mausoleum** *(closed Nov.–March, $)* of the Dietrichsteins. The 44 coffins, some of them highly elaborate, date back to Renaissance times. Mikulov is also one of Moravia's centers of white wine production.
🅜 244 D1 ✉ 30 miles (48 km) S of Brno via E461, then route 52 🚌 Bus from Brno
Visitor information ✉ Náměstí 7; e-mail tic@mikulov.cz ☎ 519 512 200; fax: 519 510 855

MORAVSKÝ KRUMLOV

Midway between Znojmo and Brno, Moravský Krumlov contains yet another **castle,** rebuilt during the Renaissance and grouped around a tiered and arcaded courtyard. One wing houses the gallery devoted to Alfons Mucha (1860–1939), who was born close by. His reputation lies with his art nouveau posters, but here the most striking exhibits are his rich historical paintings, known as the "Slav Epic."

🅰 244 D2　✉ 20 miles (32 km) SW of Brno.
E65, then S on route 394　🚌 Bus from Brno
Castle 🕐 Closed Mon. May–June &
Sept.–Oct.; & all Nov.–March　💲 $

SLAVKOV U BRNA

On December 2, 1805, in what was to become
known as the Battle of Austerlitz, Napoleon
delayed his own advance on the enemy until
the optimal moment, thereby thrashing the
Austrians and Russians in one of his most
defining moments. The site, due east of Brno
at Slavkov u Brna (Austerlitz), and in between
the two towns, is now commemorated with a
scattering of sites. At the top of the Pratzen hill
(Pracký kopec), on route 417 between Slavkov
and Brno, is Josef Fanta's **Monument of
Peace,** commissioned in 1912 by the three
combatant countries. A **museum** ($) marks
this crucial event. Napoleon stayed at the
colossal **Slavkov Castle,** built for the
Kaunitz family by Domenico Martinelli in the
18th century. Inside its neoclassic bulk, stuccoed salons display exhibits devoted to
Napoleon and his influence on the country.
🅰 245 E2　✉ 10 miles (16 km) E of Brno via
E462, W on route 50　🚌 Bus from Brno
Visitor information ✉ Palackého náměstí 1
☎ 544 220 988　**Slavkov Castle** 🕐 Closed
Mon. April–June & Sept.–Nov.; & all
Dec.–March　💲 $–$$

TIŠNOV

Near Tišnov in the valley of the River Svratka
is the Cistercian **Abbey of Porta Coeli,**
founded in 1233 and built in Romanesque
style. It has a superb, if overrestored, west
portal, richly carved, and fine cloisters.
🅰 244 D3　✉ 15 miles (24 km) N of Brno via
routes 43 and 385　🚆 Train from Brno

TŘEBÍČ

It's worth pausing at Třebíč to visit the magnificent **Basilica of St. Procopius** (Kostel sv.
Prokopa). Built in granite between 1240 and
1260, it sports a superlative Romanesque porch
(Gate of Paradise), and a chapel in the choir
contains rare 13th-century frescoes. The lovely
maze of a crypt is forested with stubby columns.
The conventual buildings house a **museum**
of Christmas crèches (closed Mon., $).
🅰 244 C3　✉ 35 miles (56 km) W of Brno via

E65, exit at Rosice, W on route 23　**Visitor
information** ✉ Karlovo náměstí 56
☎ 568 896 120

UHERSKÉ HRADIŠTĚ

Uherské Hradiště is best known for its excavations of Velká Morava, **Great Moravia,** the
oldest Slav settlement in the Czech Republic:
Follow the signs to "Památník." At the museum
(closed Dec.–March, $), an English guidebook
explains the significance of the excavations and
skeletons, weaponry, jewelry, and other exhibits.
🅰 245 F2　✉ 40 miles (64 km) E of Brno via
E462, then W on route 50　🚌 Bus from Brno

VRANOV NAD DYJÍ

Dramatically located on a crag above Vranov
nad Dyjí is the town's **château,** largely
rebuilt in the 1690s by the Austrian architect
Johann Bernard Fischer von Erlach. The present building is a hodgepodge of baroque and
neoclassic styles, and the interior includes the
domed Hall of the Ancestors, lavishly frescoed.
🅰 244 B2　✉ 14 miles (22 km) W of Znojmo
via routes 38, 408, 398　🚌 Bus from Znojmo
Château 🕐 Closed Mon. May–Sept.;
Mon.–Fri. April & Oct.; & Nov.–March
💲 $$–$$$

ŽĎÁR NAD SÁZAVOU

Just north of Žďár nad Sázavou you'll discov-
er a striking Cistercian monastery. With the
original monastery having been destroyed
during the Hussite wars in the 15th century,
the present complex was mostly built by
Giovanni Santini (1677–1723). His style is
a curious hybrid, often placing Gothic forms
within a supple baroque framework, a style
evident also at the nearby pilgrimage **Church
of St. John of Nepomuk** (Kostel sv. Jana
Nepomuckého). The church is decorated with
motifs associated with the saint. The design is
unique: Not only pentagonal but also encircled
by a zigzag of continuous arcades, making this
one of the most eccentric expressions of central
European baroque. There is a fine book museum in the monastery stables.
🅰 244 C4　✉ 40 miles (64 km) NW of Brno
🚆 Train from Prague and Brno　**Church of
St. John of Nepomuk** 🕐 Closed Mon.
May–Sept.; Mon.–Fri. April & Oct.; &
Nov.–March　💲 $$ ∎

It may be fairly remote, but northern Moravia holds much variety: From the sophisticated university town of Olomouc to the mining town of Ostrava, from the Jeseníky mountains to the open-air museum at Rožnov pod Radhoštěm.

Northern Moravia

A mosaic from the town hall at Olomouc

Area of map detail

Prague

POLAND

5▷

Javorník

Vidnava

Žulová

Mikulovice

Osoblaha

Jeskyně
na Pomezí
1125m

Lázně
Jeseník

Jeseník

Zlaté
Hory

Jindřichov

Smrk

Lipová-
Lázně

Město
Albrechtice

1423m
Kepřník

Staré
Město

H r u b ý

Vrbno
pod Pradědem

1013m
Červenohorské
sedlo

Karlovice

Krnov

Hanušovice

1491m
Praděd

Karlova Studánka

4▷

J e s e n í k

Velké
Losiny

Ruda
nad Moravou

Sobotín

Bruntál

Horní
Benešov

Koběří

Šumperk

Opava

Kravaře

Bludov

Rýmařov

N í z k y

Postřelmov

Litultovice

Libina

vod. nádrž
Slezská Harta

**Hradec
nad Moravicí**

Zábřeh

Troubelice

Dvorce

Klimkovice

35
E442

Moravský
Beroun

vod. nádrž
Kružberk

Bílovec

Mohelnice

J e s e n í k

Vitkov

3▷

Loštice

Uničov

Šternberk

Fulnek

Studénka

Litovel

Bouzov

O d e r s k é

Odry

Příbor

Horka
nad Moravou

Svatý
Kopeček

v r c h y

Potštát

Kopřivnic

Senice
na Hané

Hlubočky

OLOMOUC

35

Hranice

48

**Nový
Jičín**

Rybí

Štramb

Lutín

Tršice

Hodslavice

Plumlov

55

47

Lipník
nad Bečvou

Bečva

**Valašské
Meziříčí**

2▷

Brodek
u Přerova

Přerov

55

**Rožn
pod Radhošt**

V s e t í n s

Jablůnka

v r c h y

Kojetín

SOUTHERN MORAVIA

p. 243

Vsetín

Halenko

69

Hovězí

49

57

Francova
Lhota

EASTERN BOHEMIA
p. 221

1▷

0   20 kilometers
0   10 miles

A   **B**   **C**   **D**

Rychlebské hory

453

Béla

Opava

45

57

Morava

Oskava

Olešná

44

35

46

Morava

35

Odra

Morava

Bečva

Senice

57

56

46

47

Opava

Northern Moravia

NO ONE COULD FAULT NORTHERN MORAVIA FOR LACK OF VARIETY. THREE cities in the north are industrial but have much interest, while close by the remote Jeseníky mountains are popular with skiers. Olomouc is a beautiful central European city, where decorative gardening is a local tradition, while the country's most impressive *skansen,* an open-air museums devoted to folk and vernacular architecture, provides a glimpse into the past.

The northern area near the Polish border is historically part of Silesia. To the west, also bordering Poland, the Jeseníky mountains are home to a number of old-fashioned ski resorts. Sadly, the area has not escaped the blight of acid rain. Easily the most interesting of northern Moravian cities is Olomouc, with its two handsome squares and many churches, museums, and institutions, and it makes a good base for exploring the region.

Less rich in castles and châteaus than eastern Bohemia, northern Moravia nonetheless has some winners when it comes to brazenness and eccentricity at Bouzov and Plumlov. Visitors head to Rožnov pod Radhoštěm to see the largest and most impressive of the Czech Republic's

skansens. The town is also a good center for exploring Moravian Wallachia, one of the most durable of the regional subcultures in the country.

Moravia pays homage to its distinguished offspring in various places. At Hukvaldy, museums and memorials are devoted to the great composer Leoš Janáček (1854–1928), and the achievements of the athlete Emil Zátopek (1922–2000) are celebrated in Kopřivnice (this town always boasts the Tatra Museum, deservedly popular with car enthusiasts). Curiously, the town of Příbor has been slow to honor the renown of its most famous native, Sigmund Freud (1856–1939), father of psychoanalysis. ∎

**Hiking trails
crisscross the
Jeseníky
mountains.**

The Renaissance town hall dominates the large main square in the city center.

Olomouc

THE CAPITAL OF MORAVIA UNTIL 1641, OLOMOUC TODAY is a thriving industrial and university town of broad avenues lined with old seminaries, solid 19th-century apartment houses, leafy parks, baroque fountains, and stately university buildings.

Olomouc

- 278 B2
- 170 miles (274 km) E of Prague
- Train and bus from Prague

Visitor information

- Town hall, Horní náměstí
- 068 551 3385
  e-mail infocentrum @olomoucko.cz

The original settlement here was established in the seventh century, and the town became the seat of a bishopric in 1063. It prospered in the 16th century but suffered during the Thirty Years War. Despite losing its capital status to Brno, Olomouc remains an important and lively city.

The heart of the Old Town beats in two bustling squares, Horní náměstí and Dolní náměstí. The vast Horní náměstí encircles the Renaissance **town hall** *(Radnice),* a complex, much altered structure with a Gothic oriel window, double staircase, tower, loggia, and portal. Its famous astronomical clock was reconstructed after it was destroyed during World War II. When the hour strikes, a procession of prole-tarian figurines (the communist version of saints) parades past.

The town hall vies for attention with the colossal **Trinity column,** culminating at a height of 115 feet (35 m) in an obelisk from which carved angels seem to tumble. Built in 1754, it is the largest of the thousands of such columns throughout the Czech Republic. The neoclassic **theater,** designed by Josef Kornhäusel in 1830, is where the young composer Gustav Mahler worked in 1883.

Adjoining Horní náměstí is Dolní náměstí, with its own pair of fountains and a Marian column. Among the Renaissance mansions here, the **Hauenschild Palace** at No. 27 boasts a double-height oriel window on the corner. The Gothic **Church of St. Maurice** (Kostel sv. Mořice) has a somewhat grimy exterior and fortresslike tower. Inside, the usual baroque and neo-Gothic furnishings can't conceal the soaring Gothic piers and vaults, even though the ribs have been painted a dirty pink. The church is celebrated for its 1745 organ, and an organ festival is held here each September. On the other side of Horni náměstí, the **Church of St. Michael** (Kostel sv. Michala) may be drab outside, but inside you find a three-domed baroque extravaganza. Nearby, the tiny 20th-century **Sarkander chapel,** like a small domed baroque temple, honors the Catholic priest Jan Sarkander, who was tortured to death in 1620.

The early 18th-century Jesuit **Church of Our Lady of the Snows** (Kostel Panna Marie Sněžné) overlooks náměstí Republiky. The former Jesuit college here faces two museums: The **Art Museum** (Muzeum umění; *closed Mon., $*) displays 16th- to 18th-century Dutch paintings and exhibits relating to the history of Olomouc; the **Vlastivědné muzeum** contains a natural history collection.

In the **Archbishop's Palace** (Arcibiskupský palác), a graceful building of the 1600s, the teenage Franz Josef was proclaimed emperor of Austria in 1848.

The Romanesque origins of the **Cathedral of St. Wenceslas** (Dóm sv. Václava; *closed Mon. & Oct.–March*) are obscured by the drastic 1880s restoration that expanded the baroque cathedral. The famous treasury is housed in the reliquary-filled crypt.

Adjoining the cathedral are the remains of the old **Bishop's Palace** *(closed Mon.).* Excavations revealed Romanesque double windows, a Gothic cloister, and a chapel with 16th-century frescoes. The Romanesque work is of outstanding quality. Opposite the cathedral is the deanery; here the last Přemysl king, Václav III, was murdered in 1306. (At present, much of this site is closed for restoration.) ■

The immense baroque Trinity column in Olomouc's main square

A walk around Olomouc

Busy Olomouc is a city in which the ancient and youthful blend well together, and it's small enough to be easily and enjoyably explored on foot. This walk takes you through the two important squares at the heart of the Old Town, through the university area, and on to the cathedral. The energetic may like to continue out to the Premonstratensian monastery at Hradisko.

Start on Horní náměstí by the Renaissance **town hall** (*Radnice*) ➊ and admire its slender tower and Italianate loggia and portal. Time your walk so that you are by the town hall when the astronomical clock strikes the hour. It draws large crowds with its procession of proletarian figurines.

Walk past the **Trinity column** (Sousoší Nejsvětější trojice), and the **theater** where the young composer Gustav Mahler served a three-month stint as musical director in 1883. The comfortable Café Mahler is across the square. Its rival, Café Caesar, occupies the prestigious site of the first-floor vaults of the town hall, and in summer terraces at both establishments spill out on to the square.

Go south from Horní náměstí to Dolní náměstí, lined with Renaissance mansions,

> ◪ See area map p. 278
> ▶ Horní náměstí
> ↔ 3 miles (4.5 km)
> ⊕ 3–4 hours
> ▶ Monastery of Hradisko
>
> **NOT TO BE MISSED**
> - Town hall
> - Horní náměstí
> - Dolní náměstí
> - Bishop's Palace

notably the ornate **Hauenschild Palace** (Hauenschildův dům) ➋, on the corner at No. 27. You can pause in summer for a snack at the open-air beer hall in the middle of the square.

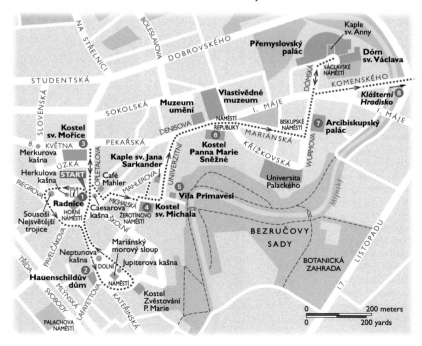

Return to Horní náměstí, bear right past the clock tower, and follow Opletalova to the Gothic **Church of St. Maurice** (Kostel sv. Mořice) ③. Pop inside to admire the soaring Gothic piers and vaults. For a view over the Old Town, you can climb the church tower. If you're here in December, you'll see traders selling live carp from huge plastic tubs outside the supermarket next to the church. Go back to Horní náměstí again, turn left after Café Mahler, then immediately right on Michalská. This leads to the domed baroque **Church of St. Michael** (Kostel sv. Michala) ④, attached to a Dominican friary. Past the church, bear left, and after 55 yards (50 m) you'll see the tiny circular **Sarkander chapel** (Kaple sv. Jana Sarkander).

Walk back toward the Church of St. Michael and follow the sign on the left to the **Villa Primavesi** (Vila Primavesi) ⑤ *(awaiting restoration)*. Continue past the villa down Univerzitní, passing a palatial 17th-century seminary before reaching Denisova and the overbearing early 18th-century Jesuit **Church of Our Lady of the Snows** (Kostel Panna Marie Sněžné) ⑥. It overlooks náměstí Republiky, where the former Jesuit college faces two museums.

From the post office on náměstí Republiky, Mariánská leads to the **Archbishop's Palace** (Arcibiskupský palác) ⑦, flanked by other baroque and reconstructed palaces and now part of Palacký University.

Bear left down Wurmova and then take Dómská to the **Cathedral of St. Wenceslas** (Dóm sv. Václava). Adjoining the cathedral are the remains of the old **Bishop's Palace** (Přemyslovský palác) that once stood here. Opposite the cathedral is the deanery, now another part of the university.

North of Olomouc is the vast former Premonstratensian **Monastery of Hradisko** (Klášterní Hradisko) ⑧. It's about a one-mile (1.6 km) hike from the cathedral. Take Komenského, the eastward extension of Denisova, in the direction away from the Old Town, cross two bridges, then take a left along an unnamed road. Soon you will see looming ahead the yellow and white of this baroque monastery. It is now a hospital and therefore not open to visitors, but you can usually walk into the courtyard to admire its sheer size. ∎

Above: An elaborate astronomical clock adorns the side of the town hall. Its mosaics depict valorous laborers.

Below: The ornate Marian column in Dolní náměstí square in the Old Town

Three villages
at Rožnov's
open-air museum
depict Wallachian
life and cultural
traditions.

Rožnov pod Radhoštěm & the Wallachians

ROŽNOV POD RADHOŠTĚM IS THE SITE OF THE SPLENDID *skansen,* or open-air museum, of Wallachia that dominates this small town. Many of the exhibits—churches, houses, schools—have been collected from Wallachian villages in the nearby Beskydy mountains.

**Rožnov pod
Radhoštěm**

⬛ 278 D2

✉ 35 miles (56 km)
E of Olomouc

🚌 Bus from Olomouc,
Prague, & Brno

**Regional visitor
information**

✉ Municipal
Information Center,
Burian Museum,
náměstí 456,
Štramberk

☎ 556 852 240

The Wallachians were a nomadic sheep-rearing people with a strong cultural tradition of their own. Nobody knows exactly where the Wallachians came from, but these herdsmen and woodsmen were possibly related to the Romanian Vlachs. With their distinctive customs and traditions, they were evidently considered outsiders, and much of their culture was wiped out by the Habsburgs in the 17th century. Even today the Wallachian people still preserve their own dialect and local customs.

Their heartland is in the Beskydy mountains northeast of Rožnov pod Radhoštěm. In villages such as **Štramberk,** there are dozens of traditional wooden cottages that are still inhabited. Despite their timeless appearance, many of these cottages were built in a range of styles in the early 19th century and are in varying states of repair. You can get an excellent view over the Wallachian countryside from the reconstructed Gothic castle tower at Štramberk *(closed Nov.–March, $).*

Other Wallachian villages that remain relatively unspoiled include **Velké Karlovice,** with its wooden church, town hall, and farmhouses, and Nový Hrozenkov, Hovězí, and Halenkov. The fiery plum brandy known as *slivovice* is not unique to Wallachia, but this region remains a center of production, with a large distillery at Vizovice.

ROŽNOV'S SKANSEN

The skansen at Rožnov was the first to be opened to the public, in 1925, and it is still the largest, an assembly of more than 90 structures, from churches to shepherd's huts dating from the 17th to 20th centuries (some are replicas). The dark logs of the houses look splendid in this wooded setting.

There are three sections to the skansen, each of which can be visited separately. The first skansen is the **Wooden Village** (Dřevěné městečko; *closed Nov., $*), the original part of the museum. If you can visit only one of the three sites, this is the one to choose. The most impressive exhibits here are the wooden town hall of Rožnov, dating from 1770, followed by a fine reconstruction of a 17th-century timber church from Větřkovice, a family house from 1750, and a collection of carved beehives; beekeeping was important in Wallachia's rural economy. Be sure to watch for these, as they are highly unusual, with lively sculptured scowling faces. The pubs are fully operational at the Wooden Village,

and light food as well as beer are served.

The second skansen is the **Wallachian Village** (Valašská dědine; *closed Oct.–April, $*), which shows what village life was like here in the past. The cattle are still raised as they would have been by Wallachian herdsmen. Horse-drawn carriages and musical ensembles featuring violins and dulcimers enliven the scene. A Wallachian carnival is staged here in February to celebrate the end of winter, and in July there are folkloric performances at Rožnov. In early July Texans of Czech descent pour into the town for a boisterous week of cook-offs and rodeos.

The most recent addition to the museum is **Mill Valley** (Mlýnská dolina; *closed Oct.–April, $); it is the only one that has to be visited on a guided tour. Here you are shown around a water mill, a sawmill, and a flour mill, in the company of cheerful guides in Wallachian peasant costumes.

Note that a combined ticket (*$$*) is available to visit all three villages. ■

Turreted and carved beehives of typical Wallachian design can be seen at Rožnov's Wooden Village.

Rožnov visitor information

✉ Palackého 484
e-mail namaste@mymail.cz

☎ 571 655 196

Jeseníky mountains

NORTH OF ŠTERNBERK RISE THE JESENÍKY MOUNTAINS (Hrubý Jeseník), the highest in Moravia, stretching eastward across the Polish border. The mountains are popular with hikers, and in winter this is a highly regarded area for cross-country skiing. In addition, there are some small spas.

Most visitors approaching the region do so from the textile-producing town of **Šumperk.** There is very little to see here, though there is a plague column in the main square. On its southern outskirts at **Bludov,** however, an immense square château has two turrets capping either end of the facade. Originally a Renaissance structure, it was given a thorough baroque face-lift in 1708.

From Šumperk continue north to the more prepossessing resort and spa town of **Velké Losiny,** a good starting point for mountain hikes. At the entrance to the village, dominating a beautiful park, is a splendid sgraffitoed Renaissance **château** with a three-tiered,

galleried courtyard; it was owned by the wealthy Žerotín family until they were ejected after the Battle of White Mountain in 1620. During the Counter-Reformation, witch trials were conducted here over a 15-year period, and 56 perfectly innocent people, their "confessions" extracted by torture, were dispatched to the stake. Along the main road on the left a **Museum of Papermaking** stands by the republic's only surviving handmade paper workshop, established here by the Žerotíns in 1516. This is a good place to find unusual souvenirs.

From Velké Losiny the road north climbs past sawmills to a mountain pass. From here the road goes, via hairpin bends, to Jeseník in the heart of the main Hrubý Jeseník range. From either side of the road you can see the principal summits, rising to 4,892 feet (1,491 m); some of them can be reached by walking trails that start at the top of the pass, Červenohorské sedlo, which itself is 3,314 feet high (1,010 m). The villages along the way are filled with low wooden cottages, usually painted green and topped by huge gabled roofs with large overhanging eaves. The landscape has suffered badly from acid rain; bleak moors, easily seen from the pass, exist where trees once thrived.

Jeseník itself is not a particularly attractive town, but above it is the little spa town of **Lázně Jeseník,** founded in 1826. From here there are fine views of the

Jeseníky mountains

⛰ 278 B4

🚆 Train from Olomouc or Opava to Jeseník

Visitor information

✉ Masarykovo náměstí 1/167, Jeseník

☎ 584 498 155

Velké Losiny château

🕐 Closed Mon. May–Sept.; Mon.–Fri. April & Oct.; & Nov.–March

💲 Guided tour: $

Left: A signpost shows walkers the way in the Jeseníky mountains.

mountains. Most of the extant buildings date from the early 20th century. The natural springs are dispersed around the spa, and you'll find numerous walks along the trails through the pleasant countryside.

An even smaller spa lies a little farther to the west: **Lipová-Lázně.** Follow route 60 north to the caves known as **Jeskyně na Pomezí** (*closed Mon., & Nov.–March, $*), with their bizarre stalactite and stalagmite formations, then continue north to the village of **Žulová,** where a fortress was converted into a church tower in the 19th century.

South of Jeseník, a particularly beautiful road (route 450) traverses the forests to the region's most enticing old spa: **Karlova Studánka.** Founded in 1785, it is noted for cold springs with a high iron content. This is easily the best of the mountain resorts, with its broad main street, handsome wooden buildings, and pleasant gardens. And at 2,543 feet high (775 m), it's an excellent base for hiking to the region's highest peak, the Praděd (4,892 feet/1,491 m), and to the waterfalls along the River Bílá Opava.

In the lower reaches of the mountains lies **Bruntál.** Its huge yellow-and-white baroque **château** (*closed Mon., & Nov.–March, $–$$*) has an entrance portal on a palatial scale from the 1760s and a lavishly furnished and frescoed interior. The charming arcaded courtyard, with its irregular shape, dates from the 16th century. ■

Grand hotels cater to visitors in Karlova Studánka and other Jeseníky resorts.

Museum of Papermaking

🕐 Closed Sat.–Sun. April & Oct., & Nov.–March

💲 Guided tour: $

The Roma plight

Nobody knows for certain how the Roma (Gypsies) ended up in central Europe, but they seem to have originated in India and migrated west during the late Middle Ages. Their nomadic way of life, communal ways, and distinctive clothing and customs cut them off from the rest of society from the start, and through the centuries they have been discriminated against and even persecuted for their dissimilarities.

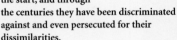
A Roma boy peers through the infamous wall at Ústí nad Labem.

In modern times, troubles for the Roma arose in 1927, when the Czechoslovak government passed the Law on Wandering Gypsies—forcing them to apply for identification and permission to stay the night. But the greatest tragedy came with World War II, when the Nazis established punitive labor camps for "Gypsies and other wandering individuals." These camps were replaced later by concentration camps at Lety u Písku in Bohemia and Hodonín u Kunštátu in Moravia, where many Roma died of starvation, malnutrition, disease, and brutality. Those who survived were subsequently transported to Nazi death camps. In the end, out of the prewar population of 6,500 Roma in Bohemia and Moravia, only 300 remained—a blight treated after the war with an embarrassed silence by the Czech nation.

Attempts were made during the communist era to integrate the Roma into society, to re-educate the Roma in the communist image—meaning, their language was suppressed and their nomadic way of life discouraged. They were forced out of their traditional occupations as weavers, musicians, and blacksmiths and drafted as unskilled construction workers. They were moved from rural settlements to tenement housing in the city. At the same time, although they were at the lower end of the socio-economic system, they were partially incorporated into the fabric of society, often forced to go to school and jobs and to participate in the greater community.

Since the fall of communism in 1989, the Roma have been left without any kind of social safety net to espouse their cause. Roma children are often denied access to normal schools. Few employers will offer adults steady work, let alone a career. Their unemployment rate is estimated to be about 70 percent. Public opinion polls show that most Czechs view the Roma minority as thieves and drunks. Racially motivated, physically violent crimes against them are commonplace. In response, many Roma have abandoned their homeland and immigrated to Canada or western Europe.

Any improvements in their living conditions, literacy rates, and employment prospects must derive from the Roma's own efforts. They have begun to organize politically, though with limited results, since they tend to think in terms of families rather than national organizations and pressure groups.

On the brighter side, there are signs that the Roma are making a proud effort to preserve their culture and traditions. There's a renewed interest in preserving their language, with the right to educate children in their mother tongue. Romani periodicals now exist, and works of original Romani literature have been published. It's a start, but there's still a long way to go. ∎

Right: A Roma boy on the wrong side of the Ústí wall, built in 1999 to segregate Roma housing; political pressure from the European Union led to its dismantling. Far right: Artistic talent flowers within the Roma community.

Above: Roma women and children don their finery for a festival at Brno.

Bouzov & Plumlov

Bouzov

 278 A3

🕐 Closed Mon.
April—Oct.,
Mon.—Fri.
Nov.—March

💲 $$

🚌 Bus from Olomouc

Plumlov

278 B2 & 245 E3

🚌 From Olomouc
take route 46 to
Prostejov, then
route 18 toward
Boskovice, & fork
left on route 377

**The neo-Gothic
extravaganza of
Bouzov castle
proved irresistible
to occupying
Nazi officers.**

IN A COUNTRY RICH IN CASTLES, BOUZOV AND PLUMLOV
stand out. They are fascinating for very different reasons: Bouzov
(northwest of Olomouc), because of its history as a favorite Nazi res-
idence during World War II, and Plumlov (just west of Prostejov), for
its sheer architectural weirdness.

BOUZOV

Bouzov is a frenzy of towers and
turrets, steeply pitched orange-red
roofs, balconies over precipitous
drops, gables and chimney stacks,
and a drawbridge, all huddled
around an immense round tower.

Set in gorgeous undulating
countryside northwest of Olomouc,
the original 14th-century fortress
became a royal property under
George of Poděbrady. In 1696 it
was acquired as the headquarters of
the hospitallers' order of the Grand
Masters of the Teutonic Knights, a
ferociously anti-Slav organization.
The castle was restyled in neo-
Gothic by the Knights in the late
19th and early 20th centuries. The

order of the Knights was abolished
in 1939, and the castle was taken
over by Nazi occupiers, who found
the Teutonic pomposity irresistible.

Three tours of the castle are
offered. The best option is the
hour-long Tour 1; although Tour 2
is more detailed, it is also much
longer. Tour 3 just visits the tower.

The interior is a medieval
dream, with suits of armor, heavy
wooden furniture, and wooden
ceilings such as the barrel-vaulted
Knights' Hall. Some of the bed-
rooms are amazingly sumptuous.
The enormous bed and other
furnishings in the Grand Master's
bedroom are riotously carved.

PLUMLOV

About 20 miles (32 km) southeast
of Bouzov is another extraordinary
building, the vertiginously tall
château at Plumlov. The 17th-
century architect was Prince-Bishop
Karl Eusebius von Liechtenstein-
Kastelkorn, a member of the
owning family. The slablike château
has so little depth that it looks as if
a gust of wind could blow it over.
This is because the prince complet-
ed only one of the four projected
wings. The facade consists of three
colossal stories, each lined with
rows of columns. It is utterly repeti-
tive, quite mad, and unforgettable.
The desperate state of disrepair
means the structure is closed to the
public, but the roof is fairly new, so
it has not been totally abandoned. ■

**Right: Only one wing of Plumlov
château was ever completed.**

A visit to Kopřivnice to tour the splendid Tatra Museum is a must for car enthusiasts.

More places to visit in northern Moravia

FULNEK

Badly damaged during World War II, Fulknek has been restored with sensitivity. Pretty houses, many of them clearly modern but blending in, line the main square. The Czech nationalist philosopher Jan Komenský (Comenius) taught at a Lutheran college here from 1618 to 1621, and the college has been reconstructed. On one side of the square is a baroque **church** set elegantly among the greenery of a wooded hillside. Atop the hill is the town's tall but shabby baroque **castle,** which was renovated in 1810 after a major fire.

278 D3 ✉ 12 miles (20 km) S of Opava via route 57

HRADEC NAD MORAVICÍ

A fortress has overlooked the town of Hradec nad Moravicí since the tenth century. The princely Lichnowsky family has owned Hradec since 1777, and in its heyday composers Beethoven, Liszt, and Paganini all stayed at the lime-green neoclassic **château.** In the 19th century the town was encircled by red-brick crenellated walls, complete with portcullis, rather like a Victorian prison.

A Beethoven music festival is held here every June.

278 D3 ✉ 5 miles (8 km) S of Opava via route 57 **Château** Closed Mon. May–Sept., Mon.–Fri. April, Oct., & Dec.

HUKVALDY

The remarkable Czech composer Leoš Janáček (1854–1928) was born in Hukvaldy, a pretty, well-maintained hillside village, with a deer park below the ruins of a medieval **castle.** His birthplace was the village school where his father taught, but the little **museum** dedicated to the composer is housed in the building where he spent his final years, having lived most of his life at Brno. Find it by turning left at the castle entrance and walking down a lane for 325 yards (300 m). It contains some of Janáček's furniture and the lectern on which he composed while standing, as was his custom.

279 E2 ✉ 4 miles (6 km) E of Příbor. E on route 48, then S on route 486 **Castle** Closed Mon. May–Sept.; Mon.–Fri. April & Oct.; & Nov.–March $ **Janáček Museum** Closed Mon. May–Sept.; Mon.–Fri. April & Oct.; & Nov.–March $

KOPŘIVNICE

North of Rožnov pod Radhoštěm (see pp. 284–285) is the unattractive industrial town of Kopřivnice, mainly taken up by the huge plants that have manufactured Tatra cars and trucks since 1897. The citizens of Communist Czechoslovakia grew used to seeing sleek black Tatra limousines, reserved for the state's favored few, overtaking their Trabants and Ladas. The **Tatra Museum** is a striking, angular, blue-and-white structure consecrated to the history of the Tatra enterprise and to the achievements of Olympic athlete Emil Zátopek, a native of the town (1922–2000).

🔼 278 D2 ✉ 12 miles (19 km) N of Rožnov pod Radhoštěm via route 58 **Tatra Museum** ✉ Záhumenní 367 🕐 Closed Mon. 💲 $

NOVÝ JIČÍN

West of Příbor (see p. 294) is Nový Jičín, in the heart of the region known as the Kuhlander, once a German-speaking agricultural area specializing, as its name suggests, in cattle raising. The sprawling town has a charming arcaded main square, with a plague column of 1710 in the center. In the much rebuilt Renaissance **castle,** nearby on Lidická, are a number of museums, one of which is devoted to the hat, a sartorial item in which the town has specialized since 1799. The **Hat Museum** (Klobourčnické muzeum) displays examples worn by such famous Czechs as President Masaryk.

🔼 278 D2 ✉ 8 miles (13 km) W of Příbor via route 48 🚌 Bus from Prague and regular services from Olomouc **Hat Museum** 🕐 Closed Mon. 💲 $

OPAVA

Opava is the former capital of Silesia, first Austrian and then Czech. Both the Thirty Years War and World War II inflicted enormous damage on this industrial city. Near Horní náměstí, the main square, is the rather ugly, and much altered, 14th-century brick **parish church,** typical of Silesian Gothic. The town hall tower dates from 1618. Two blocks behind the church is Masarykova, lined with patrician mansions; these include the shabby, buff-colored, baroque Blücher Palace, now a branch of the Silesian Museum, and the beautifully restored playful facade of the Sobek Palace, now a bank. With typical architectural insensitivity, the communist regime attached concrete apartment blocks to this lovely building. Opposite is the **Church of the Holy Ghost** (Kostel sv. Ducha), with an interesting pink-and-green baroque facade resembling Dutch stepped gables, and the neoclassic Minorite convent. The main **Silesian Regional Museum,** founded in 1814, is on the outskirts of the old town.

🔼 278 D4 ✉ 20 miles (32 km) NW of Olomouc on route 46 via Šternberk 🚃 Train from Olomouc **Silesian Regional Museum** ✉ Tyršova 1 🕐 Closed Mon.

OSTRAVA

Near the Polish border sprawls the large industrial city of Ostrava. After coal was found here in the 1760s, mines were tunneled under the city, with foundries being built perilously close to the city center. By the late 1990s most, but not all, had been closed down, and pollution levels, once dangerously high, have diminished. Many buildings, however, are still prone to subsidence.

Sigmund Freud was born in Příbor, but only in recent years has the father of psychoanalysis been honored at his birthplace.

Apart from the town hall tower (1687) in the main square, Masarykovo náměstí, there is little that's compelling in the center, even though it is the third largest city in the republic. However, the **Mining Museum** (Hornické muzeum) is of surprising interest. It is situated in the northern suburb of Pod Landekem, and based in a former colliery; visitors can even go down to the coal face itself. By car, take Sokolská north for 2 miles (3 km), following signs for the museum, which is on the right just after you cross the River Odra. One of Ostrava's best known natives is the tennis star Ivan Lendl, who was born here in 1960.

 279 E3  100 miles (160 km) NE of Brno via E462, then route 47. Train and bus from Prague.
Visitor information  Municipal Information Center, Nádražní 7/686  596 123 913 **Mining Museum**  Closed Mon.  Guided tour: $$

The magnificent church of Svatý Kopeček attracts thousands of visitors, some pilgrims, others heading for the nearby zoo.

PŘÍBOR

Příbor is the birthplace of Sigmund Freud (1856–1939), the father of psychoanalysis, at Freudova 117. The town was strangely reticent about the fact until recently, not honoring him until 1994; at that time a bust was placed between the main square and the former college, where the town **museum** is housed. The room devoted to Freud contains little more than familiar photographs and books, but the infant Freud left Příbor at the age of three and the Freud museums in Vienna and London have had first pick of letters and memorabilia. In the late 1990s the town finally got around to naming its pleasant main square after its most famous son.

 278 D3  19 miles (33 km) SW of Ostrava via route 58 **Museum**  Closed Mon., Wed., & Fri.–Sat.  $

ŠTERNBERK

North of Olomouc lies Šternberk and its **castle,** which was founded in the 13th century by the eponymous family. It was largely rebuilt in a cramped neo-Gothic style in the 1880s, though vestiges of the medieval fortifications and a tall Gothic chapel, complete with Gothic murals and a fine statue of the Madonna, remain. The interior is sparsely furnished, but it contains medieval artifacts from Olomouc.

 278 B3  10 miles (15 km) N of Olomouc via route 46 **Castle**  Closed Mon. May–Sept.; Mon.–Fri. April & Oct.; & Nov.–March  $–$$

SVATÝ KOPEČEK

Just off route 46, the road from Olomouc to Šternberk, is Italian architect Giovanni Tencalla's 17th-century **church** at Holy Hill (Svatý Kopeček). With its broad two-story facade topped with a row of statues, it resembles a baroque palace as much as a church. The interior of this fine yellow and white pilgrimage church is a feast of lilac marble, coarse stucco, and crowded ceiling frescoes. The galleried dome is impressive, and the organ gallery has a riot of decorative musical cherubs. Along the outer side of the church an array of little cafés and snack bars caters to pilgrims. You can also buy religious knickknacks and even plastic budgerigars. For the more secular-minded, there's a small zoo. The view from this hill stretches a great distance but there is not much to see in the surrounding countryside.

 278 C3  3 miles (5 km) NE of Olomouc via route 46 ■

Travelwise

Trams are still the most pleasant way to get around Prague.

TRAVELWISE INFORMATION

PLANNING YOUR TRIP

WHEN TO GO

Prague has become a year-round destination. Late spring and summer are, in many ways, the best time to visit. The climate is generally warm, occasionally hot, and you can take advantage of the city's many summer terraces in restaurants and cafés. If you enjoy music and the performing arts, you might consider visiting Prague during the annual Prague Spring Music Festival, in the second half of May. If you plan to do this, make your bookings well in advance.

But there are drawbacks to visiting Prague in the summer. The first is that it becomes extremely crowded. It is a small city, and its proximity to the German and Austrian borders has led to a steady influx of visitors from those countries. You will need to plan your stay well in advance, securing hotel reservations as early as possible. Once you have arrived, you are likely to find that the best or most fashionable restaurants are also booked up days ahead. Most visitors, especially those on day or weekend trips from Germany, crowd into the same narrow streets and squares. The crush can be fatiguing, as can the heat. And unfortunately for visitors there are often downpours in July and August.

The great advantage of visiting Prague out of season is that you will not be jostling with quite so many other tourists. You can also take advantage of low-season hotel rates, which in general apply from November through March. There are performances of operas and symphony concerts in the city's main opera houses and concert halls year-round, but the height of the cultural program is in the fall and winter. The drawbacks of coming to Prague out of season

are the drop in temperature and the short days, which limit sightseeing time.

As for the rest of the country, it does not make much sense to plan a trip through the Bohemian and Moravian countryside in the late fall and winter. Quite apart from the vagaries of the climate, many tourist attractions will be closed. Castles, châteaus, and other major sites are usually open daily from May through September, and on weekends only during April and October. Most buildings are closed to the public from November to March, with a handful of exceptions such as Karlštejn. Snow and ice are common in the countryside from December to February, making a tour of the country by car quite hazardous.

Christmas in Prague can be great fun, with open-air markets, clowns and pranksters in the streets, and the welcome possibility of crunchy snow underfoot. On the other hand, the city can become as crowded as during the height of summer, and many hotels charge their highest rates over Christmas and New Year's.

CLIMATE

The climate of the Czech Republic is varied, owing to the length of the country from east to west and variations in altitude. Local microclimates are of great importance, and climatically the republic is a distinct patchwork. Generally speaking, the climate becomes more continental as you move eastward into Moravia, whereas Bohemia has a more moderate maritime climate, comparable to that of southern Germany. Summers can be quite hot, extending into delightful falls, but winters are occasionally severe.

Rainfall also varies, again as a result of elevation. Annual

precipitation in Prague is 19 inches (487 mm), with July and August being the wettest months and February the driest. Prague enjoys a particularly mild climate, with an average temperature throughout the year of 49°F (9°C). Even in winter the temperature does not usually drop far below freezing point, although it can remain at that chilly level for many days at a time. Cold weather can set in by late October, and January and February in particular are often chilly. In July the average temperature is 66°F (19°C); in February 33°F (1.8°C).

The Moravian climate is distinct. The north is considerably wetter than Bohemia, as a consequence of the lack of high mountains to shelter the region. The south is notably mild, with long, warm fall seasons that make the region ideal for viticulture.

WHAT TO TAKE

Prague is a modern city with modern shops. Nevertheless, if you need special medication, be sure to take it with you. Medication that may be available over the counter in your own country may be on prescription only in the Czech Republic. While most hotels stock electronic adaptors (220V) for computers, hair dryers, etc., it is wise to buy them in your home country. As for clothing, be prepared for extremes, especially in winter, when the temperatures vary from mild to very cold. Take footwear that can withstand rain and slush. In summer light slacks or skirts and T-shirts should be sufficient.

INSURANCE

Although travel in the Czech Republic will not expose you to unusual risks or dangers, it is best to take out travel insurance. Your travel agent will be able to help, but the prices may not be competitive, so shop around. If your bookings are made using a major credit card, such as American Express, you will probably be covered for basic risks and losses, but check the coverage carefully.

THEFT AND LOSS

In the event of theft or other crime, make an immediate report to the police, and be sure to get a copy of the report; it will be essential in processing any claim you subsequently make.

MEDICAL

Similarly, keep copies of all bills for any medical treatment you have. The Czech Republic provides free emergency medical care for all foreigners. Medical problems not classified as emergencies will be charged for, so it is sensible to take out medical insurance.

CAR

If you are driving your own car, you should obtain a Green Card (usually free of charge) from your insurer as proof of insurance before you leave your country of residence.

ENTRY FORMALITIES

You need a valid passport to enter the Czech Republic and stay for up to 90 days. Make sure that the validity of your passport extends for at least six months from your date of entry. At present, citizens of the U.S., the EU, and some other countries do not require visas; Canadians now do, however. Check with your travel agent or Czech consulate well in advance of your journey, as visas cannot be issued at your point of entry.

FURTHER READING

If you think that the work of Franz Kafka will prove an ideal literary introduction to Prague, you will find you are wrong. Instead, if you are not familiar with their works, try the novels and stories of Milan Kundera,

Josef Škvorecký, Ivan Klima, and the late Bohumil Hrabal, whose *I Served the King of England* is a modern Czech classic. An older Czech classic is *The Good Soldier Švejk*, a celebrated novel by Jaroslav Hašek; for many readers it is the definitive delineation of the wily Czech character.

Václav Havel is not only the country's former president but also its most distinguished playwright and essayist. Volumes such as *Letters to Olga*, written during Havel's 1979-1982 imprisonment, offer unique insight into Czechoslovakia under the Communists. Timothy Garton Ash is the best modern chronicler of the politics of Central Europe *(The Magic Lantern)*, and Peter Demetz's *Prague in Black and Gold* gives a detailed cultural history of the city.

HOW TO GET TO PRAGUE & THE CZECH REPUBLIC

BY AIR

Most visitors arrive by air at Ruzyně, 12 miles (19 km) from Prague city center. For flight information in English, call 220 113 314 or try the Czech Airlines Web site www.csa.cz. The airport has been modernized, and you are unlikely to meet serious delays at immigration or in the baggage hall.

The Czech national carrier is Czech Airlines (ČSA), but many other airlines provide regular services from European cities to Prague. There are regular, though not daily, flights on ČSA to Prague from New York and Newark, or on Continental from Newark. All other airlines connect through British and European airports.

HOW TO GET TO THE CITY CENTER

"Airport vans" will take you to Revoluční trída, close to the city center, for 180 Kč. Tickets are

available at the airport newsstand. When booking your hotel room, check to see whether the hotel has its own minibus or limousine service from the airport. You can also take the local bus 119 to the terminus at Dejvická, from where it is a short metro ride into the city. Tickets at the metro station are 12 Kč for a transfer ticket (this allows you to travel on all forms of public transportation) or 8 Kč for a single ride (maximum 15 minutes). This is the cheapest option by far, but it can be slow and tiring if you have a lot of luggage.

The quickest way into town from the airport is by taxi, but drivers are notoriously dishonest. Be sure to agree on a fare beforehand; expect to pay about 300 Kč for a one-way trip. Reputable English-speaking companies include City Taxi (233 103 310) and AAA (222 333 222).

BY TRAIN

Prague has four train stations: nádraži Holešovice, Hlavní nádraži (the main station), Masarykovo nádraži, and Smíchovské nádraži. All are on metro lines. If you arrive by train from another European city, check your ticket to see where you will arrive. For train information, call 221 111 122.

BY CAR

If you drive into Prague, bear in mind that parking in the city center is strictly regulated and signs are not always fully comprehensible to non-Czech readers. Many hotels have parking lots or access to secure parking close by; expect to pay $10–$18 per day for parking.

BY COACH

One of the cheapest ways to get to Prague for U.K.-based travelers is by coach. Kingscourt Travel organizes coach travel six days a week, and the journey takes just under a day. In London call 020 8673 7500. The Prague office can be contacted at 224 234 583.

GETTING AROUND

PRAGUE

BY PUBLIC TRANSPORTATION

Prague has an extensive and efficient public transportation system employing metro, trams, and buses. Almost all the places you are likely to visit are easily accessible by frequent trams and metro trains. At night a limited tram service operates, so you will rarely be completely dependent on taxi drivers.

It is crucial to have a valid ticket before you travel. Plain-clothes inspectors check tickets often and will impose an on-the-spot fine of 400 Kč if you are traveling without a valid ticket. Ticket prices vary according to whether or not you wish to transfer from one conveyance to another. Tickets are valid for between 60 and 90 minutes only and must be punched as you enter a metro station or board a tram or bus. Buy tickets from tobacconists and station booking offices. Alternatively, a 24-hour pass costs 70 Kč, a 7-day pass 250 Kč, and a 14-day pass only slightly more, 280 Kč. Metro and tram maps are displayed at all stations and are available at some station offices.

Metro

There are three lines: A (Green), B (Yellow), and C (Red). Trains are frequent and clean; they run from around 5 a.m. to midnight.

Trams

Unlike metro lines, the trams run through the night. But they offer limited, less frequent service. Lines such as the 22 are very useful.

Buses

Buses often run from metro terminuses and provide access to suburban destinations such as the airport, Troja, and Star Castle.

The Prague Post, a weekly English newspaper, lists metro, tram, and bus information. You can also find this on www.dp-praha.cz or you can call 296 191 817.

BY TAXI

Use taxis as a last resort. Ask at your hotel about acceptable rates for trips you are planning; then, agree with drivers about rates before setting off, or insist that they run their meters (most are disinclined to do so). Demand receipts imprinted with company names; this discourages drivers from overcharging you. Try City Taxi (233 103 310) or AAA (222 333 222).

ON FOOT

Remember that Prague is a small city, and that the fastest way to get somewhere in the center is by walking. It is a 15-minute stroll from the Castle to the Old Town, and about the same from the Old Town Square to the National Museum.

CZECH REPUBLIC

BY BUS & TRAIN

The Czech Republic has a well-developed train and bus system linking the major cities, but trains in particular can be very slow. Obtaining accurate information about timetables and fares can be frustrating and time-consuming. Buses can be good for day trips from Prague to places such as Kutná Hora, but are not recommended as a way of exploring the whole country. If you plan on crisscrossing the republic for a week or more, look into the passes on offer. The Czech Flexipass is available to students, teachers, and those under 26. For information, call at Čedok, Na Příkopě 18, tel 224 197 111.

BY CAR

If your license does not include a photograph, you should obtain an International Driving Permit. In addition, you should carry a green card and your vehicle registration document if you are driving your own car (not necessary for rental cars).

Outside major cities, traffic is light and roads are maintained well, making driving largely stress-free—except when you are stuck behind a slow-moving tractor. Driving is on the right side of the road, and drivers should know it is not acceptable to have any alcohol in the blood.

Speed limits range from 30 to 50 kmh in built-up areas to 90 kmh on country roads and 110 to 130 kmh on motorways. Seat belts must be worn, and during the winter months you must keep your headlights turned on. In towns with tramlines, remember that trams always have the right-of-way.

If you plan to use the country's few motorways, you must display a special sticker. Such items are inexpensive and can be bought at gas stations and post offices. Most rental cars are provided with them. Always lock the car, don't leave valuables within view, and keep your luggage in the trunk if possible. Car theft and break-ins are not common, but opportunist crime does occur.

Breakdown & accidents

In the case of an accident, the police should be notified as soon as possible. It is advisable to contact the Czech automobile club, UAMK, for emergency phone numbers before setting out. UAMK headquarters are at Na strzi 9, Nusle, Prague 4 (tel 261 104 333), but you may find it easier to contact your own automobile association, with which UAMK may have a reciprocal agreement.

Gas

Gas *(benzin)* is cheaper than in most western European countries, and the republic is well supplied with large and well-equipped gas stations, many open 24 hours a day.

Car rental

If you plan to spend much time exploring the country, car rental is your best option. It is advisable to make reservations when you book your vacation. All the major international rental companies have offices in main towns and in such hotels as Prague's Inter-Continental. You will find local companies that are considerably cheaper (from $20 per day, including insurance), but the language barrier may prove to be a difficulty.

Hertz Karlovo náměstí 28, Prague 2, tel 220 102 444
Avis Klimentská 46, Prague 1, tel 221 851 225
National Masarykovo nádraži 4, Prague 2, tel 224 923 719

PRACTICAL ADVICE

COMMUNICATIONS

POST OFFICES

Post offices are open Monday to Friday from 8 to 5, and on Saturdays from 8 to noon. The main post office in Prague (Jindřišská 14) is open 24 hours a day. Stamps and phone cards are available at many newsstands.

TELEPHONES

The easiest way to make phone calls, both local and international, is to use a phone card. Hotel-room phone charges can be exorbitant. The entire domestic telephone system has been overhauled in recent years and many phone numbers have changed. Numbers in older guides and listings may be invalid.

Cell phones

Cellular telephones brought from other countries in Europe or from Australia will probably work in the Czech Republic, but check with your service provider to ensure they will allow calls to and from your number. Cell phones brought from North America normally use a different frequency; they will not work in the Czech Republic unless they have a dual frequency option.

CONVERSIONS

1 kilo = 2.2 pounds
1 liter = 0.2642 U.S. gallon
1 kilometer = 0.62 mile
1 meter = 1.093 yards

Women's clothing

U.S.	6	8	10	12	14	16
Czech	34	36	38	40	42	44

Men's clothing

U.S.	36	38	40	42	44	46
Czech	46	48	50	52	54	56

ELECTRICITY

Electricity in the Czech Republic is 220 volts. Plugs have two round pins. If you bring electrical equipment from the U.S. or the U.K., you will need an adaptor, plus a transformer for 110/120-volt appliances.

ETIQUETTE

Etiquette does not differ greatly from that expected in other European countries. It is customary to say "good day" (*dobrý den*) on entering an office or shop, and to say "goodbye" (*na shledanou*) on leaving. If you visit a private home, it will be much appreciated if you bring a small gift, such as a bunch of flowers or an item from your own country. In some homes you will be politely asked to remove your shoes. In pubs and simpler restaurants, you are expected to share tables during busy times.

MEDIA

NEWSPAPERS

The Prague Post is a weekly newspaper published in English. Its "Night & Day" supplement (and www.praguepost.com) has very useful listings and reviews. Various free publications can be found in hotel lobbies, but they are essentially advertisements for restaurants and clubs. Non-Czech newspapers are easy to obtain in major cities, but difficult elsewhere. European editions of the *Guardian, USA Today,* and the *International Herald Tribune* are more widely available, as are magazines such as *Time* and *Newsweek.*

RADIO

Czech radio runs the gamut from pop music to jazz to classical. English-language programs can be found on several stations, including the BBC at 101.1 FM. Radio Prague can be found at 92.6 FM and 102.7 FM, on medium wave within the Czech Republic at 1287, 1233 or 1071 KHz, and on shortwave around the world. It broadcasts programs in English Monday through Friday at 1:30 p.m. and 7:30 p.m., and on Saturday and Sunday at 1:30 p.m. and 8:30 p.m. The BBC World Service broadcasts on several SW and FM frequencies, but many of the programs are in Czech.

TELEVISION

There are two state-owned television channels, and at least two commercial channels. Česká Televize's Channel 2 shows news transmissions in English at 8 a.m. weekdays, 7 a.m. weekends.

MONEY MATTERS

Czech currency is based on the *koruna* (plural: *koruny),* abbreviated to Kč and known in English as crowns. Each crown is divided into 100 *hellers,* which you will rarely encounter since they are worth so little. Money can be changed easily, especially in Prague, where there are dozens of bureaus. Try to avoid changing money at the airport or border crossings; commission rates are often a steep 5 percent. Equally, beware of bureaus that offer "no commission"; exchange rates can be very unfavorable.

Outside major towns and cities, your best bet is to use an ATM. Most banks have currency-changing desks and charge a minimal fee, but the process can be time-consuming.

There is a marked contrast in expense between Prague and the rest of the country. It is hard to find a double room in Prague for under 3,000 Kč, which in most small towns would buy you the best suite in town. Similarly, Prague restaurants that have French chefs or cater to foreigners (there are tens of thousands of foreign residents as well as visitors) charge prices comparable to those of other European cities. Restaurants with a local clientele charge much less, simply because the average Czech cannot afford Berlin or Paris prices.

Major credit cards are widely accepted in Czech hotels, restaurants, and shops. Nonetheless, there are exceptions, so it is wise to carry a reasonable amount of Czech currency.

NATIONAL HOLIDAYS

There are relatively few national holidays. The most important are:
January 1 (New Year's Day)
Easter Monday
May 1 (May Day)
May 8 (National Liberation Day)
July 5 (Sts. Cyril and Methodius)
July 6 (Jan Hus Day)
September 28 (St. Václav's Day or Czech Statehood Day)
October 28 (Foundation of the Czechoslovak Republic, 1918)
November 17 (Student's Day)
December 24–26 (Christmas).
Most castles and some museums are closed on national holidays and the day following.

OPENING TIMES

Opening times are irregular, but, broadly speaking, shops, offices, and banks open from 8 to 5 or 9 to 6. Some close for an hour or more at lunchtime. In general, shops and banks are closed on Sundays and holidays, and often on Saturday afternoons. A few shops offer later opening times, and even 24-hour "nonstop" hours. Pharmacies are open from 7:30 a.m. to 6 p.m. on weekdays; in major cities there will be one or two 24-hour pharmacies.

Most restaurants are open for lunch and dinner, seven days a week, and do not have the variable day off that is common in countries such as France and Germany. Many churches are open all day, especially when they are in use for regular services, but others have more quirky opening times. Some are open only during services (usually early morning and late afternoon); others close for a number of hours during the day.

PLACES OF WORSHIP

Many churches are tourist attractions as well as places of worship. Times of services are normally posted on the door. They are also listed in the classified section of *Prague Post*. No formal dress is required, except for yarmulkas in synagogues and at the Jewish cemeteries (paper ones are usually available at the synagogues). Many churches also function as concert halls. In some cases, the only way you can see inside a church without paying is to attend a service.

REST ROOMS

Public rest rooms are usually clearly marked "WC"; a small charge (around 5 Kč) is levied for admission and some sheets of toilet paper. Standards vary, but most restrooms are clean and properly maintained. Women should look for the words Dámy or Ženy; men for Páni or Muži (however, be aware that Paní means "women" and is sometimes used on WC doors). Additional facilities, sometimes free and better maintained, are available at many metro stations, department stores, museums, restaurants, and cafés.

SAFETY

There was a time when an evening stroll down Václavské náměstí (Wenceslas Square) required you to be fully alert to the attentions of roaming gangs of pickpockets. Those days are over, and Prague is no more threatening or dangerous than any large European city.

Pickpockets are still at work in the metro, and on trams and at tramstops. Trams 22 and 23 are popular with tourists—and with pickpockets. Tourist attractions such as the Charles Bridge are also prime spots. Speaking English or German is enough to draw attention to yourself. Keep wallets in front pockets; close purses and hold them near the body. Similarly, be careful when withdrawing cash from an ATM.

Unsavory characters, including drug addicts, often congregate at the main railway station, the park in front of it, and the Florenc bus terminal, especially late at night. So take particular care if you find yourself at these locations, although they are not in themselves dangerous.

TIME DIFFERENCES

The Czech Republic runs on CET (Central European Time), one hour ahead of GMT (Greenwich Mean Time), six hours ahead of New York, and nine hours ahead of Los Angeles. Clocks change for daylight saving on the last Sunday in March (one hour forward), and go back one hour the last Sunday in October.

TIPPING

In general Czechs do not tip, but they do round up the bill in restaurants. For example, if your bill comes to 282 Kč, you might hand the waiter 300 Kč in notes and tell him to keep the change. If it comes to 235 Kč, you could ask for 50 Kč back.

TRAVELERS WITH DISABILITIES

Special provisions for the disabled are still the exception rather than the rule, but Prague hotels, restaurants, and museums are becoming increasingly aware of the need to cater to such special needs. Some of the hotel listings that follow indicate wheelchair accessibility. The major problem for people with disabilities arises when using public transportation. You cannot get a wheelchair onto a tram.

The Prague Wheelchair Association publishes *Accessible Prague*, a guide to facilities for the disabled. They can be contacted at Benediktská 6, Staré Město, Prague. Tel: 224 827 210.

VISITING CASTLES AND CHÂTEAUS

A castle is known in Czech as a *hrad,* whereas a *zámek* denotes a building akin to a French château, i.e., the country residence of an aristocratic family, varying in scale from a modest mansion to a palace. Opening times of castles and museums vary considerably. Except for the most popular attractions, all such places are closed on Mondays, national holidays, and the days following national holidays. Although a castle may advertise its open hours as 9 to 5 in summer, bear in mind that there is often a lunch break from noon to 1, and if the site can be visited only on a guided tour, the last tour is likely to leave an hour before the official closing time. Guided tours range in duration from 45 to 90 minutes.

The more popular attractions offer guided tours in languages other than Czech, usually German and English. The admission fee is usually double that for a tour in Czech, but well worth the extra cost, for obvious reasons. Some larger châteaus offer as many as three separate tours, each focusing on different features of the building.

VISITOR INFORMATION

Visitors to the Czech Republic are served well by information bureaus, which are readily identifiable by a large, bright-green, lowercase letter "i." There is scarcely a provincial town of any interest that does not have such an office, usually in the main square or within or near the town hall. Some bureaus are extremely useful, and can assist with hotel and campsite bookings. Others are essentially glorified sales outlets for local postcard producers. Overall, however, they are mines of information, offering maps, booklets, and verbal guidance.

In Prague the main visitor information centers are located at the main station, Hlavní nádraží at Na Příkopě 20, and in the Old Town Hall (Staroměstské náměstí). If you are planning an excursion out of Prague, it is worth visiting the latter, where staff have access via their computers to the opening times of all castles and museums throughout the republic. The Prague information center has its own Web site (www.prague-info.cz).

EMERGENCIES

EMBASSIES IN PRAGUE

United States
Tržište 15, Prague 1, tel 257 530 663. Open Mon.–Fri. 8–4:30 (consular hours 9–12).
Canada
Muchova 6, Prague 6, tel 272 101 800. Open Mon.–Fri. 8–4.
United Kingdom
Thunovská 14, Prague 1, tel 257 402 111. Open Mon.–Fri. 9–noon.

EMERGENCY PHONE NUMBERS

Police	112
Prague Police	112
Fire	112
Ambulance	112
Automobile emergencies	1230

HEALTH

If you think you need a doctor during your stay, consult your hotel reception desk. For minor ailments, go to any pharmacy *(lékárna);* if the language problems can be overcome, you can often obtain advice and inexpensive medicines there. Most pharmacies close at 6 p.m. but some remain open 24 hours:
Palackého 5, Prague 1, near Mustek metro station, tel 224 946 982.
Belgická 37, Prague 2, near Námesti Míru metro station, tel 222 519 731.
Stefánikova 6, Prague 6, near Andel, tel 257 320 918.

By western European and North American standards, charges for non-emergency treatment and medication are low. If you do not have health insurance, you can apply for short-term coverage from the Czech Central Health Insurance Office, Tyřeova 7, Prague 2 (tel 221 972 111).

In Prague, recommended clinics include the First Medical Clinic, Tylovo náměstí 3, Prague 2, tel 224 251 319, and No Homolce Hospital, Roentgenova 2, Smíchov, Prague 5, tel 257 271 111. Both have English-speaking staff. For dental emergencies: Palackého 5, tel 224 946 981 (24 hours).

The American Medical Center in Prague is at Janovského 48 (open 24 hours), Prague 7, tel 220 807 756. The Canadian Medical Center (24 hours) is at Veleslavínská 1, Prague 6, tel 235 360 133; after hours tel 724 300 301 (general practice) and tel 724 300 303 (pediatrician).

LOST PROPERTY

Prague's central lost property office is at Karoliny Svetlé 5, Prague 1, tel 224 235 085. Open weekdays 8–noon, 12:30–5:30.

If you lose your credit card, telephone the relevant provider:
American Express tel 222 800 111
Visa tel (410) 581-3836 (U.S.)
Eurocard/Mastercard tel 261 354 650
Diners Club tel 267 197 450

HOTELS & RESTAURANTS

ACCOMMODATIONS

Prague has hundreds of hotels and pensions, but at certain times of the year a room is very difficult to find; it's best to make reservations well in advance if possible. Czech tourist offices provide fairly complete lists of hotels in Prague, and local tourist offices outside the capital usually have information about accommodations in their regions.

Standards are high, especially in Prague, where almost all rooms have bathrooms and basic facilities such as telephones and televisions. While you can assume rooms will be comfortable and clean, don't always expect light, airy rooms with modern furnishings in Prague or the Czech Republic: Decor and furniture tend to be traditional, which means dark and heavy.

You will find a huge price differential between hotels in Prague and those outside the city. For 2,000 Kč you will get a large, comfortable room in the provinces, but this will pay only for rock-bottom accommodations in the capital. Prices should include all taxes, but it's sensible to check before making a reservation. Almost without exception, the room rate includes breakfast. Major credit cards are accepted in all but the smallest and most remote hotels.

Price ranges indicated in the listings below are official "rack rates." Except during the high season, it is usually possible to negotiate a discount, especially at some of the luxury hotels that have high overhead costs and, out of season, when occupancy rates are fairly low.

There is little clear difference between a hotel and a pension. Indeed, the City Hotel in Prague manages to be both. A pension will usually be family-run, and it may not have a reception desk; guests are provided with a key to the front door as if to a private house.

If you are planning a stay of a week or more, it is worth considering a "residence" or private accommodations. A residence provides a fully furnished apartment, often centrally located, with cooking facilities. Prices vary enormously, depending on location, quality of facilities, and the degree of independence and privacy.

A few agencies specialize in locating accommodations in private apartments. Try Ave Travel at the main train station (Hlavní Nádraží, tel 224 223 226), at the airport in the transit hall (tel 220 561 817) or in the arrivals hall (tel 220 114 674), and at Staroměstské náměstí 2, Prague 1 (Old Town Square, tel 224 482 018). From the U.S., call 1-415-479-5581, or visit www.avetravel.cz.

RESTAURANTS

A *restaurace* is a proper restaurant, sometimes formal and relatively expensive, but not necessarily so. For simpler food a *pivnice*, *hostinec*, or *hospoda* (all essentially pubs) will usually be adequate; if you wish to drink wine with your meal rather than beer, look for a *vinárna* (wine bar). In practice, beer and wine are equally available in a restaurace and a vinárna, but the latter should offer a better range. You can get snacks at *bufets*.

In simpler establishments, cooked dishes may be rudimentary—sausages or stews—and you often get better value from *chlebíčky*, open sandwiches made from sausage, ham, other meats, and cheese, usually topped with sour cream, gherkins, radishes, and other garnishes. Some of the grander coffeehouses (*kavárna*) also serve simple meals. The quality and hygiene are generally better than you will find at roadside stands selling sausages and a roll. Fast-food chains are sadly becoming more common in all the towns, but there seems little point in coming all the way to Prague or Brno to end up eating a Big Mac.

PRICES

HOTELS
An indication of the cost of a double room without breakfast is given by $ signs.

$$$$$	Over $200
$$$$	$130–$200
$$$	$80–$130
$$	$50–$80
$	Under $50

RESTAURANTS
An indication of the cost of a three-course dinner without drinks is given by $ signs.

$$$$$	Over $35
$$$$	$25–$35
$$$	$15–$25
$$	$10–$15
$	Under $10

Dining etiquette & times

Eating out is made simpler if you understand the local etiquette. In basic restaurants and pubs it is common to share a table, which is a good way of meeting local people—if you can find a common language.

Lunch is served from about 11:30 onward, and Czechs tend to eat their evening meal at around 7 p.m. Except in the cities and tourist centers, it can sometimes be difficult to order hot meals after 9 p.m.

Menus

The menu (*jídelní lístek*) can be an obstacle. A few standard terms stand out: *Vepřové* means "pork," *hovězí* "beef," *klobásy* "sausages," and *hranolky* "French fries" or "chips." Cooking terms include *na rostu* (roasted), *smažený* (fried), and *řízek* (breaded). But the dish descriptions in which these staple terms are embedded are often unfamiliar and either denote special methods of preparation or are fanciful terms invented by the chef. Even with a basic command of Czech culinary terms, you will almost certainly need to ask the waiter for advice. And waiters tend to recommend the more expensive

---

KEY 🏨 Hotel 🍴 Restaurant ⓘ No. of guest rooms ➕ No. of seats Ⓜ Metro 🅿 Parking 🕐 Closed 🛗 Elevator

dishes, and those, like schnitzel or steak, that are likely to be familiar. Thus the chances of sampling original cooking, where it is available, are remote.

Fortunately almost all restaurants, except the most basic establishments such as country pubs, have menus in German and sometimes English. Even though translations are not always reliable, they will certainly help you make your choice.

Privatization has led to an improvement in overall quality. Under the state-owned system, service was poor, menus were indecipherable, and cooks had no incentive to excel. Meals were often dull and marred by mediocre ingredients. Today the problem is very different, since some modern cooks try to bring together all kinds of ingredients in an attempt at originality or exoticism, with often chaotic and indigestible results.

Outside Prague, most visitors will find a great deal of similarity among restaurants. Establishments vary in comfort, decor, and quality of food and service, but their menus tend to focus on the same types of dishes, with a few of the chef's own concoctions. Some may offer specialties such as fish or game. There is also very little variation in price. On the other hand, quality is usually dependable.

In Prague, however, the situation is different. In the working-class suburbs, and even in the city center, you will find smoky pubs that serve basic food at lunchtime to hordes of regular customers. Such establishments are not focused on foreign visitors, so the menus may be in Czech only. You can eat very cheaply, but you may not feel particularly welcome.

In contrast, the tourist-frequented areas such as the Little Quarter (Malá Strana), Old Town (Staré Město), and the Jewish Quarter (Josefov) have numerous restaurants that are expensive by Czech standards, but some of them are very high-quality, serving international

Notes: The hotels and restaurants listed here have been grouped by area (in Prague) or region (in the Czech Republic). They are then listed alphabetically by price category. The postal address Prague 1 covers the central part of the city—the Castle District, Little Quarter, and Old Town. Visitors with disabilities should ask the establishment about facilities.

Abbreviations:
L = lunch   D = dinner
AE American Express
DC Diner's Club
MC MasterCard
V Visa

dishes to international standards. There should be no problem with communication with the waiting staff, and the selection of drinks is wide. Such restaurants can be excellent, but over a long period they will be a drain on most budgets. In smart residential districts such as Vinohrady, visitors will find a plethora of small, cozy, neighborhood restaurants serving up mostly Czech dishes with a modest selection of beers and wines. These places are inexpensive, and the food is usually delicious and served in generous portions. Plenty of restaurants offer pasta, French, and even Indian dishes as well.

Paying for your meal
Unfortunately, many waiters in Prague feel it is their patriotic duty to cheat foreign customers. In modest establishments such as pubs, the waiter will tot up the bill on a slip of paper and present it to you. Close scrutiny will often reveal that the bill has been padded. Have an idea of what your bill should be before you ask for it; if there's a clear discrepancy, check it. You may be charged extra for accompaniments that are in fact included in the cost of the meal. Often the sums involved are

trifling, but these attempts to defraud are perpetuated because many visitors will not challenge questionable calculations.

You should be aware that there is no "service charge" in any Czech restaurant, although many that cater to foreigners try to rip their customers off by imposing one. The size of the charge varies and can be as high as 20 percent. Refuse to pay the charge, and instead slip some money to the waiter or waitress in person. You can be sure that any "service charge" will not end up in the pockets of the restaurant's staff.

PRAGUE

CASTLE DISTRICT & LITTLE QUARTER

HOTELS

HOFFMEISTER
$$$$$
POD BRUSKOU 7
PRAGUE 1
TEL 251 017 111
FAX 251 017 120
E-MAIL hotel@hoffmeister.cz
www.hoffmeister.cz
The Hoffmeister, Prague's only Relais & Châteaux group member, offers luxury and excellent service. The rooms are very richly furnished, with heavy draperies, but the location along a busy tramline beneath the castle may not be ideal. There's a fine and tasteful restaurant, the Ada, and the terrace is delightful in summer.
🛏 38 Ⓜ Malostranská Ⓟ
🔁 Ⓢ Ⓧ All major cards

SAVOY
$$$$$
KEPLEROVA 6
PRAGUE 1
TEL 224 302 430
FAX 224 302 128
E-MAIL info@hotel-savoy.cz
www.hotel-savoy.cz
This is an art nouveau building near the Strahov Monastery. Its elegant public rooms include a lobby bar,

with curved banquettes, where you can have a wide range of snacks and light meals, and the glass-roofed Hradčany restaurant. The bedrooms are among the largest in the city, with complimentary mini-bars and spacious marble bathrooms. Guests have free use of the fitness center. The hotel is extremely popular with celebrities, but the location at some distance from the city center may be a disadvantage for most visitors to Prague.

🏨 61 🚇 Malostranská 🅿️
🔄 🚫 ♿ 📺 🐾 All
major cards

🏨 U TŘÍ PŠTROSŮ
🍴 $$$$$
NÁMĚSTÍ DRAŽICKÉHO 12
PRAGUE 1
TEL 257 532 410
FAX 257 533 217
E-MAIL info@upstrosu.cz
"The Three Ostriches," in the shadow of the Charles Bridge, is one of Prague's best-established luxury inns. It was the city's first coffeehouse, and until the 1960s was run by the Dundr family, who regained possession in the 1990s. The interior retains precious Renaissance features including a painted wooden ceiling. The U Tří Pstrosů restaurant offers a good selection of fish, including carp filets and salmon with caviar sauce. Game dishes, such as leg of boar with rosehip sauce, traditional Czech dishes, and ostrich specialties are also on the menu. There's a cheaper lunchtime selection.

🏨 18 🚇 Malostranská 🅿️
♿ All major cards

SOMETHING SPECIAL

🏨 U ZLATÉ STUDNĚ
🍴

T ucked away in a cul-de-sac beneath the castle, this 16th-century mansion, once the property of Rudolph II and the astronomer Tycho Brahe, was skillfully converted in 2000 into a luxury hotel. It's certainly among the best of Prague's top hotels. All rooms are furnished differently and to the highest standards, with a Jacuzzi in every bathroom. The equally luxurious restaurant offers a short menu of dishes that often blend different European cuisines. The decor is essentially modern, and in summer a roof terrace adjacent to the Ledebur Gardens has what is surely the best view of all the roofs of the Little Quarter.

$$$$–$$$$$
U ZLATÉ STUDNĚ 4
PRAGUE 1
TEL 257 011 213
FAX 257 533 320
E-MAIL hotel@zlatastudna.cz
www.zlatastudna.cz

🏨 20 🚇 Malostranská 🅿️
♿ All major cards

🏨 SAX
$$$$
JÁNSKÝ VRŠEK 3
PRAGUE 1
TEL 257 530 172
FAX 257 534 101
E-MAIL hotelsax@bon.cz
www.hotelsax.cz
This discreet hotel is located on a quiet square off Vlašská in the heart of the Little Quarter. The rooms are simply but attractively furnished, and the stylish lobby bar in a courtyard atrium is decorated with modern art.

🏨 22 🚇 Malostranská 🅿️
♿ All major cards

🏨 U PÁVA
$$$$
U LUŽISKÉHO SEMINÁŘE 32
PRAGUE 1
TEL 257 533 573
FAX 257 530 919
E-MAIL hotelupava@iol.cz
www.romantichotels.cz
U Páva is located on a quiet square just a short distance from the Charles Bridge. Try to see the rooms before making a reservation; some can be a bit gloomy, especially in winter. The dark wood furnishings and heavy drapery are not to everyone's taste, but the rooms are sumptuous. It is worth investigating the suites, which are only slightly more expensive than the double rooms.

🏨 27 🚇 Malostranská 🅿️
🔄 ♿ AE, MC, V

🏨 ZLATÁ HVĚZDA
$$$$
NERUDOVA 48
PRAGUE 1
TEL 257 533 833
FAX 257 533 624
E-MAIL hvezda@ok.cz
The grand Zlatá Hvězda in the heart of the Little Quarter occupies a magnificent 1730s baroque building. It was reconstructed in 2000, but original features such as the ornate plasterwork were not disturbed. The rooms vary in size, and all have period wooden furnishings.

🏨 26 🚇 Malostranská 🅿️
🔄 ♿ AE, MC, V

🏨 U MODREHO KLICE (THE BLUE KEY)
$$$–$$$$
LETENSKÁ 14
PRAGUE 1
TEL 257 534 361
FAX 257 534 372
E-MAIL bluekey@mbox.vol.cz
This old but renovated building lies close to Malostranské náměstí. The rooms are cozy rather than luxurious. Some have a kitchenette. Ask for a room away from the noisy main road. Service is friendly and helpful.

🏨 28 🚇 Malostranská 🔄
♿ All major cards

🏨 PENSION 🍴 DIENTZENHOFER
$$$
NOSTICOVA 2
PRAGUE 1
TEL 257 311 319
FAX 257 320 888
E-MAIL dientzenhofer@volny.cz
Kilián Ignác Dientzenhofer's birthplace, close to Kampa Island, now flourishes as a small hotel and restaurant. The location is appealing and quiet, but the rooms, although

quite spacious, are in need of a makeover. There is wheelchair access, and a pleasant garden terrace.
(1) 9 **(R)** Malostranská **(P)**
(S) **(⊘)** All major cards

RESTAURANTS

🍴 U MALÍŘŮ
$$$$$
MALTÉZSKÉ NÁMĚSTÍ 11
PRAGUE 1
TEL 257 530 000
FAX 257 530 318
The restaurant claims to date back to 1543. The food is solidly French except for the Menu Bohemia, which includes venison terrine and roast goose. Good selection of pricey French wines.
🔢 60 **(R)** Malostranská
(⊘) AE, MV, V

🍴 CIRCLE LINE
$$$$
MALOSTRANSKÉ NÁMĚSTÍ 12
PRAGUE 1
TEL 257 530 021
FAX 257 530 023
E-MAIL circleline@zatisigroup.cz
The chef is French, so even the Czech food has a slight Gallic accent. Most of the dishes are French, with a strong emphasis on fresh fish: mille feuille of ray features alongside Tournedos Rossini. There are two charming dining rooms, quite formal. The wine list is international, but dominated by bottles from Moravia.
🔢 65 **(R)** Malostranská
(⊘) AE, MC, V

🍴 PÁLFFY PALÁC
$$$$
VALDŠTEJNSKÁ 14
PRAGUE 1
TEL/FAX 257 530 522
E-MAIL palffy@seznam.cz
This luxurious establishment occupies part of the second floor of a large palace, which has served as the Prague music conservatory since 1989. In summer, opt to eat on the terrace overlooking the palace gardens rather than

in the faded grandeur of the main dining room. The cooking is essentially French and includes skewer of sea bass, shallots, and bacon served with chestnuts, lamb cutlets with mint aspic, and beef filet with roasted forest mushrooms. Salads are good and there are a number of tasty vegetarian options as well. It's a popular venue for brunch. The selection of French wines is better than at most Prague restaurants.
🔢 60 **(R)** Malostranská
(⊘) AE, MC, V

🍴 U ZLATÉ HRUŠKY
$$$$
NOVÝ SVĚT 3/77, PRAGUE 1
TEL 220 514 778
FAX 220 515 356
E-MAIL info@zlatahruska.cz
www.zlatahruska.cz
The restaurant occupies three wood-paneled rooms on the first floor of an old house. In summer you can eat in the garden. Most of chef Karel Brázda's dishes are inter-national, but there are also local specialties such as tripe cooked in Bohemian style, a stew served as an appetizer, and venison roulade with pear purée. All dishes are freshly prepared, so you may have a wait of 20–50 minutes. The desserts are solidly Bohemian, from noodles with poppy seed and curd to dumplings with plum sauce. The international wine list is less exciting than the menu.
🔢 70 **(⊘)** AE, MC, V

🍴 BAZAAR
$$$
NERUDOVA 40
PRAGUE 1
TEL 257 535 050
FAX 257 534 848
E-MAIL info@restaurantbazaar.cz
The eclectic menu calls itself Mediterranean. Dishes include risotto, sole, coq au vin, osso buco, and steaks, as well as a few Moroccan specialties. There is an extensive list of Bohemian and Moravian

wines, including older vintages, and some well-chosen wines from France. Summer terrace; live music in the evenings.
🔢 250 **(R)** Malostranská
(⊘) All major cards

🍴 U MALTÉZSKÝCH RYTÍŘŮ
$$$
PROKOPSKÁ 10, PRAGUE 1
TEL/FAX 257 533 666
With its medieval cellars and piano bar, this small, cozy restaurant has a devoted following. The menu is sensibly short, featuring Continental dishes such as Chateaubriand steak for two, lamb fillets, duck, quail, and sole.
🔢 30 **(R)** Malostranská
(⊘) AE, MC, V

🍴 U ŠEVCE MATOUŠE
$$$
LORETÁNSKÉ NÁMĚSTÍ 4
PRAGUE 1
TEL 220 514 536
This is a grand Czech restaurant, located in vaulted chambers, with staid furnishings. The menu is enormous, and so are the helpings. Chicken and steak are prepared in a number of different ways, but the wine list is limited.
🔢 45 **(R)** Malostranská
(⊘) All major cards

🍴 WALDŠTEJNSKA HOSPODA
$$$
VALDŠTEJNSKÉ NÁMĚSTÍ 7
PRAGUE 1
TEL 257 531 759
FAX 257 532 195
This Czech restaurant specializes in game, but also serves some international dishes. The specialty is the "Valdštejn sword"—various meats skewered onto a sword, for two people or more. Try the steak with port wine sauce. Most of the wines are Moravian. The decor of the three rooms is traditional, with dark wooden banquettes.
🔢 100 **(R)** Malostranská
(⊘) MC, V

HOTELS & RESTAURANTS

▌ U LABUTI
$$–$$$
HRADČANSKÉ NÁMĚSTÍ 11
PRAGUE 1
TEL 220 511 191
FAX 220 511 190
The U Labuti is based in a historic building that has over the years been home to Johannes Kepler, Tycho Brahe, and the young Madeleine Albright, former U.S. Secretary of State. It has two rooms—one, the principal restaurant, focuses on international cuisine, while the other, more like a pub in atmosphere, offers Czech cuisine and Plzeň beer. The house specialty is the Old Prague Platter, which consists of duck, rabbit, smoked pork, red and white cabbage, and three kinds of dumplings. The vaulted rooms, pretty tapestry chairs, and pink tablecloths make for an elegant setting. The wine list is international.
🔳 100   🚇 Malostranská
🃏 All major cards

OLD TOWN

HOTELS

🏨 PAŘÍŽ
$$$$–$$$$$
U OBECNIHO DOMU 1
PRAGUE 1
TEL 222 195 195
FAX 224 225 475
E-MAIL booking@hotel-pariz.cz
www.hotel-pariz.cz
This gorgeous secessionist hotel has been completely renovated to combine comfort with beauty. Public rooms include the stylish Café de Paris, with its art nouveau light fittings. Admire the lovely ironwork on the staircase.
ⓘ 94   🚇 Náměstí Republiky
🅿 🛗 🔲 🎴 📺 🃏 All major cards

🏨 UNGELT
$$$$–$$$$$
MALÁ ŠTUPARTSKÁ 1
PRAGUE 1
TEL 224 828 686

FAX 224 828 181
E-MAIL hotel@ungelt.cz
www.ungelt.cz
The Ungelt hotel, behind the Týn church, offers spacious apartments. All have a kitchenette. Some have two bedrooms, sleeping four.
ⓘ 10   🚇 Náměstí Republiky
🛗 🃏 All major cards

🏨 RESIDENCE MASNÁ 9
$$$–$$$$
MASNÁ 9
PRAGUE 1
TEL 222 312 257
FAX 224 815 551
E-MAIL info@pragamagica.cz
Dating from 1937, the renovated building has been converted into apartments, making it ideal for visitors planning to stay for an extended period. You can also rent apartments for just a few days. They have kitchenettes and a maid service. Prices compare favorably with most 4-star hotels, especially given the excellent location.
ⓘ 10   🚇 Náměstí Republiky
🛗 🃏 All major cards

🏨 BETLEM CLUB
$$$
BETLÉMSKÉ NÁMĚSTÍ 9
PRAGUE 1
TEL 222 221 574
FAX 222 220 580
E-MAIL betlem.club@login.cz
www.betlemclub.cz
This represents one of the few bargains left in the Old Town. The location opposite the Bethlehem Chapel is convenient, and the rooms are comfortable and of a reasonable size. All have bathrooms. Those with four beds are ideal for families.
ⓘ 22   🚇 Národní Třída
🛗 🔲 🃏 MC, V

🏨 CENTRAL
$$$
RYBNÁ 8
PRAGUE 1
TEL 224 812 041
FAX 222 328 404
E-MAIL central@orfea.cz
Built in 1931, the Central, near

PRICES

HOTELS
An indication of the cost of a double room without breakfast is given by $ signs.

$$$$$	Over $200
$$$$	$130–$200
$$$	$80–$130
$$	$50–$80
$	Under $50

RESTAURANTS
An indication of the cost of a three-course dinner without drinks is given by $ signs.

$$$$$	Over $35
$$$$	$25–$35
$$$	$15–$25
$$	$10–$15
$	Under $10

náměstí Republiky, was renovated in the late 1990s. Rooms are simply furnished. The best and priciest, on the top floors, have balconies with views over the city. There's an attractive lobby bar.
ⓘ 68   🚇 Náměstí Republiky
🅿 🛗 🔲 🃏 MC, V

🏨 U KRÁLE JIŘÍHO
$$$
LILIOVÁ 10
PRAGUE 1
TEL 222 220 925
FAX 222 221 707
E-MAIL kral.jiri@telecom.cz
www.kinggeorge.cz
The small King George hotel occupies an old house at the heart of the Old Town. The rooms are simply furnished and prices are low for the area. In the same building is a pub of the same name and the James Joyce Irish pub.
ⓘ 12   🚇 Staroměstská
🃏 All major cards

🏨 RESIDENCE ŘETĚZOVÁ
$$–$$$$$
ŘETĚZOVÁ 9
PRAGUE 1
TEL/FAX 222 221 800
E-MAIL info@residence
retezova.com
www.residenceretezova.com

Centrally located in the maze of streets in the Old Town, this renovated 15th-century building offers a range of accommodations in self-catering units—making this a good choice if you are staying in Prague for more than just a few days.

(1) 9 🚇 Staroměstská ⬇
🗝 All major cards

🏨 UNITAS
$
BARTOLOMĚJSKÁ 9
PRAGUE 1
TEL 222 327 700
FAX 222 327 709
E-MAIL cloister@cloister-inn.cz
This is a clean but spartan budget choice, with twin and triple rooms and some dormitory-style rooms in what used to be convent cells. All bathroom facilities are shared, and the rooms are hardly spacious, but the location, just a short walk from the Charles Bridge and the Old Town, is good.

(1) 34 🚇 Národní třída 🅿
🚭 🗝 No credit cards accepted

RESTAURANTS

🍴 BELLEVUE
$$$$$
SMETANOVO NÁBŘEŽÍ 18
PRAGUE 1
TEL 222 221 443
FAX 222 220 453
The cooking is Continental, and primarily French. Dishes include New Zealand lamb, turbot, and venison—all richly prepared and very expensive. Guests appreciate the spacious views of Hradčany. Live jazz on Sundays.

🍴 120 🚇 Staroměstská
🗝 AE, MC

🍴 V ZÁTIŠÍ
$$$–$$$$$
BETLÉMSKÉ NÁMĚSTÍ, LILIOVÁ 1
PRAGUE 1
TEL 222 221 155
FAX 222 220 629
E-MAIL vzatisi@zatisigroup.cz
This exceptionally pretty and

acclaimed restaurant occupies several rooms, with mottled Provençal decor. The menu, which changes regularly, is international, but there are also Bohemian specialties such as goose, and venison with foie gras. House specialties include New Zealand lamb chops, duck, and John Dory. The strength of the wine list lies in good Czech wines. Service is excellent.

🍴 105 🚇 Národní Třída
🚭 🗝 AE, MC, V

🍴 REYKJAVIK
$$$$
KARLOVA 20
PRAGUE 1
TEL 222 221 218
FAX 222 221 419
E-MAIL reykjavik@mbox.vol.cz
www.reykjavik.cz
The compact, galleried Reykjavik, in the heart of the Old Town, offers fresh seafood flown in daily. Specialties include Icelandic salted cod prepared in various ways; tuna; and cod. Meat dishes include ostrich medallions. The most popular dessert is the cheesecake. Near the entrance is a small area where you can eat sandwiches. The wines are relatively expensive.

🍴 150 🚇 Staroměstská
🗝 All major cards

🍴 RYBÍ TRH
$$$$
TÝNSKÝ DVŮR 5
PRAGUE 1
TEL 224 895 447
FAX 224 895 449
The tanks ranged round the restaurant's two rooms are a clear indication of what to expect on the menu here: live lobster, octopus, squid, cod, halibut, and tuna. Steamed mussels, bouillabaisse, sushi, and oysters all feature. The location is in the smart Ungelt courtyard. In summer you can eat in the garden.

🍴 60 🚇 Náměstí Republiky
🗝 All major cards

🍴 ARCHIV
$$$
MASNÁ 3
PRAGUE 1
TEL/FAX 224 819 297
The vast menu includes seafood prepared in French ways, fondue, Surf and Turf, oysters, steaks, and game in the autumn. The decor is Provençal-style beige walls, plain wooden tables and chairs, and parquet floors. In summer the restaurant expands into the garden at the back.

🍴 80 🚇 Náměstí Republiky
🗝 All major cards

🍴 DON GIOVANNI
$$$
KAROLÍNY SVĚTLÉ 34
PRAGUE 1
TEL 222 222 062
E-MAIL dongio@mbox.vol.cz
www.dongiovanni.cz
Prague has numerous pasta and pizza joints but only a few serious Italian restaurants. Don Giovanni, close to the Charles Bridge, is one of these. It features seafood, carpaccio, risotto with porcini mushrooms, and other Italian classics. The interior is sober, with photographs of Czech celebrities adorning the walls. The wine list is largely Italian and reasonably priced, with an excellent selection of *grappa*. Watch for a wide range of set menus at lunchtime.

🍴 80 🚇 Národní Třída 🔆
🗝 All major cards

🍴 LE SAINT-JACQUES
$$$
JAKUBSKÁ 4
PRAGUE 1
TEL/FAX 222 322 685
www.saint-jacques.cz
Devotedly Francophile, Le Saint-Jacques offers oysters and mussels in season, while the full menu includes scallops, steaks, lamb, and Basque chicken. The mostly French wine list is fairly limited.

🍴 50 🚇 Náměstí Republiky
⏰ Closed Sun. 🗝 AE, MC, V

🍴 KLUB ARCHITEKTŮ
$$
BETLÉMSKÉ NÁMĚSTÍ 169/5A
PRAGUE I
TEL 224 401 214
This is a basement restaurant with bare stone walls and wooden tables. The large menu includes odd dishes such as chicken with peaches, plus Thai dishes, burritos, and BBQ. A good selection of wines from individual growers.
🪑 100 🚇 Národní Třída
💳 MC, V

🍴 RED HOT & BLUES
$$
JAKUBSKÁ 12
PRAGUE I
TEL 222 314 639
Simply furnished, this large restaurant with many rooms offers a home-away-from-home to hundreds of (mostly American) expats who can't get enough of its burgers and Creole and Tex-Mex dishes. Live jazz every evening; filling brunches over the weekend.
🪑 130 🚇 Náměstí Republiky
💳 AE, MC, V

🍴 U RUDOLFA
$$
TÝNSKÁ 19
PRAGUE I
TEL 224 808 270
E-MAIL foks@volny.cz
www.rest2000.cz/urudolfa
This sensibly priced Czech restaurant in an increasingly pricey area offers a good selection of goulash dishes. It's not the lightest and brightest of settings, but the service is pleasant and efficient, and portions are generous.
🪑 45 🚇 Náměstí Republiky
💳 AE, MC, V

🍴 U SUPA
$$
CELETNÁ 22
PRAGUE I
TEL 224 212 004
FAX 224 223 929
Behind the facade along Celetná are two spacious vaulted halls that have long been a popular traditional restaurant. U Supa is very much on the tourist trail, but the food is authentic and excellent. Such staples as cabbage soup and duck with red cabbage are rich and tasty. If you are part of a large group, consider ordering the house specialty a day in advance: whole suckling pig. Service is swift and professional, but check your bill for extra "service charges."
🪑 160 🚇 Náměstí Republiky
💳 No credit cards accepted

🍴 AMOS
$
MASNÁ 17
PRAGUE I
TEL 222 323 933
This neighborhood restaurant and pub offers succulent beef prepared in a number of ways, as well as more standard pork dishes and pasta. The wine list is short but inexpensive. Prices are low, and there are few frills. Make sure you check the bill for extra charges.
🪑 30 🚇 Náměstí Republiky
💳 No credit cards accepted

JOSEFOV

HOTEL

🏨 INTERCONTINENTAL
🍴 **$$$$$**
NÁMĚSTÍ CURIEOVÝCH 43/5
PRAGUE I
TEL 296 631 111
FAX 224 811 216
E-MAIL prague@interconti.com
Quite a few of the international chains have hotels in Prague, but this has the best location: on the river just a few minutes' walk from Josefov. As well as having all the restaurant and business facilities one expects from a hotel of this caliber and price (most notably the rooftop restaurant, Zlatá Praha), the hotel has wheelchair access and a Casa del Habano cigar shop.
🛏 364 🚇 Staroměstská
🅿 🔄 🚫 🔄 📶 📺
💳 All major cards

RESTAURANTS

🍴 PRAVDA
$$$$$
PAŘÍŽSKÁ 17
PRAGUE I
TEL 222 326 203
FAX 222 312 042
E-MAIL bgoff@anet.cz
Right next to the Old-New Synagogue, this fashionable restaurant offers "specialties of the global villages"—from Vietnam to Mexico. Highlights include pea and leek soup with fresh oysters; tea-smoked Atlantic scallops with bell pepper and orange sauce; and baked lamb loin with sweet corn, tomatoes, and goat's cheese. Pravda occupies a vaulted room in a corner building. One arm is a well-stocked bar; the other, the restaurant. There's a good range of French wines and champagnes.
🪑 100 🚇 Staroměstská
💳 All major cards

🍴 BAROCK
$$$$
PAŘÍŽSKÁ 24
PRAGUE I
TEL 222 329 221
FAX 222 321 933
E-MAIL bgoff@anet.cz
Owned by the same group that created Pravda a few doors farther up the road, Barock places the emphasis on Asiatic cuisine, notably sushi and sashimi. The restaurant's walls are plastered with photographs of supermodels, which tells you a bit about the market it is targeting. The front of the restaurant also functions as a bar, and in summer there's extra seating in the garden.
🪑 50 🚇 Staroměstská
💳 All major cards

🍴 CAFÉ COLONIAL
$$$$
ŠIROKÁ 6
PRAGUE I
TEL 224 818 322
This Josefov restaurant offers eclectic cooking and a chic

---

ambience. Starters may be duck carpaccio and marinated seafood; main courses include elaborate salads, pasta dishes, satay, fondue, fresh fish, chicken curry, and steaks. The setting is informal, with cane chairs and low lighting. It's a popular place for breakfast, but prices, even by Prague standards, are quite high.

85 Staroměstská
All major cards

CARTOUCHE
$$$
BÍLKOVA 14
PRAGUE 1
TEL 224 819 597
FAX 224 819 598
E-MAIL cartouch@quick.cz
www.cartouche.cz

A newcomer to the Prague restaurant scene, Cartouche occupies a 16th-century, brick-vaulted cellar just off Pařížská. It's an atmospheric place, candlelit and illuminated by log fires. Specialties are cooked on the spit: stuffed duck on some days, a whole suckling pig on others. There are also plenty of fish dishes and oysters in season. The wine list is mixed and reasonably priced.

100 Staromestská
All major cards

NEW TOWN

HOTELS

JALTA
$$$$$
VÁCLAVSKÉ NÁMĚSTÍ 45
PRAGUE 1
TEL 222 822 111
FAX 222 213 866
E-MAIL jalta@jalta.cz
www.jalta.cz

Built in the 1950s, the Jalta has successfully converted from a fairly soulless place to a comfortable 4-star hotel. The rooms are well appointed and spacious, although the public areas lack charm. There is a good Japanese restaurant within the hotel for those

with a craving for sushi.

94 Můstek
AE, DC, JCB, MC, V

AMBASSADOR ZLATÁ HUSA
$$$$–$$$$$
VÁCLAVSKÉ NÁMĚSTÍ 5–7
PRAGUE 1
TEL 224 193 111
FAX 224 226 167
E-MAIL hotel@ambassador.cz
www.ambassador.cz

The location on Wenceslas Square is hard to beat, and the guest rooms are comfortable and well equipped, although the public rooms are lacking in atmosphere. The hotel adjoins the nightclub and casino.

160 Můstek
All major cards

CITY HOTEL MORAN
$$$$–$$$$$
NA MORÁNI 15
PRAGUE 2
TEL 224 915 208
FAX 224 920 625

The rooms in this attractive building are spacious and well equipped, though bland. Just off Charles Square, it is a good choice in this location.

57 Karlovo Náměstí
All major cards

PALACE PRAHA
$$$$–$$$$$
PANSKÁ 12
PRAGUE 1
TEL 224 093 111
FAX 224 221 240
E-MAIL palhoprg@palacehotel.cz
www.palacehotel.cz

This 1906 secessionist building is perfectly located just off Wenceslas Square. One of Prague's first luxury hotels, it is still holding its own. It's expensive, but has personality, and is very well equipped and effortlessly comfortable. Many of the rooms are individually decorated; all are stylish, with fine-quality fabrics for curtains and bedspreads.

124 Můstek
All major cards

EVROPA
$$$
VÁCLAVSKÉ NÁMĚSTÍ 25
PRAGUE 1
TEL 224 228 117
FAX 224 224 544

An old building, only partly renovated, Europa has lots of character—even though the 18th-century (Louis XVI-style) furnishings in some rooms jar with the art nouveau structure. Rooms with bathrooms are spacious; avoid the rooms without bathrooms, which are dreary and can be hot. The café downstairs is a perfect meeting and gathering place, and the location is as good as it gets.

93 Můstek
AE, MC, V

PRAGA 1
$$$
ŽITNÁ 5
PRAGUE 1
TEL 222 233 149
FAX 222 231 898
E-MAIL praga1@anet.cz
www.praga1.cz

There's an emphasis on service in this small hotel close to Charles Square. The rooms are well equipped, with TV, radio, phone, safe, and minibar, but furnishings are spartan. Most rooms have showers rather than baths.

31 Karlovo Náměstí
All major cards

CITY
$–$$
BELGICKÁ 10
PRAGUE 2
TEL 222 521 606
FAX 222 522 386
E-MAIL hotel@hotelcity.cz
www.hotelcity.cz

The City, a five-minute walk from náměstí Miru, is one of the few bargains in the city center. The rooms are large and bright, but sparsely furnished. The cheaper rooms have separate, shared bathrooms. Service is exceptionally helpful.

19 Náměstí Miru
All major cards

RESTAURANTS

SOMETHING SPECIAL

🍴 LA PERLE DE PRAGUE

It was inevitable that the avant-garde "Fred & Ginger" building on the banks of the Vltava would have to be topped with a chic restaurant, and La Perle de Prague fits the bill perfectly. The seventh-floor restaurant has a spectacular view over the city, and in summer you can step out onto an idyllic terrace. Begin your evening at the bar on the ground floor, before moving up to the restaurant. The food is classic French, and, as in France, there is a choice of set menus, the simplest at 900 Kč and the more elaborate degustation menu at 2,500 Kč. À la carte dishes include such specialties as foie gras with cognac, langoustines with red mullet, or sea bass with lentils. The wine list is superb, and includes some good Moravians. The room has stylish furnishings and tableware.

$$$$$
RAŠÍNOVO NÁBŘEŽÍ 80
PRAGUE 2
TEL 221 984 160
FAX 221 984 179
E-MAIL laperle@volny.cz
🍽 60 🚇 Karlovo Náměstí
🕐 Closed Sun. and L Mon.
♿ 💳 All major cards

🍴 BUFFALO BILL'S

$$
VODIČKOVA 9
PRAGUE 1
TEL 224 948 624
FAX 296 238 083
www.buffalobills.cz
The ribs, tacos, burritos, and country music served up at this Tex-Mex hangout are popular with expats.
🍽 65 🚇 Můstek 💳 AE, MC, JCB, V

🍴 PIZZERIA DI CARLO

$$
KARLOVO NÁMĚSTÍ 30
PRAGUE 2
TEL 222 231 374
FAX 222 231 381
In addition to pizza, this popular basement with its summer garden offers a full range of pasta dishes. Portions are generous and the salads impressive. Busy at lunchtime with local office workers.
🍽 120 🚇 Karlovo Náměstí
💳 AE, JCB, MC

🍴 U ČÍŽKŮ

$$
KARLOVO NÁMĚSTÍ 34
PRAGUE 2
TEL 222 232 257
FAX 222 232 609
www.restauranttucizku.cz
U Čížků, with its cozy wood-beamed interior, offers good Moravian wines and rich Czech cooking such as pig's trotter in beer. There are also vegetarian dishes.
🍽 100 🚇 Karlovo Náměstí
♿ 💳 AE, MC, V

🍴 U KALICHA

$$
NA BOJIŠTI 12–14
PRAGUE 2
TEL/FAX 224 912 557
E-MAIL ukalicha@ukalicha.cz
Josef Švejk and the novelist Jaroslav Hašek, who created him, have made this pub famous. It is extravagantly Czech, serving goose, pork knuckle, and steaks, and specializing in large platters for groups. It is decorated with Švejk memorabilia, and its walls are scribbled with signatures of celebrities. The menu is in 22 languages. Music in the evening.
🍽 240 🚇 I. P. Pavlova
💳 AE, DC, JCB, V

FARTHER AFIELD

HOTEL

🏨 MÖVENPICK

$$$
MOZARTOVA 261/1
PRAGUE 5
TEL 257 151 111
FAX 257 153 131
E-MAIL reservation@moevenpick.cz

PRICES

HOTELS
An indication of the cost of a double room without breakfast is given by **$** signs.

$$$$$	Over $200
$$$$	$130–$200
$$$	$80–$130
$$	$50–$80
$	Under $50

RESTAURANTS
An indication of the cost of a three-course dinner without drinks is given by **$** signs.

$$$$$	Over $35
$$$$	$25–$35
$$$	$15–$25
$$	$10–$15
$	Under $10

www.moevenpick-prague.com
Pink and starkly modern, Mövenpick is in one of the city's least attractive districts, but there is little choice in this area. This hotel is especially useful for travelers with cars, because access is easy and there is ample parking. Moreover, prices are fair. The rooms have discreetly modern furnishings and the beds have thick mattresses and luxurious duvets.
🛏 434 🚇 Andel 🅿 🛗
♿ 🚭 💳 All major cards

RESTAURANT

🍴 DONG DO

$$
VÍTĚZNÉ NÁMĚSTÍ 4, DEJVICE
PRAGUE 6
TEL/FAX 220 981 318
This large hall next to Dejvická metro station may have standard-issue "Chinese" furnishings and lamps, but it is a Vietnamese restaurant. The menu includes grilled snails, crab, and carp; the food is good and portions are generous. The restaurant is popular with the local community—a good sign.
🍽 120 🚇 Dejvická 💳 All major cards

DAY TRIPS FROM PRAGUE

KUTNÁ HORA, 28401

ZLATÁ STOUPA
$$
TYLOVA 426
TEL 327 511 540
FAX 327 513 808
The hotel is located close to the city center, and facilities include a restaurant and wine bar. All rooms are equipped with a safe, minibar, and satellite TV. Secure parking is available.
[i] 25 [P] [S] V

U GROŠE
$
KOLLÁROVA 313
TEL 327 515 330
This Czech restaurant occupies a much renovated medieval building in the historic center of town. The menu is extensive; dishes to try include trout and, for dessert, pancakes.
[+] 70 [S] No credit cards accepted

MĚLNÍK, 27601

U RYTÍŘŮ
$$
SVATOVÁCLAVSKÁ 17
TEL 315 621 440
FAX 315 621 439
E-MAIL jansladecek@seznam.cz
Located right next to the castle, this renovated old building offers comfortable accommodations with kitchenettes. Some of the rooms have four beds, making the hotel a useful option for families. In summer ask for a room with a terrace. The hotel has a restaurant, which has a terrace for dining al fresco in summer; and a less formal café.
[i] 5 [S] All major cards

PODĚBRADY, 29001

BELLEVUE
$$
NÁMĚSTÍ MASARYKA 654
TEL 325 616 483
FAX 325 614 584
E-MAIL hotel@bellevue.cz
The Bellevue has the best location in town, overlooking the park. It's a comfortable hotel, with a restaurant and a wine bar. The rooms are not lavishly decorated, but they are modern; each comes with a shower or bath and has satellite TV.
[i] 60 [P] [S] [H] [S] All major cards

CZECH REPUBLIC

SOUTHERN BOHEMIA

ČESKÉ BUDĚJOVICE, 37001

GRAND HOTEL ZVON
$$
NAMĚSTÍ PŘEMYSLA OTAKARA 11, 28
TEL 387 311 383
FAX 387 311 385
This well-established hotel is on the main square and offers a number of restaurants and snack bars. Try to get one of the rooms that face onto the square; they have some of the best urban views in Bohemia. Several rooms have four-poster beds. The kitchens produce the rich cakes that are sold in the hotel's excellent pastry shop—which may explain why the hotel is especially popular with sweet-toothed Austrians. Other facilities include a business center.
[i] 75 [P] [S] [S] All major cards

BOHEMIA
$–$$
HRADEBNÍ 20
TEL/FAX 386 352 097
E-MAIL hotel-bohemia@volny.cz
Located on the edge of the old town, the Bohemia

occupies two renovated buildings. Rooms, although far from luxurious, all come with bathroom, minibar, and satellite TV. The hotel offers good value and a restaurant, and you can leave your car safely in the courtyard.
[i] 16 [S] All major cards

PANSKÝ SENK
$$
PLACHÉHO 10
The Panský Senk, set in vaulted rooms with a medieval ambience, specializes in game.
[S] No credit cards accepted

ČESKÝ KRUMLOV, 38101

SOMETHING SPECIAL

RŮŽE
Without question, this is the best hotel in town, and one of the best in all of southern Bohemia. It's away from the main tourist throng in a very beautiful sgraffitoed Renaissance building that was once a Jesuit college. It has been exquisitely renovated, and its Renaissance character has been maintained. Rooms are furnished with dark wooden beds, heavy draperies, and in some cases, beamed wooden ceilings and brass chandeliers. There's a delightful and spacious terrace high above the river with a café and live music in summer. The hotel can arrange sporting activities such as cycling and rafting in the surrounding region.
$$$$
HORNÍ 154
TEL 380 772 100
FAX 380 713 146
[i] 81 [P] [S] [H] [S] All major cards

DVOŘÁK
$$$
RADNIČNÍ 101
TEL 380 711 020
FAX 380 711 024
E-MAIL dvorak@ckmbox.vol.cz
Although it's in the city center, the Dvořák spreads along

the banks of the River Vltava. The rooms come with marble bathrooms, and some are furnished with antiques. A treasured feature is the terrace overlooking the river, a lovely spot for a summer drink.

🛈 20 🅿 ⬍ 📺 🚫All major cards

🏨 THE OLD INN
🍴 $$
NÁMĚSTÍ SVORNOSTI 12
TEL 380 772 500
FAX 380 772 550
E-MAIL info@hoteloldinn.cz
This hotel has been created from three old houses in the main square, and it has access to the facilities of the costlier Růže hotel (see above). Some of the rooms have plain furnishings, but the pricier ones are more luxurious, with antique-style beds and cupboards. Parking is not available at the hotel, but the staff will park and return your car for you. The restaurant spills out onto the square, and there's a beer cellar dating back to the 13th century. Guests are also entitled to use the pool and fitness center of the Růže, a few minutes' walk away—all of which makes this hotel quite a bargain.

🛈 52 🅿 ⬍ 📶 📺
🚫All major cards

🍴 NA OSTROVĚ
$
NA OSTROVĚ 171
TEL/FAX 380 711 326
Avoid the touristy restaurants on the town's main streets and come straight to this inexpensive fish restaurant just beyond the castle viaduct. Don't expect elegantly presented food or refined service; the emphasis is on good fresh ingredients and simple cooking. The menu features carp, eel, trout, and other fish.

🪑 80 🚫No credit cards accepted

FRYMBURK, 38279

🏨 VLTAVA
$$
FRYMBURK 45
TEL 380 735 605
FAX 380 735 603
E-MAIL info@hotel-vltava.com
The Vltava fronts the main square of this pretty little resort, but terraces behind the building extend to the shore of the lake. In summer you can eat outdoors. The rooms are bright and cheerful, and there are a few apartments that have kitchenettes. The staff will help to arrange excursions and various sporting activities.

🛈 25 🅿 ⬍ 📶 🚫All major cards

JINDŘICHŮV HRADEC, 37701

🏨 BÍLÁ PANÍ
🍴 $
DOBROVSKÉHO 5
TEL/FAX 384 363 329
This tiny, family-run hotel is close to the castle and has a restaurant. The atmosphere is pleasant, but ask to see the rooms; some are more comfortable than others.

🛈 6 🅿 🚫All major cards

🏨 GRAND HOTEL
🍴 $
NÁMĚSTÍ MÍRU 165
TEL 384 361 252
FAX 384 361 251
The Grand is well situated on the town's main square and has been here for centuries. It doesn't quite live up to its name, but the rooms are adequate for a night or two. It has a restaurant and wine bar.

🛈 25 🅿 🚫All major cards

PÍSEK, 39701

🏨 CITY HOTEL
🍴 $
ALŠOVO NÁMĚSTÍ 35
TEL/FAX 382 215 192
E-MAIL lala@cityhotel.cz
Its central location in the

heart of the old city is this hotel's chief attraction. It occupies a medieval house, and the rooms are reasonably well equipped. There's a restaurant, as well as a pretty little courtyard for drinks and meals in summer, but service is hit and miss.

🛈 19 🅿 🚫All major cards

PRACHATICE, 38301

🏨 PARKÁN
$
VĚŽNÍ 51
TEL/FAX 388 311 868
E-MAIL pavel.hlavac@iol.cz
This reconstructed hotel in the city center occupies a renovated medieval house. The rooms are equipped with shower, satellite TV, and refrigerator. There's a pleasant summer terrace, and the friendly staff can help you organize hiking and other activities in the nearby Šumava mountains.

🛈 23 🚫All major cards

TÁBOR, 39001

🍴 U KALICHA
$
SVATOŠOVA 25
TEL 381 251 927
Set in a large vaulted room near the church, U Kalicha offers a fairly sophisticated version of Czech cooking.

🕐 Closed Sun. 🚫No credit cards accepted

TŘEBOŇ, 37901

🏨 ZLATÁ HVĚZDA
🍴 $–$$
MASARYKOVO NÁMĚSTÍ 107
TEL 384 757 111
FAX 384 757 300
E-MAIL mailbox@zhevzda.cz
This fine Renaissance house stands on the main square. The decor is not exciting, but rooms are well equipped. The restaurant features both local and Continental cuisine.

🛈 42 🅿 🚫All major cards

▦ BÍLÝ KONÍCEK
▥ $
MASARYKOVO NÁMĚSTÍ 97
TEL/FAX 384 721 213
The Bílý Koníček is in one of
the oldest buildings on the
main square (it dates from
1544) and offers the best
deal in town. Some of the
rooms are small, but all have
bathrooms. You can rent bikes
here, and a restaurant serves
typical Czech dishes.
🛈 10   🅿   ⊗ No credit
cards accepted

▥ ŠUPINKA
$
VALY 56/155
TEL 384 721 149
This small restaurant, away
from the crowds of the
square, specializes in fish. The
Šupina restaurant facing it
serves an identical menu.
Despite their location off the
well-beaten track, both
restaurants are popular and
are often full.
🅿   ⊗ No credit cards
accepted

WESTERN
BOHEMIA

CHEB, 35002

▦ HVĚZDA
$
NÁMĚSTÍ KRÁLE JIŘÍHO Z
PODĚBRAD 4–6
TEL 354 422 549
FAX 354 422 546
E-MAIL hotel-hvezda@email.cz
In an excellent location on
the main square, the Hvězda
is the best place to stay in
Cheb. Ask for one of the
rooms with a private
bathroom; the slight extra
cost is worthwhile.
🛈 90   🅿   ⊗ All credit
cards

DOMAŽLICE, 34401

▥ CHODSKY HRAD
$
CHODSKÉ NÁMĚSTÍ 96
TEL 379 776 010
This spacious and lively

restaurant adjoining the
castle serves typical Czech
food. The pork dishes are a
good option.
🔢 100   🕒 Closed Sun. D
⊗ All credit cards

FRANTIŠKOVY LÁZNĚ, 35101

▦ BOHEMIA
▥ $
KLOSTERMANNOVA 92
TEL 354 403 811
FAX 354 403 844
The bustling Bohemia, on the
edge of the spa gardens, is just
a few minutes' walk from the
spa and casino. The rooms are
modern and very clean,
and the restaurant is friendly
and informal.
🛈 27   🅿   ⊗ No credit
cards accepted

▥ GOETHE
$$
CASINO, NÁRODNÍ 1
Located within the casino, this
opulent restaurant offers
mostly Czech dishes in a
sumptuous setting. With
prices to match.
⊗ All major cards

KARLOVY VARY

SOMETHING
SPECIAL

▦ GRANDHOTEL PUPP
This immense and luxurious
hotel is **the** place to stay in
Karlovy Vary. It was founded
in 1701, though the present
buildings date mostly from the
19th century. As a gathering
place for the rich and famous in
times past—former guests
include J. S. Bach, Ludwig van
Beethoven, Franz Liszt, Karl
Marx, Franz Kafka, and Rita
Hayworth—it was built to
impress. Its palatial halls can be
intimidating, but the rooms are
richly furnished and as luxurious
as any hotel in Prague. If the
prices are too daunting for you,
consider the annex, Parkhotel
Pupp, where 140 rooms are done
up in a slightly less opulent

manner; rates there are about
60 percent lower than those at
the Grand Hotel.
$$$$$
MÍROVÉ NÁMĚSTÍ 2, 36091
TEL 353 109 111
FAX 353 266 638
E-MAIL reserv@pupp.kpgroup.cz
🛈 110   🅿   ⊟   🔽   ⊗ All
major cards

▦ DVOŘÁK
$$$–$$$$
NOVÁ LOUKA 11, 36021
TEL 353 102 111
FAX 353 102 119
E-MAIL dvorakkv@vol.cz
A grand and well-equipped
hotel with comfortable
rooms, near the Grandhotel
Pupp, the Dvořák is very
popular option with
visitors who are taking spa
treatments in Karlovy Vary.
🛈 106   ⊠   ⊗ All
major cards

▦ OSTENDE
▥ $$$–$$$$
STARÁ LOUKA 60, 36001
TEL 353 585 216
FAX 353 585 230
E-MAIL Info@ostende.cz
Deceptively plain from the
outside, the Ostende is a
small but luxurious hotel that
offers spa treatments as well
as comfort. The rooms,
furnished in an old-fashioned
style, are ideal for long-term
stays; they are equipped with
fully fitted kitchenettes. The
restaurant has a pleasant
terrace facing the museum.
The Ostende is located near
the Grandhotel Pupp.
🛈 20   🅿   🔽   ⊗ AE,
MC, V

▦ CENTRAL
▥ $$$
DIVADELNÍ NÁMĚSTÍ. 17, 36003
TEL 353 225 251
FAX 353 229 086
E-MAIL central@mbox.vol.cz
This spacious hotel is in a
relatively tranquil setting next
to the theater, yet close to
the springs and the town
center. While the Central

HOTELS & RESTAURANTS

cannot be described as chic, the rooms are spacious and are painted in attractive pastel shades. It has a pleasant outdoor café and two restaurants.

🛏 64 🅿 🛗 🖾 All major cards

🏨 EMBASSY
$$–$$$
NOVÁ LOUKA 21, 36021
TEL 353 221 161
FAX 353 223 146
E-MAIL embassy@mbox.vol.cz
This is a small, perfectly located, family-run hotel with comfortable rooms and a few apartments. It has an attractive restaurant, which is decorated with old stoves and painted alcoves and offers traditional Bohemian cooking and beers.

🛏 18 🅿 🖾 All major cards

🏨 PALACKÝ
$$–$$$
STARÁ LOUKA 40, 36001
TEL 353 222 544
FAX 353 228 122
E-MAIL palacky@seznam.cz
Well located near the Spring Colonnade, this modest hotel has spacious and comfortable rooms. The hotel can arrange for spa treatments and will provide special dietary meals.

🛏 7 🅿 🛗 🖾 All major cards

🏨 PROMENÁDA
$$–$$$
TRŽIŠTĚ 31, 36001
TEL 353 225 648
FAX 353 229 703
E-MAIL hotel@hotel-promenade.cz
The charming Promenáda has pleasant rooms and its restaurant, which occupies an inner atrium, serves both international and Czech cuisine. Very good wine list.

🛏 21 🅿 🖾 All major cards

🍴 NAPOLEON
$$
NOVÁ LOUKA 25, 36021
Located just across from the Grandhotel Pupp, the cozy Napoleon has an enjoyable ambience. Despite the name, most dishes are Czech, and there are various set menus as well as à la carte items.

🍴 40 🕐 Closed Sun. D
🖾 No credit cards accepted

MARIÁNSKÉ LÁZNĚ

🏨 BOHEMIA
$$–$$$
HLAVNÍ 100, 35301
TEL 354 623 251
FAX 354 622 943
E-MAIL hotel.bohemia@orea.cz
This grand, old-fashioned hotel epitomizes the appeal of the spa: luxurious, but with an emphasis on health-enhancing treatments. The rooms have satellite TV, minibar, safe, and shower room. Some of the rooms have balconies that overlook the spa garden.

🛏 77 🅿 🖾 All major cards

🏨 VILLA BUTTERFLY
$$–$$$
HLAVNÍ TRIDA 655, 35301
TEL 354 654 111
FAX 354 654 200
E-MAIL villabutterfly@badmarienbad.cz
Kitsch comes to Marienbad, as the skinny nudes gesticulating from the hotel roof confirm. Despite the flamboyant exterior, the rooms are conventional, with large beds and desks. Some of the pricier ones have Jacuzzis and Internet access. Villa Butterfly also has a coffeeshop and a chic lobby bar that provides snacks as well as drinks.

🛏 96 🅿 🖾 All major cards

PLZEŇ

🏨 CONTINENTAL
$$
ZBROJNICKÁ 8, 30534
TEL 377 235 292
FAX 377 221 746
E-MAIL mail@hotelcontinental.cz
Originally built by the Plzeň brewery in 1895, this hotel

---

has a location that's hard to beat, just off the main square. The rooms have been redecorated, though the interior decor and furnishings have deliberately been kept old-fashioned so as to harmonize with the turn-of-the-20th-century exterior. Not all rooms have WCs, so be sure to specify when making a reservation.

🛏 40 🅿 🖾 All major cards

TEPLÁ

🏨 KLÁŠTER TEPLÁ
$$
U TOUŽÍMĚ, 36461
TEL 353 392 264
FAX 353 392 312
When the monks returned to this vast Premonstratensian foundation in the 1990s, they reconstructed a wing of the ancient monastery with the aim of providing simple but comfortable accommodations. All the rooms have private bathrooms but are not lavishly fitted out. On the premises are a restaurant and tavern, and a golf course is nearby.

🛏 50 🅿 🛗 🖾 All major cards

NORTHERN BOHEMIA

DĚČÍN, 40501

 U ZÁMKU
$
NÁROŽNÍ 21
TEL 412 513 481
FAX 412 513 482
E-MAIL spus@praha.czcom.cz
Rooms offer little more than a bed and bedside table, but they are clean and the hotel is in an excellent location next to the castle. A good choice for budget travelers.
🛈 86 ⬌ 🚭 **No credit cards accepted**

HŘENSKO

🏨 **PRAHA**
$$
HŘENSKO 37, 40717
TEL 412 554 006
FAX 412 554 162
An old resort hotel in this touristy village, the skillfully modernized Praha is the best place to stay. Rooms are comfortable, and the terrace is popular in summer. There's a sauna to relax in after a day's hiking. Wheelchair access.
🛈 34 🅿 ⬌ 🚭 **All major cards**

LIBEREC, 46001

🏨 **PRAHA**
🍴 **$$**
ŽELEŽNÁ 2
TEL 485 102 655
FAX 485 113 138
The hotel is in an exceptionally well restored, impressive 1905 art nouveau building. Its excellent facilities include a restaurant, coffee bar, casino, and night club. Staff will help organize sporting and tourism activities. Wheelchair access.
🛈 62 🅿 ⬌ 🚭 **All major cards**

LITOMĚŘICE, 41201

🏨 **SALVA GUARDA**
🍴 **$–$$**
MÍROVÉ NÁMĚSTÍ 12

TEL 416 732 506
FAX 416 732 798
E-MAIL
hotel.restaurant@salva-guarda.cz
The rooms in this remarkable Renaissance house dating from 1560 are not stylish, but the comfortable apartments have good-size bathrooms. A few rooms have four beds and are ideal for families. Salva Guarda also offers a good restaurant and wine bar.
🛈 16 🅿 🚭 **All major cards**

TEPLICE, 41501

🏨 **PRINCE DE LIGNE**
🍴 **$$–$$$**
ZÁMECKÉ NÁMĚSTÍ 136
TEL 417 514 111
FAX 417 537 727
E-MAIL info@princedeligne.cz
Completely renovated in 1991, this 1824 building is situated near the spa and gardens—the most pleasant corner of a town that sees more people visiting on business than on holiday. If you feel like a splurge, ask for the suite done out in sumptuous 18th-century style. Worth a try are the Italian Leone Venezia restaurant, and the smaller Cabana Mexicana.
🛈 32 🅿 ⬌ 🚭 **All major cards**

ŽATEC, 43801

🏨 **U HADA**
🍴 **$**
NÁMĚSTÍ SVOBODY 155
TEL 415 711 000
E-MAIL uhada@email.cz
The town's only real draw for visitors is its fame as the source of the world's best hops. If you come to its hop festival, you will find the U Hada conveniently situated on the main square. It is a well-restored, ancient building—be careful not to bang your head on the low wooden beams—with a restaurant and wine bar. Parking is secure.
🛈 21 🅿 🏥 🚭 **All major cards**

EASTERN BOHEMIA

HRADEC KRÁLOVÉ, 50001

🏨 **U JANA**
🍴 **$**
VELKÉ NÁMĚSTÍ 137
TEL 495 512 355
U Jana, attractively located on the main square, has been renovated in an unusually minimalist and elegant style. The hotel's restaurant specializes in fish dishes and Czech cuisine.
🛈 7 🅿 🚭 **All major cards**

🍴 **SPORT CAFÉ**
$
VELKÉ NÁMĚSTÍ 151
TEL 495 514 202
This is just the spot when you tire of Bohemian food and fancy pizza, chili, or pasta instead. In summer, enjoy the terrace jutting out onto the square. The café is deservedly popular with town residents and visitors alike for its friendly service and reliable food.
🚭 **All major cards**

HRUBÁ SKÁLA

🏨 **ŠTEKL**
$
HRUBÁ SKALÁ, TURNOV, 51101
TEL 481 389 684
FAX 481 389 410
E-MAIL stekl@proaktiv.cz
The Štekl occupies a former castle in the middle of the Český ráj (see pp. 236–239). Its location is exemplary, making it a perfect base for exploring the region. Rooms are basic, but the Štekl has the merit of being inexpensive. Some of the cheapest rooms have shared bathrooms.
🛈 25 🅿 🚭 **All major cards**

JANSKÉ LÁZNĚ, 54225

🏨 **LESNÍ DŮM**
🍴 **$**
KRKONOŠSKÁ 208
TEL 499 875 167

🚭 Nonsmoking 🆒 Air-conditioning 🏊 Indoor/🏊 Outdoor swimming pool 🏥 Health club 🚭 Credit cards **KEY**

FAX 499 875 167
E-MAIL lesni.dum@tiscali.cz
Though just a modest chalet hotel, the Lesní Dům has a good deal of charm. Service is friendly and hospitable. The hotel also offers a decent and inexpensive restaurant, a summer terrace, a tennis court, and a sauna.
🛏 21 🅿 ⛔No credit cards accepted

LITOMYŠL, 57001

🏨 ZLATÁ HVĚZDA
🍴 $$
SMETANOVO NÁMĚSTÍ 84
TEL 461 615 338
FAX 461 615 091
E-MAIL zlata.hvezda@lit.cz
This stylish hotel on the main square is reasonably priced, and the staff is efficient and helpful. The management makes much of the fact that President Havel once stayed here. Ask for a room with a view of the castle. Serious Czech and Oriental cooking is served in the somber dining room.
🛏 24 🅿 ⇄ 🚭 ⛔All major cards

NÁCHOD, 54701

🏨 U BERÁNKA
🍴 $
NÁMĚSTÍ TGM 74
TEL 491 433 118
FAX 491 433 119
The hotel dates from 1914, which explains its essentially secessionist decor. The rooms have parquet flooring and are high-ceilinged and airy. The restaurant has a splendid pristine secessionist interior. Given the hotel's small size, it is impressive that there is 24-hour room service. Overall, the Beránka has much more character than most Czech hotels.
🛏 16 🅿 🚭 ⛔All major cards

🏨 U MĚSTA PRAHY
🍴 $
NÁMĚSTÍ TGM 66

TEL 491 421 817
A good choice for the budget traveler, this hotel offers simple rooms, a popular restaurant and wine bar, and a terrace on the square in summer.
🛏 10 🅿 ⛔No credit cards accepted

TURNOV, 51101

🏨 KORUNNÍ PRINC
🍴 $
NÁMĚSTÍ ČESKÉHO RÁJE 137
TEL 481 313 520
FAX 481 313 522
The Korunní Princ enjoys an excellent central location in a town that is a popular base for visiting the Český ráj. The rooms are comfortable if not luxurious. The restaurant offers a wide range of dishes, specializing in fish and game.
🛏 24 ⇄ ⛔No credit cards accepted

VRCHLABÍ, 54301

🏨 LABUT
🍴 $
KRKONOŠSKÁ 188
TEL 499 421 964
FAX 499 421 700
E-MAIL hotellabut@krkonose.cz
Vrchlabí is an excellent base for visiting the Krkonoše mountains, and the Labut has perfectly adequate accommodations. Its spacious restaurant presents international as well as Czech dishes, and there's an attractive courtyard where you can enjoy a beer after a day's hiking.
🛏 25 🅿 ⇄ ⛔All major cards

> **SOUTHERN MORAVIA**

BRNO

🏨 GRAND HOTEL
🍴 $$$
BENEŠOVA 18
65783
TEL 542 321 287
FAX 542 210 345
E-MAIL grandhotel-brno@

austria-hotels.telecom.cz
This is the city's leading international hotel, offering health club, sauna, hairdresser, all laundry requirements, and room service. The cheerful bedrooms all have minibars, satellite TVs, safes, and telephones. As well as a restaurant and grill room, the hotel has its own nightclub and casino. The Grand is located right on the edge of the Old Town, with parking immediately outside.
🛏 110 🅿 ⇄ 🚭 ⛔All major cards

🏨 INTERNATIONAL
🍴 $$$
HUSOVA 16
65921
TEL 542 122 111
FAX 542 210 843
E-MAIL hotel.international.cz
Well located opposite the Špilberk hill, this modern hotel offers reasonably sized, brightly furnished rooms and a range of services and facilities that includes two restaurants, a casino, a hairdresser, a fitness center, and a car repair shop. There's a car rental facility on the premises.
🛏 271 🅿 ⇄ 🚭 ⛔All major cards

🏨 SLAVIA
🍴 $$
SOLNIČNÍ 15
66216
TEL 542 321 249
FAX 542 211 769
The Slavia is in a 19th-century building on the edge of the old town, not far from the Špilberk fortress, and has been here for over a century. It has high-ceilinged, spacious bedrooms, and the public rooms include a restaurant, wine bar, and coffee bar.
🛏 82 🅿 ⇄ ⛔All major cards

🏨 AVION
$–$$
ČESKÁ 20
60200
TEL 542 215 016

FAX 542 214 055
A famous building designed in 1928 by Brno's leading modernist architect of the day, Bohuslav Fuchs, the Avion offers reasonably priced rooms. It's in a pedestrian zone, so reasonably tranquil, but there is no easy parking.
🛈 31 ⬛ 🖾 All major cards

🍴 **TAJ**
$$
BĚHOUNSKÁ 12/14
60200
TEL 542 214 372
When dumplings pall, it's worth considering this fairly authentic, light and airy Indian restaurant in the city center. You can also enjoy a drink at the thatched bar.
🅰 🖾 All major cards

🍴 **POD ŠPILBERKEM**
$
HUSOVA 13
60200
TEL 543 211 669
Typical and unpretentious, this Czech inn is perfectly located should you need reviving after a tour of the Špilberk or the Moravian galleries.
🛉 80 🅿 🖾 No credit cards accepted

🍴 **ŠPALÍČEK**
$
ZELNÝ TRH
60200
TEL 542 211 526
This straightforward city-center restaurant serves traditional Czech food. In summer there's a terrace at the top of the square.
🖾 No credit cards accepted

KROMĚŘÍŽ, 76701

🏨 **BOUČEK**
$–$$
VELKÉ NÁMĚSTÍ 108
TEL/FAX 573 342 777
The Bouček enjoys an excellent location on the main square, and the rooms are cozy. No-smoking rooms are available. Parking can be a

problem during the day, but there is short-term, meter parking outside.
🛈 10 🅰 🖾 All major cards

MIKULOV, 69201

🏨 **PENSION ELISKA**
$
PIARISTŮ 4
TEL/FAX 519 513 073
The popular Pension Eliska is a simple, no-frills hotel that fills up fast in the summer. A bonus is the Irish pub on the ground floor.
🛈 20 🅿 🖾 No credit cards accepted

SLAVKOV, 68401

🏨 **SOKOLSKÝ DŮM**
🍴 **$**
PALACKÉHO NÁMĚSTÍ 75
TEL 544 221 103
Half an hour's drive from Brno, this modern, clean, pleasant hotel on the main street is an excellent option for those who would prefer not to stay in the big city. Rooms are very comfortable and offer good value for the money. Service is friendly and efficient. It's best to reserve ahead for a summer visit. The restaurant offers good steaks and a few Mexican dishes.
🛈 20 🅿 🖾 No credit cards accepted

STRÁŽNICE, 69662

🏨 **FLAG HOTEL**
🍴 **STRÁŽNICE**
$
PŘEDMĚSTI 3
TEL 518 332 059
FAX 518 332 099
E-MAIL agflag@flag.cz
The building is dull and the rooms are standard, but the hotel is right in the town center. It is the best base for those planning to visit the annual folk festival (see pp. 258–259)—as long as you can get a room. A restaurant and wine bar are on the

premises; parking is secure.
🛈 57 🅿 ⬛ 🖾 All major cards

TELČ, 58856

🏨 **ČERNÝ OREL**
🍴 **$$**
NÁMĚSTÍ ZACHARIÁŠE Z HRADCE 7
TEL 567 243 222
FAX 567 243 221
This 16th-century building right on the main square has been a hotel since 1907 and is now the top choice in Telč. A few of the rooms don't have a private rest room, so check when making a reservation. There's a restaurant, but, like the bedrooms, it lacks any real atmosphere or style.
🛈 28 🅿 ⬛ 🖾 All major cards

🏨 **HOTEL TELČ**
$–$$
NA MŮSTKU 37
TEL 567 243 109
FAX 567 223 887
This small hotel is perfectly adequate, but the rooms are sparsely furnished.
🛈 10 🅿 🖾 All major cards

🍴 **U ZACHARIÁŠE**
$$
NÁMĚSTÍ ZACHARIÁŠE Z HRADCE 33
TEL 567 223 872
FAX 567 223 887
On the main square, the cozy Zachariáše serves fish, beef, and pork, all in generous portions. The menu often includes imaginative dishes such as sliced steak stewed with white asparagus. Regent beer is on tap.
🛉 60 🖾 All major cards

VALTICE, 69142

🏨 **APOLLON**
🍴 **$**
PETRA BEZRUČE 720
TEL 519 352 625
FAX 519 352 009
Located in a quiet spot on the

HOTELS & RESTAURANTS

outskirts of the town, the Apollon is nevertheless within walking distance of the center and the château (see pp. 256–257). The hotel offers simply furnished and comfortable rooms, a pleasant restaurant, and a summer terrace.

🏨 21 🅿 🖾 All major cards

NORTHERN MORAVIA

KARLOVA STUDÁNKA, 79324

🏨 DŽBÁN
$
KARLOVA STUDÁNKA
TEL 554 772 014
FAX 554 772 013
The unique feature of the centrally situated Džbán is that it offers training in rock climbing on its own rock face. Rooms are comfortably if cheaply furnished. There are a few rooms that have four beds, which are ideal for families or groups.

ⓘ 25 🅿 🖾 🖾 All major cards

OLOMOUC, 77200

🏨 GEMO
🍴 $$$–$$$$
PAVELČÁKOVA 22
TEL 585 222 115
FAX 585 231 730
E-MAIL gemo@hotel-gemo.cz
This modern hotel is just a few steps from the main square. Rooms are attractive, decorated mostly with modern pine furnishings and brightly colored floral and abstract fabrics. The Gemo also has a good, if pricey, seafood restaurant.

ⓘ 100 🅿 🖾 All major cards

🏨 PALÁC
$
1 MÁJE 27
TEL 585 224 096
This looks like a grim Stalinist exercise in hospitality from

the outside, but the Palác's rooms are clean and reasonably spacious, and the location, near the cathedral, is excellent. A good option for the budget traveler.

ⓘ 24 🅿 🖾 🖾 All major cards

🍴 CAESAR
$
HORNÍ NÁMĚSTÍ
TEL 585 229 287
In a splendid setting in the undercroft of the town hall, this is now a lively Italian restaurant. Pizzas are the most popular choice, but there is also a wide selection of pasta dishes.

🪑 120 🖾 All major cards

🍴 U CERVENÉHO VOLKA
$
DOLNÍ NÁMĚSTÍ 39
This restaurant is on one of the town's two main squares, next to Hauernschild Palace. It serves mostly Czech food and some Italian and Chinese dishes. The conservatory-style room is an attractive setting.

🪑 100 🖾 All major cards

OSTRAVA, 70200

🏨 POLSKÝ DŮM
🍴 $
PODĚBRADOVA 53
TEL 596 122 001
FAX 596 125 062
E-MAIL polskydum@volny.cz
It may not be in the most salubrious location, but this art nouveau mansion has been beautifully restored. Most of the rooms are large and comfortable. The restaurant offers a small discount to hotel residents and serves large portions of typical Czech food. Secure parking is available.

ⓘ 20 🅿 🖾 🖾 All major cards

ROŽNOV POD RADHOŠTĚM, 75661

🏨 EROPLÁN
🍴 $$
HORNÍ PASEKY 451, ROŽNOV

TEL 571 648 014
FAX 571 648 222
E-MAIL hotel-eroplan@iol.cz
The Eroplán is a large, modern, chalet-style hotel close to the skansen (see pp. 284–285). It is comfortable and offers excellent facilities and services. All rooms have bathrooms and Internet connections. The complex includes a restaurant and snack bar, as well as a fitness center with a sauna and solarium. Some evenings feature live music and dancing. Secure parking is available.

ⓘ 39 🅿 🖾 🖾 🖾 All major cards

VELKÉ LOSINY, 78815

🏨 PRADED
$$
LÁZEŇSKÁ 4
TEL 583 248 215
FAX 583 248 415
The Praded is very close to the spa center in this attractive resort town. The rooms are decorated in bright and cheerful colors. The staff can help to arrange sporting activities such as tennis and mountain biking.

ⓘ 35 🅿 🖾 All major cards

SHOPPING

It would be wrong to claim that the Czech Republic is a shopper's paradise, but even through the communist period it continued to produce the items for which it has always been well known—notably crystal glassware and garnets. The quality of clothing before 1990 was dire; however, in recent years there has been a resurgence of design, and a few boutiques, almost entirely in Prague, are now selling high-quality products of local design and manufacture. The price of beer is kept low because the local population demands it, and beer remains a tremendous bargain (assuming you are able to take it home with you).

ANTIQUES

Prague has plenty of antique shops, varying in content from junk to fine-quality furniture and clocks. If you are serious about finding bargains, take a preliminary tour of the Dorotheum auction house to get an idea of the going price for desirable items, and seek specialized advice about the most reliable antique dealers. Some luxury hotels, such as Růže in Český Krumlov, incorporate antique shops; outside Prague it is worth inquiring at the front desk of your hotel about local antique shops where you just might find something rare or interesting. Book collectors can pass many fascinating hours browsing in one of the country's many *antikvariát* (secondhand bookshops).

Antik Mucha Národní třida 25 (Palace Metro). This is a new address during reconstruction due to flooding. Call 210 853 300 for details. Specialties are art nouveau and art deco items.
Antikvariát Galerie Mustek Národní třida 40, Prague 1, tel 224 949 587. Open Mon.-Fri. 10–1, 2–7, and Sat. 10–2. One of the best secondhand bookshops in the city, with an excellent selection of art books.
Antiques & Auction House Slezská 24, Prague 2 (opposite "Vinohrady" Pavilion), tel/fax 222 512 512. Open Mon.-Fri. 10:30–6. This shop specializes in paintings and furniture from the 18th to the 20th century.
Art Deco Galerie Michalská 21, Prague 1, tel 224 223 076. Open Mon.-Fri. 2–7. As well as

clothing from the art deco period, there is usually a fine and affordable collection of costume jewelry.
Dorotheum Ovocný trh 2, Prague 1, tel 224 222 001. Open Mon.–Fri. 10–7 and Sat. 10–5. Carries crystal, glass, jewelry, pictures, furniture, and more.

BEER

Prices of bottled beer are a fraction of those charged for the same products elsewhere in Europe. The best buys are the classics such as Pilsner Urquell and Budvar (see pp. 184–185); also watch for Krušovice, Radegast, Regent, and other labels. Just about any beer that you sample on tap in a pub will be available in a bottled version, so just follow your personal tastes.

CDs

These can be good value, especially recordings of classical music and ethnic Czech music on the local Supraphon label. But in recent years prices in Europe and the U.S. have become highly competitive, so CDs are not the bargains they once were.

Kafkovo kuihkupectví Staroměstské nám 606/12 (Old Town Square), tel 222 321 454. Open Mon.-Fri. 10–7. This has an interesting selection of ethnic music, as well as classical and jazz. It also has good books.
Philharmonia Pařížská 13, Prague 1, tel 222 324 060. Open Mon.-Fri. 10–6. Shop has big selection of classical, jazz, ethnic, and folk music; it is affiliated with Prague Philharmonic orchestra.

CLOTHING

Fashionable streets such as Pařížská in Prague are lined with clothes boutiques, but you are unlikely to find anything that is not available at home. However, some local workshops are now beginning to produce clothing and accessories of good quality.

Army shop Ripská 22, Prague 3, tel 224 251 232. Open Mon.–Fri. 9–6. This Vinohrady shop sells army surplus items, especially clothing, at low prices.
Klára Nademlýnská Dlouhá 7, Prague 1, tel 2481 8769. Open Mon.-Fri. 10–7 and Sat. 12–6. This Czech designer is based in Paris, but her designs, many of them haute couture, are on sale in this sumptuous shop.
Mýrnyx Týrnyx Saská, Prague 1, tel 2492 3270. Open Mon.–Sat. 12–7. Prague's best outlet for good-quality secondhand fashion clothing, with constantly changing stock.
Piano Betlemské náměstí 6, Prague 1, tel 222 220 210. Manufactures and sells stylish handbags and leather goods. Fairly expensive.
Romantik Karoliny Svetlé, Prague 1, tel 222 221 632. Open Mon.–Fri. 10–6 and Sat. 10–4. Romantik specializes in inexpensive evening wear. It also rents out these items.
Taiza Na Příkopě 31, Prague 1, tel 221 613 308. Open Mon.–Sat. 10–8 and Sun. 1–6. The Cuban-born designer Osmany Laffita produces extravagant and expensive women's wear. There is also a branch in Karlovy Vary, Vridelní 57, tel 353 224 828.
Timoure et Group V Kolkovně 6, Prague 1, tel 222 327 358. Open Mon.–Fri. 10–7 and Sat. 12–6. The outlet for two Czech designers who create chic business-style clothing.

CRYSTAL

The Czech Republic produces glassware that is high quality and widely available. Indeed, for many visitors Bohemia is synonymous with crystal. There are glassware shops in every major town, but the best selection and most competitive prices are in Prague. Commercial streets such as Karlova have countless glass shops. Most Bohemian crystal is cut glass and often colored, too. With such a vast range on offer, you are bound to find something that suits your taste—unless you are looking for classic, unadorned wine glasses. Many shops will pack and dispatch your purchases.

Celetná Crystal Celetná 15, Prague 1, tel 222 324 022. Open Mon.–Thurs. 10–8, Fri.–Sun. 10–10. This large shop offers a classic selection of good-quality Bohemian crystal, displayed in attractive surroundings.

Moser Na Příkopě 12, Prague 1, tel 224 211 293; fax 224 228 686. Also Malé náměstí 11. Since 1957, when the firm was founded in Karlovy Vary, Moser has been the leading producer of fine Bohemian glassware. Prices are very high, but the products are handmade. Even if you have little interest in crystal, it is worth visiting the showrooms on the first floor. This building was once the home of Bohumil Bondy, a rich industrialist who decorated his mansion in lavish 19th-century style, and the wood paneling, wood inlays, and chandeliers are all immaculately preserved.

Moser Tržiště 7, Karlovy Vary. The firm's leading showroom in this spa town. To learn more about the glassmaking process, visit the factory and museum in Karlovy Vary at Jaroše 19, tel 353 416 111. Also visit www.moser-glass.com. Open Mon.–Fri. 8–5, Sat. 9–3.

Moser Náměstí Svobody 15, Brno, tel 542 514 300. Same stock, different city.

DELICATESSEN

The range of both Czech and imported food products available in Prague has expanded and improved in quality over

recent years, and visitors will find plenty to tempt them.

U Italia Hastalská 10, Prague 1, tel 224 812 832. Open Mon.–Fri. 11–7 and Sat. 9–2. The best Italian deli in town, with good olives, salami, and pasta.

Fruits de France Jindřišská 9, Prague 1, tel 224 220 304. Also Bělehradská 94, Prague 2, tel 222 511 261. Well-established French deli with fine vintage Bordeaux wines, cheeses, fruits, vegetables, mustards, and oils. Expensive.

Ocean Zborovská 49, Prague 5, tel 9000 1517. Open Mon.–Sat. 10–8. This fish shop flies in fresh fish and shellfish twice weekly. Quality and prices are high.

GARNETS

These semiprecious stones come from Turnov in northern Bohemia and are very decorative and relatively inexpensive. Modest in size, they rarely exceed two carats; larger stones are imported from India. Color does not affect the value of garnets as it does with other precious and semiprecious stones. There are many garnet shops in Prague.

Granát Turnov Dlouhá 30, Prague 1, tel 222 315 612, www.granat-cz.com. Also Panská 1. Open Mon.–Fri. 10–6, Sat. 10–1. This factory store is the best place in Prague to buy garnets: Buyers can be sure they're getting Bohemian (Czech) garnets, not stones from elsewhere. The company, a cooperative based in Turnov, produces an evolving range of 3,500 items, with garnets set in silver or gold. There are other branches of this company in the following towns:
České Budejovice: Dr. Stejskala 9
Český Krumlov: Latrán 53
Liberec: nám. E. Beneše 12/4
Turnov: nám. Ceského ráje 4.

MARIONETTES

Marionette theaters have been popular in the Czech lands since the 17th century, and to this day

puppets are crafted with sophistication and humor. Unfortunately, with the exception of the establishment listed below, you will find only mass-produced examples for sale. Though perfectly acceptable if inexpensive, they give little idea of the refinement of the best handmade marionettes.

Firma Ami Nerudova 51, Prague 1, tel 257 532 735. An excellent selection of quality handmade original puppets from up to 30 different craftsmen and producers. Some are one-offs and can be as costly as 10,000 Kč, but most are priced between 600 and 5,000 Kč. There is also a small selection of older puppets.

WINE

The quality of Bohemian and Moravian wine is improving. Most towns have at least one wine shop with a fair selection of local bottles, and there is a growing number in Prague. Many stock wines from all over the world as well as from the Czech Republic. (If you order the "house red," you'll get Frankovka; the most common "white" is Ryzlink.) The best Czech wines tend to come from small growers with limited production and distribution. Some labels worth watching for are Baloun, Château Melník, Klas, Kolby, Kromeřiž, Lechovice, Mádl, Mikros-Vín, Patria Kobylí, Na Vinici, Skoupil, Valtice, and Znovín.

Monarch Na Perštýně 15, Prague 1, tel 224 239 602. This shop has a fine selection of Czech, French, and Italian wines.

Vinotéka Carrefour Mall, Plzeňská 8, Prague 5, tel 257 329 257. This shop carries a large range of reasonably priced Czech wines from good producers.

Wine Shop Ungelt Týnský dvůr 7, Prague 1, tel 224 827 501; fax 224 895 449. An extensive international range, and some good Moravian white wines, too; prices are high.

ENTERTAINMENT & ACTIVITIES

The Czech Republic has always been a hotbed of cultural activity. The love of music of all kinds is profound, and there are dozens of festivals featuring classical music, jazz, and folklore. Nightclubs and jazz clubs are common in every major town. The Czechs are enthusiastic about sports, and Prague and the Czech Republic offer a wide variety of sporting and other recreational activities. There is something to suit all tastes, ranging from spectator sports such as horse racing or ice hockey to active sports—for example, cycling or hiking in the Český ráj region. The country boasts a network of well-marked trails for hiking, and skiing is also a popular pastime.

PRAGUE

ENTERTAINMENT

The English-language weekly *Prague Post* is invaluable for checking all listings.

CLASSICAL MUSIC & OPERA

Lovers of classical music and opera are well served, especially in the fall and winter (there are few performances during the summer months). The city has two first-rate orchestras, the Czech Philharmonic and the Prague Symphony, and a renowned annual music festival.

Music-lovers enjoy the many concerts held in Prague's churches and chapels, in the beautiful Chapel of Mirrors at the Klementinum (see p. 90), and, in summer, in the gardens of some of the city's loveliest palaces. Opera is performed regularly at Prague's two opera houses, **Státní Opera** (State Opera), Wilsonova 4, Prague 1, tel 224 227 266, and **Národni Divadlo** (National Theater), Narodní 2, Prague 1, tel 224 901 668. The National Theater also administers the **Starovské Divadlo** (Estates Theater), Ovocný trh 1, Prague 1, tel 224 215 001. Another notable theater is **Klementinum**, Zrcadlová kaple, Mariánské nám, Prague 1, tel 272 766 902. For general information about concerts, also see www.concerts-prague.cz.

THEATER & MIME

Language is often an obstacle to enjoying theatrical performances abroad, but this does not apply to the celebrated multimedia **Laterna Magika** productions at the National Theater in Prague (see p. 119), nor to the many puppet theater companies across the country. Best known in Prague are the **National Marionette Theater**, Žatecká 1, and **Spejbl and Hurvínek**, Dejvická 38, Prague 6, tel 224 316 784. Many puppet productions are ideal for children; they tend to be mounted at a sophisticated level, so adults enjoy them, too. Mime is another strong Czech tradition (see p. 51).

Prices for cultural events are reasonable, even inexpensive. **Tickets** can be obtained from TicketPro, Řytířska 31, tel 221 610 162, www.ticketpro.cz; Bohemia Ticket International Malé náměstí 13; and box offices.

NIGHTLIFE

Prague has the most vibrant nightlife in the republic, with a good selection of discos and jazz clubs, as well as clubs where live music can be heard until the early hours of the morning. The largest and most popular disco is **Music Park** at Francouzská 4, Prague 2, a complex combining a large dance floor, casino, pub, café, and steak house. The **Reduta** (Národní 20, Prague 1, tel 224 933 487) is the city's best-known jazz club (performances start at 9 p.m.), along with **Jazz Club Železná**

(Železná 16, Prague 1, tel 224 239 697, open 3 p.m. to 1 a.m.). Theme nights can provide some unintended entertainment as the crowds dress up in their finest approximations of Western cowboy gear. Better music and a wilder clientele can be found at clubs such as **AghaRTA** (Krakovská 5, Prague 1, tel 222 211 275, open 7 p.m. to 1 a.m.) or the **Rock Café** (Národní 20, Prague 1, tel 224 933 945). **Roxy** (Dlouhá 33, Prague 1, tel 224 826 296, www.roxy.cz) combines music, a gallery, performing arts, and film with an Internet café. The gallery and café open from 1 p.m. until 1 a.m., the club from 8 p.m. until 5 a.m. Other clubs include **CZ Beat** (Balbínova 26, Prague 2); **Radost FX** (Bělehradská 120, Prague 2, tel 224 254 776), which is a restaurant, gallery, and dance club; **Újezd** (Újezd 18, Prague 1, tel 257 316 537, open 11 a.m. until 4 a.m.); and **Palác Akropolis** (Kubelíkova 27, Prague 3, tel 296 330 913). The club situation is very volatile, with new ones opening as swiftly as others close.

Coffeehouses have returned to Prague and other main cities. Some, such as **Slavia** (Národní trida 1, Prague 1) and **Kavárna** (Obecní dům in Prague), are in the Viennese mold—places to talk, snack, drink coffee, and read newspapers; others are closer in style to Italian espresso bars. Internet cafés have sprung up in most Czech towns, but are often gloomy basement dives. In Prague you can enjoy the excellent facilities of the **Hermes Café** (Nekázanka) and the **Bohemia Bagel** chain (Ujezd 16 and Masna 2, Prague 1), which is popular with U.S. visitors and expats.

FESTIVALS & EVENTS
January
Prague International Dance Week (Part 1; Part 2 is in November) Both weeks are organized by Taneční centrum Praha, U Větrníku 3, 16200 Prague 6, tel 220 611 980.

April
Prague Writer's Festival
Started in London in 1980, nowadays this festival draws names such as Alain Robbe-Grillet, Jiří Gruša, and Ludvík Vaculík (Křemencova 7, Prague 1, ww.pwf.pragonet.cz).

May
Prague Spring International Music Festival This is the biggest and best-known music festival of the year; it was first held in 1946 (Hellichova 18, Prague 1, tel 257 312 547, www.festival.cz).

August
Prague Open Tennis Championship

October
International Jazz Festival
This week-long festival of concerts is held at various venues in the city (Pragokoncert Bohemia, Peckova 13, Prague 8, tel 224 818 277).

November
Prague International Dance Week Part 2. See January.

December
Eve of St. Nicholas (Dec. 5). People dressed as angels and devils tease children and give them sweets. Old Town Square in Prague is a good place to be, although most of the festivities take place at home. St. Nicholas Day (Dec. 6) itself is comparatively quiet.

ACTIVITIES

GOLF
There is a 9-hole course in Prague's 5th district (Plzeňská, tel 257 216 585). For more information, visit www.golf.cz.

HEALTH & FITNESS
Fitness centers and gyms are spreading like wildfire. Some of the best-equipped clubs in Prague are at the **Hilton Hotel** (Pobrezní 1, Prague 6, tel 224 841 111), the **Holiday Inn** at Dejvice (tel 261 175 000), and

the **Intercontinental Hotel** (nám Curieovych 43/5, Prague 1, tel 296 631 111). Non-residents can pay to use the facilities. Other clubs advertise widely on the metro and buses.

HORSE RACING
In the Prague suburb of **Radotín**, about 3 miles (5 km) south of the city, various types of races take place at the Velká Chuchle track (tel 257 941 431) from May through October. To get there from the city center, take the metro in from Smíchovské nádraží, then bus 129 or 172.

ICE HOCKEY & SKATING
Ice hockey has become a very popular sport, especially since the Czech team has triumphed at an international level. National league games usually take place in the early evening on Tuesdays and Fridays, and sometimes on Sunday afternoons. The best stadia are the **Sparta Stadium** in Bubeneč, close to Holešovice metro station, and **Slavia Praha** winter stadium (Na hroudě, Vršovice, Prague 10). Ice rinks are also used for skating between October and April.

SOCCER
This is the most popular sport in the republic. Most matches are played on Sundays, September through November and April through June. The two leading Prague-based teams, Sparta Praha (tel 220 570 323) and Slavia Praha (tel 233 081 751), are bitter rivals. The most important games are played at the **Sparta Stadium** in Prague, which is easily accessible from Hradčanská metro station.

SPORTS COMPLEXES
Southeast of Prague, the **Club Hotel** (Plzenská, Prague 5) on the Prague–Plzeň road has a golf course and facilities for tennis, riding, squash, badminton, and other activities. Fees for the use of recreational facilities are very reasonable.

SQUASH
Squash is very popular in Prague, especially with young executives resident in the city. There are courts available at the **Fitness Forum International** (Kongresová 1, Vysehrad, Prague 4, tel 261 191 326), which stays open until 10 p.m. Slightly cheaper is the **Squash Centrum Strahov** (Strahov 1230, Prague 6, tel 2051 3609), open Mon.–Fri. 7–11, weekends 8–11.

SWIMMING
Plavecky Stadion Podolí (Podolská 74, Prague 4, tel 241 433 952) has modern indoor and outdoor facilities. The **Aquacentrum** pool (Tupolerova 665, Prague-9-Letňany, tel 283 921 799) has waterslides and children's pools, as well as a fitness center.

TENNIS
The Czechs have excelled at tennis for decades, producing champions such as Ivan Lendl, Martina Navratilova, Jana Novotna, and the late Jaroslav Drobny. The Club Hotel (see Sports Complexes) has courts, as do some hotels. For further information, contact the **Czech Tennis Federation,** Ostrov Štvanice 38, Prague 7, tel 224 810 108, www.cztenis.cz.

CZECH REPUBLIC

ENTERTAINMENT

CLASSICAL MUSIC, OPERA, & THEATER
Ostrava and Olomouc have their own orchestras, and Olomouc and Brno hold music festivals. Many smaller festivals, held in châteaus, specialize in baroque music or the works of individual composers such as Janáček, Smetana, and Beethoven. In many towns, including Brno and Plzeň, delightful 19th-century theaters have been restored; they offer a wide repertoire of drama, opera, and ballet. Brno is home to the **National Theater**

(Dvořákova 11, tel 542 321 285) and the **Janáčkovo Divadlo** (Rooseveltova, tel 542 321 285). Puppet and mime theater companies are found in many towns across the republic.

NIGHTLIFE
In the smaller towns people tend to go home early, so don't expect late-night carousing outside the cities. Because nightspots come and go all the time, look for the detailed listings in local newssheets and promotional brochures.

Today even small towns are likely to have **casinos**, which may be incorporated into local hotels. Smaller casinos, called *herna*, are ubiquitous and remain open until dawn. They consist of little more than slot machines and a bar.

FESTIVALS & EVENTS
April
Flora Olomouc international garden exhibition, Olomouc. This weekend-long exhibition has been running since the early 1980s; indoor and outdoor displays (www.flora-ol.cz).
Jazz Pramět Šumperk, Šumperk. This international jazz festival is well regarded (tel 649 214 276).

May
Beer festival, Karlovy Vary.
Janáček International Music Festival, Ostrava. Some of Janáček's lesser-known works can be heard at this festival held not far from his native village of Hukvaldy (Masná 10, 70200 Ostrava, tel 596 122 300, www.czech-festivals.cz).

June
International Festival of Records, Curiosities, and Budvar Beer, Pelhřimov. Enjoy the beer as you watch people vie for a place in the *Guinness Book of Records* (Agency Dobrý den Pelhřimov, Slovanského bratrství 1664, 39301 Pelhřimov, tel 565 321 226, www.dobryden.cz).

Music in Gardens and Châteaus, Kroměříž. A summer series of concerts (Kovářská 1, 76701 Kroměříž, tel 573 331 473, www.hudba-kromeriz.cz).
Olomouc Beer Festival, Olomouc. A four-day festival of beer olympics and music ranging from jazz to blues, rock, and folk. Most of the major breweries are represented, and it's all free (www.pivnifestival.cz)!
Smetanova Litomyšl International Opera Festival, Litomyšl. This open-air classical festival, held over two weekends at the castle in Smetana's home town, is one of the Czech Republic's oldest (www.smetanovalitomysl.cz).
Strážnice International folk festival Held the last weekend of June, this has been attracting dozens of folk dancers, singers, and musicians from all over the Czech Republic and the rest of the world since the 1940s (Ústav lidové kultury, 69662 Strážnice, tel 631 332 092, www.straznice-mesto.cz).

July
Karlovy Vary International Film Festival The most important film festival in Central and Eastern Europe, the 10-day Karlovy Vary festival dates back to the mid-20th century. Lots of famous faces to see (tel 224 235 412, www.iffkv.cz).
Puppet festival, Chrudim. A week-long festival is presented by the city's Puppet Museum (tel 469 620 310, www.puppets.cz).

August
Brno Grand Prix motorcycle race This is part of the World Championship of Road Motorcycles (Automotodrom Brno, Ostrovice 201, 664 81 Brno venkov, tel 546 216 111, www.brnograndprix.com).
Chodské slavnosti, Domažlice. This folk festival is devoted to the Chod people and their traditions.
International Bagpipe Festival (dudácký festival), Strakonice. Bagpipers, singers, dancers, and artists come

from all over Europe to perform (tel 383 321 540, www.must.cz/english/menu_H.htm).

September
Hop festival, Žatec. The festival celebrates the Czech Republic's most famous product—beer (Chmelarské museum, Mostecká 2580, 43819 Žatec, tel 397 626 125).
Moravsky podzim international music festival, Brno. The two-week "Moravian Autumn" festival of classical music has a good showing of Czech composers (www.mhfb.cz).

October
Jazz Goes to Town, Hradec Králové. An international Jazz Festival (tel 495 513 858, www.jazzgoestotown.com).
Pilsnerfest, Plzeň. This two-day festival is the granddaddy of all beer festivals, put on by Pilsner Urquell brewery (tel 377 062 888, www.pilsnerfest.cz).
Velká pardubická steeplechase, Pardubice (second Sunday in October). This world-famous cross-country steeplechase has been running for over a century (tel 466 797 111, www.pardubice-racecourse.cz).

November
Blues-Alive international blues festival, Šumperk. Three days of blues from around the world (www.bluesalive.cz).

ACTIVITIES

BOATING
Lakes such as Lipno provide good boating and windsurfing. Contact the **Czech Yachting Union,** Atletická 100/2, Prague 6, tel/fax 220 513 656, www.yachting.cz. At the same address is the **Czech Canoeing Union** (www.kanoe.cz).

CYCLING
Mountain bikes may be rented at many resorts in the Český ráj or Krkonoše mountains. It can also be pleasant to hire a bicycle and explore the gentler terrain of southern Bohemia and

ENTERTAINMENT & ACTIVITIES

Moravia, on mostly uncrowded roads. Details of facilities and competitive events for serious cyclists are available from the **Czech Cycling Union,** Nad Hliníkem 4, Prague 5, tel 257 214 613. For cycling routes, contact **CDV Olomouc** (Žilinská, 77900 Olomouc, tel 685 725 255, www.cdv.cz) and see the cycling section of the Czech Republic Web site (www.czecot.cz).

FISHING

Lakes, mountain streams, and major rivers provide excellent opportunities for fishing. Besides trout, there are catfish, common walleye, perch, carp, pike, and river eels. Fishing permits, available from many tackle shops and the Czech Fishing Association, are required, and regulations determine seasons and the size of the catch. Contact: **Czech Angling Union** (Nad Olšinami 31, Prague 10, tel 7811 7513) and **Moravian Angling Union** (Soběšická 83, Brno, tel/fax 05 4522 3838).

GOLF

The best golf courses are at Mariánské Lázně (where a large, comfortable hotel adjoins), Karlovy Vary, and Ostrava. There is a 9-hole course at Pardubice. The latest 18-hole course to open is at Karlštejn (tel 311 684 716 or 311 684 717). The game is becoming increasingly popular, so book in advance. For more information, contact the **Czech Golf Federation** (Strakonická 510, Prague 5, tel 5415444, fax 544586).

HEALTH & FITNESS

Many hotels in larger towns are equipped with fitness centers and gyms. Alternatively, your hotel concierge should be able to tell you about local health clubs.

HIKING

Most of the republic is hilly or mountainous, and there are ample opportunities for hiking. Some of the many parks offer inexpensive accommodations in chaty (hostels) and horské hotely (mountain hotels; check with the local information office). Many prefer the comfortable base offered by a spa, from which there are always well-marked trails exploring the surrounding hills and woods. Regions such as the Český ráj (Czech Paradise) and České Švýčarsko (Bohemian Switzerland) are popular. Maps giving details of hiking trails are available from most bookshops. For more information contact **1st Municipal Map Shop** in the Prague City Hall (Žatecká 2, Old Town, Prague 1) or **Klub Česýck turistů**, the Czech Hiking Club (Jaromírova 9, Prague 2, tel 235 514 529). Experienced hikers seeking details of more challenging activities should contact the **Czech Orienteering Association** (Strahov, Prague 6, tel 354679).

HORSE RACING

The major event in the Czech Republic is the Grand Steeplechase at Pardubice, which has been in existence since 1874 and takes place annually on the second Sunday in October. There are 39 jumps, making a race that both horses and jockeys find extremely demanding. The most notorious jump is the Taxis Ditch, which many an experienced horse and jockey fail to clear. Increasing awareness about animal welfare issues has led to improvements that should make the course less dangerous for horses.

HORSE RIDING

There are stables in Poděbrady, Třeboň, Karlovy Vary, and other towns. You can obtain further information from the **Czech Horse Riding Federation** (Atletická 100.2, Prague 6, tel 2051 1105, fax 3335 4399).

HUNTING

During the Habsburg empire, the Austrian nobility maintained hunting lodges in Bohemia and farther east. Game birds may be less plentiful nowadays, but there is good year-round sport on offer for those with a license. Game includes pheasant, wild duck, deer, wild boar, and hare. For further information, contact **Pragolov** (Národní 37, Prague 1, tel 224 218 119; fax 224 218 467). This private company organizes permits and accommodations.

ICE HOCKEY & SKATING

Almost every town has a winter stadium (zimní stadion), where ice hockey matches are held regularly. In the winter months ice rinks are also used for skating, and there is good outdoor skating in rural areas when some reservoirs freeze over.

MOTOR SPORTS

Two outstanding events are the Motorcycle Grand Prix in Brno (www.brnograndprix.com), which takes place in August, and the Golden Helmet Speedway Race in Pardubice a month later.

SPORTS COMPLEXES

Facilities are good, and every town of any size has a sports complex, a beneficial legacy of the Communist era. One of the largest sports complexes in the Czech Republic, at Roudnice, north of Prague, also has a good hotel and restaurant. Fees are very reasonable.

SWIMMING

Most towns have swimming pools. Sometimes standards of cleanliness and hygiene may be suspect, so in summer it is often preferable to head for the lakes and reservoirs. Many have excellent sandy beaches—for example, **Slapy reservoir,** south of Prague on the Vltava river.

TENNIS

Many hotels, especially in spa towns, have courts for casual players. In Prague, you'll find first-class clay courts open to the public at Tenisové Haly Uhříněves (Prague 10, tel 267 711 440 to reserve a court). Also contact the **Czech Tennis Federation** (Ostrov Štvanice 38, Prague 7, tel 224 810 108).

LANGUAGE GUIDE

Czech belongs to the Slav family of languages and, as such, is highly inflected. Even if you learn a good deal of vocabulary, you still will find it difficult to speak or understand the language effectively without some knowledge of its grammatical structure. Nonetheless, even a limited knowledge of the language can prove helpful.

Most English-speakers find pronunciation a problem, but the system of accents should make it clear. Acute accents (or in the case of "u," ů) lengthen the vowel. The stress usually falls on the first syllable. There are some clear differences from "English-style" pronunciation:

á = as in far
c = ts as in cats
č = ch as in cheek
ch = ch as in loch
ě = ye as in yet
é = ea as in pear
í and ý = ee as in see
j = y as in yawn
ň = ny as in banyan
ř = as in bourgeois (combined rolled r and ž sound)
š = sh as in shabby
ú and ů = oo as in zoo
y = j as in fit
ž = zh sound as in measure

GENERAL CONVERSATION
Good day/hello dobrý den
Goodbye na shledanou
Please prosím
Thank you děkuji
Yes ano
No ne
Good/OK dobře
Sorry/Excuse me promiňte
Where? kde je?
When? kdy?
Why? proč?
Large/Small velký/malý
More/Less více/méně
Hot/Cold horký/studený
Here/There tady/tam
Right/Left vpravo/vlevo
Straight ahead jděte přímo

SIGNS
vchod entrance
východ exit
otevřeno open
zavřeno closed
pozor danger
toalety rest rooms

muži/páni men/gentlemen
ženy/dámy women/ladies

TIME
Today dnes
Tomorrow zítra
Yesterday včera
Morning ráno
Afternoon odpoledne
Evening večer
Night noc

SHOPPING
Cash desk pokladna
Post office pošta
Bank banka
Supermarket potraviny
Chemist lékárna
Expensive/Cheap drahý/levný
How much is it? Kolik to stojí?

TRANSPORTATION
Airport letiště
Railway station nádraží
Bus station autobusové nádraží
Metro station stanice
Aeroplane letadlo
Train vlak
Bus autobus
Tram tramvaj
Seat místo
Ticket lístek
One-way jednosmeřnou
Return zpáteční

GEOGRAPHY & PLACES
Tourist office informační centrum
Theater divadlo
Garden zahrada
Church kostel
Museum muzeum
Bridge most
Avenue třída
Square námesti
Street ulice
Castle hrad
Château zámek
Mountain hora
River řeka

HOTELS
Hotel hotel
Room pokoj

Breakfast snídaně
Key klíč
Reservation mistenka
Toilet toaleta
Bath koupelna
Shower sprcha

EMERGENCIES
Help! pomoc!
Doctor doktor/lékař
Dentist zubní lékař
Hospital nemocnice
Police Station policie

NUMBERS
1 jeden
2 dva
3 tří
4 čtyři
5 pět
6 šest
7 sedm
8 osm
9 devět
10 deset
15 patnáct
20 dvacet
25 dvacet pět
50 padesát
100 sto
1000 tisíc
1,000,000 jeden milión

DAYS OF THE WEEK
Monday pondělí
Tuesday úterý
Wednesday středa
Thursday čtvrtek
Friday pátek
Saturday sobota
Sunday neděle

MONTHS OF THE YEAR & SEASONS
January leden
February únor
March březen
April duben
May květen
June červen
July červenec
August srpen
September září
October říjen
November listopad
December prosinec

Spring jaro
Summer léto
Autumn podzim
Winter zima

MENU READER

GENERAL TERMS
restaurant *restaurace*
menu *jídelní lístek*
table *stůl*
lunch *oběd*
dinner *večeře*
appetizer *předkrmy*
main meal *hlavní jídlo*
side dish *přílohy*
dessert *moučník*
wine list *nápojový lístek*
the bill *účet*

BASICS
chléb bread
máslo butter
sukr sugar
vejce eggs
sýr cheese
smetana cream
ovoce fruit
maso meat
zeleniny vegetables
polévka soup
sůl salt
pepř pepper
ocet vinegar
olej oil

COOKING METHODS
grilované grilled
piněné stuffed
pečené baked
smažené fried
uzené smoked
špíz skewered
vařené boiled

MEATS
drůbež poultry
kuře chicken
husa goose
kachna duck
bažant pheasant
krocan turkey
hovězí beef
vepřové pork
teleci veal
šunka ham
králík rabbit
játra liver
klobása sausage
vepřový řízek schnitzel
Bepřové koleno pork knee

SEAFOOD
ryby fish
uzený losos smoked salmon
kapr carp

pstruh trout
treska cod
tuna tuna
krevety prawns

SIDE DISHES
brambory potatoes
knedliky dumplings
rýže rice
hranolky french fries
bramborová kaše mashed potatoes
salát salad

FRUIT
jablko apple
banán banana
pomeranč orange
citrón lemon
jahody strawberries
hrozny grapes
hruška pear
ananas pineapple
rozinky raisins

VEGETABLES
hrášek peas
rajčata tomatoes
špenát spinach
cibule onion
česnek garlic
okurka cucumber
karotka carrot
zelí cabbage
žampiony mushrooms
květák cauliflower

DESSERTS
palačinky pancakes
zmrzlina ice cream
závin strudel
dort cake
buchty curd cakes
čokoláda chocolate

DRINKS
voda water
minerální voda mineral water
  nešumivá still
  šumivá sparkling
mléko milk
čaj tea
káva coffee
pomerančový džus orange juice
červené víno red wine
bílé víno white wine
pivo beer

OTHER
chlebíček open sandwiches
omeleta omelette
smažený sýr fried cheese

INDEX

Bold page numbers
indicate illustrations

ILLUSTRATIONS CREDITS

CREDITS

The author wishes to thank the Czech Tourist Authority for their assistance in researching this book.

Published by the National Geographic Society
John M. Fahey, Jr., *President and Chief Executive Officer*
Gilbert M. Grosvenor, *Chairman of the Board*
Nina D. Hoffman, *Executive Vice President,*
             President, Books and School Publishing
Kevin Mulroy, *Vice President and Editor-in-Chief*
Elizabeth L. Newhouse, *Director of Travel Publishing*
Barbara A. Noe, *Senior Editor and Project Manager*
Cinda Rose, *Art Director*
Carl Mehler, *Director of Maps*
Joseph F. Ochlak, *Map Coordinator*
R. Gary Colbert, *Production Director*
Richard S. Wain, *Production Project Manager*
Lawrence Porges, *Editorial Coordinator*
Kay Hankins, Carolina E. Averitt, Judith Klein, *Contributors*

Edited and designed by AA Publishing (a trading name of Automobile Association Developments Limited, whose registered office is Millstream, Maidenhead Road, Windsor, Berkshire, England SL4 5GD Registered number: 1878835).
Virginia Langer, *Project Manager*
David Austin, *Senior Art Editor*
Catherine Hatley, *Editor*
Keith Russell, *Designer*
Keith Brook, *Senior Cartographic Editor*
Cartography by AA Cartography Department
Richard Firth, *Production Director*
Sarah Reynolds, *Production Controller*
Carol Walker, *Picture Research Manager*
Picture Research by Kathy Lockley
Drive maps and Prague area maps drawn by Chris Orr Associates, Southampton, England
Cutaway illustrations drawn by Maltings Partnership, Derby, England

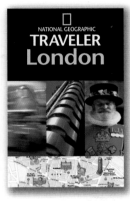